THE PLATONIC TRADITION IN ANGLO-SAXON PHILOSOPHY

STUDIES IN THE HISTORY OF IDEALISM IN ENGLAND AND AMERICA

by

JOHN H. MUIRHEAD

LL.D. Glasgow and California
Professor Emeritus of Philosophy in the
University of Birmingham

"The safest general characterisation of the European philosophical tradition is that it consists of a series of footnotes to Plato."—A. N. WHITEHEAD

LONDON: GEORGE ALLEN & UNWIN LTD
NEW YORK: THE MACMILLAN COMPANY

FIRST PUBLISHED IN 1931

PRINTED IN GREAT BRITAIN BY
UNWIN BROTHERS LTD., WOKING

TO THE MEMORY

OF

EDWARD CAIRD

THOMAS HILL GREEN

AND

BERNARD BOSANQUET

PREFACE

It is a common view of the course of British philosophy that, starting from the empirical basis laid down by Bacon, Hobbes, and Locke, its chief and characteristic contribution to Western thought has been the development this received from their time to that of Mill, Spencer, and Sidgwick; that in the 'sixties of last century this tradition was broken into by an influx of foreign ideas which diverted it for a generation from its own natural bed into that of Kantian and post-Kantian idealism; finally, that the paradoxes of the absolutism to which it has thus been led have created a strong counter-current under the influence of which it is returning repentantly to the older, safer, and more national lines.

The present Studies were undertaken in the conviction that, if not wholly mistaken, this view gives a very one-sided picture of the work of the national genius in the department of philosophy and of its contribution to Western thought. Long before the time of Bacon, and before the freer manner of thought inherited from Greece had passed under bondage to Mediæval Scholasticism, the seeds of quite another order of thought had been planted in England by John Scotus Erigena. In the early part of the century of Hobbes and Locke, the influence of the Platonic revival that had taken place in Italy was making itself powerfully felt in Oxford and Cambridge, and had issued in the latter University in a movement which gave expression to Neo-Platonic ideas with a freedom, an energy, and a grace unequalled anywhere else at the time in Europe.

If, in the century that followed, the seed thus replanted and copiously watered by the Cambridge writers failed to show above the ground except in the pale form of the later speculations of Bishop Berkeley, this was owing partly to the mixture with it of elements derived from a form of Malebranchean mysticism to which English soil was essentially uncongenial, partly to the growing domination of the mind of the time by Locke's "new way of ideas" as more in harmony with its secular interests, but most of all to the fertility in the physical sciences of the Cartesian idea of mechanical law. If this was valid for matter, why not for life? And if valid for life, why not for mind? The credit of breaking the spell both of Lockean empiricism and Cartesian materialism is usually given to Kant, and it is impossible to exaggerate the influence of his *Critique* on contemporary and later thought. But Kant's merit, so far as England was concerned, consisted rather in his having worked out with hitherto unequalled analytic power ideas that had already found expression and been made the foundation of a whole system in some of her own earlier writers. When, accordingly, the work of Kant came to be known in England, as it first effectively did in the talk and writings of Coleridge, it was in no mere spirit of self-defence that the poet-philosopher was able to declare that he only found in it the confirmation of what, with their aid, he had "toiled out for himself". In the end, the system Coleridge himself wrought out is far more rightly conceived as a genuine product of his own essentially English genius than as a development of German Idealism.

What is true of Coleridge is, I believe, true also of the idealistic revival of a generation later. The writer who by common consent was the pioneer of this movement, James Frederick Ferrier, owed little or nothing to Kant and Hegel, and traced his inspiration rather to Plato and Berkeley. Even when in the following decade the Hegelian philosophy took hold (in Coleridge's phrase for the influence of Kant upon himself), "as with a giant's hand", upon the Scottish writers Hutchison Stirling and Edward Caird, there were others, like T. H. Green, not less representative of the new movement, who profoundly suspected it, and in Oxford at least the new thought owed at least as much to the revival of Platonic study, initiated by Benjamin Jowett, as to German philosophy. Even in the case of the more pronounced Germanizers, the stress that was laid on personality both in man and God, on freedom and self-determination both in individuals and communities, linked them more closely with the older British writers than with anything they found explicitly stated in Schelling and Hegel. That they themselves were largely unconscious of this affinity, and that allusions to the work of Cudworth and Norris, Berkeley, Coleridge, and his disciple Joseph Henry Green, are conspicuous by their absence, only makes the coincidence the more noteworthy as an illustration of the national bent that has all along given a special character to Anglo-Saxon idealism.

Finally, as regards the reaction against the form that this took in the developments it received from such writers as Bradley and Bosanquet, I believe that it can be shown to be the result rather of their failure to do justice to an important side of the Platonism they had inherited than of any exaggeration of influences that came from Germany, and we may see a certain poetic justice in a situation that has left it to a distinguished leader of the realistic reaction to claim to be on'y adding one more to "the series of footnotes to Plato" of which he holds the European philosophical tradition to consist. "If we had to render Plato's general point of view with the least changes made necessary by the intervening two thousand years of human experience in social organization, in æsthetic attainments, in science, and in religion," writes Professor Whitehead, "we should have to set about the construction of a philosophy of organism"—the suggestive name that this writer has chosen for his own.

Be the apostolic succession with whom it may, these Studies will have served their main purpose if they succeed in convincing the reader of the continuity of that great tradition in Anglo-Saxon philosophy. They make no pretence of being a history of English and American Idealism. This remains to be written. They deal with a few of the main periods, of which such a history will have to take account, and with a few of the outstanding names in these periods. Imperfect as they are as comprised in this book, they are still more imperfect than they were originally intended to be, owing to the omission from them of the writer who forms the link between the first and the second of these periods. In the course of preparation for the section on Coleridge, the author became aware of the existence of material which had only to a small extent been previously utilized, and found that, if justice were to be done to the poet's work in this department, a far fuller treatment than was compatible with inclusion in this volume must be given to him. As this has been attempted in a separate volume, already published, I do not need to ask the reader of this one to accept intention for deed, but merely to forgive me for having to refer him elsewhere for what should fill the obvious gap. For one or two other equally obvious omissions I may perhaps be allowed to refer to what I have written on Edward Caird in *The Life and Philosophy* of that writer, on T. H. Green in my little book with the title *The Service of the State*, and on Bernard Bosanquet in *Mind*, N.S. xxxii, No. 128. It was my privilege to know and to learn from these men, particularly from the first, more than I can tell as to the meaning of the great tradition which is the subject of these studies; and I have ventured, with great diffidence in view of their manifold imperfections, to dedicate them to their memory.

I have to acknowledge the kindness of the Editor of *Mind* in permitting me to republish the chapters on "The Cambridge Platonists" and "How Hegel Came to England", of the Editor of the *Philosophical Review* for the same permission in reference to those on "Hegel in America" and "Charles Peirce's Pragmatism", which have already appeared in their journals. But especially am I indebted to my friend Professor J. S. Mackenzie for his assistance in reading the whole in proof and in making valuable suggestions for the clarification of the point of view from which it is written.

January 1931

CONTENTS

B

PART ONE

EARLY IDEALISTIC MOVEMENT IN
ENGLISH PHILOSOPHY

CHAPTER I

THE CAMBRIDGE PLATONISTS. THE SCHOOL

I. CONTEMPORARY INFLUENCES

It was mentioned in the Preface, as the initial error of the view of British philosophy there criticized, that it ignores the powerful speculative movement that preceded Hobbes in its origin, and, so far as it came later to be influenced by him, took the form of an energetic repudiation of his ideas. It is therefore in the interest of historic justice, as well as of a more balanced estimate of the debt which idealism in England owes to native and foreign influences respectively, to recall, in more detail than has hitherto been done from this point of view, the critical and constructive work of the men who led this reaction.

Whence precisely the particular impulse came that stimulated and inspired them, it is perhaps difficult to say. It is tempting to connect it with the name of Descartes. Cambridge University had the honour of being the first to welcome the new thought. Between Descartes and the Cambridge writers there was a certain identity of aim in that both sought for a basis in reason for man's moral and religious experience. One of the latter, Henry More, corresponded with Descartes and at one time professed himself his devoted disciple. But we have the evidence of the poet Milton writing in 1644 that tradition at that date still reigned in Cambridge, providing only "an asinine feast of sow-thistles and brambles", and there is no evidence that Whichcote, the founder of the school, was at all influenced by Descartes.[1] As a body, moreover, as Tulloch has pointed out,[2] these ardent theologians had little in common with the detached sceptical spirit of the French philosopher. So far from leaving their Christian beliefs outside the sphere of their thought even temporarily, as Descartes sought to do, their whole endeavour was to find the ground for them within it. If it could not fairly be said that they were theologians first and philosophers only secondarily, yet to them philosophy and theology were the same thing, namely, the conceptual expression of the ideas that underlie essential religious experience. Nor was it long before, with

[1] He was already preaching and teaching in 1636. Descartes' *Discourse on Method* only appeared in 1637.
[2] *Rational Theology in England in the Seventeenth Century*.

all the points of affinity which they found between the Cartesians and themselves, they came to recognize a fundamental difference of tendency. "The Cartesians", wrote Cudworth, "have an undiscerned tang of the mechanic Atheism hanging about them." Descartes, he held, had even "outdone" the Atomists in their "mechanizing humour".[1] Even Henry More lived to repent his early enthusiasm.

For these reasons it seems to be equally misleading to represent Cambridge Platonism, as J. A. Stewart[2] does, as a correction of Cartesianism by the insertion of certain Platonic elements into a fabric otherwise accepted as in harmony with it. We are on surer ground in seeking for the roots of the movement, on the one hand, in the deep-going connection which has existed from the first between Christian and Platonic thought, and on the other, in the antagonism which the entirely contrary teaching of Hobbes excited in the minds of those who had the intelligence to perceive its real drift.

It is difficult to exaggerate the essential unity of principle and spirit that pervades these two great systems. Both start from the assumption of the affinity between the structure of the world and the mind of man. To Plato it was the same principle that was the source both of the being and the knowledge of the world. "The Platonic theory of knowledge", writes Professor Perry,[3] "was both retained and reinforced by Christianity." Similarly from the side of practice. A philosophy whose ultimate principle was the Good was committed as deeply as Christianity to the supreme reality of the moral and religious life. To neither could the ultimate opposition be between knowledge and faith. To both the fundamental antithesis was between merely natural knowledge or the unenlightened conscience and the higher light into which the soul might rise by the Grace of God. Platonism might indeed be called the intellectual side of Christianity. Wherever, from the author of the Fourth Gospel to St. Augustine, from St. Augustine to Thomas Aquinas, and from Aquinas to Dean Inge, the spirit of Christian theology has been really alive, it has tended to fall back upon Platonism.

The last named of these writers[4] has sought to trace this tradition

---

[1] The True Intellectual System of the Universe, Eng. Tr., London, 1845, vol. i. p. 275. Cudworth, however, is always ready to make a distinction between Descartes' conscious object and the unconscious tendency of his thought.
[2] Art., "Cambridge Platonists" in Encyclopædia of Religion and Ethics.
[3] Present Philosophical Tendencies.
[4] In The Platonic Tradition in English Religious Thought, London, 1920.

itself to the new spiritual enlightenment "that came to all the civilized peoples of the earth in the millennium before the Christian era". Delivered from the primitive worship of outward things of nature, the mind of man sought refuge from the flux of appearances in an unseen reality underlying them, with which it could enter into communion because this reality was none other than its own deeper self. Beginning in Asia, this mystical faith swept over Greece and Southern Italy in the form of Orphism and Pythagoreanism. It found an intelligent sympathizer in Socrates, and under his inspiration reached its highest expression in the *Dialogues* of Plato. Revived in a form more suited to "the poignant longing" of the time in the Neo-Platonism of the Roman Empire, it passed into the theology of the Christian Church. Dean Inge is not himself prepared to accept Bruno Bauer's dictum that "Christianity is a Græco-Roman phenomenon in a Jewish mask"; nor even Havet's view that "Christianity though Jewish in form is Hellenic at bottom". But in the central Pauline and Johannine conceptions of the eternal Christ and of Love as "the great hierophant of the divine mysteries" he finds a closer affinity to Plato's Idea of the Good and the teaching of the *Phædrus* than to anything that is to be found in the "Palestinian tradition".

It is not, therefore, surprising that at a time when the Platonic revival was spreading from Italy over Europe, and among such men as Cambridge was then producing, there should have been a movement of independent, if somewhat uncritical, study of Plato. Coleridge said of them that they were "Plotinists rather than Platonists", and Professor Stewart [1] has pointed out the mingling of the Christian religion and the Platonic Philosophy in "the doctrine and experience of ecstasy". But it is an exaggeration to say, as Stewart does, that they put this doctrine in the very centre of their philosophy. The theory of knowledge which is central in Cudworth is essentially Platonic, and even with respect to the "experience", John Smith, perhaps the most really representative of them all, is ready to declare that a true Christian "is more for a solid peace and a settled calm of spirit than for high raptures and feelings of joy or extraordinary manifestations of God in him".[2]

But their Platonism might have taken no organized aggressive form nor been known outside their lecture rooms had it not been for the challenge to the whole basis on which both Christianity

[1] *Loc. cit.*   [2] See *The Excellency and Nobleness of True Religion.*

and Platonism stood, that came from the new thought on the nature of the physical world, as interpreted by such writers as Gassendi, and the application of it to the origin of law and morality by Hobbes. While it took some time to discern the "tang of mechanic atheism" in Descartes, the danger that threatened not only the Christian but all religion, and the morality which was believed to be bound up with it from this source, was obvious from the first. To any who believed, as did these inheritors of the best traditions not only of Puritanism but of English liberty, that the authority of law and government rested in their intrinsic justice and the response to them of man's reason and conscience, nothing could be more antipathetic than a theory which taught that nothing was good or bad in itself, and that the only right in the end was might. It was the vigour with which, as against this attack upon them, the principles underlying the Platonico-Christian scheme of thought were reasserted (unsystematically in the teaching of the whole school, with an attempt at system, however ponderous and over-laid with erudition, on the part of at least one member of it), at a time when it may be said to have been the sole witness to them, that gives philosophical significance to the work of the Cambridge men.

We are not here concerned with the differences of style, personality, method of approach, or details of doctrine in separate individuals,[1] but *first* with the main features of the singularly attractive theology which in the light of their central principles they succeeded in sketching out and which remains to this day the highest expression of Christian theology in England; and *secondly* with the extent to which the thought of the more speculative of them broke through any mere dogmatic limits and can be credited with a real addition to idealistic philosophy.

2. COMMON FEATURES OF THE SCHOOL

Though, as already said, it is a mistake to represent mystic ecstasy as the centre of its teaching, it is true that the main interest of the school was religious. Its philosophy, however much it might extend to include a theory of knowledge and of nature, was a "philosophy of religion".[2] It differed from the dogmatic system of the times, *first* in the interpretation it gave of what was quintessential

[1] See on this Dr. Powicke's admirable book, *The Cambridge Platonists*.
[2] A phrase which Cudworth seems to have been the first to use.

in religious experience; *secondly*, in the direction in which the foundation of belief in God as the object of religious experience was to be sought; *thirdly*, and as a corollary, in the view of the relation between reason and faith.

(*a*) Religion was indeed to them, as to the neo-Platonist, "a flight of the alone to the Alone". But the Alone, while never conceived of in any narrow anthropological way, was not left in the vague as a "splendid kind of nothing".[1]

After the manner of the Fourth Gospel, which was the source of so much of their inspiration, God was conceived of as the unity of love and knowledge. "Wherever it (true religion) finds beauty, harmony, goodness, love, ingenuousness, wisdom, holiness, justice, and the like, it is ready to say here and there is God; wheresoever any such shine out, a holy mind climbs up by these sunbeams and raises itself up to God." "God is not better defined to us by our understandings than by our wills and affections; He is not only the eternal reason, but He is also that unstained beauty and supreme good to which our wills are perpetually aspiring."[2] Heaven and Hell are not things or places without us but states of our own souls: the one consisting of "a true conjunction of the mind with God in a secret feeling of His goodness"; the other of an evil spirit arising "from the bottom of our own soul". More desirable than to hear a voice from heaven giving assurance of salvation is "to find a revelation of all from within rising up from the centre of a man's own soul in the real and internal impressions of a godlike nature upon his own spirit".[3]

(*b*) It is thus from no external witness but from the nature of the soul and its experiences that we can learn of the existence and nature and operation of God. "The spirit of man", they were fond of quoting, "is the candle of the Lord." "*Nullus spiritus*," wrote Henry More, "*nullus deus*." "Though the whole of this visible universe be whispering out the notions of a Deity, yet we cannot understand it without some interpreter within."[4] It is this that makes it so important, the author declares in the same passage, to inquire "what that knowledge of a Deity is, into which a due converse with our own naked understandings will lead us".

[1] A phrase of John Smith's in another connection.
[2] John Smith, *The Excellency and Nobleness of True Religion*, c. viii, and *Discourse of the Existence and Nature of God*, c. viii.
[3] *The Excellency*, etc., c. vii.
[4] John Smith, *Of the Existence and Nature of God*, c. i.

(c) Leaving this for the moment and confining ourselves to the general doctrine, what, we may ask, by the aid of this interpreter within, may be discovered in the whispers of the world without? Granted we cannot find God in the world unless we find Him in our own souls, can we really find Him if we do? It was a fundamental part of these men's teaching that we can. Though the spirit of man is the candle of the Lord, yet is its light a derivative one. "All created excellency shines with borrowed beams."[1]

The ideas of the reason (Culverwel mentions especially that of Obligation) imply the actual reality of a reason transcending ours, and therewith a belief in a Providence in Nature and History. There was no point in which they believed themselves more in harmony with the great Christian as well as the great philosophic tradition than in holding that "nature is that regular line which the wisdom of God Himself has drawn in being, whereas that which they called fortune is nothing but a line fuller of windings and varieties; and as nature was a fixed and ordinary kind of providence, so fortune was nothing but a more abstruse and mysterious and occult kind of providence".[2] "It is not worth the while to live in a world devoid of God and of Providence", John Smith was fond of quoting from Marcus Aurelius. He seemed even to regard it as possible for human wisdom, looking from the beginning to the end of things, to behold them all, in spite of apparent digressions, "acting that part which the Supreme Mind and Wisdom that governs all things hath appointed them".[3]

From all this two things followed as corollaries, the one fundamental to morality, the other to religion.

It followed in the first place that there could be no antagonism between freedom and determination. Man is free because he has the power not merely of choosing—this is merely the condition of real liberty—but of determining himself by his idea of good; he is *more fully* free according to the fullness of the good with which he identifies himself and the fullness of his knowledge of it. The discussion of freedom is apt with them, as Tulloch says, to be mixed up with the question of the nature of will in God, but this was only because it was seen how closely the questions were connected; and there are passages in which the vital element in human freedom is stated as well as anywhere else in the whole literature of philo-

---

[1] Culverwel, *The Light of Nature*, c. xi.   [2] *Ibid.*, c. iii.
[3] *The Excellency*, etc., c. ix. *Cp. Short Discourse on Atheism.*

sophy. "When we converse with our own souls," writes John Smith,[1] "we find the spring of all liberty to be nothing else but reason; and therefore no unreasonable creature can partake of it; and that it is not so much any indifference in our wills of determining without reason, much less against it, as the liberal election of and complacency in that which our understandings propound to us as most expedient; and our liberty most appears when our will most of all congratulates the results of our own judgments. And therefore the more the results of our judgments tend to our indifference, the more we find our wills dubious and in suspense what to choose, and all the while the soul's liberty is nothing else but a fluctuation between uncertainties and languisheth away in the impotency of our understandings." On the other hand: "Then is it most pregnant and flows forth in the fullest stream when its object is most full and the acquaintance with it most ample; all liberty in the soul being a kind of liberality in the bestowing of our affections, and the want or scarce measure of it parsimoniousness."

As the antithesis between freedom and determinism is thus constructively solved, so that between faith and reason. Religion is committed to the honouring of reason. It was not in vain that these men were Protestants. "Every man", declared Whichcote, "hath a right to judgment, if he be capable; yea, can a man, ought a man, to believe otherwise than he sees cause? Is it in a man's power to believe as he would or only as the reason of the thing appears to him?"[2] To the same effect Culverwel protests that religion is no "bird of prey that comes to peck out the eyes of men, no extinguisher to put out the candle of the Lord".[3] But they were also bound to recognize in the name of reason that its own was a derived light, and that it might have to trust in the Source of that light where it could not see. But this was an entirely different thing from declaring the object of faith wholly beyond knowledge (in a sense they were ready to hold that the Infinite Source was the more known); a fortiori from declaring that it was contrary to knowledge.

This in outline was the theory of the nature of religious experience and of the object and foundation of it that these men held. It

---

[1] *Discourse concerning the Existence and Nature of God*, c. ii (condensed), The passage is quoted at length in E. T. Campagnac's *Cambridge Platonists*. p. 170.
[2] See Tulloch, ii. 70.
[3] *Op. cit.*, p. 19.

seemed to them the fine flower of what was best in the thought of the past. Could it maintain itself against the new thought, whether in the open materialism of Hobbes or in the subtler form of scepticism represented by the Cartesians? This was the question with which Ralph Cudworth and the younger men found themselves faced.

CHAPTER II

CUDWORTH (i). INTELLECTUAL SYSTEM

1. The Design of His Work

While the movement owed its origin and the range of its influence to men peculiarly gifted with religious insight and powers of literary expression, and while they all at times showed themselves alive to the kind of evidence which in the end must be appealed to in support of their system,[1] Cudworth was the first fully to realize what was required by a "philosophy of religion confirmed and established by philosophical reasons in an age so philosophical", demonstrated "not *a priori*, which is impossible and contradictious, but by necessary inference from principles altogether undeniable".[2]

This was the enterprise on which he embarked in his work on *The True Intellectual* (as contrasted with the visible and corporeal) *System of the Universe*. Its aim, as he tells us in the Preface, was to establish the three things which he conceived as "the fundamental or essentials of true religion. *First*, that all things in the world do not float without a head and governor; but that there is a God, an omnipotent understanding Being, presiding over all. *Secondly* that, this God being essentially good and just, there is a φύσει καλὸν καὶ δίκαιον, something in its own nature immutably and eternally just and unjust; and not by arbitrary will law and command only. And, *lastly*, that there is something Ἐφ'ἡμῖν or that we are so far principles or masters of our own actions as to be accountable to justice for them". His original idea had been to write a treatise on liberty and necessity, which he rightly conceived of as the central point of the whole argument, but he found that this could not be treated apart from the nature of the physical world on the one hand, and the relation of the Will, of which this was the expression, to goodness, justice, and truth, on the other. Once grasped in its entirety, the argument was seen to involve the above three problems, which were also three steps in the development of it, and three faces which it must present to the rival systems of the time. As against a materialism of the kind represented by

---

[1] See John Smith's appeal to the constitution of the "naked understanding" which might be compared to Kant's "pure reason".
[2] Preface to *The True Intellectual System*.

Hobbes, it might be sufficient to prove the presence of a spiritual principle in the world. But this might be admitted while yet it might be possible to maintain with Descartes that the principle was that of an indeterminate will, and thus after all leave goodness and justice without other support than arbitrary divine decrees. Hence the necessity of the second step. Finally, the existence of divine justice might be acknowledged as by "the Stoics and divers modern writers" and yet leave "no liberty from necessity anywhere". Hence the necessity of the third.

It was a noble design worthy of the age and the man. Unfortunately, though he recognized in words what was required by "an age so philosophical", and had before him the example in Hobbes of a method which was entirely independent of traditional opinion, and against which mere learning was entirely wasted, he was unable to free himself of the heavy panoply he had inherited.[1] One result was that he never succeeded in completing more than the first part "wherein all the reason and philosophy of Atheism is confuted and its impossibility demonstrated". Realizing the necessity, as his health failed, of condensing what was to have been the second part, he wrote the short *Treatise Concerning Eternal and Immutable Morality*, which, however, was not published till 1731, forty-three years after his death. If we cannot say with its first editor that "it is drawn up with that beauty, clearness, and strength as must delight as well as convince the reader", we may perhaps agree with him in the claim for the English quality of "good sense" in the conduct of the argument, which among other things contains what Sorley describes as "a striking contribution to epistemology".[2] Yet how constantly the third part of his great design occupied his attention in later life can be seen from the lengthy manuscript remains that have come down to us in an unfinished and disorderly form.[3]

[1] See W. R. Sorley's *History of English Philosophy*, p. 89. With which we may compare Bolingbroke's saying that Cudworth "had read too much to think enough and admired too much to think freely". It is possible that Hobbes had him in view when he said of himself that "if he had read as much as other men he would have been as ignorant as they".

[2] The First Part of the *Intellectual System* was published in 1678; an abridgement of it by Thomas Wise in 1706. It was translated into Latin with notes almost as long as the text and published in 1733 by Dr. J. L. Mosheim. This work was translated into English by John Harrison, M.A., and published in three volumes, including the *Eternal and Immutable Morality*, in London, 1845. It is from this translation that quotations are made in the text.

[3] See on these Note below, p. 70.

Confining ourselves in the present chapter to his chief book, and cutting ourselves free both of his order and detail.[1] there are three points in Cudworth's work which may be said to be of permanent interest and to give him a claim to be the real founder of British Idealism. (1) The view of nature which he pressed against the mechanical systems both of other times and of his own; (2) the theory of mind as an active participant in the process of knowledge, referred to by Sorley; (3) his view of the divine principle in the world as the action, not of an arbitrary Will acting on it from without, but of an immanent will to good, whether conceived of as beauty, justice, or truth. If in none of these he succeeded in emancipating himself from traditional views or reaching perfect clarity, it is still possible to distinguish what is essential and what accidental in his thought.

2. THEORY OF NATURE

Its treatment of Nature has been something of a scandal to idealist philosophy up to the present day. In Cudworth's philosophy of it there is much that already in his own time was an anachronism and is entirely foreign to modern modes of thought. Though he was prepared to accept mechanical explanations wherever they seemed to rest on sufficient evidence, he was not prepared wholly to discard design, where this evidence seemed wholly lacking or insufficient. To us his favourite example of the angle of inclination of the plane of the ecliptic which is responsible for the seasons is unconvincing, but we can understand the temptation to exploit what seemed so mysterious an arrangement in the interest of Theism as then understood.[2] On the other hand, his criticisms of

[1] For an epitomized account of his argument, see Charles E. Lowrey's *Philosophy of Ralph Cudworth*, New York, 1884.
[2] In one of the few allusions in Continental writers to British Philosophy of the seventeenth century, Leibniz in a letter of 1714 accuses the Platonists of neglecting efficient and material causes: "The Idealists, like Plato and Aristotle, are right when they find the source of all things in final and formal causes; but they are wrong when they neglect efficient and material causes, and conclude, as Henry More and other Platonists have done, that there are phenomena which are incapable of mechanical explanation. The Materialists, on the other hand, are wrong in engaging themselves simply with a mechanical philosophy, rejecting the metaphysical view and trying to explain everything by what affects the senses only." He goes on to claim that he has himself "penetrated to the harmony of the two realms". It is only justice to Cudworth to note that he held that "the mechanic powers are not rejected, but taken in so far as they could comply serviceably with the intellectual model and platform" (ii. 594). Is Leibniz's "harmony" essentially different from this?

contemporary theories which sought to explain all natural, including organic, phenomena either on purely mechanical principles or by appeal to the direct intervention of God, as in the theory of Occasional Causes, have a permanent interest; while there is no part of his system in which he strikes a more modern note than in the view of the presence of a plastic principle in nature which he sought to substitute for these theories.

i. Against the purely fortuitous origin of nature he urged, on the one hand, the appearance of order (τὸ εὖ καὶ καλῶς) in the whole which it seemed impossible to attribute to mere chance and the struggle for existence, and, on the other, in the spirit of modern neo-vitalism, the existence of phenomena such as respiration, reparation, etc., in animal organisms which "plainly transcend the powers of mechanism". Against the doctrine of Occasional Causes he urged, quaintly but effectively, that it had no advantage over its materialistic rival in that, equally with it, it left us with "a dead and wooden world that hath nothing vital nor magical at all in it". To this, he held, it added the defect that it ignored "that slow and gradual process that is in the generation of things, which would seem to be but a vain and idle pomp or a trifling formality if the agent were omnipotent, as also those errors and bungles which are committed". But his chief argument is that the hypothesis would altogether fail of its object as a support of theism, seeing that it would render divine Providence "operose, solicitous, and distractious, and thereby make the belief in it more difficult".

ii. The problem of phenomena that seemed in Cudworth's language to "transcend the powers of mechanism" was of course no new one. It was to meet it that hylozoism, both in the form of the endowment of every atom of matter with a soul of its own and in the form of one single all-permeating soul, was devised. Cudworth would have nothing to do with either. The former, besides committing us to the absurdity of unconscious purpose and failing to explain how the souls of the separate cells could unite in the single soul of the organism, seemed to be of no use as a basis of religion. On the contrary, it was the destruction of religion by "the breaking and crumbling of the simple Deity".[1] The latter, though not in the same way violating every principle of science by the multiplication of entities, yet, in denying conscious purpose, was equally destructive of any form of theism.

[1] *Op. cit.*, iii. 455. *Cp.* on the whole subject i. 106 and 144, ii. 620 foll., iii. 405.

His own solution was to conceive of nature as the repository of a plastic energy, akin to what recent writers have called a *nisus, hormé*, or *élan vital*—an organizing principle in things, ever integrating and reintegrating them in a manner wholly transcending the powers of mechanism. "Though there be no vegetative soul in separate things or in the earth", he held "there may be one plastic, inconscious nature in the whole terraqueous globe, by which vegetables may be severally organized and framed and all things performed which transcend the power of fortuitous mechanism." Its general nature and mode of operation he tries further to define by contrasting it with human art. "Whereas human art acts from without, cumberously, moliminously, with tumult and hurly-burly, nature acting from within does its work easily, cleverly, and silently." Again, "whereas human artists are often to seek and at a loss, and anxiously consult, not as artists but only for want of art, nature is never to seek, nor unresolved what to do, nor doth she ever repent afterwards of what she hath done." On the other hand, nature falls behind art in that it "never intends those ends nor understands the reason of what it doth"; and further, because "it acts without express con-sense and consciousness and is devoid of self-perception of self-enjoyment".[1] For nature is at best "no God or Goddess but a low and imperfect creature". Its art is not the divine reason and art "pure and abstract, but *ratio mersa et confusa*, reason immersed and plunged into matter, and as it were fuddled in it and confounded with it".

In all this Cudworth is conscious that he may be accused of appealing, in mediæval style, to an "occult quality", but he defends himself vigorously on the ground that, while this amounts to assigning no cause at all for a phenomenon and only declares our ignorance, "he that asserts a plastic nature assigns a determinate and proper cause, nay the only intelligible cause of that which is greatest of all phenomena in the world, namely the τὸ εὖ καὶ καλῶς, the orderly, regular, and artificial (= artistic) frame of things in the universe; whereof the mechanic philosophers, however pretending to solve all phenomena by matter and motion, assign no cause at all".[2] It is not he but those who would make confusion the cause of order, or chance of constant regularity, that "must

---

[1] i. 235 foll. *Cp.* 281-282. The emphasis is on the *con* and the *self*. He does not of course intend to deny sense and feeling to animals.
[2] Much that he says on the theme, if there is no self-activity there is no activity at all, reminds us of Bergson's treatment of mechanism.

resolve it into an occult quality". If objection be taken to this as an unconscious purposiveness, Cudworth appeals to the analogy of instinct in the lower animals, habits in human beings, putting aside the question as to whether these are to be called "thought" as one merely of words. If Nature, as Plotinus said, is "a lover of contemplation", the contemplation is of a "drowsy, unawakened, or astonished kind".[1] What is essential in his doctrine is *first* that nature as a whole should be conceived of not as dead matter but as spirit that is asleep, *ratio mersa et confusa*; and *second* that for the hard and fast division of reality into thought and extension should be substituted the idea of a hierarchy of being "climbing stairs of entity and perfections";[2] starting from resisting extension, rising thence first to unconscious then to conscious life. It is no contradiction of this that he elsewhere speaks of it as a "descent and not an ascent".[3] What he is there thinking of is the necessity of supposing that in some sense the end must be in the beginning, that "Knowledge is older than sensible things, mind senior to the world, and the architect thereof".[4]

From this outline it will be seen where at once the strength and the weakness of this form of Neo-vitalism lie. Cudworth is on strong ground in insisting on the impossibility of resolving life into mechanism, the impossibility, as he himself puts it with regard to animal life, of making "sense and reason in animals to emerge out of a senseless life of nature by the mere modification and organization of matter".[5] No one has ever stated more clearly that life must precede organization and cannot come out of it. Nor is there any point in which the teaching of Cudworth is more in harmony with recent biological theory.[6]

On the other hand, the point in which the theologian is supremely interested, namely the relation between the "plastic nature" and the Divine Mind, is full of difficulty, and can hardly be said to have received more than a dogmatic solution. It is not surprising that Boyle in a celebrated controversy with Cudworth's disciple, Le

[1] iii. 432.   [2] ii. 246.
[3] See below, under heading "Theology". There is nothing the whole school held to so consistently as νοῦς προγενέστατος.
[4] iii. 420 and *passim*.   [5] *Op. cit.*, iii. pp. 283–284.
[6] See, *e.g.*, Julian Huxley's *The New Philosophy*, where mind, or "something of the same general nature as mind", is said to be "inherent in all life", and J. S. Haldane's *Mechanism, Life, and Personality*, where besides that "we cannot resolve life into mechanism", it is suggested that "behind what we at present interpret as physical and chemical mechanisms, life may be hidden for all we know".

Clerc, should have attacked him on this point and pressed on him the alternative *either* of separating the Divine Mind from nature and so incurring all the difficulties which attach to the Cartesian doctrine and which the plastic theory was designed to meet; *or* of substituting an unconscious purposiveness for the conscious design of a Divine Intelligence, and so failing to provide the support to religion which his theory was intended to give. But it is still less surprising that Cudworth should have failed to solve what to this day may be said to be the main problem of speculative Theism—that of bridging the gulf between self-integration and self-transcendence, as principles undeniably operative throughout nature, and anything that is recognizable as a Divine Mind.

3. THEORY OF KNOWLEDGE

Coleridge criticizes the whole school of Cambridge Platonists, Cudworth included, for its want of "a pre-inquisition into the mind, as part organ, part constituent of all knowledge, an examination of the scales, weights, and measures themselves, abstracted from their objects".[1] It would, of course, be vain to look in these seventeenth-century writers for anything[2] comparable to the analysis in Kant's *Critique of Pure Reason*. But in the sections of his works[3] dealing with knowledge or, as he called it, "epistemonical" theory, Cudworth not only starts the pre-inquisition, but carries it farther than had anywhere yet been done, and farther than any critic of empiricism carried it up to the time of Kant—farther, it may be added, than Coleridge himself, in his published works, anywhere attempts to do. From the point of view, moreover, of what was to follow in the later rejection of Kant's dualism between understanding and reason, Cudworth has the merit of giving the cue to British Idealism in this respect. If this has consistently refused to draw any hard and fast line between the unitive function of the mind in physical knowledge, whether perceptual or conceptual, in the apprehension of life and in the speculative grasp of the world as a whole, it was only carrying on the true Platonic tradition as interpreted by Cudworth. He saw in the work of the reason no merely regulative and provisional structure, but the completion of the systematizing, and therewith objectifying work of the under-

---

[1] *Notes on English Divines* (London, 1853), pp. 128 and 351.
[2] *Pace* Dugald Stewart. See below, p. 150 *n*.
[3] *Intellectual System*, iii. 417 foll. *Eternal and Immutable Morality*, pp. 557 foll.

standing, which, as he had the signal merit of clearly seeing, must
furnish us with the criterion both of truth and reality.

As Plato had developed his theory of knowledge in opposition
to the sensationalism of Protagoras, so Cudworth found himself
faced with a modern revival of Protagoreanism in Hobbes's contention that knowledge and understanding are "in us nothing else
but a tumult in the mind raised by external things that press on
the organical parts of man's body", and that this pressure being
what we call "sensation" "is *nothing more* than a motion among
the particles of the sensing body". His task, therefore, is conceived
by him as that of proving that knowledge "is not a passion from
anything without the mind, but an active exertion of the inward
strength, vigour, and power of the mind". His proof consists in
showing that, besides what is passively received through the senses
or survives as an image or "phantasm", we have to recognize
noemata, ideas, cogitations, or concepts, requiring an activity of
the mind apart from which what is received would be entirely
meaningless. What and whence, he asks, are these ideas?

We are tempted to explain them as merely modified phantasms,
seeing that these seem to be their normal accompaniments: "As
we ourselves consist of soul and body united together, so are the
cogitations that we have of corporeal things usually both noematical
and phantasmical together, the one being as it were the soul and
the other the body of them." But Cudworth was not prepared to
commit himself to the dogma which denied "imageless thoughts".
On the contrary, he held that "there are many conceptions of
which we can have no genuine phantasms at all", and even where
phantasms are present the concept is something entirely different
and cannot "by any strange chemistry" be extracted from them.[1]
Whence then do these conceptions come?

It would still have been in order before the appearance of Locke's
Essay in 1690 to appeal to the doctrine of "innate ideas" which
was supposed to have recently received the benediction of Descartes.
Cudworth is specially careful to avoid all allusion to innate ideas.[2]

[1] He gives a witty caricature of the ordinary doctrine which sought to explain
concepts as the results of abstraction, "by separation of the individuating
circumstances, as it were by hewing off certain chips from them, or by hammer-
ing, beating, and anvelling of them out into thin intelligible ideas; as if solid
and massy gold should be beaten out into thin leaf-gold". *Op. cit.*, iii. p. 614.
[2] That this was the attitude of the younger men to the doctrine of innate or,
as they called them, "connate" ideas is evident from the remarkable passage
in which Culverwel anticipates Locke's criticisms of it. "Do but analyse your

His own expression for the relation between sense and idea is "invitation"; the ideas are "invited and elicited" by a process which he compares to what we should call apperception. If we could conceive of him using the phrase "transcendental apperception", this would have exactly expressed what he appears to have meant. In other words, the source of the conceptual element in knowledge is traced by him, not to any storehouse of ready-made ideas, but to the nature of the mind itself. Concepts proceed "from the unitive power and activity of the mind itself". The examples he gives are a somewhat uncritical medley of mental processes (thought, volition, memory), ideals (justice, duty, truth), relations of real things (cause and effect), modalities (possibility, impossibility, necessity), ideal constructions (the triangle and the cube), logical principles like that of non-contradiction, none of which carry us beyond the commonplaces of the School. It is only when he comes to the detailed illustrations from concrete instances of what he means by the "unitive" action of the mind that a note is struck which is new and constitutes a real contribution to an idealistic theory of knowledge.

It illustrates at once the range of his thought and the imperfect division of the field of philosophy at this period that he draws his examples indifferently from politics, æsthetics, and epistemology

own thoughts; do but consult your own breasts; tell us whence it was that the light first sprang in upon you. Had you such notions when you first peeped into being? Had you these connate 'ideas' in the cradle? And were they rocked asleep with you? or did you meditate upon these principles: 'The whole is greater than its part'; and 'nothing can be and not be at the same time'? Never tell me that you wanted (? lacked) organical dispositions, for you plainly have recourse to the sensitive powers and must needs subscribe to this that all knowledge comes flourishing in at these lattices." While Culverwel will have nothing to do with connate ideas, but looks upon understanding "as a glass not prepossessed with any connate tinctures but nakedly receiving and faithfully returning all such colours as fall upon it", these colours are conceived of as coming from other sources than the objects of sense and meeting with a response from other powers than the senses. These powers are "the beginning of the soul's strength, espoused to their virgin objects, closing and complying with them long before discourse (*i.e.* reasoning) can reach them—nay with such objects as discourse cannot reach at all". (*Cp.* Wordsworth's—

> "All that, lost beyond the reach of thought,
> All human knowledge, to the human eye
> Invisible, yet liveth in the heart.")

In this sense he held "the Platonists were commendable that they looked upon the spirit of man as 'the candle of the Lord', though they were deceived as to the time when it was lighted". See *Of the Light of Nature*, chapter xi.

in the strict sense. His first is from the conception of the State, made prominent at the time of writing by the individualism of Hobbes. It seemed quite natural to Cudworth that a sensationalist theory of knowledge should go along with an atomic theory which treated society as consisting of units externally bound together by contract, and was blind to the deeper bond which united the members, "as it were by one will for the good of the whole". For, "though the eye may see the particular persons (or at least their outsides) that are the respective members thereof, yet it can neither see the bond which unites them together, which is nothing but relation, nor comprehend the *totum*, 'whole' that is made up of them, that is a polity or commonwealth according to the formal (= essential) nature of it; which is an idea that proceeds merely from the unitive power and activity of the mind itself".[1]

Cudworth and his friends were not primarily political writers. Where they touch on the theory of the State, it is usually to disown and denounce a view like that of Hobbes, which subordinates morality and with it liberty of conscience to State authority founded on power. But here his thought takes a wider sweep and penetrates more deeply to the foundations of all forms of society, as resting on the idea of a common good which transcends all forms of selfish interest. Undeveloped as the thought is, and with what he would call a "tang" of subjectivism, as though the unity were conveyed into society by the individual mind, it is not difficult to see in it one of the earliest statements in English literature of the political theory which is perhaps the most distinctive contribution of British writers to Idealistic philosophy. It is here all the more striking, coming, as it does, as a deduction from the central principle of his philosophy as a theory of knowledge.

His next illustrations, taken from the products of art and organic nature, are hardly less suggestive in view of later developments. Artifects, he points out, are no mere collections of materials. What makes a house or a palace is the idea which it embodies. "The very essence, formal *ratio*, reason of it, is made up of relative or schetical notions, in which there is a logic of whole and parts." This "print of intellectuality", so far from being a mere imaginary addition to the parts, is something which enters into their constitution, by reason of which they have "more entity" in them. "The eye or sense of a brute, though it have as much passively impressed

[1] *Op. cit.*, iii. p. 593.

upon it from without as the soul of a man hath, if it should see all the inside also as well as the outside, could not comprehend from thence the formal idea and nature of a house or palace, which nothing but an active intellectual principle can reach unto."[1]

What is true of artificial things is still more obviously true of organic creatures. It is only by a creative act of the mind that the parts can be seen in their organic unity. "Sense can give us colours either on the outside or the inside of any animals, but doth not sum them up into one *totum* or whole. Such an idea that hath something of logic in it is only conceivable by the unitive action and comprehensive power of the intellect."[2]

His last example of such "action and comprehensive power" in the field of knowledge is that of the cosmos itself. Here he is in his element. As perceived through the senses, the world is pluralistic. Its unity, indeed, he held, "pierces loudly into the ears of the mind, but in such an indiscernible manner that sense, listening never so attentively, could not perceive the least murmur of it". On the other hand, to "the intellectual mind", it is full of all manner of "logical scheses that unite the parts to one another, the whole with the mind" (this would have been enough for his immediate purpose; but theology was never absent from the mind of these men, and he adds), "and the mind of man to one infinite and eternal mind as containing the plot of the whole mundane music".

The "logical schesis" merging thus in an æsthetic one, he is led, naturally enough, to illustrate his main thesis in terms of feeling, as he has already done in terms of intellect and will. The delight which the mind of a man, as compared with that of the brute, or, again, the trained, as compared with the untrained, takes in these "harmonious airs" he declares to be only explicable on the supposition of the pre-existence in nature, on the one hand, of something akin to itself, "some footsteps and resemblances of itself"; on the other hand, of "anticipations" in the mind "gratefully closing" with these resemblances. "For which cause the ancients",

[1] iii. p. 594 (condensed).
[2] P. 595. This passage as well as that which precedes it on the sense of unity in objects of art reminds us of the treatment of these judgments in Kant's *Critique of Judgment*. We have, of course, nothing approaching the range of thought in Kant, but we have also none of the entangling ambiguities of a theory which, while insisting that the only concepts by which we can make organic nature intelligible to ourselves are those of mechanism, yet admits that living organisms inevitably carry us beyond all merely mechanical principles of explanation.

he concludes, "made Pan, that is nature, to play upon a harp; but sense which only passively receives particular outward objects doth here, like the brute, hear nothing but mere noise and sound and clatter, but no music or harmony at all; having no active principle and anticipation within itself to comprehend it by, and correspond or vitally sympathize with it; whereas the mind of a rational and intellectual being will be ravished and enthusiastically transported in the contemplation of it and of its own accordance to this pipe of Pan, nature's intellectual music and harmony."[1]

Returning to the theory of knowledge: Cudworth has hitherto been dealing with complex structures wherein the mind, in his own words, "comprehends by something of its own that is native and domestic to it that which is passively perceived by the senses", and so combines objects into wholes by an "anticipatory judgment" upon them: "displaying itself gradually after this manner".[2] He has spoken of sense as "passively receiving particular outward objects". He now carries the argument a step farther, in going on to show that there can be no knowledge of *individual objects of any kind*, except on the assumption of the activity of a unifying intelligence.

Taking the instance of a white triangular surface, he shows that to sense alone there is merely "the appearance of an individual thing, without any distinctions, concretely and confusedly together". Before it can be really anything to us, the mind has to "analyse and resolve this concrete *totum* and take notice of several distinct intellectual objects in it", *e.g.* whiteness and triangularity. These, by a further act of judgment, it refers to a common or corporeal substance. Herewith, inasmuch as all these are universals and may be considered apart from "individuating circumstances", the mind may be said to "bid adieu to sense and singularity", but only to return to them, "that so from thence with a descending view it may comprehend under the universals those individuals that now

[1] *Op. cit.*, iii. p. 600. In connection with such passages we naturally think of Coleridge's view of Nature, and the theory of art which he based upon it. What must always seem strange is that he should have had to go to Schelling for a doctrine that was staring him in the face in his own Cambridge predecessors. "The judgment that men have," wrote Cudworth, continuing the thought of the present passage, "of pulchritude and deformity is not merely artificial from institution or instruction or of taught things, but such as spring originally from nature itself."

[2] Pp. 603 and 609. "If there were no inward anticipations, the spectator would not judge at all but only suffer." The active element is essentially *judgment*.

affect the sense". Finally, bound up with the whole process, there is the judgment of actual external existence, without which it would remain merely "a notion or objective[1] cogitation". At the beginning of the passage he speaks of the object being given to sense "as existing without it", but the later explicit statement that objectivity (in our sense) is itself a function of judgment seems to put his meaning beyond doubt.

In the whole account there is doubtless much that is metaphorical and, from the point of view of modern psychology, mythical—as when he speaks of the process he is describing as one "whereby the mind first reflecting upon itself and its own ideas, virtually contained in its own uniform cognoscitive power, and thence descending downwards comprehends individual things under them". In this last phrase, moreover, there still survives too much of the idea of the concept as a mere class notion, instead of the unifying scheme with which he has already identified it: too much of the "abstract" instead of the "concrete" universal, as we might say. But such mythologizing is perhaps an incident in any attempt to draw out the process, as in the slowing down of movements in a cinematograph, while the other is only the survival in language of an idea of the universal which his own account has virtually superseded. In any case the general sense is clear, and the whole passage[2] is significant as the first statement in British philosophy of the necessary implication in the apprehension even of the simplest objects, as individual existences, of an element of judgment without which we cannot be said even to perceive them: that, in fact, as he puts it in conclusion, "knowledge doth not begin in individuals, but end in them".

In the passage which follows he goes on to deal with qualities like colour and sound, emphasizing the difficulty of explaining them on any theory which treats sense as merely the passive recipient of impressions from extended substance, and defining them in the end as "a species of cogitation or an half-awakened perception". Passing over this anticipation of a real difficulty with regard to secondary qualities, we have in the last part of this section what again must rank as perhaps the first clear statement of the constructive function of thought in mathematical concepts and propositions.

[1] In the terminology of the time "objective" = our "subjective".
[2] Pp. 603 foll.

In the proof that apart from "the actual strength and vigour of the intellect itself, comprehending its own intelligible ideas", there could be neither mathematical objects (triangle, circle, pyramid, cube, or sphere) nor mathematical truth, it is noteworthy that he recalls the reader not to the semi-mythological treatment in Plato's *Meno*, but to the classical statement in Aristotle's *Posterior Analytics*: "Since these demonstrations are of a universal, it is plain that there is no knowledge of the universal theorems of geometry by sense. For is it manifest that, if we could perceive by sense that the three angles of a triangle were equal to two right angles, yet should we not rest satisfied with this, as having therefore a sufficient knowledge of it (as some say), but would seek further after a demonstration hereof: sense reaching only to singulars, but knowledge to universals."[1]

To sum up Cudworth's doctrine of knowledge: while essentially Platonic in insisting on the presence of universals in all knowledge, he sees the futility both of mediæval discussions as to their separate existence and of facile appeals in his contemporaries to innate ideas. His argument throughout is an appeal to experience, none the less so because he sees that for any true account of what experience means he has to go beyond contemporary empiricism. That his teaching was lost on his immediate successors, and was only recovered after long wanderings in the mazes of Locke's "new way of ideas", is doubtless partly to be explained as due to the ponderous framework of learning in which it was encased; but it also shows that philosophies, like individuals, may be born out of due season. The uncriticized empirical point of view was too congenial to the spirit of the age to be lightly set aside. It had to work itself out to its own conclusions and exhibit its own inherent contradictions before men could be ready to go back upon its assumptions, and submit them to a thoroughgoing examination. But merit belongs none the less to those who, like Cudworth, anticipated by a century the general result of such a criticism.

4. THEOLOGY

The circumstances of Cudworth's time secured that all philosophy should have a direct theological bearing, affirmative or negative as the case might be. They had secured further that the issue should be seen to involve more than the truth of Christianity or

[1] P. 619.

any particular form of theism; and further still, that it should be profoundly influenced by the work of both Hobbes and Descartes. What impressed the Cambridge thinkers in the work of Hobbes was the blow that it had struck not only at theology but at the morality and civic loyalty which were conceived of as bound up with it. But not less did the spiritual world, as they conceived it, seem to be endangered by the would-be friends of theism, who taught that truth and goodness depended upon the arbitrary will of God and were able to draw support for this doctrine from certain elements in the Cartesianism of the day. While, therefore, in his own work, Cudworth had the inspiration of feeling that the whole cause of civilization, as he and his contemporaries in England understood it, depended on the success of his enterprise, he felt also that his task had a wider bearing as a reassertion of a doctrine of the nature of God with which the very existence of truth itself was essentially bound up.

As it lies out in the two treatises, his argument here consists of two parts, in the first of which he seeks to refute the objections that may be brought against any theology, in the second to set out the ground on which he would establish his own. Needless to say, the parts are not kept clearly distinct, and there is much in both sections that is negligible by the modern reader; but in both important issues are raised which are of permanent interest to philosophy and which are treated in a genuinely speculative spirit, making it worth while to follow his statement of them in some detail.

i. The negative arguments which he had to face were founded on the incomprehensibility of the idea of God and the difficulties involved in the whole conception of the infinite.[1]

(a) It was argued that the idea of God is incomprehensible, that what is incomprehensible is inconceivable, and that the inconceivable is as good as nothing. Cudworth was too good a Platonist to challenge the last of these statements. Seeing that the mind must be conceived of as a "diaphanous and crystal sphere" in some way reflecting whatever is in the real world,[2] anything that falls outside its range (and what more certainly does than what is self-contradictory?) *is* as good as nothing. But he is not prepared to admit that the incomprehensible is synonymous with the inconceivable. It may merely mean that to which our ideas are inadequate, and in that sense must in the end include the being not only of God but of ourselves,

---

[1] *Op. cit.*, ii. 517 foll.   [2] He quotes Aristotle's ψυχή πως πάντα.

and indeed of anything to which we attribute substantiality, *e.g.*, body, or even accidents themselves, such as time and motion.[1] "Truth", he finely says, "is bigger than our minds, and we are not the same with it, but have a lower participation only of the intellectual nature, and are rather apprehenders than comprehenders thereof." Though, therefore, we may not exhaust the fullness of the divine perfection, we may have the idea of a Being which is absolutely perfect, "as we may approach near to a mountain and touch it with our hands, though we cannot encompass it all round and enclasp it within our arms". Our reach, as we might say, is farther than our grasp. "Whatsoever", he sums up, "is in its own nature absolutely inconceivable, is nothing, but not what is not fully comprehensible by our imperfect understandings. It is true, indeed, that the Deity is more incomprehensible to us than anything else whatsoever, which proceeds from the fullness of its being and perfection, and from the transcendency of its brightness; but for the very same reason may it be said also, in some sense, that it is more knowable and conceivable. As where there is more of light there is more of visibility, so where there is more of entity, reality, and perfection there is there more of conceptibility and cognoscibility, such an object filling up the mind more and acting more strongly upon it."[2]

The suggestion, with which he ends this passage, that the presence in us of a sense of something adorable along with "a kind of ecstasy and pleasing horror"[3] "seems to speak thus much to us in the silent language of nature that there is some object in the world so much vaster than our mind and thoughts that it is the very same to them that the ocean is to narrow vessels"—belongs rather to the positive side of the argument.

(*b*) The second argument against theism founded upon the inconceivability, and therefore the unreality, of the *Infinite* is only a particular form of the first. Cudworth meets it again by admitting that anything which is self-contradictory must be unreal, and, further, that the idea of an endless time or space or body is self-contradictory. Such an idea involves that a thing which never can be (*e.g.*, a whole of time) actually is, and this justifies us in denying

---

[1] This in spite of the fact that, as we have seen, he was prepared to treat substance as one of the unitive or schetical ideas.

[2] ii. pp. 518 and 519, condensed.

[3] *Cp*. Rudolf Otto's "Numinal" in his *Idea of the Holy*. Cudworth himself uses *Numen* frequently in this connection.

the reality of infinite time: all we can say is that time must be conceived of as that which can be indefinitely increased, which is an entirely different thing.[1] This might seem, as it did to Kant, to be a surrender of the whole position and an admission that the infinite to us is unknowable. On the contrary, Cudworth maintains, just because we must reject the idea of the absolute reality of time, we are constrained to believe in a being who "is in the order of nature senior to time and so without time and before time". Therefore he concludes: "Though we, being finite, have no full comprehension and adequate understanding of this infinity and eternity, yet can we not be without some notion, conception, and apprehension thereof, so long as we can thus demonstrate concerning it that it belongs to something and yet to nothing neither but a perfect immutable nature."[2] Put in another way, though the word infinite, when applied to the Deity, is negative in form, yet in sense it is positive, meaning, as it does, "that which in order of nature is before the finite". It is in reality the affirmative of which the finite is the negative. If we reverse this and conceive of the infinite as mere endlessness, we substitute a counterfeit and imitation for the real thing.[3]

All this is of course good Platonism, according to which time is only "the moving image of eternity", but it is Platonism brought up to date. It is not difficult even to see in it an early statement of the later idealist distinction between the true and the false infinite. Applied to the attributes of Deity, it means that it is a mistake to look for these (e.g., wisdom and power) in the mere removal of all limits, assigning to God the power to make truth untruth, good evil, and so "to deny and baffle his own wisdom and understanding which is the very rule and measure of his power". The correction of the error consists again in conceiving of perfection not as the mere negation of all limits, but as the positive fullness of that which by reason of its limits falls short of it. The statement that only on the supposition of the reality of such a positive idea of perfection as the standard of comparison is it possible to explain the divers degrees of perfection revealed to us in things—the "scale or ladder of perfections" which we see in nature,[4] belongs again rather to the constructive part of the argument.

---

[1] Time and space are, in fact, functions of the *System*, *i.e.*, of Spirit. See Lowrey, *op. cit.*, pp. 128, 140

[2] P. 531.   [3] *Loc. cit.*, p. 537.   [4] P. 538.

Meantime it is interesting to find him following out this line of thought so far as to denounce the ordinary idea of the "attributes" of God as "a bundle of inconceivables and impossibles, huddled up together, attributes of honour and compliment only", nothing, in fact, "but the religious nonsense of astonished minds expressing their devotion towards what they fear". In opposition to all this, he claims for them that they are "all of them attributes of nature and of most severe philosophic truth", being in reality "nothing else but so many partial and inadequate conceptions of one and the same perfect being, taken as it were piecemeal, by reason of the imperfection of human understandings". We are left to infer that Cudworth would not have objected to the elimination of the term "atrributes of God" from the theological vocabulary altogether in favour of the interpretation of them as the aspects which nature presents to us when regarded as the source of our ideals of truth, beauty, and goodness.

(c) From the point of view thus developed, Cudworth is able to meet the negative argument which is founded upon the psychological origin of religion in fear, ignorance of causes, and the fictions of politicians, and which finds in it nothing but the "confounded nonsense of astonished minds". Though he held that religion could be justified as reasonable, Cudworth was far from holding that it was rational in the sense that everything in it could be reduced to logic. There is in man a sense of Deity "urging itself more immediately upon us, a natural *prolepsis* or anticipation in the minds of men concerning it", often "preventing ratiocination". There is, moreover, an element of fear in all religion, but it is a mistake to conceive of this as springing from an "antecedent fear concerning good and evil fortune". On the contrary, "none are less solicitous concerning such events than they who are truly religious"—the reason being their conviction that "their chief good is nothing that is in another's power but in that which is most truly their own, namely, the right use of their own will".[1] The source of this fear is "the sense that there is a natural difference of good and evil" and an "impartial justice which presideth over the same". As contrasted with the other kind of fear, which is mere superstition,[2]

---

[1] P. 569.
[2] To seek to dispel it, as the old atomists did, leaving the course of the world to accident, is merely to substitute one terror for another, and "running from fear, to plunge themselves into fear" (574). In other words, we have not a

this is an altogether wholesome and salutary affection and the beginning of wisdom. "The true fear of God (as the son of Sirach speaks) is the beginning of love, and faith is the beginning of cleaving to him." If from the point of view of a psychology which traces religion to atavistic complexes, or, again, which recognizes an "evolution of religion", Cudworth's treatment is elementary, his perception of the inadequacy of anything short of the sense of the infinite within to explain the phenomena of religious consciousness is wholly sound. He may be said to have been the first to formulate what Eucken has finely described as "the constant presupposition of all idealism that a spiritual life which is a unified whole is at work in the depths of our soul".[1]

ii. Coming to the positive grounds of theistic belief, there was for a writer of the time no escape from the glamour of the ontological argument, recently re-stated by Descartes. What Cudworth says of it has more than historic interest as an anticipation of Kant's destructive criticism and the virtual substitution of something entirely different not only from it but from anything that could properly be called Kantian. He sees that to conclude from the idea of a perfect being to its actual existence may be the merest sophism amounting to saying that "God is because he is".[2] Yet he is loth to part with so ancient a sheet-anchor of the faith. He is convinced of the validity of the principle, on which Bradley has recently insisted and which perhaps Cudworth was the first to state, that what is possible and at the same time necessary must be.[3] Upon the basis of it he makes several attempts at a re-statement of the Cartesian argument, but sets them aside successively as unlikely to bring conviction to his readers. In the end he sees that the real question is not of the existence of *some* necessary and eternal being (this is common ground with himself and his materialistic opponents), but of the *character* that we must assign to it: "whether that which existed of itself from all eternity and was the cause of all other things was a perfect Being and God, or the most imperfect of all things whatsoever, inanimate and senseless matter". In the rest of the earlier

conscience because we are cowards, but "conscience doth make cowards of us all". He would have added, with Coleridge, that it can also, on occasions, make heroes of us.

[1] Quoted by Perry, *op. cit.*, p. 118.　　　　　　　　　　　[2] iii. 41.

[3] "From these two things put together, the possibility of such a Being and its necessary existence, will it according to reason follow that he actually is." iii. 48–49.

work and in the later one we hear, accordingly, no more of the ontological argument, but we have instead what purports to be an argument founded on "the nature of existing things".

We have already seen that experience shows the world to be no dead level of things all on one plane, but a hierarchy or "climbing stairs of entity and perfection" leading from inorganic matter up through all stages to self-conscious intelligence. Is such a world, Cudworth asks, explicable on any other assumption than that of the reality of a being, who contains all perfections somehow in himself? On the principle that "no effect can possibly transcend the power of its cause", he was convinced that "there could be no ascent which was not also a descent", no "emergence" (the phrase is his) where there was nothing to emerge from. The question he is raising is not that between emanation and evolution (an issue that was yet in the future), but of the possibility of life and mind being posterior in reality to the lifeless and the senseless, the lower to the higher perfection. It seemed to him axiomatic that, unless we are to suppose that something can come out of nothing, all actual generated perfections must have their ground in one that is all—inclusive and ungenerated. But could it be demonstrated that Knowledge was an element in such a perfection? And granted that it was, was the world of truth, that was revealed in knowledge, of the essence of the divine mind, or was it dependent rather on the divine will conceived of as omnipotent over truth as over everything else? It was these questions that had been raised both by Hobbes and by Descartes, and our interest in Cudworth's theology consists in the way in which he meets them respectively.

(a) If, as Hobbes maintained, "the world and all sensible things must be before there can be any knowledge of them", if, that is, "things make knowledge and not knowledge things", it was impossible to represent knowledge as a perfection. Rather it is a sign of dependence, and therefore of imperfection, in the being to whom it is attributed.[1] We have seen how in his own theory of knowledge Cudworth seeks to establish the priority of knowledge to things, and we may here go directly to the application of this theory to the proof of the existence of God.

There is no more interesting point in the history of idealism as a philosophical theory than what Hoernlé[2] has called the subtle change of emphasis that took place when the doctrine of the ideas

[1] iii. p. 60.   [2] *Idealism as a Philosophical Doctrine*, p. 31.

passed from Plato into Christian theology. "For Plato, the ideas and not God are the supreme realities. On the other hand, when the Theism of Jewish and Christian thought came into contact with Greek philosophy in the resulting give-and-take, the balance shifted in favour of God." If God is the supreme and indeed the all-inclusive reality, the "ideas must somehow be conceived as part of His being and essence".

Whether the Cambridge Platonists were conscious of this shift is doubtful; anyway it does not prevent Cudworth from appealing to the authority of Plato in support of the direct inference from the *noemata* as immutable entities which are implied in all human knowledge to the existence of a supporting mind. As noemata they "can exist" (quoting the Parmenides) "nowhere but in the soul itself".[1] On the other hand, they cannot be dependent on our individual minds, seeing that they "have a constant being, when our particular created minds do not actually think of them, and therefore are immutable in another sense likewise, not only because they are indivisibly the same when we think of them, but also because they have a constant and never-failing entity, and always are, whether our particular minds think of them or not". For these reasons, "It is all one to affirm that these are eternal *rationes*, essences of things, and verities necessarily existing, and to say that there is an infinite omnipotent and eternal Mind necessarily existing that always actually comprehendeth himself the essences of all things and their verities".[2] And lest this should seem to reduce the Divine Mind to a system of merely passive perfections—a block universe of static types—or, again, to that of an artist forming things as copies of eternally existing archetypes, he goes on to insist that "the rationes and essences of things are not dead things like so many statues, images, or pictures hung up somewhere by themselves alone in a world: neither are truths mere sentences and propositions written down with ink in a book, but they are living things, and nothing but modifications of mind and intellect". It is only to "our particular, imperfect understandings, which are many times ignorant, doubting, erring, and slowly proceed by discourse and ratiocination from one thing to another", that truth can seem to stand still and look at us with dead eyes waiting for us to put it to use.[3]

[1] P. 625.   [2] P. 626.
[3] See Martineau's excellent statement of this point, *Types of Ethical Theory*, vol. i. p. 447.

Cudworth does not deal with the central problem of theism which
is thus raised as to the relation of "particular understandings",
conceived of as lodged in finite persons, to the universal mind; but
the general intention of these passages is clearly inconsistent with
any ultimate dualism between the divine and the human. In the
passage which follows he even gives a hint of how the union might
be made intelligible, by dwelling finally on the Ideas, thus actively
conceived, as the basis of the union of finite minds with one another
in a common understanding. Conceived of in any other way, men's
minds would be divided from one another by their individual
perspectives as they are in the world of sense. If they are to be
capable of "presently perceiving one another's meaning and having
the very same conceptions of things in their minds", there must
be a real community of intelligences made possible by their power
of participating in a system of mind-sustained truth. It is in this
sense that he would interpret Aristotle's saying that "that which
knows and that which is known (reason and the world of reason)
are really the same thing".[1]

(b) But in maintaining this he was aware that he was challenging
the central doctrine of the Cartesian philosophy, according to which
the world of truth, in which the human reason thus found itself at
home, was conceived of as the arbitrary creation of the Divine
Will. To Cudworth and his friends by destroying the possibility
of knowledge this was the destruction of everything, and it was
necessary to carry the argument into the enemy's camp and to
prove the essential unity of thought and reality. Short as it is,
there is no passage in his works which shows a truer apprehension
of the basis of a sound idealism than that in which he meets
Descartes on his own ground and shows the untenableness of the
whole position.

Descartes had maintained, in opposition to the sceptical suggestion
that the faculties in which men trusted might deceive them, that
they had the guarantee of the truthfulness of God: "God does not
deceive us". Cudworth has little difficulty in showing the fallacy
of this argument. "It is plain that it is but a circle and makes no
progress at all, for as much as all the certainty they have of the
existence of God and of His nature depends wholly upon the
arbitrary make of their faculties, which for aught they know may

[1] 'Επὶ μὲν γὰρ τῶν ἄνευ ὕλης τὸ αὐτό ἐστι τὸ νοοῦν καὶ τὸ νοούμενον,
de An., iii. 4, 12.

be false. Nay, according to this doctrine no man can certainly know that there is any absolute truth in the world at all, because it is nothing but his faculties which make him think there is, which possibly may be false. Wherefore, upon this supposition, all created knowledge, as such, is a mere fantastical thing."[1] Cudworth, with the rest of the school, accepted whole-heartedly the principle that only what is clearly intelligible can be true and in correspondence with reality,[2] to which he here adds the converse that "whatsoever is clearly understood has an objective entity in it and must be true". By this criterion we must stand if we are to have any world at all. "To make the certainty of all truth and knowledge not to be determined by the clearness of apprehensions themselves, but a supposed unaccountable truth and rectitude of faculties, and so by the uncertainty thereof quite to baffle all our clearest intellections, is quite to pervert the nature of knowledge, which is κατάληψις τοῦ ὄντος, 'the comprehension of that which absolutely is', which is not terminated in the τὸ φαινόμενον appearance only as sense is, but in that τὸ ὄν, 'which is', and whose evidence and certainty is no extrinsical, adventitious, and borrowed thing, but native and intrinsical to itself." His conclusion is: "Be our faculties what they will, and let them be supposed to be made how you will, yet, notwithstanding, whatsoever is clearly understood and conceived has an objective entity in it and must of necessity be true. For a clear concept cannot be nothing."

It might still be urged that men can never tell for a certainty when they have clear apprehensions. To this Cudworth replies that, while it cannot be denied that men are often deceived and think they clearly comprehend what they do not, it does not follow that they can never be certain that they do clearly comprehend anything, any more than that "because in our dreams we think we have clear sensations, we cannot therefore ever be sure, when we are awake, that we see things as they really are".

In the absence of a more definite statement of what was meant by "clear apprehension", the reply, it must be admitted, is not wholly convincing. Descartes had himself set the fashion of appealing to "clearness and distinctness" as the criterion of truth. But neither he nor his contemporaries realized sufficiently that "clearness and

[1] P. 635.
[2] This does not exclude, as we have seen, realities which are beyond our comprehension. The existence of these may be clear and distinct, though their full nature may not be.

distinctness" was itself anything but a clear and distinct idea.[1] What they doubtless meant was the clearness and distinctness that comes, as in the typical case of mathematics, from the perception of the complete interrelatedness of the parts in any whole, but this was never clearly stated or universally applied as it has been in recent idealistic philosophy.

Cudworth saw that inner connection in a logical whole was the clue to the intelligibility of the world along the whole gamut from particular things as given to sense to the Cosmos itself; he saw that to be fully intelligible was to be true, and that truth was the form that reality took as apprehended by mind; finally, he saw that reality, though always present in part, could never fully appear to finite minds, whose thought it always transcended, and from that he drew the conclusion of the existence of an intelligence in which truth and reality, thought and being, were somehow one. But he cannot be said to have brought these elements together in a coherent system of what might be called pure or non-theological metaphysic. What can be claimed for him is that he saw that the foundation of any true system and the starting-point of sane philosophizing must be the validity of knowledge as guaranteed by reason itself. In the statement of this faith at the conclusion of the present passage, in opposition both to materialism and to what seemed to him a fanatical and misguided theism, the seeds of both of which he found in the Cartesianism of his time, he happily quotes Origen against Celsus: " 'Μόνον τῶν ὄντων βέβαιον ἐπιστήμη', 'Science and knowledge is the only firm thing in the world', without a participation of which communicated to them from God, all creatures would be mere *ludibria* and vanity."

---

[1] See, however, John Norris on this below, p. 93.

CHAPTER III

CUDWORTH (ii). IMMUTABLE MORALITY

I. THE BOOK

Although Cudworth's whole philosophy had for its motive the vindication of moral distinctions, and although, after his failure to come to a detailed application to them of his long argument in the *Intellectual System*, he sought to remedy this defect by planning a shorter work with precisely this object, he succeeded in leaving in the end only the merest fragment with direct bearing on the subject. The *Treatise on Immutable Morality*, in fact, comes to little more than a later statement of the argument of the earlier work. Moral theory plays little more part in it. As Martineau puts it, the two books "present the same philosophy twice over".[1] History has in a sense compensated by causing his name to be chiefly associated with the plea for an "eternal and immutable morality". But in doing so it has done him also the ill-service of diverting attention from what is of real value in his work to a phrase which seems to place him in antagonism to all that modern ethics teaches as to the varying forms in which morality presents itself and the essential relativity to circumstances of the values it represents.

To do Cudworth justice in respect to his sins both of omission and commission, we have to remember, in the first place, that even the shorter treatise is only a portion of the work he was engaged on at the time of his death.[2] In the second place, we have to remember that the eternity and immutability he speaks of do not attach to the details of what he calls "positive" or "thetical" moral and legal injunctions, but only to the principles of ethics and politics, as resting, in the one case, on "the intellectual and rational nature of man", in the other, on the reality of a common good which, in virtue of that nature, the members of human society are pledged to realize. In the account which he actually gives in the text we have to remember finally that, as in the case of his theory of knowledge, the argument takes its form from the theories with

---

[1] *Op, cit.*, p. 434.
[2] See the "Account of the Life and Writings of Ralph Cudworth, D.D." by Thomas Birch, M.A., F.R.S., in his edition of the *Intellectual System*, p. 32 foll. Birch also tells the story of More's deference to Cudworth in publishing his *Enchiridion Ethicum* in Latin, so as the less to interfere with his friend's projected work.

which he found himself face to face; on the one hand, the general theory (connected with Descartes) that made good and evil depend on the mere fiat of the Divine Will; on the other, that which (as in Hobbes), holding to their dependence on will, ignored or denied the operation in human affairs of any will higher than that of man. We shall get the best idea of what he both did, and, so far as our material goes, failed to do, by following shortly his argument under these two heads.

2. PRIORITY OF GOOD TO THE WILL OF GOD

His treatment of the more general subject of the dependence of good and evil on arbitrary will, as we find it in Book I, Chapter II, of the *Eternal and Immutable Morality*, does not open very hopefully. Everything, he declares, must be determined necessarily and immutably by its own nature, over which mere will "can have no control". Will, whether in God or man, is only an efficient cause; its action presupposes entities with a nature of their own (in his language, which are formal causes or essences). Seeing then that justice and injustice are entities with such a nature they cannot be "arbitrarious things". If this were all that Cudworth had to say, his critics[1] would be justified in setting the argument aside as merely an egregious case of begging the question. The whole question turns upon the existence of a "natural" justice. To assume that it comes under his principle that "the nature of things must be that which it is and nothing else" is to assume the very point at issue.

But Cudworth goes on in the sections which follow to analyse the idea of "law" in order to show that wherever we have law, by whomsoever promulgated, there is an assumption of an *obligation* to observe it. "Obligation to obey is older than all laws and previous and antecedent to them." In all laws, therefore, whether of God or man, "it is not mere will that obligeth, but the nature of good and evil, just and unjust really existing in the world". He is aware, however, that this is still precisely what is denied by the philosophy he is criticizing and that more is required to justify it. It is here that his previous analysis of the place of mind and reason in knowledge comes to his aid, and he is able boldly to appeal as the basis

[1] See Tulloch, *in loco*.

for the assertion of a real justice in practice (as he had there been able to appeal for the assertion of a real truth in knowledge) to the "rational and intellectual nature of man". Finally, in a passage reminding us of Kant's categorical and hypothetical imperatives, he draws the distinction between things that "the intellectual nature obliges to immediately, absolutely, and perpetually, and upon no condition of any voluntary action that may be done or omitted intervening", and those that "natural justice or the intellectual nature obligeth to accidentally and hypothetically upon the condition of some voluntary act of another person invested with lawful authority in commanding".

In these statements it is easy to see the spirit of the sturdy English and Puritan Divine putting lawfulness before all laws and carrying his claim before the high tribunal of Heaven itself. But it is here a matter of philosophy, and we should have expected from him at least some attempt at a definition of goodness in terms of the "intellectual nature". There is no pretence of this, but Cudworth goes off *more suo* to the ever present theological issue between himself and Descartes as to the priority of will or goodness in the nature of God, and therewith as to the real nature of the infinity and freedom we are to assign to Him.

In opposition to the Cartesian theory of the unlimited independence and the liberty of indifference that a false piety would assign to the divine wisdom, he ends the section with the claim that "There is in the scale of being a nature of goodness superior to wisdom, which therefore measures and determines the wisdom of God, as his wisdom measures and determines his will. . . . Wherefore, altho' some novelists (= innovators) make a contracted idea of God consisting of nothing else but will and power; yet his nature is better expressed by some in the mystical representation of an infinite circle, whose inmost centre is simple goodness, the rays and expanded plat thereof all-comprehending and immutable wisdom, the exterior periphery or interminate circumference omnipotent will or activity by which everything without God is brought forth into existence. Wherefore the will of God is always free, tho' not always indifferent, since it is its greatest perfection to be determined by infinite wisdom and infinite goodness."[1] Powerful and

[1] *Eternal and Immutable Morality*, in vol. iii. p. 540 of work as quoted above (condensed).

convincing though this is as an assertion of the true nature of freedom against the abstractions of the Cartesianism of the day, it still leaves the idea of goodness, whether in God or man, undefined, and it is particularly tantalizing to be referred to what is to "follow afterward in another place"—which never comes.

Yet, with all its defects, it is possible to see in Cudworth's treatment of the general question a clear grasp of what must always be the central point in a sound idealism. In the Volitionism which Coleridge was to bring the whole power of his genius to vindicate, still more in that of our own time, which seeks to vindicate the reality of the spiritual world by the discovery of spontaneity and contingency in nature, we have the legitimate successor of the Cartesian theology which exalted will above rational purpose. At the best, this philosophy contains only a part of the truth; at the worst (in other words, when insisted on as the whole to the neglect of that to which by its nature as rational activity the will is committed), it merely brings us back in the end to the "naturalism" it seeks to escape. Why, we ask, apart from what is spontaneously done, should spontaneity have more value than necessity? A Bishop may prefer a nation free to a nation compulsorily sober, but the freedom that ends in insobriety is only another kind of bondage. In opposition to all this, Cudworth's claim for the priority of goodness in "the scale of being", even as the essence of being itself, is an anticipation of what may be said to contain the central contention of present-day idealism as represented by such writers as Green, Bosanquet, and Bradley.

3. NATURAL JUSTICE

Cudworth's criticism of Hobbes's ethical and social theory has the merit of being the first systematic refutation, and is not unworthy of that place. Following on what he had said in the *Intellectual System* on the psychology of religion, we have, to begin with, a vigorous denunciation of the supporters of Hobbes on the ground that "as they first of all slander human nature and make a villain of it, so do they, in the next place, reproach justice and civil sovereignty also, making it nothing but an ignoble and bastardly brat of fear, or else a lesser evil, submitted to merely out of necessity for the avoiding of a greater evil, that of war with every one by reason of man's natural imbecility". He next goes on to expose, as has often been done since, the fundamental inconsistency of the contractual theory of social justice.

It is true that if there be a natural justice, covenants will oblige. Yet "without natural justice they are nothing but mere words and breath, and therefore can they have no force to oblige". If, to avoid this difficulty, these "justice-makers" fly to "laws of nature", as Hobbes himself does, "this is not to make justice, but clearly to unmake their own hypothesis, and to suppose justice to have been already made by nature or to be in nature. These their laws of nature are indeed nothing but juggling equivocation and a mere mockery. For they who have courage and generosity (= high spirit) in them, according to this hypothesis, would never submit to such sneaking terms of equality and subjection but venture for dominion, and resolve either to win the saddle or lose the horse. Here, therefore, our atheistical politicians plainly dance round in a circle; first deriving the obligations of civil laws from that of covenants, and then that of covenants from the laws of nature, and, lastly, the obligations both of these laws of nature and of covenants themselves again from the law, command and sanction of the civil sovereign, without which neither of them would at all oblige. And thus is it manifest how vain the attempts of these politicians are to make justice artificially, when there is no such thing naturally (which is indeed no less than to make something out of nothing); and by art to consociate into bodies politic those whom nature had dissociated from one another; a thing as impossible as to tie knots in the wind or water or to build up a stately palace out of sand. Indeed, the ligaments by which these politicians would tie the members of their huge Leviathan or artificial man are not so good as cobwebs, they being really nothing but mere will and words; for, if authority and sovereignty be made only by will and words, then is it plain that by will and words they may be unmade again at pleasure."[1]

We have already been told what Cudworth would substitute for this "dissociate" idea of political society. We have seen how he finds in society a premier instance of the idea of a whole, whose parts in spite of their apparent discontinuity as physical bodies yet, as he here puts it, "are joined by scheses, relations, and habitudes to one another (founded on some actions of them as they

[1] Pp. 505 foll., condensed.

are cogitative beings), and by order all conspiring into one thing".[1]

If asked what this "one thing" is, Cudworth is prepared to define it as "the good of the whole", which, as the object of "one will", is that which makes the commonwealth a spiritual unity and, so far as its laws and institutions embody this good, constitutes the real source of their authority over the many wills of the individuals. But again we have to be content with little more than the mere statement, in this case not even co-ordinated with the general ethical motive of the treatise.

Even if we try to eke out Cudworth's ethical theory by a reference to the brilliant apperçus of John Smith and to the more methodical but less philosophical *Enchiridion Ethicum* of Henry More, we have a very imperfect outline, in which it is again easier to see the sturdy British protest against arbitrary law and government than anything that could be called an articulated social ethics.

What was necessary was that Cudworth should carry over what he had succeeded in partly doing in the analysis of knowledge into the sphere of conduct and see in the idea of goodness in the individual just the counterpart of the "schetical" element that he had shown to be present in all knowledge and, in the search for truth, to dominate the details by its "logic". Substituting the instincts, appetites and habits for sensory data, it would then have been possible to see in morality the domination of these by the idea of a practical order prescribed by "the intellectual and rational nature of man", committing him to realize the good as a coherent whole of purposes, precisely parallel to truth as a coherent whole of thoughts.

If we had only his published works before us, we should have to admit that while the germ of all this is contained in them, the fuller development of it had to await a later age. But in his manuscript remains we have the record of his persistent attempt in failing health to work out the theory of the Will on which he had recognized from the first that his whole philosophy depended, and the present study would be still more incomplete than it is without some more detailed reference to their contents.[2]

---

[1] P. 593.   [2] See note at the end of this Study.

4. THE FREEDOM OF THE WILL

It was one of the strong points in the teaching and preaching of the Cambridge men that to them freedom and rationality were not two different things, but one and the same. To be free was to be determined by reason, and to be determined by reason was to be determined by what was most real in oneself—in other words, to be self-determined.[1] This teaching Cudworth held was fundamental to any true morality. But it had to be vindicated against the opposite tendencies of that of Hobbes and Descartes, the one towards an absolute necessitarianism, the other towards a spurious form of absolute liberty of choice. On the former, what becomes of conscience and inward struggle? On the latter, what becomes of the determining power of habit and acquired disposition, on which all moral progress depends?

These questions required to be settled by a fuller account of what is meant by will and the freedom that is claimed for it than was anywhere extant. It was the clearness with which Cudworth recognized the scope of the problem, and the method by which alone it could be solved, together with the breadth and consistency of his own solution of it, that gives value to what we are able to rescue from the manuscript remains of his treatises on the subject.

"That faculty of the human soul", he writes in the opening passage of what seems to be the second part of the first of five books,[2] "commonly expressed by the name *liberum arbitrium* or free will, is a matter of great consequence as to the doctrine of morality to be assured and vindicated; but it is a thing of no small difficulty to do clearly and convincingly as may appear from the objection made against it in the former part. And this is not only true in a moral sense that the most difficult knowledge is to know a man's self, but also in a philosophical." After explaining that the source of the difficulty lies in the difference between the self and all other objects, which, unlike it, may be put at a distance and observed from an external point of view, he goes on: "Hence, if what I shall say concerning free will seem unsatisfactory to any, I shall think it no marvel at all, for I never was myself fully satisfied in any discourse which I read of it." Following on this modest

[1] See the passage quoted above from John Smith.
[2] MS. British Museum Add. No. 4981.

introduction, he proceeds to give an outline of the method he intends to adopt. "We will endeavour to lay down some intelligible hypotheses tending to the clearing of this point, and then compare the phenomena with them and demonstrate the truth of them from thence. The first thing that we shall propound is that the human soul is a self-active being, by which we mean a being who has a spring and fountain of activity within itself." This may be said to be the "hypothesis" which all he here writes is meant to maintain and explain.

i. It has to be maintained first against those who, like Hobbes, would resolve all action into "mere swinges and impetuosities of nature which have no internal self-flexibility in them". Just as in perception we are not merely passive, but employ imagination, which is "a motion or action of a different species such as does not belong to body but to an incorporeal substance wholly distinct from local motion—an autocinecy, not a heterocinecy, occasioned and invited, but not caused from something without", so "besides appetites there are ambition, emulation, pride, desire for honour and applause, which only a madman can consider merely mechanical motions". Even when unmastered and unregulated, there is manifested in these a single self-activity of the soul. But that there is such a power of mastery is as evident as that there are appetites and passions to be mastered. "What", he asks, "is this ruling principle?"

He rejects the definition of it as a rational or intellectual appetite as contrasted with that which is the result of mere fancy and imagination on the ground first that we may will the irrational, and second that this would not secure the required "self-flexibility": reason imposes a necessity of her own. "Wherefore we have proposed another psychological hypothesis: that whereas there are in the soul lower and higher principles of life and action: appetites, passions, and inferior reason, which is a comprehension of our own utility, and superior reason or the instinct of honesty, besides the speculative understanding and other powers, there must of necessity be in the soul one common focus or centre in which all these kinds may meet, some one thing in which all is recollected and knit together, something that is conscious of all congruities, both higher and lower, of all the cogitations, powers, and faculties of the soul . . . which also can wield, steer, and guide the whole soul and exercise power and dominion over the several faculties of it.

Now this is the whole soul redoubled on to itself, which both comprehends itself and, holding itself as it were in its own hands, turns itself this way and that way. This in all free-willed, self-powerful beings is the head and summit or top of them, the τὸ ἡγεμονικόν, the ruling principle in them, and not the notional or speculative understanding as some conceit. This is the αὐτοέκαστος, that which is properly called I myself in every man; and, according to the disposition of it as it converts and turns itself, frames and fabricates itself, as it exerts its own activity towards the higher principle in the soul, more or less so is every one morally denominated good or bad. This is commonly called will when that word is taken properly, not for any lubency in general, but as distinct from animal appetite—the soul redoubled and reflected upon itself, recollected and knit up together into itself, hanging tight and loose, hovering and suspended, active upon itself and determining itself, and being nimbly self-flexible this way and that."[1]

It is this fact that explains the apparent duplicity of the soul indicated by such phrases as being superior to oneself; as also the presence of *judgment* as an element in all determination, an element, however, which is not something different from the will, but its concluding form and identical with it. Will, in fact, is not, as Hobbes called it, "the last appetite", but "the last practical judgment" in deliberation. What distinguishes it from judgment of opinions, which Cudworth describes as, in comparison with it, "natural", is that "it belongs rather to the doubled self-active soul, and is the act of the man or the whole soul". This is indicated in common language by the use of the word "conscience" for that which is said to approve, condemn, arbitrate, etc.—all of these merely "different ways in which one and the same thing displays itself".[2]

(ii) But to have established the reality of this power of self-determination is not sufficient in view of the exaggeration of it in the ordinary doctrine of free will as something wholly indeterminate, and the writer returns to the criticism of this error with a view to showing how it fails to take account of the "phaenomena".

In the first place, looking at the facts in general, it is a mistake to conceive of this "redoubled activity of the soul which governs

[1] MS., vol. iv. p. 106.
[2] He compares it elsewhere to "the same air in an organ passing through several pipes and making several noises" (see *Treatise of Freewill*, p. 25).

its activity" as indifferent to everything. Just as motion is a mani-festation of something one and the same, so the will must be of some natural and necessary inclination.[1] Cudworth, like a true Platonist, finds this "natural and necessary inclination" in the idea of "good": "We do not will merely because we will, but it is always for the sake of some good. . . . There is talk of hating good as good and loving evil as such. But it is rather to be thought impossible that there should be any such being in the world." The will "cannot possibly pursue after any(thing) or will any(thing) as it is incongruous to it, but only as taking notice of something of good in it". To pain, for instance, as such, "aversion is as necessary as the descent of a stone downwards".

In the second place, there are instances in which the case is so clear and the balance of good so all on one side that there is no conscious choice between alternatives. In these, as Cudworth puts it, "goods of utility, of pleasure, honour and honesty do so conspire as that the will doth in a manner naturally and necessarily without any wavering or hesitation embrace the same". "Finally, there is a factitious nature of the will which is liable to habitual dispositions, which do strongly incline it one way more than another, and are not whensoever we please immediately vincible and destroyable by us." In all these cases we have will, yet in none of them pure in-difference and contingency. They do not, however, exhaust the facts, and there are undoubted cases into which choice and apparent contingency enter.

While it is true that the idea of "good" or of what is "in con-gruity with the soul" is always present, it is only so as a "general and confused notion". It has to be particularized and defined. In this process many cases occur where good is mixed with evil, evil with good; dishonesty is mixed with pleasure, ease and profit; even the greatest bodily pain may be mixed with "the good of honesty in undergoing them". Hence there is "a great latitude and compass for the will to exercise contingent liberty and in activity to determine itself to this or that particular good". If we are going to act at all, "there must be some power in the soul to compound and arbitrate these differences and to determine the loose infinitude or capability of nature one way or other". Where there is an equal balance, the will seems even to have the power of adding "some-thing of its own to the moments of reason so as to rest the scale,

[1] See *op. cit.*, p. 30.

so that the opportunity of action may not be lost". There are, moreover, different degrees in which the powers of thought and judgment may be called upon in deliberation, which is itself an exercise of will.

"For the soul may more or less introvert itself or turn the way of its cogitation inward upon itself, attend to its own actions, and expone the different sentiments of its own mind and weigh them within itself; it may be more or less watchful and careful and circumspect, excite or quicken itself more or less to the use of endeavours, fortify itself by resolution, wake considerations both rational and fantastical more or less to confirm its purposes. In the contest between the higher and lower principle, the animal instinct and the instinct of honesty and morality, the soul, as redoubled and self-active, hath plainly in it a power or strength to promote itself toward the higher good which is self-determinable, and may be more or less exerted by it; it may either put forth a vigorous force of *conatus* to resist the lower animal inclinations when repugnant to the dictate of honesty, or determine itself to a sluggish, lazy, languid compliance with them. . . . According as it is either in such an exerted or non-exerted condition, it will be apt to have different judgments of things and consequently to act differently. When it is recollected into itself and stands upon its watch it will immediately repel those assaults and temptations, which at another time it would be easily vulnerable by. It will have different sapors, tastes, and relishes of things, and be apt to make different judgments not only in practical but also in theoretical matters according as it doth screw up itself to a higher pitch or let itself down to a lower peg." In a word, as Scripture has it, it may "gird up the loins of its mind" or leave them ungirt. Lastly, "when designs of great consequence are taken up, the soul may determine itself to attend more to some one consideration than another, and thereby add more or less weight to some reasons and considerations, and so resolve otherwise than it should do if it had maturely and impartially examined it".

All this has to be admitted, yet none of these instances proves the contingency of the will in general, or that there is no more certainty of doing one thing than another. Any such contingency "would be a mere monstrosity in nature". So much may indeed be granted that "in all free-willed beings which are neither essentially good nor bad there may be a contingent possibility in length of time[1] of their changing from virtue to vice and vice to virtue, of their ascending to the divine life or of their again descending from it—which are those *circuitus animarum*, those circuits of souls, which some philosophers have supposed". Souls need constant self-active exertion, as animals need continual refection and reparation to preserve them in the same state of health and strength. But the important thing is that *this contingency arises from their imperfection and from their occupying a middle place between perfection and brutish animality*. "Self-power or free will is in fact of mixed nature, a mongrel compound of perfection and imperfection like the monster of the poet *mulier formosa superne definit in piscem*—an amphibious thing according to the different use of it. Though vigour is its true nature, through sluggish compliance it becomes unnatural and degenerate."[2]

What gives the vulgar view of freedom as consisting in unconditioned liberty of choice its attraction, is the appearance of dominance over action which it seems to promise, and the idea that such freedom must belong to God as His special glory "assisted by infinite power of operating the same". But this is "a spurious and adulterate notion" of free will—a description not of a power but of a weakness, seeing that it means the power to "defy and abandon not only wisdom and goodness moral, but also the reason of his own good, the reason which dictates what is most agreeable to his own private utility". "To conclude, therefore, *liberum arbitrium* is not indifferency but self-power, a power which the soul as redoubled and self-active hath of exerting a vigorous *conatus* towards the higher principle of honesty and reason, or of not exerting the same, of determination to follow towards the better or the worse."

This being so, it is clear that this power cannot belong to God, "in whom is no variableness or shadow of change, who can neither transcend himself nor fall short of himself, who never consults or deliberates as having to seek what to do, who doth not keep up or repair his flitting being by any new exerted *conatus*, contention or tugging with himself, but comprehends and is all his possibility with ease at once; lastly, who is liable to no uncertain contingency,

---

[1] This he conceived as extending into the next life. See what he says of eternal punishment below, p. 71.

[2] In this connection he elsewhere quotes *Sirach*: "Before man is life and death, and whatever him liketh shall be given him."

blame, or commendation." "Howbeit," he adds, "God may be said in a pure and refined sense to be most perfectly αὐτεξούσιος, *sui dominus*, Lord and master of himself, and most truly free not in a compound manner as if there were such a duplicity in him as in free-willed beings, or as if he were so much distant from himself and hung so loose together, but as being essentially simple goodness, the root of all wisdom, excellency, and perfection."[1]

In the doctrine here outlined the modern reader will be apt to find much that belongs to a primitive psychology. What is remarkable is not so much the extent to which Cudworth has suffered from the limitations under which he worked as the extent to which by sheer force of intellect he has been able to break through them.[1] As an attempt to develop a rational theory of volition equally remote from ordinary determinism and libertarianism, it stands alone, so far as I know, in English philosophical literature, not only of his own but of the following century. Till the time of Coleridge there was no equally strong and clear assertion of the implication in voluntary action of the idea of the self as a whole and all that this carried with it for the interpretation of the moral life; while for a like analysis of the process of deliberation, with its powerful emphasis on the part that the movement of attention to ideas plays in it, we have had to wait till our own day. That in the main portion of the manuscript work the old defects of philosophical style show themselves even in exaggerated form ought not to prevent us from recognizing the clearness with which, in these excerpts, he realizes what is meant by philosophical method, and the strictly philosophical spirit he brings to the development of his own argument.

SUMMARY

Attempting to sum up the general significance for philosophy of this early Cambridge movement, we should, I think, be justified in claiming for it that it stands in the *first* place, when regarded as a whole, for the first modern attempt to unite the essential spirit of Christianity with that of Greek Philosophy by interpreting the nature of God and of faith in Him in terms of the Idea of the

[1] See, *e.g.*, his criticism of "the scholastic jargon of faculties" in *Treatise of Freewill*, p. 25.

Good. Where you have faith in the supremacy of truth and goodness, there you have faith in God; where you have not, you have either an empty form or, worse still, a degrading superstition. In the *second* place, in its leading philosophical writer, it stands for an attempt at an up-to-date statement in opposition, on the one hand, to a pronounced form of Naturalism (in Hobbes), on the other, to an empty Spiritualism (in Descartes), of the essential elements of an idealist philosophy: (*a*) the reality of the form or underlying identity of principle in things as that which gives the clue to their nature; (*b*) as a consequence of this, the necessity for a constructive act of thought in the apprehension of them over against the passive reception of sense and the associations of memory; (*c*) the unity of these forms themselves in an all-comprehensive form or pattern, in which their apparent discords are ultimately harmonized—variously describable as truth, goodness, or beauty, of which our own sense of these things, as intermittently revealed to us under finite conditions, is a presentiment.

The movement as sketched above, when we look back upon it, has the appearance of something isolated and largely abortive. It was indeed in a sense born out of due season. The main tide of British philosophy was setting strongly in the direction of the empiricism, which was destined during the greater part of the next century to dominate thought. But the tradition lived on well into that century in two writers who have hardly received justice from historians as at once continuing and closing this early outburst of idealistic thought.

NOTE ON CUDWORTH'S MANUSCRIPT REMAINS

In the British Museum Manuscript Room, under the numbers Add. 4978–4985, are seven folio volumes of more than a thousand pages, entitled on the flyleaf of the first "The Ethical Works of Ralph Cudworth", with a reference to John Nichol's *Literary Anecdotes* (vol. ix. p. 276) for their story. This is also given in fuller form in the *Gentleman's Magazine* of 1788 (p. 1186). They were left in the possession of Cudworth's daughter, Lady Masham, the friend of John Locke. On his second marriage, Lord Masham, her grandson, sold them to Robert Davies, a bookseller in Piccadilly, in order to make room in his library for "books of polite amusement".

Apparently under the impression that they were Locke's, Davies gave some of the Scriptural parts to embellish Dr. Dodd's Commentary on the Bible, in which he was interested, and thus secured the success of that undertaking. The remainder, long left in neglect, he afterwards sold for forty guineas. The purchaser, on discovering that they were Cudworth's and not Locke's, returned them; but on receiving the money back, in consideration of Davies's disappointment, gave him ten guineas, and recommended them to the British Museum by which they were purchased in 1796.

For some account of the contents of these volumes, see Thomas Birch's Edition of the *Intellectual System* (London, 1820), vol. i. pp. 32 foll. The short treatise in No. 4978 on Freewill was edited by John Allen in 1838, and is referred to above. The statement of Cudworth's doctrine in the text follows the "Summary View of what we have to say concerning *Liberum Arbitrium*", in vol. No. 4981, itself a part of a longer treatise. An interesting illustration of the essentially Platonic theory of the will, here set forth, is the application of it in No. 4983 to the ordinary doctrine of Eternal Punishment, which is rejected as wholly incompatible with the existence of the natural and indestructible "tendency of the soul towards good".

CHAPTER IV

THE OXFORD AFTERMATH. JOHN NORRIS (i)

THE IDEAL WORLD ABSOLUTELY IN ITSELF

I. PLATONISM IN THE REVOLUTION ERA

Although the movement known as Cambridge Platonism may be said to have exhausted itself by the 'eighties of the seventeenth century, it was, as we have seen, part of a larger European movement, and the impulse that gave rise to it could hardly fail to have similar effects elsewhere. In Cambridge itself, if little of the spirit, something of the philosophy survived to the end of the century in the works of John Sergeant.[1] But it is to two Oxford writers that the task of carrying on the Platonic tradition into the new century fell. If the first word came from the powerful Cambridge group, the last came from two somewhat isolated Oxford men (the one of All Souls, the other of Balliol)[2] whose work, if not whose names, are now wellnigh forgotten. Both have suffered from the greater fame of contemporary writers, the elder from the eclipse which idealistic

[1] John Sergeant was born in 1622, and entered St. John's College, Cambridge, in 1639. Subsequently converted to Roman Catholicism, he spent the rest of his life, "the very genius of controversy", in the ardent defence of the faith he had embraced. He was struck, as Kant afterwards was, by the contrast between the progress that the mathematical sciences had made and the stagnant state of philosophy. He traced it, as Kant did, to the absence of a true method in the latter, whether represented by the Cartesians or the empirical school. Cartesianism is criticized by him for the want of any self-evident principle which may be taken as the criterion of truth, the experimental method for its incompetence to beget scientific knowledge. The errors of Locke all spring from "the way of ideas", which it was therefore of prime necessity "to stub up by the roots". Faithful to this congenial task, he devotes himself to a criticism of Locke, which, like that of Norris, anticipates much that was to come, and probably had considerable influence on Berkeley, who in his *Commonplace Book* (*Works*, vol. i. p. 54) alludes to him under the initials J. S., though only to dissent from his doctrine that "we see solids".
Of his numerous works, *The Method to Science* (London, 1696) and *Solid Philosophy asserted against the Fancies of the Ideists or the Method to Science further Illustrated with Reflections on Mr. Locke's Essay on the Human Understanding* (London, 1697), give him his main claim to rank as a philosophic thinker.
[2] John Norris, 1657–1711, Arthur Collier, 1680–1732. If we wanted a picturesque name for this aftermath of the main and central glow we might call it Avonian Platonism. It was close by the Wiltshire Avon, and within a few miles of each other, that Norris (himself a successor of George Herbert in the church at Bemerton) and Collier lived.

methods of thought were about to undergo through the work of John Locke, the younger from the philosophic and literary gifts of Bishop Berkeley. But it is all the more important on that account to rescue what was significant in their work from an unjust oblivion.

"Norris", writes Tulloch in his *Rational Theology in the Seventeenth Century*, "stands by himself in the history of English Philosophy, the solitary Platonist of the Revolution era, who handed on the Torch of Idealism into the next century till it was grasped by the vigorous and graceful hand of Berkeley." There is both truth and error in this description. It is true that by the time his chief work appeared Norris was a solitary figure in a great line of thought. But it would be a mistake to find any direct connection between him and Berkeley,[1] or to regard the latter as in the same sense a representative of the Platonic tradition. What is grasped by Berkeley in his earlier period is only Locke's "new way of ideas". By the time he grasped Plato's old way, whatever we are to say of the grace, the vigour has departed. While in the early phase of his philosophical development Berkeley clearly saw that on the principles he had adopted there could be no place for "eternal truths", in his later he never seems clearly to have seen that there could be no place for *esse est percipi*. Norris's work, in fact, began where Berkeley's ended. "His goal", as Dr. Powicke puts it, "is Norris's starting-point. Norris assumes what Berkeley attains. He comes down from the Mount with the Heavenly patterns already in his hands and knows how to apply them to everything."[2]

2. Philosophical Affinities

Though, owing to the weight of the Aristotelian tradition, there was in Oxford no such enthusiastic revival of Platonic study as there was in Cambridge, Norris, who was in residence from 1676

[1] Berkeley, so far as I can find, never once mentions Norris. He was familiar with Malebranche, but mentions his theory of seeing all things in God only to reject it. (See *Principles of Human Knowledge*, Pt. I. par. 148.) It is nevertheless true that Berkeley has been treated far too much as merely a link in a chain of writers whose service to philosophy was mainly the negative one of showing the impossibility of a consistent sensationalism, and Mr. G. A. Johnston has done well to dissent from the dictum that "Berkeley is only Locke purged". See *The Development of Berkeley's Philosophy*, p. 4.

[2] *A Dissertation on John Norris of Bemerton* (London, 1894), by F. J. Powicke. Though as a doctor's thesis a youthful work, this gives the best account I know of Norris's work. See also F. I. MacKinnon's (Master's Thesis) on *The Philosophy of John Norris* (*Psychological Review Publications*, 1910).

to 1689, could claim in an early essay on Plato's Ideas "a more than ordinary acquaintance with Plato's works"; and we know from his correspondence with the aged Henry More, begun in 1684, when he was himself twenty-seven years old, that he had "read all the Doctor's works and had them placed in our (presumably All Souls) Library". But we also know from his later correspondence with Lady Masham[1] that his Oxford studies had failed to take any real hold of him. "I have spent thirteen years", he wrote, "in the most celebrated University in the world. . . . But truly I cannot say that I have ordered my studies in that seat of learning so much to my own satisfaction as to my reputation with others. To be free with you I must declare that when I reflect upon my past intellectual conduct I am as little satisfied with it as I am with that of my morals." He does not tell us what it was that had now given him "a very different taste and apprehension of things", or what were the books, "sapid, pathetic, and Divinely relishing, such as warm, kindle, and enlarge the interior and awaken the divine sense of the soul", to which he was resolved thenceforth chiefly to apply himself. But there is abundant evidence as to at least one of these latter from all that he subsequently wrote. In his *Spiritual Counsel*[2] he speaks of Malebranche's *De la Recherche de la Verité* as a book "that is alone a library", and as "one of the best books that is in the world." Thenceforth the French Mystic may be said to have been one of the main influences in his life.

As Norris has suffered as well as profited by the description of him as "the English Malebranche", it is right to recall that, as a glance at his chief work can easily convince us, the Malebranchean growth came only as a graft upon a deeper root of Platonic Idealism, and that "the English St. Augustine" would have been an equally good description of him. We know, indeed, from the *Essay on the Ideal World*[3] that Norris recognized in Malebranche "the Galileo of the intellectual world", and that the "ideal philosophy", of which Norris was the exponent, appealed to him, not merely from the side of edification, but as something in essential harmony with the spirit of the age: "the strange awakenings of thought and reflection and the modern enlargement of the world out of the servile straitness of authority and commonplacing into the liberty of

[1] Daughter of Ralph Cudworth, and in after years friend of Locke.
[2] London, 1694. It was addressed to his children, the eldest of whom at the time could barely have reached the mature age of four.
[3] Pt. I. p. 4.

meditation and good sense". Yet we know also from the Preface to the same work that already while he was still in Oxford, and before the awakening to which reference has been made, he had begun a treatise in Latin which he elsewhere tells us was to be called *Theoria Mundi Idealis sive Metaphysica Platonica*. He had laid it aside at the time because of "the difficulty of the undertaking and other avocations", and when later he returned to it he found that the "edifice" had to be rebuilt "from the very ground". While he everywhere acknowledges the debt he owed to Malebranche in this task, he held that the work had been left by him only half done ("This great Apelles has drawn the celestial beauty but half way"), and, though he modestly fears that "the excellent piece will suffer whatever other hand has the finishing of it", he sets this before him as his own task. Even with regard to the "seeing of all things in God" we have Norris's own word for it that it was "a notion which he very early lighted upon by the natural parturiency of his own mind before he had consulted with any authors that might imbrue him with it", and that he was only confirmed in it by finding it in the Platonists both ancient and modern, though in none "so copiously, so purposely and dexterously managed as by the incomparable M. Malebranche".

There is no reason to doubt this statement. The natural partiality, if not the parturiency of his own mind, inclined him to the mystic doctrine from the first. Of Malebranche himself, Sir William Hamilton wrote that his "philosophical theory is nothing but the extension of a theological hypothesis long common in the schools".[1] What seems to be the truth about this and his whole relation to Malebranche is that (as in the case of Coleridge in relation to Schelling) ideas which vaguely haunted his mind as the result of his own Platonic studies received at once definiteness and new direction from the French writer. The difference was that, while to Coleridge there came a healthy revolt from the pantheism in which the Philosophy of Identity seemed to end,[2] Norris was never visited by any such saving compunction with regard to the like feature in Malebranche. He was, indeed, prepared to criticize his celebrated formula as open to dangerous misunderstanding, but this does not prevent him from returning in the end to a doctrine practically indistinguishable from the Master's.

[1] Quoted by Powicke, *Dissertation*, etc., p. 37 *n*.
[2] See the Author's *Coleridge as Philosopher*, Chapter I, pp. 48 foll.

Be all this as it may, and even granting a far greater degree of dependence than I believe there actually is, it is worth while to trace the outlines of this English reflection of a notable phase of Continental philosophy, if for no other reason than to correct the impression that is apt to be conveyed by Dr. Powicke's judgment, that while Norris the moralist as revealed in his sermons is a "tonic," Norris the Metaphysician as revealed in his Theory of the Ideal and Intelligible World is a "fantastic".[1] Fortunately, it is an easier and shorter task than the corresponding one in the case of the leader of the Cambridge movement.

3. THE ESSAY[2]

In Norris we pass not only into a new political and ecclesiastical but into a new literary atmosphere. As compared with Cudworth he has the merit of freeing the Platonism which is the common basis of both from the mass of mediæval learning with which its main outlines are obscured. Norris is still too fond of what he calls "the bed of authority"—a soft enough one often for a thinker of his type—and, in spite of his censures on "commonplace" writers, he has filled whole pages with quotations from the Christian Fathers. But he is aware of the contempt the "new philosophy" has for them, and is always careful to distinguish between what rests on reason and what on authority, and to emphasize the dependence of the latter upon rational approval. In spite of its repetitions and many survivals in it of mediæval method, his book is readable to-day in a sense in which Cudworth's is not, and Dr. Powicke is even prepared to apply to him what James Martineau says of his French Master: "Few philosophical writers present their thoughts in so lucid and attractive a style."[3]

But it is not only in the literary style, in the matter also we have a notable simplification. In Cudworth there is a wide grasp of the scope of philosophy reflecting something of Aristotle's encyclopædic method, and we have found it possible to trace the outlines in his work of a philosophy of nature and art, morals and politics, as well as of metaphysics and theory of knowledge. The scope of

---

[1] Cambridge Platonists, p. v.
[2] An Essay towards the Theory of the Ideal or Intelligible World, Designed for two Parts. The First considering it Absolutely in itself, and the Second in Relation to Human Understanding. London, MDCCI.
[3] Dissertation, etc., p. 142.

Norris's work is more restricted. He concerns himself with the theory of the Ideas, first as he conceives of them in themselves, secondly as they are instruments of the understanding, "representative", as he expresses it, of things. With that longing for clarity, which, whatever success he had in achieving it, he struggles everywhere to attain, he confines himself to an outline without attempting to fill in the details of "the two globes", the celestial and the terrestrial, of the Ideal world.[1] The method of the "cosmography" of that which is for the most part "a *terra incognita*, a mere question, an intellectual America", is, as he tells us,[2] to begin with a confused notion of our subject, thence to proceed to the question of its reality, finally to return to a more explicit and distinct consideration of its nature.

Following this excellent method with regard to the Ideas, he begins by remarking on the reason for the obscurity of the subject to our ordinary vision in our "union with the Sensible" and the dazzling abstractness of the intelligible object. Even to talk of it seems to be "a subtilizing upon a fine nothing". Yet it is not difficult to give a general indication of it by pointing to the familiar contrast between "the natural state", or world of what is contingent and mutable, and an ideal state conceived of as permanent and immutable which is not only antecedent to the natural, but exemplary and representative of[3] it—the measure of what is true and beautiful in it. Otherwise viewed, it is the contrast between the one and the many, the simple and the various, yet conceived of not as exclusive the one of the other, but as differing as the virtual from the actual. *How prove* the reality of this state? *Where* must we suppose it to be? *How is it related* to the sensible state?

4. THE EXISTENCE OF THE IDEAS

As the first and most easily recognized proof we have the fact that our world presents the appearance of "a considerate system, a very thoughtful composure", which is sufficient to suggest the idea of a mind that views it as we do ourselves, yet with exactness instead of our confusedness, entireness as contrasted with our partialness, ease and repose, instead of our labour and study.

[1] In what follows, the orthography is modernized and the superabundance of capitals reduced.

[2] *Ideal World*, pp. 224–226.

[3] It is essential to remember that this in Norris means *giving validity to*, not *receiving it from*, another.

Coming to particular created things, we have in the second place the measures within which they keep. "What is it", we ask, "that stints and retrenches them?" It is not enough to refer to the limited capacity of the creature as contrasted with the unlimited power of the creator. There must be some inner reason and necessity coming from their essential nature or idea. And similarly of their figures and the uniformity they preserve. Irregularities, even monstrosities, we indeed have. But the difficulty these raise is not confined to the Ideal Hypothesis. Moreover, it is difficult to see how it could be otherwise if (as we must conceive) God acts by the fewest and simplest ways, leaving room for creatures, as He elsewhere expresses it, "to step out of the track". The notable thing is not that there are divergences, but that things on the whole remain true to type, and that we have degrees of being or perfection, according to the degree in which they do so. The most obvious case is that of geometrical forms or species for the types of which we must go not to the natural but to the ideal object. How otherwise are the propositions about them to be solved? What is the ground and pillar of their truth?

The existence of these propositions, therefore, and of a "pillar" of eternal truth in general, provides a third argument which possesses the merit of being one which even sceptics are forced to admit, seeing that in denying they in reality assert it. Some modern idealists, like Royce,[1] have been willing to rest their whole case on this argument. It is interesting to find one of the best statements of it in this early writer. Even sceptics, he points out, "suppose themselves in the right (as other disputants do), and their adversaries in the wrong, which they cannot do if there is no truth, since error is a departing from the truth, and where there is no truth there can be no error, even as where there is no law there can be no s n. Such sceptics then would overthrow themselves, allowing that truth in hypothesi, which they deny in thesi. They contradict the doctrine they maintain and in pretending to prove it disprove it".[2]

Granting the existence of truth as a necessary and therefore eternal relation between ideal terms, we have a new argument for the existence of the terms. "It is indeed", Norris exclaims, "a great conclusion and such as would appear to be of most momentary importance were we to consider it in its full power and extent." On the other hand, "If this foundation be removed," he sees "nothing

[1] See below, p. 363.   [2] P. 63.

but a vast and frightful ruin to which the dissolution of 10,000 worlds bears no proportion". True, "Science abstracts from existence", but only from existence "according to the present state of things," not from "existence at large". This is always assumed (all judgment, as we might say, has reality for its ultimate subject). "Demonstration, tho' it produces knowledge, yet it supposes the thing known. . . . All that our reason can do is only to follow the nature of things with which, as it agrees or disagrees, it is true or false".[1] He goes on to contrast these ideal propositions, which are identical with truth in the object, with "mental propositions", "the late offspring of time and contingency", and merely "participations" in the other, "that divine and substantial truth whose spring rises in the Intelligible and whose remoter streams reach and glide through the barren regions of our natural and sensible world".

He is only putting this more clearly when he claims as a further argument that the Ideas stand or fall with Science, which consists of nothing else than a set of principles or conclusions—in other words, necessary and eternal truths—"only with the connotation of a certain order of dependency and a common formality of consideration in which they agree, fixing the bounds of the sciences and distinguishing one science from another".

All this is implied in the admission of the Schools that Science is not of singulars, which are contingent, but of universals, which are necessary. "But why will they not speak out? What means this mincing and this disguising of a plain and unavoidable truth? For what are these universals and these essences that science is so much beholden to? Are they only abstractions or inadequate conceptions in the mind? But then they will be as contingent and mutable as the mind itself is wherein they are formed. Or are they really in things themselves that exist in nature? But then again, they will be as contingent and mutable as these things, and no more capable of being the objects of science than the things themselves are. Here then is a confuse intimation of those very ideal reasons of things we are contending for."[2]

5. THE PLACE OF THE IDEAS

Passing therefore from the question of the existence to the question of the "place" of the ideas, to those who ask "where is

[1] P. 105.   [2] Pp. 130-131.

this ideal world you speak of?" Norris replies, "Where is it not?" As truth is everywhere, so the ideas which truth implies are everywhere, "compresential as well as coeternal with it". But "everywhere" can only mean in the end in the mind of God, not indeed as something existing separately, as some falsely think that Plato held, but really in it and of it. Here, with the authority not only of the old scholastic but of the new Cartesian philosophy behind him, Norris feels himself on safe ground. "Were I disposed for the way of quotation and to plant my margent thick with authorities, I need not desire a better opportunity." But he would still have to ask, "Has this acknowledg'd principle *reason* enough on its side to deserve so much countenance from authority?" And he goes on to give his own reasons for accepting it.

First and foremost he puts the identity of God with "All-being". "If God is All-Being, it necessarily follows that there is no degree of being in the creatures, whether collectively or distributively taken, nor any so much as absolutely possible, which does not some way or other pre-exist in God, at least as to the intelligible order and kind of it."[1] This he takes to be Descartes' meaning when he argues that God must be and must contain all perfections, seeing that otherwise it is impossible that we should have any idea of Him. Descartes' mistake was to make our idea of God one of His effects. On the contrary, "we see God in himself, and not by any idea distinct from him, or that is an effect of him—it being impossible that God should be represented by anything other than himself". The point was fundamental in Norris's philosophy. God had not to look outside Himself for the patterns of creation. It is even incorrect to think of the ideas as in God's mind, in the sense of being formed by Him. They are part and parcel of the mind of Him who *is* the truth and the life. The doctrine raises difficulties enough (as the reservation "at least in so far as the intelligible order and kind of it" shows) both as to the relation of the ideal to the actual and as to the relation of the divine ideas to ours, but in itself it is not the piece of fantastic mediævalism that it seemed at the time and has continued to seem to his critics.

His own argument is founded on the idea of the Wisdom of God taken in the sense of the knowledge of all things possible as well as actual, and therefore of their ideas or reasons. In speaking of possibilities, Norris sees with admirable plainness that potentiality

[1] P.143.

involves reality of some sort. To this he adds that the only way in which we can assign reality to that which is not actual, is to conceive of it as present in and to the All-Being, which he identifies with God. But he develops the point here only so far as to prove that if God knows possibilities, *a fortiori*. He knows actualities, in order to proceed at once to the question of the *way* in which God knows, which he rightly sees to be the crucial one.

God's knowledge must differ from ours, for whereas in our case knowledge succeeds and is dependent on created being, this cannot be so with God, who cannot be supposed to know in one way before, in another way after creation. Hence, while to ourselves we can only assign what St. Augustine calls *cognitio vespertina*, to God we must assign *cognitio matutina*—the knowledge that is possible only to a being who knows all things in Himself as Creator, before He knows them as created. What then of God's knowledge of Himself? Is it the same as His knowledge of His creatures? In both cases it is indeed knowledge of Himself, but in the latter case it is an inadequate, in the former an adequate knowledge. Yet there is no hard and fast lines of distinction between these; for, as there are degrees of perfection in created things, degrees that is of their being in God, so there are degrees of adequacy in God's knowledge of Himself in them. It is by this proviso that Norris thinks to avoid "that stupid conceit of taking the world for God. . . . Not 'Whatever you see is Jupiter', but 'Jupiter is whatever you see' ". He makes no mention of Spinoza, and, if he knew of his work, ignores it throughout the book. It is all the more interesting to find him anticipating in his own case the objections that were urged against Spinoza, and meeting them by an appeal to the same principle of the degrees of reality, or of the reflection of divine perfection, in things. The conclusion of the whole he sums up in Plato's words: "It is altogether necessary that this world should be the Image of Something."

Going on to the comparison of the reasons there are for believing in the existence of the Intelligible and of the Sensible or Natural World respectively, he holds in harmony with what he has already said of it, that there are *more* and *better* reasons for believing in the existence of the former. There are *more*, seeing that, in contrast to the many he has given, there is only one argument for the existence of the sensible world, namely, the impression of it upon our bodies. True we may be said to have Revelation, but Revelation depends on sense knowledge, and must share its defects. There are *better* reasons in proportion as rational evidence, involving as it does necessity, is superior to sensible resting on contingency, and is always necessary to correct the errors of sense. Rational evidence itself indeed rests in the end on the principle of non-contradiction, but, as distinguished from anything in sense, this principle is intuitively clear and derives support from human science, of whose "firmitas" it is the source.

The discussion raised a point which was a fundamental interest to the philosophy of the time and has remained so ever since: What is meant by the evidence of sense? If sense be taken as equivalent to mere immediate feeling or "sentiment", Norris insists that this of itself involves no judgment, not even that of existence. On Cartesian principles we may go from it to the existence of the self that feels, but not to the existence of an external body that is felt. "It goes no farther than a *sensation*, and that sensation goes no farther than my *soul*. And what is either of these as such to the existence of bodies that are without me?" Do I not upon such sensations naturally judge that there are such bodies? "That", replies Norris, "indeed I do; and now you have hit it. But then this amounts to a plain confession that what you call the evidence of sense is indeed not the evidence of *sense*, but the evidence of reason. Instead then of comparing sensible with rational evidence in order to the better determining on which side lies the advantage of certainty, we must compare *rational* evidence with *rational*."[1] But all reasoning from feeling to bodies as the causes of our feelings, "as the best philosophers now admit", is at least questionable. Vision may seem an exception. But even in the case of vision we have no direct knowledge of external objects, and it was not on vision but on the veracity of God—in other words, on a rational principle—that Descartes founded his belief in their existence. "Even the author of the *Essay of Human Understanding*, as great a patron as he otherwise seems to be of the senses, does yet with good judgment make sensible knowledge to be the lowest form of knowledge, and indeed will hardly allow it a place among the degrees of it, there being no knowledge properly so call'd but what is the result of intuition and demonstration."[2]

[1] P. 200.   [2] P. 212.

6. Manner of the Existence of the Ideas

Philosophy, Norris goes on to urge, can prove a great deal more than it can explain. Ours may fall short of "a perfect scheme of ideal cosmography". We can only know in part and prophesy in part. Yet *something* may be known and said. And to bring a subject of such "vast and most diffused amplitude" within as contracted a compass as may be, he proceeds to divide it into the four questions: What the Divine Ideas are; How the Ideas of things are in God; What part is assignable to them in the formation of the sensible world; How they consist with the simplicity, immateriality, and infinity of the Divine Nature.

i. He rejects the view that the Ideas are in any sense copies of other originals. They *are* the originals or archetypes of which everything else is a copy according to the degree of its perfection: "the intellectual hinges upon which the sciences turn", "the essences which furnish Logic with its definitions, Metaphysics with its abstractions, and to which Physics is beholden for its station among the sciences", independent of the creature—and in some measure even of the Creator.

The last point is the most important. There was none on which early English idealism was more insistent or on stronger ground as against Descartes.[1] Norris later submits the Cartesian doctrine of the dependence of the ideal world upon the will of God to thorough and trenchant criticism. He is here content to reject it on the ground that if the Ideas depended on the mere will and pleasure of God, "they might either not have been or they may now have their whole system cancel'd and absolutely cease to be"—a supposition which "threatens us with a darkness to which that of Egypt would be the very brightness of glory". To the objection whether it will not hence follow that they *are* God, he answers, "Yes, it will, and so far is it from being an objection that 'tis the very consequence I have been all this while driving at." But he adds that they are of the essence of God only in relation to the creation, and that this does not exclude Ideas or perfections that belong to the Divine nature considered absolutely and in itself. Again there is no mention of Spinoza, but the argument follows the same logic as issued in Spinoza's doctrine that thought and extension are only two of the infinite attributes of God.

[1] See above, p. 59.

ii. Leaving this, he comes to the crucial question of *how* the Ideas of things are in God. Disclaiming again any exact knowledge on so high and wonderful a subject, he thinks that such "a general and gross delineation of it as may serve to show the intelligibility of the notion" may be possible, and finds guidance in the hypothesis before hinted at that God "has Ideas of things as he is imitable by them. The Divine Essence, conceiv'd as imitable in such a degree, is in God such an Idea or the Idea of such a thing; the same Divine Essence conceived as imitable in another degree is in him another Idea or the Idea of another thing; and so on throughout the whole scale of being from first or mere matter (the nearest to nothing and the furthest creatural projection from God) to the most excellent of created intelligences".[1] Like his predecessors, he exhausts himself in metaphors to explain his meaning, using among others that, of which Bergson has made use, of a cone extending from "the most excellent and enlarg'd beings" to "the very last reality that is contracted as it were into a mathematical point", that "touches on the very confines of nothing", and yet, as "a metaphysical unit", has some degree of reality in it and must be conceived of as having its ideal counterpart (Malebranche's "intelligible extension") in the mind of God. God, in a word, "represents *things* in the same proportion as they imitate *Him*". But again, Norris is careful to add that He represents them, from the side of being, only in their perfections; from the side of knowledge, He represents them in a way very different from our confused apprehension of them.

iii. In reply to the question of the *part assignable* to the Ideas in the formation of the natural world, it is admitted that, while Ideas concur in the "what" of things (their *tale esse*), they do not possess the will and power to give things actual existence or *esse*. They are only "plastic principles"[2] regulating the otherwise indefinite operation of the Omnipotent Agent, which without them would have acted "exorbitantly and at random". Yet there is a sense in which the Ideas may be said to act. "Tho' every efficient be not as such an exemplary, yet every exemplary (as directly regulating and specifying the work) is also as such a kind of efficient cause." Thus, while for the generation of things we must have motion and its laws as "the fixed and general will of their author", yet "rule and hand still go on together. Nature can no more proceed

[1] P. 247.   [2] *Cp.* Cudworth's use of the term to which he does not allude.

than begin without the Ideas". "The chest", he quotes from St. Augustine, "not the chest as it is made, but the chest in the mind of the maker, is the living thing." In this connection he returns to the question of aberrations in Nature, and naïvely suggests that there may be a purpose in them: "Since we will not admire the regularity of her procedure, Nature tries to assure and stir up our wonder by irregular births." Her "wheel gives us a jogg by stepping a little out of the track". Be this as it may, aberrations and monsters are no argument against the Ideas, but really are arguments for them, seeing that we should not know them as such except for the ideal patterns.

iv. Coming finally to the difficulties raised by the *simplicity*, *immateriality*, and *infinity* of the divine nature as contrasted with the compositeness, materiality, and finitude of the natural world, he disposes of the first by an appeal again to the principle of degrees of reality. The composite he explains is that which is made up of things altogether distinct from one another. But Nature is not a composition in this sense, but a hierarchy of orders possessing all degrees of the *same* perfection which is God Himself. He has greater difficulty with materiality. Matter had not yet been resolved into the abstraction it appeared to Collier and Berkeley. Kant's doctrine of extension as a form of the sensory was yet further in the future. To represent material things as in God would be, as Arnauld had urged against Malebranche, to make God to be material. Norris is prepared to accept the explanation that things may be in God in one form but not in another, as they may be in the design of the artist without being materialized—*eminenter* as the scholastics had it. But he feels its vagueness, and in the end confesses himself unable to explain precisely "how an Idea purely spiritual can represent *body*".[1]

The difficulty, lastly, of reconciling the apparent finitude of the Ideas with the infinitude of God is solved by recourse to the similar distinction between their *formal* being as they are in our minds and their *real* being as they are in the mind of God. In our minds they are "prescinded or abstracted" so as to exclude one another; in God's mind they exist in a form in which each includes all the others. Just as (again to take St. Augustine's instance) paternity to us is a definite and exclusive relation, whereas, as an attribute of God, it penetrates all His other attributes and includes the whole of the divine nature.

[1] P. 296.

7. ETERNAL TRUTHS

(*a*) *Relation to the Ideas.*—While in considering the Ideas proof of existence is more necessary than explanation, in considering Eternal Truths the opposite is the case, seeing that their existence is generally admitted, the chief question is as to their nature. The first point to be here made clear is the distinction between what he calls truth in the object—truth as something which "the understanding finds and does not make", and truth in the subject or conformity between the "mental" and "the real proposition". The eternal truths "are no creatures of ours nor yet of God's neither. God is what he is and they are what they are, and they can neither not be, nor be otherwise, but remain in their steady and immutable order, the same yesterday, to-day, and for ever".[1]

Their more precise nature, and particularly their relation to the Ideas, is "a neglected and uncultivated piece of speculation", on which Norris has much to say. They are really relations or "habitudes" between the Ideas, standing to them as the Ideas themselves stand to the essence of God, emanating (developing as we might say) from them, as the Ideas emanate from Him. From this it follows that all that has been proved with regard to the existence and nature of the Ideas belongs to them also. Hence the mistake of separating between them and the Ideas or things themselves and conceiving of them as something externally added. "They do not add any new reality to their Absolutes or to the things said to be related, but are only the things themselves under a certain order of consideration to one another." Norris will have nothing to do with the view that "likeness", for example, is something made by our comparison of things, seeing that it is "just the very quality that a thing has in reference to another thing".[2] All that can be said, therefore, of the Ideas, as the foundation of science and art, can be said equally of the Truths: "Here the arts originally flourish; here the ancient family of metaphysical truths derive their pedigree, and here geometry was a science before any lines or figures could be drawn upon matter." Finally, they share the *necessity* of the Ideas: "The necessity of Fate is but contingency to that of truth, that being owing to decrees, whereas this is from the very nature of things themselves." Do what you may, "you cannot disimagine them. They still return upon us with a strong and irresistible spring".[3]

[1] P. 314.   [2] P. 330.   [3] Pp. 318-319.

All this is again brought home by contrast with the Cartesian doctrine, which makes them an effect of God's arbitrary will and with Regis's[1] reduction of them to *entia rationis* existing only in our understanding. Descartes' doctrine, he argues, is inconsistent with his own definition of God as the sum of all perfection. Upon it all demonstration would be impossible, and he "would ruin his own beloved and admired science" of mathematics. Against Regis he presses the question, valid against all forms of subjectivism: how, if the understanding makes truth, it comes about that all understandings make it the same. Such a theory is the destruction of the very idea of immutable truth. "Men may wink and they may spurn against the Sun, but they cannot put out his light."[2]

(b) *Place of Truth.*—The answer to the question, "Where is the place of understanding?" as to the similar question of the Ideas, is "she is everywhere". Truth is a "*sphere* whose centre is everywhere and whose circumference is nowhere". More particularly she is where the Divine Ideas are, that is in God. "If this does not satisfy, she is in thyself", and Norris goes on to expound the commonplace which was also the paradox of all Platonism, the union of "interiority" with "community" in truth. It dwells in the head and in the heart of each, in the one not less than in the other. ("The studious head must also bring with it a pure heart and a wellrectified spirit. . . . I could almost say that Ethics is the best Logic."[3]) Yet she is none the less common to all, "since the greatest excellencies have also the greatest community". As St. Augustine puts it: "Thou dost not inclose anything to thyself out of her communion, but what thou takest from her remains also to me entire."

For the rest: "The figure of a house is a very natural and lively image of truth which for the order and harmonious arrangement of the whole and the settled dependencies and coherencies of one part with another is not unlike a great and goodly system or structure." The ideas must be said indeed to be the foundation of it, but in reality "it cannot properly be said to have any ground or foundation, but is a ground and foundation to itself", self-centring as

[1] Pierre Silvain Regis (1632–1707), author of *Cours entier de Philosophie*, and for long regarded as the chief representative of Cartesianism in its purest form.
[2] P. 387.
[3] P. 393; *Cp*. Cudworth (Pref. to I.S.) who quotes the Philosopher "ἡ κάθαρσις ποιεῖ ἐν γνώσει τῶν ἀρίστων εἶναι, Purity possesses man with an assurance of the best things".

God Himself.[1] If it be said that on this showing our whole argument is a circle: the existence of eternal truth being made to depend on the existence of God, and the existence of God on eternal truth, the objection might hold of a theory like Descartes' which proves the effect from the cause and the cause from the effect. It does not hold as against ours in which the dependence of truth upon God is a dependence for *being*, whereas by the dependence of God upon truth is meant our dependence for *knowledge* of Him. In His being He *is* truth.

8. ESSENCE AND EXISTENCE

This leads Norris in the last of the expository chapters to a discussion of the relation of essence and existence. He admits the distinction, and the problem it raises of the relation between them, and does his best to solve it by proving that in each of the two fields of the ideal and the natural world the one involves the other. In the world of temporal things it is just their essence to exist in time. In the world of essences these apart from existence are "very unintelligible. It would be a very romantick system that would be built in such essences". "Science indeed abstracts from the existence of things in *Nature*", and considers only the essences of them; "but then this is so far from excluding, that it the more strongly infers the real existence of these intelligible essences *elsewhere*".[2]

There is much in this crucial passage that is of real value, especially, the insistence of the implication of existence in essence, of reality in thought. Yet we cannot help feeling that we are left in the end with the difficulty of the relation between what he calls "constitutive" and "representative" essences very much as he found it, or, as we ought perhaps to say, as he *made* it. So long as Norris held, as he thought himself bound to do, that there is a real "outworld" of nature, which, on account of its necessary imperfections, is not involved in the essence of God, he left the problem of their relation unsolved. St. Augustine was prepared to speak of God as the "*sinus naturæ, in se ipso continens omnia*", and the Schoolmen had their distinction between a "formal" and an "eminent" manner of this *continentia*; but Norris rejects these solutions, and ends in the Postscript by putting the problem aside, as he had previously done with regard to matter, as one which his "present light does not serve

[1] P. 398.   [2] Pp. 425–426.

him to unfold". The point at which he comes nearest to an answer is in his conception of degrees of being. But unless the possession of "degrees of being" could itself be interpreted as involved in the perfection of God—the existence of creatures in the essence of the creator—the answer is incomplete, and left a hiatus in his Ideal World.

The last chapter on the Beauty of the Intelligible World and the Happiness of those that have their Conversation in it, with concluding Reflections upon the Advantages of a Retired and Contemplative Life—fine though it is in conception and interesting as throwing light on the man, adds nothing to his philosophy.

CHAPTER V

JOHN NORRIS (ii)

THEORY OF THE IDEAL WORLD IN RELATION TO THE HUMAN UNDERSTANDING

1. THE SECOND PART OF THE IDEAL WORLD

Though portions of the same original design, the first and second parts of Norris's work were divided by an interval of three years. In the Epistle Dedicatory and in the long Preface of the latter, the Author makes us feel, as he himself felt more and more, how the flowing tide was against him in his effort to maintain the interest in metaphysical questions, and what "a great disadvantage" it was "to come abroad in a discovering age". But he feels all the more the importance of keeping philosophy alive at this its fountain-head: "Sure the stream of philosophy, and divinity too, must quickly run low, if not fed by a metaphysical spring." He sustains himself further with the reflection that he has something to contribute to it, seeing that "'tis a great thing that is now taken in hand to explain the way of our Understanding", and that, so far as he knows, "this is the first time that this hypothesis has appear'd in the form of a System". It was indeed "a great thing" with Locke's mighty Essay already in the field, founded on a diametrically different hypothesis, and with the advantage of appealing to the spirit of just that "discovering age", which Norris felt to be antagonistic to himself. His mind occupied with problems, which, in the form in which he states them, had ceased to be of interest, and employing a method largely out of date, he might well seem to be engaged in an unequal conflict. But in the larger perspective of our own time we can give him credit for perceiving that his own "hypothesis" was of wider scope than that of his great opponent, taking account of elements in the work of the Understanding which Locke had either overlooked or failed to explain, and for being the first to apply it directly to this particular problem. On this ground it is, I believe, a mistake to regard what constitutes the main section of this Part as merely an exercise in scholastic method.[1] In the lonely furrow he there draws, besides opening up fresh soil in an old field, he was a pioneer in a work which had sooner or later to be done. It is this that makes it worth while

[1] See Powicke, *Op. cit.*, p. 58.

to follow him in the discussion of the questions of the *bearer*, the *nature*, the *object* of thought as seen in the light of the Ideal world, whose reality they illustrate.

2. WHAT IS IT THAT THINKS?

"The great question", as Norris calls it, "whether Matter can think" was raised by the materialistic theories of his time. In reply to them he might have been prepared to fall back upon the Cartesian argument for the separate existence of thinking substance. But he finds it "too dispatching a demonstration", and embarks on a proof of the impossibility of attributing thought to matter, which, with a lively digression upon the souls of animals, occupies a fifth of the whole volume. Much in it is out of date. What is still of interest is the frankness with which he insists, as far as regards Nature, on the efficacy of the principle of mechanical action. Great and strange as are the works of Nature as compared with those of Art, yet "they proceed ordinarily from Mechanism, the wise disposition of Matter and Motion; and then do we understand them most perfectly and philosophize upon them with best satisfaction when we can resolve them into their *natural*, that is, their mechanik, causes. . . . This you may call, if you please, the New Philosophy, but 'tis what should have been the old . . . in opposition to those imaginary principles of substantial forms and qualities introduced by the school of Aristotle".[1]

The only question is now far merely mechanic causes extend. With some hesitation, and with an earnest protest against supposing that it gives any encouragement to cruelty, he is prepared to extend it to the lower animals. But he is clear that there *is* a limit to its application, and he draws a definite line at the point where the repetitive processes of nature give place to deliberation and thought, with the possibility of variety and improvement that these bring with them. The whole of his own work was regarded by him as an essay in proof of an order of being, whose characters, as actually experienced, are inexplicable except on principles wholly different from those of matter and motion.

3. WHAT THOUGHT IS

Passing to the question of the nature of thought, Norris modestly disclaims any power of explaining what thought is *per se*. Yet he

[1] P. 88.

holds that there are some distinctions that throw light on the subject and "are not unworthy of our consideration nor beside the limits of our present design". First and foremost, and giving the clue to all the others, is the distinction between the mental or "formal" act and the object in which it "terminates". Of the former, he holds, we have "only a confuse interview like the glimmering light that trims the edge of a dark cloud", knowing only sufficient by a reflex use of it to distinguish it, *e.g.*, from will and desire, and to see that there are differences in the intentness of its application on different occasions. It is from the side of the object as something essentially different from itself, and not, as Descartes held, merely a part or aspect of the formal act, that we can get forward in further definition of the nature of thought itself.

i. Thus it is in the light of differences in the object that we must explain the distinction between "thought of perception" and "thought of volition". These are not two separate processes. Thought is essentially judgment, and judgment as involving assent is a matter of the will: "Why may there not be a willing and a nilling that belongs to Truth as well as that which respects good?" The only difference is in the objects: "Truth is that *absolute* relation which things have among themselves, whereas Good is that relation of agreement or, as the schools say, *convenience* which they have to us."[1] This explains why we may have different degrees of perception and understanding (faith, opinion, knowledge), corresponding to the degrees of completeness in the evidence. And, further, it explains the distinction between ignorance and error: ignorance being a defect of perception, and sometimes therefore excusable, error proceeding from judging further than we perceive, and always therefore a fault.

ii. From this it follows with regard to the common distinction between "active" and "passive" thought that, while thought is not active in the sense of *making* its object, it is active so far as it involves attention to it. Little as psychology owes to Norris as compared with Locke, the place he assigns to *attention* is all to his credit.[2] To him this was a matter of first-rate importance, seeing that, anticipating modern views, he found the seat of the freedom of the will not in the power of directly determining to overt action

[1] P. 129.
[2] The word does not occur in the Index of the Globe Edition of the *Essay on the Human Understanding*.

(this necessarily follows the dictate of understanding), but in the power of attending or not attending more or less to an objective.[1]

iii. Equally important from the side of the criterion of thought was the Cartesian distinction between "clear" and "confuse" thought, itself depending on intensitiveness of attention. He agrees that distinctness is "the greatest excellency and perfection of understanding: next to divine grace the greatest blessing Heaven can bestow on any man". But he is dissatisfied with Descartes' attempt to distinguish between clearness and distinctness on the ground that that is "clear" which is present and open to the mind with a strong impression, as an object in a clear light is to the eye, that "distinct" which is severed and disjoined from other things so as to contain in itself nothing but what is clear.

Norris admits the helpfulness of the comparison of thought to vision as the sense which is likest to it, and happily illustrates from a vivid impression of the moon, which yet is compatible with seeing the fantastic resemblance to a human face in it, and only becomes "distinct" when, with the aid of a telescope, we descry rocks and hills and valleys and plains in clear relation to one another. But he denies that in the application to thought we can say there is any real difference between the two. There can be no clearness unless we perceive "plainly, perfectly, and fully those Ideas or those relations of Ideas which are the objects of our thought", and, given this clearness, we have also determinateness or distinction from other things. The only valid distinction is between the object as it is in itself and the same object seen by us in its differences from other things. It is clearness and distinctness in this sense (determinateness and individuality, as we might say) that Norris means by "intelligibility" or rationality, and that he is prepared to accept as the only criterion of truth. All that is true is not, indeed, clearly perceived; "but all that is clearly perceived is true". From which he draws the congenial conclusion that, while we may entertain beliefs as to things *above* reason, we cannot entertain any that is *contrary* to reason, "though the authority it pretends to be never so great".

iv. A like historic interest, in view of Berkeley's polemic against abstract ideas that was about to appear, attaches to what he says

[1] See "Letters Philosophical and Moral between the Author and Dr. Henry More", published in Norris's *Theory and Regulation of Love* (1688), and what Cudworth, unknown to Norris, says on Freedom of the Will (above, pp. 63 foll.).

of the distinction between "abstract" and "concrete" thought. Abstraction is defined by him as the consideration, not of one entire and complete being apart from another, but of one part of such a being without another. This may be *either* when the modes of a substance are taken apart from it or from one another (*e.g.*, length apart from an object or from its breadth) *or* when a habitude or relation is taken as possessed in common with another thing, in other words, as a general or universal. The former is incident on the infirmity of our minds and serves for thought, as spectacles for our eyes, to give distinctness to its object and to aid discovery. It was by taking motion by itself in this way that the reflection and refraction of light were discovered. Generalization in turn serves for the extension of thought. The more general *contains* less but *represents* more, and so contributes to the enlargement of our thought—a distinction which the student of the relation between the connotation and denotation of terms might still find useful.

v. The distinction between "pure" and "impure" thought had special importance for Norris, corresponding as it did to that between understanding or thought proper and imagination. True to his conception of the formal unity of thought, he refuses to assign these to different faculties, or even to the same faculty operating on different objects, the one immaterial, the other material. They both operate on immaterial objects, namely Ideas.[1] The difference is that in imagination the immediate object of our thought is the Idea as representative of a material object (having reference, as we might say, to a spatial world); in thought proper the immediate object is the same Idea taken as representative of an immaterial object, referring purely to the intellectual world—the world, as we might say, of meanings.

Discussing in this connection the difference between sensation (another form of thought in the larger sense[2]) and imagination, Norris finds it to consist, from the side of its *physical* origin, in that between agitation of the fibres of the nerves in the extremities and agitation of their terminals in the brain, the one caused by the external object, the other by the "sole efflux of the spirits"; from the side of the *psychical* effect the difference consists in the comparative strength and liveliness of the image. Vision, for

---

[1] *Cp*. Browning's Essay on Shelley: "The Ideas of Plato, seeds of Creation, lying burningly in the Divine Hand—it is towards these (the poet) struggles."
[2] See p. 109.

instance, "is a stronger sort of imagination, as imagination is but a weaker and fainter kind of vision".[1] The whole passage is a crucial one for Norris's theory of knowledge, and is all the more interesting because of the incidental criticism it contains of Malebranche.[2]

From the insistence on the doctrine that the immediate objects of knowledge are Ideas, one might suppose that he is committing himself to a pure subjectivism. Yet nothing could be farther from his meaning. The Ideas are neither sensations nor images nor thoughts as a mental product, but objective elements in the world of truth, and these are something that we *find* and do not in any sense *make*. True, they have to be appropriated by an active intelligence. Only those that seek find. Yet this does not make them mental. What he is here insisting on is that in the process of search we may employ images which are derived from and are "representative" of material things; but, so far as we do this, we mix our thought with an element which is really foreign, or at any rate only remotely related to the world of truth and reality, and may be a hindrance to the apprehension of it. He thinks that cerebral affections of some kind are indispensable, but he holds that sensory images, even in the form of words,[3] may be unnecessary in pure thought. The important point with him here, as elsewhere, is not psychological analysis, but the reality of a conceptual world or whole of truth more immediately present to us, however confusedly apprehended, than that of materially existing things.

"Stepping", therefore, "again into the track before it closes", he willingly returns to the question of the object of sensation and the resulting imagery as forms of thought. He has admitted that we may be purely passive with respect to it, and this raises the question "passive to what?" There are only two alternatives, either to those bodies upon whose impression we have sensation or to the settled will and order of some other being. He rejects the former on grounds similar to those on which modern psychology rejects the action and reaction theory of the relation of mind and body, and ends with the view that Divine Activity is the true cause not only of

---

[1] P. 201.

[2] See p. 186, where he rejects as "extremely gross and unmetaphysical the notion favoured by Malebranche", that imagination means 'converting' the soul to material impressions in the brain.

[3] *Cp.* what he says of the possibility in the case of the angels of "darting pure and immediate thoughts into each other without the vehicle of words", vol. ii. p. 163.

the impressions the soul receives from experience, but of the physical movements that result from the voluntary activity of the mind.

In this connection the statement of the theory of Occasional Causes and of the arbitrary and "incongruous" relation between physical motions and the resulting qualitative world of experience, with its pains and pleasures, its colours, tastes, smells, touches, temperatures, and sounds, is, to my knowledge, one of the best extant. It wants only the addition of figure, solidity, motion, and magnitude, which, by a failure in logic, he still left to "matter", to be an anticipation of Berkeley's theory of natural phenomena as the language of God to our souls.

4. THE OBJECTS OF THOUGHT

True to the modesty of his programme, again disowning in the discussion of the question, How we think, the attempt to penetrate to the "manner of our thinking" as it is in its own essence, Norris again confines himself to the discussion of it in relation to the objects of thought. These he divides into those which are known immediately and are therefore self-intelligible, and those which are known only through the medium of ideas.

i. The first thing is to be assured of the existence of the former both in ourselves and out of ourselves. Within ourselves, so far is it from being true that there is nothing in the intellect which was not in the senses, that we have sensations, desires, affections, intellection itself, which are immediately perceived without the intervention of sense. But the main interest of the section centres in the "out-being" of God and the Ideas as immediate objects of thought.

"A philosopher of great name has offered a demonstration of God's existence from his Idea." But this cannot be in the sense in which we derive the existence of men or horses from the idea of them. In their case we apprehend by something different and representative of them. In the case of God there can be nothing of this kind. "We may beat the field of Nature over and over" for Ideas that represent God. We shall not find them. All the Ideas men pretend to are mere idols of the imagination. On the contrary, it is by the idea of Him as the immediate object of our thought and that which is most intimately present to our souls that we perceive all other things. Yet Descartes' argument only needs amendment.

We have a notion or perception of God, and from this we may argue to His existence, as we may not from the idea of any creature. For in their case there is something superior to them and inclusive of them. This is not so in the case of the Divine Being, which is all-inclusive and has nothing superior to it on which its existence depends. While the immediacy of our knowledge of God is proved from the presence in us of the notion of an all-inclusive principle of being, the immediacy of the Ideas is proved from their reality as principles of knowledge. Without them we should run on to infinity, vainly seeking in what is itself merely contingent and conditioned for the necessary and unconditioned. True, we see the Ideas in and through God, but not as something different from Him, but as parts of the whole which He is.

The passage is interesting as an anticipation of later idealistic attempts to rehabilitate the ontological argument for the being of God as against Kant's criticism that it rests on a confusion between the idea of a hundred dollars and their existence in one's purse. The essence of Norris's contention is that if 'God' means, as he took it to mean, All-Being, and if in All-Being are included both the potential and the actual, as they also must be, existence in the sense of actuality is not something that requires to be added. It was only gradually that he came to see that, granted the validity of the argument, the God whose existence was proved by it might satisfy the pantheist, but hardly the theist.

ii. In contrast to what is thus immediately perceived, all material and most spiritual objects are only mediately known. That material things are so, follows from the Cartesian doctrine that extension is removed by the whole diameter of being from thought and is wholly disproportionate to it. But it follows also from the contingency and instability of material objects. "For the salving of science", and the reality of the physical world, of which otherwise we should have no real knowledge, it is necessary that material things should be perceived not by themselves but by their Ideas, and that "we should think of corporeal things according to incorporeal reasons". That we have such ideas and reasons in their case he still held with ordinary realism. Coming to spiritual things and taking ourselves as an example, Norris holds that these have an essence or Idea of their own. But he holds also that "as intimately united as we are with ourselves, the Ideas of them are hid from us", and that what is true of ourselves is still more true of other selves. If, therefore, we are to have any real knowledge with regard to them, it must be through Ideas which indirectly *represent* them to our understanding and which are "the formal principles of our knowledge". The important questions therefore are: (i) what these ideas, both in the case of material and spiritual objects, are, and (ii) whence they are derived.

Assuming, as perhaps he may, that we are sufficiently familiar with the answer to the former of these questions, Norris devotes himself in the rest of the book to the question ("and a very great thing indeed it is") of the source whence the Ideas are derived. In the discussion of it he is the more willing to avail himself of another's guidance, "considering what moderate assistance he has had hitherto in the prosecution of this work from other men's thoughts". He only takes the liberty to express what he borrows in his own way, "the better to accommodate it to the contexture of his own discourse and the order of his general design".

5. The Source of the Ideas. (a) Norris and Locke

Adopting, therefore, Malebranche's division of the views that are possible as to the origin of the Ideas "whereby we perceive such objects as are mediately intelligible, namely, that they come from the objects themselves; that the soul produces them; that God produced them when He created the soul; that He produces them on the occasion of our thinking of an object; that they are perfections resident in the soul itself; that the soul is united to an all-perfect Being who includes in Himself all the perfections of created beings"—he proceeds to discuss them one by one. Both because of the close reproduction of the French master's arguments, and because these have been already anticipated in what has gone before, it is the less necessary here to follow his treatment of them. It will be sufficient to note what he says in connection with the first and the last of the above alternatives. The first gives occasion to a reference to Locke, the second to a stricture on Malebranche himself. These, taken together, serve to give a clearness of outline to his own view otherwise unattainable.

On the appearance of the *Essay on the Human Understanding* in 1690, it was sent to Norris by a friend with the request that he should give him his opinion of it. Norris replied with some "cursory reflections" which were added as an Appendix to the *Discourses*

on the Beatitudes and published in the same year. They have thus
the distinction of being the first published criticism of the great
Essay.

They go straight to the root of the matter in remarking on
Locke's failure to provide us with an analysis of the work of the
Understanding, and on the substitution of an account of the origin
of ideas for a definition of what they really are. If it be true, as
Locke tells us, that "the Understanding, like the eye, whilst it
makes us see and perceive all things, takes no notice of itself, 'the
Essay' must be very unaccountably undertaken". Whence, in that
case, can the material for it be drawn? Similarly with the ideas.
Before going on to account for their origin, we might have expected
Locke to give some account of their nature. Till we know this, "all
further discourse is but talk in the dark".

Turning to Locke's attack on *innate* ideas, how, asks Norris,
can the author fairly object to innate principles on the ground
that "there are none to which mankind gives universal assent",
seeing that he himself appeals to propositions which are self-evident
both in logic and ethics? Thus to the question, "Where is the
practical truth which is universally received?" Locke gives his own
reply when later on he tells us: "I doubt not that from principles
as incontestable as those of Mathematics, by necessary consequences the Measure of Right and Wrong may be made out to
anyone." Moreover, it is no argument against implanted laws that
"there is none whereof a man may not justly demand a reason".
Implanted truth may get confirmation from reason. Nor is it an
argument that there may be a breach of them. (Why may there
not be a breach of innate as of written law?) Nor, finally, that such
truths ought to be easily distinguishable. "A man", Norris acutely
observes, "may be sensible of a Truth impressed and yet not of
the impression, but think it came some other way." Even from
the side of Locke's own psychology, the principle that "it is
impossible for truths to be imprinted on the soul, which it perceives not", is untenable. For he himself admits that there may
be unconscious impressions in the pre-natal state, during the
absorption of attention with something else, or in memory as a
"repertory of ideas", from which not the ideas themselves but the
consciousness of them is retrieved. Finally, "if nullity of perception
will not conclude against innate principles, neither will lateness of
perception". Locke himself admits that "there is a time when

children begin to think". Why, then, may there not be a time for the awakening of particular thoughts?

Norris feels himself all the more at liberty to press these points against the critic of innate ideas because, with his idealistic predecessors in England, he himself rejects the whole doctrine and relies upon the direct evidence of the operation of thought in the structure of experience. All talk of "mental impressions or characters written upon the mind" he regards as "mere jargon and unintelligible cant". All that holds is something of near analogy to innate ideas: "some particular truths of the Ideal World" exhibited "more clearly and constantly to the view of the soul than others, that by these she may be the better directed to the good of the reasonable life, as animals by their sensitive instincts and inclinations are to the good of sense".

While thus rejecting the letter of Locke's teaching as defective and inconclusive, Norris ends with a fine appreciation of the spirit of the thinker—the generous tribute, we might call it, of the last representative of the old way of Ideas to the first of the new way, in which for a century in England men were chiefly to walk. In spite of all he has said, "The Author", he writes, "is just such a kind of writer as I like: one that has thought much and well, and who freely writes what he thinks. I hate your commonplace men (*i.e.*, men who keep commonplace-books) of all writers in the world who, though they happen to say things that are in themselves not only true but considerable, yet never write in any train or order of thinking, which is one of the greatest beauties of composition. But this gentleman is a writer of a very different genius and complexion of soul, and whose character I cannot easily give, but must leave it either to the description of some finer pen or to the silent admiration of posterity."[1]

[1] Locke made no reply at the time to Norris's "reflections", but later wrote "Remarks upon some of Mr. Norris's books" (chiefly *Reason and Religion*), the finishing of which "he deferred to another season", which never came. They will be found in the 1823 edition of his *Works*, pp. 247 foll. The main points attacked by him are:—

1. The idea of seeing all things in God "as if we understood what Ideas are in the understanding of God better than when they are in our own". The real difficulty, he explains, is not as to the nature of ideas "this no man can tell", but "what alteration is made in a man's mind when he sees a marygold and sees not a marygold, whether we call it the marygold in the garden, or the divine ideas of it".

2. The dogma of the simplicity of the ways of God's action on which this whole system is built. How is this compatible with "the curious structure of

In the passage of his own Essay which is before us, Norris concludes what he has to say on the view that the Ideas are derived
from natural objects, with a criticism both of the scholastic maxim
that "there is nothing in the understanding but what was first in
the sense", and of Locke's particular application of it.[1]

To what he has already said of the former,[2] he adds that, if the
phrase means that everything is transmitted to the understanding
from sensible objects through the senses, he is prepared to say, on the
contrary, that "there is nothing in the understanding that was first
in the sense". But if it means that the Understanding *perceives*
nothing but by the occasion of sensible impressions, this may in great
measure be allowed. Yet not so freely or so far as to include such
objects as "seem to carry no relation to matter or motion, such as
Ideas of Order, Truth, Justice, Goodness, Being, with a numerous
multitude of abstract and purely intelligible objects of metaphysical
and moral consideration".[3]

Turning to Locke, his theory of the origin of Ideas in the senses can
only at best hold of ideas of *bodies*. But, even taking it with this
limitation, Norris holds it to be obvious "by the whole tenour of
this discourse" that if it be meant that sensible objects send or
carry ideas in the sense of principles of knowledge to our minds
by the medium of the senses, "he has derived them from a false
original". But "if his meaning merely be, as perhaps it may, that
sensible objects by the impression they make upon our outward
senses serve to excite Ideas in our minds, so that we are beholding
to them as the *occasions* of our having such ideas, there is nothing
either so dangerous or so extraordinary in it but that we may without
the eye and ear, not to mention the other parts of the body? . . . as if it were
possible for the Almighty to produce anything but by ways we must conceive
and are able to comprehend".

3. The doctrine of universals as anything more than "in representation
abstracting from particulars. The immutability of essences lies in the same
sounds supposed to stand for the same ideas. Whatever exists, whether in
God or man, is singular."

4. The doctrine of Occasional Causes, leading to the consequence that "God
produces all our thoughts, let it be infidelity, murmuring, or blasphemy. The
mind doth nothing".

The criticism is illuminating both as to Norris and Locke. In 1, 2, and 4 of
the above it attacks points that were really excrescences from the main idealistic tradition, and Locke finds an easy victim in his critic. On the other hand,
we have in 3 a clear statement of the great issue between Lockean nominalism
and Platonic realism, and there are perhaps few to-day who would claim an
easy victory for the former.

[1] I reverse the order of the text.   [2] See above, pp. 96–99.   [3] Pp. 374–375.

scruple in great measure allow it him". This hypothesis is "a sort of *Transcendental* too common to all to be set up in opposition to any". Granting it, it is still open to doubt whether the Idea of extension itself can owe its origin to sense instead of being one always present with us independently of any bodily impression and, as in mathematics, modifiable in our thoughts.[1]

It is not difficult in all this to see how far Norris goes in anticipating later developments of the idealistic theory of knowledge. He is clear about the reality of "forms of the sensory and understanding" which cannot be derived from sense perception, but, on the contrary, are presupposed in anything that can be called knowledge of objects that impress the senses. Yet, owing to his failure to carry his analysis far enough, he is unable to drive his point home, as Kant was able to do, by showing that these forms and principles are involved in the very conception of an object of experience; still more to anticipate the objections to which Kant's theory is exposed.

6. (*b*) Norris and Malebranche

Arrived at the last of the above alternatives, namely, that the Ideas whereby we understand are actually identical with the divine Ideas, the first thing he has to prove is that this is a *possible* view. "Possibility", he remarks, "is a considerable offer if it is the only explanation which is open."[2] After all that has gone before, he thinks himself justified in asking whether it is not at least possible that the Ideas, which must have been in God the patterns of creation "coessential with him tho' representative of things without him", may be intelligible to us, and be the very ideas, by which we make the things, of which they are the patterns, intelligible to ourselves. The only obstacle is "the disproportion of our faculties" to them. But if, as Norris held, God actually does discover Himself and "we have any intellectual sight (tho' never so imperfect) of his *absolute* nature, much more may we see his *relative* nature or that in him which respects his creatures".[3]

Having demonstrated the possibility, the way is open to him for affirmative argument. We know by this time the line it is likely to take. Its centre, as always with him, is the existence of science, as a light which "undivisibly communicates itself to all that is

---

[1] Pp. 370–373.
[2] *Cp.* what Cudworth says as to the reality of that which is possible and at the same time necessary. P. 51 above.   [3] P. 419.

intellectual", as the sun communicates itself to all that is capable of vision, and which on this account "cannot be less than divine".[1] It is this that "M. Malebranche was pleased to express by our seeing all things in God". But Norris is dissatisfied with this way of speaking, not, as Dr. Powicke seems to think,[2] on the ground that it revives scholastic memories—the authority of Aquinas, which he quotes for it, was a point in its favour—but because of its fatal ambiguity and the offence it gives to "common ears". Were it taken as meaning merely that things themselves are "immediately and properly seen, this *strikes in* with the vulgar presumption rather than *opposes* it". But if it be taken to mean, as it is too apt to be, that things as they are in Nature and according to their sensible appearances are really in God and are seen in Him, it must be rejected. All that we are justified in saying, and all that Malebranche himself really intends to say, is "that as things are in God after an intelligible manner, viz. by those essential perfections or ideas of his which represent them, so they are those divine Ideas which are the immediate objects of our thoughts in our perception of things". In this there is nothing to give offence, seeing that "'tis generally allow'd that the things without us are not perceived immediately by themselves but by their Ideas. The only question is by *what* Ideas or what these Ideas are? Some assign one sort of ideas and some another sort. All that this hypothesis of seeing all things in God adds to the vulgar and has peculiar to itself from any of the rest is precisely that these ideas are the divine Ideas or that the divine Ideas are the ideas whereby we understand".

With this he holds himself free to go on to give a "compendious view" of the arguments used by Malebranche to prove the doctrine as so interpreted. But he is soon again in difficulty over his claim for it as involving the "entire dependence" of created spirits upon God, "since upon this supposition we cannot only see nothing but what God is willing we should see, but we can see nothing but what God himself makes us see".[3] Does this mean that we are dependent on God *immediately* both for the object and for the formal act of understanding? On this view, and with a theory like his own of the necessary connection of will and understanding, what becomes of human freedom? Norris feels the difficulty, but either has not the courage to face it squarely or is visited by the

[1] P. 433.   [2] *Dissertation*, p. 30.   [3] *Ibid.*, p. 450.

ghost of an earlier Calvinism; and, not to be behind His master in attributing "the entire glory of our thoughts to God", concludes that he "knows not whether the one sort of dependence may not be as necessary as the other".[1]

He feels himself on stronger ground in using the argument founded on the immediate presence to our minds "confusely" of the totality of being and the freedom implied in the selective character of thought.[2] "We find by experience that when we have a mind to think of any particular thing, we forthwith cast our view upon all Beings, and then afterwards apply ourselves to the consideration of the object we propose to think on. But now it is certain that we cannot desire to see any object, but that we must first see it already, although confusely and in general. And therefore, since we may desire to see all beings sometimes one and sometimes another, it is certain that all beings are present to our minds; and it seems that all beings cannot be present to our minds any otherwise than because God is present to them, who in the simplicity of his being contains all beings."

This is quaintly expressed, but it is not difficult to see in it an anticipation of the later idealist doctrine of the immediate presence of Reality to experiencing mind.[3] Following it out, Norris is prepared to go beyond Malebranche and the view to which he had formerly leant[4] of the indeterminateness, and therewith the unknowableness, of the divine essence. For if God be thus the All of Beings, and if the Whole known in the parts is more than their sum, there is a true sense in which we may be said to know God. In opposition, therefore, to Malebranche's view that we see not God but with relation to creatures,[5] Norris reiterates the view that "tho' we cannot *comprehend* God, yet 'tis plain and acknowledg'd we have some notion or perception of him, and since this perception cannot be any idea distinct from him, we must perceive him immediately himself". Malebranche, indeed, himself seems to admit this in declaring that "Infinite is to itself its own Idea. It has not any archetype. It may

---

[1] P. 453. Elsewhere he has some trenchant remarks in the same spirit on "the bold and forward offers that have been made by some men towards the setting up of the creature upon a bottom of its own," p. 556.

[2] The passage has the additional interest of being one that (as anticipated in *Reason and Religion*) Locke attacked in his criticism of Norris. (See above, p. 100.)

[3] See below, pp. 263 foll.   [4] See *Reason and Religion*, p. 15.

[5] See *Dialogues on Metaphysics*, III. "Tho' you see the Infinite without restriction, you do not see it as a single being."

be known, but it cannot be made." Finally, he clinches his own argument with the reflection that if we did not see God in some degree, as we could not *talk* of Him, neither is it possible we should *love* Him. "For I think it in the general a certain truth that we can love nothing but what we see."[1]

Though Norris founds his doctrine on metaphysical reasons alone, as in the First Part, so here he finds it at the end a comfort "to repose a little on the bed of authority", and to reflect on the support which morality and religion derive from a theory such as his. Interesting as these reflections are for an estimate of the learning and character of the man, they add nothing to his philosophy.

7. NORRIS AS TRANSITIONAL THINKER

It is impossible to claim for Norris that he was an original thinker in the sense that may be claimed for his contemporary Locke. There is little in his philosophy the source of which it is not easy to recognize. From Plato he derived the contrast between the Ideas or Essences, as permanent elements in being and knowledge, and the contingent matter of sensory experience; from Descartes the dualistic scheme of the two worlds of thought and extension; from Malebranche, the religious interpretation of the Ideas as no mere patterns to which God, as it were, looked in the creation of the world, but as a part of the divine essence itself; from Philo and St. Augustine, the co-ordination of all this with Trinitarian Theology. He had too little historic and critical sense to feel the incompatibility of some of these and similar borrowed elements with one another: of the Platonic Logos with the historic Christi; of the Greek ὕλη with the Cartesian extension; of Malebranche's mysticism with Descartes' criterion of clearness and distinctness; even of his own earlier view of the indeterminateness of the divine essence as we have it in *Reason and Religion*, with that of its essential knowableness in the *Theory of the Ideal or Intelligible World*. But we have to remember that the absence of historic sense was a defect which he shared with the greatest of his contemporaries, and that there are other merits in a philosopher than that of consistency. Inconsistencies, by being brought to the surface, may point forward to the next step.

What may be claimed for this retired thinker is, *first*, that he saw that the Platonic doctrine of ideas or essences, so deeply

[1] P. 506.

interfused with Christian theology, deserved and was capable of a more independent and systematic statement than it had hitherto received; *secondly*, that he felt that such a statement was all the more necessary in view of the growing influence of a sensational philosophy that left the truth this tradition contained entirely on one side; and *thirdly*, that he had the courage to attempt, and the perseverance to carry through, this "great thing", in spite of persistent bad health and the drizzle of petty, uninspiring interruptions that came from his parish work, and to add one more to the "foot-notes on Plato", of which Professor Whitehead finds European philosophy to consist. The form he gave to his Idealism may appear too like one of Plato's own myths. But we have to allow for the absence of a vocabulary, that had still to be created, as well as of the fuller analysis of the work of the understanding, that had still to be made. Even taking it as it stands, his work emphasizes with hitherto unexampled clearness elements in reality and in our knowledge of it for which the "new philosophy" as represented by Locke was to show itself more and more inadequate to account, and to which a newer still was in the end to return. Devastating as the irony of Locke's criticism of him, above condensed, must have appeared on its publication, it left untouched and in a great degree misunderstood the real point of Norris's contention. It was not his fault that the times were metaphysically out of joint, and that while Locke was to increase he was to decrease.[1] What may more justly be laid to his charge is that out of deference to a foreign authority he allowed his statement to remain cumbered with a doctrine he had himself in reality undermined and that, in one or two fundamental respects at least, left it seriously ambiguous.

1. While his Platonism separated him, as it was bound to do, from the Cartesian doctrine of the Ideas as arbitrary creations of God, it did not prevent him from embracing that of the independent existence of matter. He failed to see that by reducing the data of sense to "sentiments" or impressions suffused with subjective elements, by arguments which were equally applicable to vision as to the other senses, to primary as well as secondary qualities, and by assigning the source of them to God, he had deprived the idea of an independent matter of any real significance. If God did

[1] Within the next century Locke's *Essay* went through some twenty editions; no second edition of Norris's was ever called for.

everything by the simplest way, what need had He of this otiose intermediary? There were solid reasons in the case of the Catholic Father for holding at all costs to the independent existence of matter. Without it the doctrine of Transubstantiation would cease to have any meaning. There was no such reason in the case of the Protestant divine, but, on the contrary, there was every reason to deny it. It was on this account all the more remarkable that he should continue to cling to it, and leave to his more consistent neighbour and admirer the credit of arriving along his lines at the conclusion which Berkeley, at the same moment, was reaching by a different and far more compromising route.

2. We have seen the difficulties in which he became involved in the effort to escape the pantheistic implications of Malebranche's formula. By insisting on the distinction between the ideal and natural order he escaped from the impiety of making the created and contingent a part of the Creator. But to assign them a being independent of Him and beyond His control was equally repugnant to one who was committed to the entire dependence of the creature upon the Creator so that "God may be all in all". In the doctrine of degrees of being and of the union in all reality of the potential and the actual, he had himself provided a clue to the solution of this difficulty. It is all the more regrettable that he failed to follow it out in a reinterpretation of the nature of All-Being as at once immanent and transcendent, at once appearing in and always breaking through the limits of the finite. Again, the source of his failure was the extent to which he had committed himself to an abstraction. As in the case of matter, he was obsessed with the idea of its independent existence as a principle of multiplicity, so here he was obsessed with the idea of essence as a no less abstract principle of unity. That Spinozism was the logical completion of Malebranche's development of Cartesianism is, I suppose, a commonplace of the schools. To dig philosophy out of this pit required a more powerful logic than Norris possessed. Here, also, there was something to which his more logical neighbour might have helped him. Yet as preparing the way for a further step, and as what an American writer on it has called "the only expression in English of the philosophy of the transition between dualistic and idealistic conceptions",[1] his work deserves more attention in his own country than it has hitherto received.

[1] Mackinnon, *op. cit.*, p. 92.

CHAPTER VI

ARTHUR COLLIER

1. COLLIER AND HIS BOOK

Arthur Collier was born in 1680 at the Rectory of Langford Magna, of which he was afterwards himself the Rector for the last twenty-eight years of his life. We have no account of his early education. We know, however, that he entered Pembroke College, Oxford, in July 1697, whence, after a year's residence, he removed to join his brother at Balliol. We have no direct knowledge of the studies which interested him there. From his allusions to Aristotle, we should judge that his knowledge of the Stagyrite was derived chiefly from the schoolmen Suarez, Scheibler, and Baronius.[1] As his brother William left minute analyses of the writings of Descartes and Malebranche, and as Arthur afterwards showed himself well acquainted with these, we may presume that they followed the same lines. Though there is no evidence that he was on familiar personal terms with Norris, it is impossible that, as members of the same University and for several years near neighbours in Wiltshire, they should not have known each other. Collier was certainly familiar with the older man's writings, to which there are several marked allusions in his own.

What is more remarkable than the absence of these details is the obscurity into which his chief book[2] had sunk in the century after his death. Reid gives a short account of its contents,[3] apologizing for doing so on the ground that "the book is rare and little known. I myself have only seen one copy of it, which is in the University Library of Glasgow".[4] Dugald Stewart, after mentioning Norris as "a very learned divine of the Church of England whose

---

[1] See *Clavis*, pp. 26, 28, 30, 62. No one who had any direct acquaintance with Aristotle would have assigned to him the theory of material images scaling off from external objects, as Collier does in the last of these passages.

[2] *Clavis Universalis*; or, *A New Inquiry after Truth, being a Demonstration of the Non-existence or Impossibility of an External World*, by Arth. Collier, Rector of Langford Magna, near Sarum. London, 1713. It bears the characteristic motto, *Vulgi assensus circa materiam difficilem est certum argumentum falsitatis istius opinionis cui assentitur*. An edition with Introduction and Notes by Ethel Bowan was published in Chicago in 1909. Campbell Fraser (Berkeley's *Complete Works*, vol. iii. pp. 385 foll.) prints the Introduction.

[3] See *Intellectual Powers*, c. 1785, Essay III, chap. x.   [4] *Ibid.*

name has unaccountably failed to obtain that distinction to which his acuteness as a logician and his boldness as a theorist justly entitle him", refers in a note to Collier in the words: "Another very acute metaphysician has met with still greater injustice. His name is found in none of our Biographical Dictionaries."[1] Writing in 1837, his biographer, Robert Benson,[2] knew of only seven copies of the original edition of the *Clavis Universalis*, no one of which was in the Oxford or Cambridge Libraries. To its honour, the Edinburgh Press had in the previous year issued a fine edition of forty copies.[3] But the book did not become generally available till it was included by Dr. Samuel Parr in his collection of *Metaphysical Tracts by English Philosophers of the Eighteenth Century*, published in 1837.

This neglect is only partly to be explained by the greater fame of Berkeley's contemporary writings, in which the same doctrine of the non-existence of an external world is set forth with a literary brilliancy to which Collier, approaching his reader, as he tells us, with no "better art of gaining him on my side than that of dry reason and metaphysical demonstration", had no claim. Though on this one point his philosophy coincided with Berkeley's,[4] and might have been expected to share in a degree of its fame, it had been arrived at from an altogether different point of view and was part of an altogether different scheme of metaphysics. The real reason of this neglect, as in the case of Norris, was the indifference of the new age to speculations that took their start from the reality of a world, access to which might be *through* the senses, but which was not to be found *in* them. This being so, the cause of the obscurity which overtook him in his own time may be said in reality to constitute his claim to a more important place than has hitherto been accorded to him in the development of that deeper strain of English thought which is the subject of these

[1] See Hamilton's Edition of Stewart's *Works*, vol. i. p. 349.
[2] *Memoirs of the Life and Writings of the Rev. Arthur Collier, M.A.*, London, 1837.
[3] I have been unable to discover whether the beautifully bound copy in the Glasgow University, which presumably is the one that Reid mentions, was one of this edition.
[4] The question of priority hardly rises. Though Collier's book was published four years after Berkeley's *New Theory of Vision* (1709), there is evidence that the theory it develops had formed itself in his mind so early as 1708. See R. Benson's *Memoirs*, and what he himself says of the "ten years' pause and deliberation" which preceded the publication of the *Clavis* (Introduction, p. 1).

Studies; and it is for this reason that it is worth while recalling
the argument of his chief book and the application he made of his
conclusions in his other still less known writings.

2. THE VISIBLE WORLD NOT EXTERNAL

The book falls into two parts, the first directed to show that the
visible world is not external in the sense of having an existence
which is "independent of mind, thought, or perception"; the second
to showing more at large that a world external in this sense is
"a being utterly impossible". But he is careful at the outset to
explain that he does not deny that bodies exist or that he does
not "see bodies just like other folk". What he denies is that they
have an "extra-existence". Nor does he intend to imply that the
material world in any way depends on our individual minds or
wills. "There is an universe or material world in being which is at
least numerically different from every material world perceived by
mere creatures . . . the great mundane idea of created (or rather
twice created) matter . . . by which the great God gives sensations
to all his thinking creatures, and by which things that are not are
preserved and ordered in the same manner as if they were."

The first thing to prove is that the appearance of being external
is no proof of real externality. This is clear in the case of imaginary
objects, e.g., a centaur. We imagine them in a form just as external
as any actual object. Seeing then that the difference between perception and imagination is merely a matter of vividness,[1] and we
could conceive the vividness of the latter increased by God so as to
equal that of the former without its becoming other than internal,
the appearance can give no more than a "quasi-externality".

It is the same with what is actual. Descartes has proved that
the qualities of sound, smell, taste, and heat are within the souls
of those who perceive them. To these we have to add pain that is
located in a member which has been lost, as an instance "which
is very home to this purpose". He cannot understand how after
this the Cartesians "should yet happen to overlook the same conclusion with relation to the bodies, subjects, or extensions which
sustain these accidents? Shall we say that the subjects exist
without, and the accidents within, the soul?"

Leaving the further consideration of this to the Second Part,

[1] Here following Norris (see p. 94 above), and followed later by Hume.

he next appeals to visual illusions, such as those of the drunkard and the looking-glass, which support the same conclusion. Even normal vision is based upon illusion, as when we see the moon as bright, flat, semicircular, no bigger than a trencher, and as different at different times. If, as is assumed, all that we know of these objects is that they are seen, in other words that they exist as visible, their visibility is their existence. "This therefore destroys all or any distinction between their *being* and their being *seen* by making them both the same thing; and this evidently at the same time destroys the externeity of them." This is the true inference from the doctrine of those who see all things, including extension, in God. If sometimes they do not seem to admit it, "how can I help it if men will speak inconsistently with themselves; or explain their meaning so by halves, as that the same thing shall appear to be both affirmed and denied by them". While it is in the argument as to visibility that Collier comes nearest to Berkeley's identification of *percipi* with *esse*, the criticism of Malebranche, here implied and further developed in the Second Part, shows the entirely different orientation of his mind.

He ends the Part with a defence against the objections that he saw "rising up everywhere", for "a whole world against one is too considerable an adversary to be despised". The objection founded on "the universal consent of mankind" was not likely, as we judge from the motto of the book quoted above, to weigh much with him. It is only valid after the point has been considered. When it is considered, the appeal is to reason, which constantly shows that "a proposition may be true which is contrary to universal consent". On the objection founded on the appeal to *feeling* (*i.e.*, touch), he refers to Norris's proof of the presence of an element of *judgment* in the apprehension of objects by this sense, as involving the denial of any immediate knowledge of externality. But he prefers to stick to vision as the crucial test, and to insist that his argument as to the visible world stands on its own bottom. Returning, therefore, to the attack on the general Cartesian position founded on the assurance our involuntary judgments give us of externality, to doubt the veracity of which is to impugn the truth and goodness of God, he replies that it is altogether a question of the truth of his own theory. If it be true, God surely is not concerned that "that should be false which is and must be supposed to be true". But he denies the existence of any such involuntary judgment, and urges that, even though it existed, "we should come to a fine pass of reasoning indeed, if this manner of it were allowed to be good, viz., *I am inclined to judge such or such a thing to be so or so*; ergo: It is as I would have it because God will not deceive me".

Whatever view the reader of to-day may take of the validity of the reasoning in this Part of Collier's book, what is likely to strike him most forcibly, in contrast to Norris, is the entire modernity of the atmosphere into which as at a step he has passed. We not only hear no more of the "bed of authority", but its accoutrements are everywhere ruthlessly trodden underfoot. At every turn authority is defied, and the argument is pursued with a strictness of appeal to psychological fact and a rigour of logic which is a new thing in idealistic literature. While in both these respects it anticipates, on however small a scale, the work of Berkeley, the argument in the Second Part, founded on considerations more metaphysical than psychological, bears a similar relation to conclusions that Kant was to draw from the same premises.

3. Impossibility of the Existence of an External World

It was the apparent contradiction involved in the view, that all we know of the external world is derived from impressions which only differ from ideas in degree, that had led Descartes, Malebranche, and Norris to distinguish the visible world from an invisible one, *i.e.*, the phenomena which lie accessibly within ourselves from the unknowable reality behind them. But if, Collier urges, the external world is unknowable, this, upon the principle *eadem est ratio non entis et non apparentis*, establishes the presumption of its non-existence. True, a thing may exist though we know nothing about it, but in asserting the opposite in this case one does not at least beg the question: "I have the same advantage as if I were girt about with ever so many demonstrations." If the Cartesians persist in asserting the existence of an unknowable matter, they charge God with having created that which has no use or purpose. To the answer that he still has no right to say that it is impossible that matter should exist, Collier replies by distinguishing between intrinsic and extrinsic impossibility: that which is asserted on the ground of the conception and that which is traceable to some impediment or some cause forbidding its existence. Though the existence of matter might be intrinsically possible, yet "when we regard its cause, viz. God, who can do nothing to no purpose by reason of his wisdom", we must regard it as extrinsically impossible. "But", he goes on acutely to observe, "I have often found upon examination, that where an extrinsic impossibility lies against any point, we need but search to the bottom of it, and we shall find an intrinsic repugnancy in the thing itself. And this I think I have seen to be the case of an external world, as, I suppose, will appear from some of the following chapters."

With this introduction, he goes on in two of the most remarkable chapters of the book to what has with justice been claimed[1] as an anticipation of Kant's famous antinomies in proof of precisely the same point. Taking first the *"maximum naturale,"* he writes: "An external world whose extension is absolute, that is, not relatively depending on any faculty of perception, has (in my opinion) such a repugnancy in its extension as actually destroys the being of the subject (= object) world. The repugnancy is this: that it is, or must be, both finite and infinite. Accordingly then I argue thus. That which is both finite and infinite in extent is absolutely non-existent, or there is or can be no such world. Or thus, an extent or expansion which is both finite and infinite, is neither finite or infinite, that is, is no expansion at all. But this is the case of an external expansion, ergo, there is, or can be, no such expansion." "I know not", he adds, "what will pass with some men for argument, if both the matter and manner of this be not approved of."

The passage that follows is too long to quote. The conclusion of it has a peculiarly Kantian ring: Both sides suppose the material world to be external, both suppose it to be created. "One side, from the idea of its being external, has proved it to be infinite; the other, from the idea of its being created, etc., has proved it to be finite. . . . At the same time neither of them so much as pretends to answer the arguments on the side opposite his own, but only to justify his own point directly. And yet both will grant that, if an external world be both finite and infinite, it is the same thing as to say there is no such world." This, Collier interposes, is the real conclusion, and "here the honour of both is salved".

From the *maximum,* Collier turns to the *"minimum naturale"*, or the question of the divisibility of matter, and again develops

---

[1] See Professor Lovejoy's article on "Kant and the English Platonists" in *Essays Philosophical and Psychological in Honour of William James,* 1908. The quotation in the text constitutes what Collier calls his "Third argument".

the argument for both sides: "External matter as a creature is evidently finite, and yet as external is as evidently infinite in the number of its parts, or divisibility of its substance; and yet nothing can be more absurd than such an infinite divisibility." The conclusion, as before, is that "the thing or matter, concerning which the question proceeds, is a mere nothing or contradiction". If it be said that it has been the least of the thoughts of the philosophers who have argued each side to draw the conclusion which he does, Collier answers, first, "Perhaps so; but who can help this?" and, secondly, that the descriptions they themselves are used to give of external matter should make them very ready to subscribe to this conclusion for its own sake.

It is useless to urge, in answer to all this, that we ought to have the humility to admit things to be whose manner of existence we cannot comprehend, as in the case of the Trinity. Collier will not admit the parallel: it is "to talk of chalk with those who talk of cheese". In the doctrine of the Trinity there is no real contradiction as there is in this case. For the rest, "If it be humility to hold that the same thing may both be and not be, then humility is no virtue. . . . To boggle at this is not reasoning. But refusing to reason is not humility of judgment, but open and avowed scepticism."

While in these metaphysical sections Collier may be said to go beyond Berkeley, in the passage following, in which he criticizes the current "hypothesis of vision", he must be admitted to fall very much behind him. Besides the historical blunder already mentioned of attributing to Aristotle the image theory, and the more serious one of confusing physical and psychological theories, he fails to see that, whatever our view of the ultimate nature of the material world, all these questions remain for the idealist precisely as they were before, and that some positive theory of vision is required to account for the apparent or "quasi-externality" which he himself admits.[1]

---

[1] This failure, as well as the absence of any mention of Berkeley's theory, might seem all the more remarkable as the *New Theory of Vision* had already been before the world for some four years. But we must remember that Berkeley at the time was a young and unknown writer, and that Collier lived in a remote country district, and seems to have been singularly incurious as to what was going on in the larger world outside of it. One is reminded of the similar problem of the relation between Jonathan Edwards' early speculations and those of his great Irish contemporary. (See Fraser's edition of Berkeley's *Works*, vol. iii. Appendix C.) The same circumstances may explain the apparent ignorance of Berkeley's work in both cases.

He is on safer ground when he goes on to show that an absolute and "self-consistent" external world is incompatible with the idea of creation and preservation. While upon the theory of such an absolute space we may suppose that individual objects, like houses and trees, are relative to Ideas and cease to be on the abstraction of a supposing power; this cannot be so of space itself, when taken as a whole. Its extension must be infinite whether God pleases or not. Let Him try to confine it in a cube "about the bigness of a common die", "this, I say, is impossible in fact, and this draws another impossibility after it, which is that by this the will of God is overruled or frustrated by the work of his hands". So of its existence. We cannot conceive it annihilated even by God. "For annihilate it in supposition as often as you will, yet still it returns upon you; and whilst you would conceive it as nothing, it becomes something to you against your will; and it is impossible to think otherwise, whatever you may say." After a further argument to show that the doctrine of the existence of an absolute space leaves no room for the omnipresence of God except on the assumption of two infinite extensions, "So unfortunate", he concludes, "are the stars of this idol of our imagination."

Finally, he clenches the whole by an appeal to the definitions of matter which have come down to us from Aristotle through St. Augustine, Porphyry, and others, which reduce it to a *prope nihil*, a series of negations, "*nec quid, nec quale, nec quantum*, to which I may fairly add *nec aliquid*". If they say that we know at least *that* it is, if not *what* it is, we may ask them to produce their reasons instead of the kind of argument with themselves, which is "only grimace and banter". None of these, we may be sure, will stand, least of all the argument "*materia habet essentiam quia ens est*". For when we ask how we know that it is an *ens*, we are told *quod habet essentiam*, which "is round about our coal-fire, in other words, arguing in a circle or no arguing at all".

The last chapter is devoted to answering objections founded, like Malebranche's, on Genesis, on Descartes' appeal to natural inclination, and on the argument of "the late judicious Mr. Norris" that it is "no other than errant scepticism to make a serious doubt of the existence of an external world".

Against the first he urges that if Malebranche means the visible world (the world of light and colour), the argument holds against himself, seeing that he teaches that this depends upon our sensations. But if he means the external world in general, all that Scripture intends is that all things derive their existence from God. Besides, how do we know that there are not other beings, *e.g.*, angels, to see and live in the world? In any case, "*the* heaven and earth" need not mean anything that to the vision of all is precisely identical.

In answering the second objection, he does little more than repeat what he has already in the First Part said of the appeal of Descartes and, as he now adds, "the late ingenious Mr. Norris, to involuntary judgments." He admits that common language seems to support it, but "common language is extremely corrupt". The Truth makes us free of this as of other things, and permits us to use language "altogether Ptolemaic" in speaking of light as a property of the sun or as "afflicting our eyes instead of our souls".

To Norris's accusation of scepticism: "Is not this", he asks, "the way to be betrayed into the very dregs of scepticism to make a doubt of one's own most evident perceptions for fear of this imputation?" What Norris was really interested in proving was the existence of a natural world and of bodies. But this is not the moot point, but the *extra*-existence of the natural world. Norris is himself prepared to throw doubt on the former, as the very title of his fourth chapter shows: "That the Existence of the Intelligible World is more certain than the Existence of the Natural and Sensible World?" "What can be more evidently inconsistent, more evidently sceptical, than this manner of proceeding? . . . Well may this be called indulging a sceptical humour under the colour of philosophical doubting."

Speaking, in the Conclusion, of the "consequences" of his theory, Collier believes that it involves a whole "new system of general knowledge". But he "knows himself unqualified for so great a task", and modestly adds: "Perhaps the little which I have here supplied may move some more comprehensive genius to begin where I conclude, and build something very considerable on the foundation which is here laid."

In what he writes of the use of his theory to religion, acute Protestant divine as he was, it was not likely that he should overlook its bearing on the doctrine of Transubstantiation, or fail to see that "to remove an external world is to prick it in its *punctum saliens* or quench its very vital flame. For if there is no external matter, the very distinction is lost between the substance and accidents or sensible species of bodies, and these last will become the sole essence of material things. So, if these are supposed to remain as before, there is no possible room for the supposal of any change, in that the thing supposed to be changed is here shown to be nothing at all".

4. COLLIER'S MONISM

Although at the end of the *Clavis* Collier disowns the ability to follow its implications by a reconstruction of the theory of knowledge, he has left us in no doubt as to the metaphysical theory, on which such a reconstruction must be based. Already, four years before the publication of his book, he had drawn out a confession of his philosophical faith, preserved to us by his biographer, which is one of the most interesting documents of the period in the history of English Idealism with which we are now dealing.[1] The only other of the kind at all comparable to it is Jonathan Edwards' almost contemporary "Notes" on Being, which may be said to bear the same relation to free speculative thought in America as Collier's Confession does in England. It consists of some fifty clauses, of which the first five contain the essence:—

"1. I believe the existence of true perfect being, meaning by this the same as being absolute, or being possessed of all degrees (if there be any such) of being or true existence.

"2. I believe that true, perfect, absolute being is universal being, because no particular being can be possessed of all degrees of being. By universal being I mean the same as being in general, in which are included all the reality and perfection of all particular beings, and on which they all depend in all manner of senses.

"3. I believe this universal being to be God, whom we acknowledge to be the maker and preserver of all the particular things that are; or, in other words, I believe God to be no particular being, but being itself, all being, universal being, which with me are words of the same signification.

"4. I believe that God, as universal being, is one, and but one only God; in other words, that it is impossible that there should be more Gods than one, because it is so that there should be more universal beings than one. For universal being is plainly all being

[1] Robert Benson's *Memoir*, pp. 191 foll.

in one, in which are and on which depend all particular beings *quatenus* particular.

"5. I believe this universal being, called God, is the maker of all particular beings, as efficient cause, as formal cause, as material cause, as final cause. By his being maker of all things as efficient cause, I mean that his will was and is the true sole cause of their beings; as formal cause, that he made all things according to the platform of his own wisdom; in other words, that their forms or essential differences stand necessarily related to the different ideas exhibited or represented in his own infinite mind. By standing necessarily related, etc., I mean the same as to say, that the perfection and goodness of their being consist in their similitude to their original ideas in the mind of their efficient cause, God. As material cause, etc., I mean that the will that created is the very substantial matter of their being; in other words, that particulars, as such, have no distinct substances of their own, but only different forms or similitudes to the one true substance, which one substance is the common substratum to all particulars, which, as such, are creatures. As final cause, etc., I believe and mean that God made all things for himself, though not all equally, because all creatures are not equally and immediately related to him."

So far we may be said to have a purely metaphysical development of the ideas he had inherited from his idealistic predecessors. Taken along with the teaching of the *Clavis*, it carries the doctrine farther at precisely the points where Norris had stopped short: first, in breaking down the last remnant of dualism between matter and spirit; and secondly, in conceiving of degrees of being, not as a limitation of the eternal perfection, but rather as a part of it, and as necessary in order that its power might be more fully displayed. But with Christian writers of his time metaphysics was still too closely bound up with theological dogma to be separated from it, however much the dogma might have to submit to reinterpretation. From such reinterpretation Collier was the last man to shrink, as he goes on to show in the remaining clauses.

The essence of their teaching is the identification, first, of the Trinity with the "differences" in the Universal Being, without which it "cannot be considered to exist: (1) absolute and perfect, (2) exhibitive, representative or ideal, (3) active or volent, Being"; and secondly, of the work of redemption, not with the acquisition by the Son of merit for those who are justified through Him, but

with the "representation" of "a suffering obedience" as something
in its very nature "more perfect than a bare and simple righteousness without suffering". The double contrast of this application of
a monistic metaphysic with that made of it by Spinoza, the "God-
inebriated" Jewish philosopher, and by Jonathan Edwards, the
New England Calvinist, is a study in theology to which justice has
still to be done.[1]

Taking the earlier clauses of the Confession along with the
Clavis, the point at which Collier's work is of interest and, I believe,
importance in the history of English philosophy has been already
indicated. It is not, or at any rate not merely, as is usually stated,
that he arrived at the same doctrine as to the existence of the
"external" world as Berkeley. It is that he carried the Platonism
of his time to its logical issue by ridding it of dualistic adhesions.
If Norris was the "English Malebranche", Collier was the English
Spinoza. It is true that there is much in the *Clavis* that reminds
us rather of Berkeley than of Spinoza, but enough has been said
to show that the resemblance is superficial, and we do him less
than justice in confining attention to any merit there may have
been in anticipating Berkeleian idealism.

Comparing the process by which Berkeley, starting from Locke,
and Collier, starting from Norris, reached the same conclusion,
Campbell Fraser[2] remarks upon the proof which this offers "that
the intellectual atmosphere of the Lockian epoch in England contained elements favourable to such a result. They are both the
genuine produce of the age of Locke and Malebranche". But we
have to remember that as this result was reached by different
paths, it had an entirely different significance in the two cases.
To Berkeley, starting from the ideas that all that can be known
comes from the senses in particular impressions, it meant merely
another nail in the coffin of universal ideas—an additional proof
that they were merely *entia rationis*, abstractions of the human
mind. To Collier, starting from the doctrine that universals stood
for the essences of which particular things are merely the temporal

---

[1] With the statement in the *Credo* should be taken the tract entitled *A Specimen of True Philosophy* in a Discourse of Genesis i. 1 (published in 1730, and
included in Dr. Parr's edition of the *Clavis*), which was intended as an Introduction to his *Logology* on John i. 1, 2, 3 and 14 (published two years later),
of which Dr. Parr gives an abridgment at the end of the *Specimen*.
[2] Berkeley's *Works*, vol. i. p. 369.

"representatives", it meant the rooting of the world of Nature still more effectually in the world of Ideas, and the removal of the last obstruction to finding the essence of all things physical as well as mental in the one Reality which is God. While therefore, in the rejection by a succeeding age of the dogma of the nominalistic basis of knowledge, the philosophy to which Berkeley's results pointed may be said to have fallen to ruin, Collier's idea remained, as he prophesied it would, to be the starting-point of a new form of realistic Idealism.

PART II

NINETEENTH-CENTURY IDEALISM
IN ENGLAND

CHAPTER I

CARLYLE'S TRANSCENDENTAL SYMBOLISM

1. PHILOSOPHICAL SPIRIT OF THE EIGHTEENTH CENTURY

In the first part of these Studies we were occupied with the new interest in the metaphysical foundations of man's moral and religious experience, which was the result of the revival in Europe of Platonic study, but which gained point and vigour from developments in contemporary philosophy both in England and on the Continent that seemed to threaten what was vital in that experience. The main product of this earlier movement may be said to have been in the broad sense of the word a *Moral* Philosophy, which found its centre in and again radiated out from the human conscience, as that which connected the individual man with society and with God. But it allied itself also with forms of intellectual and social life that were already losing their hold of the mind of the time. Its exponents were Churchmen, some of them Tories and ardent reactionaries in all that concerned political and ecclesiastical doctrine and government. In both respects—both in being dominated by an interest in man's spiritual experience and in its attachment to established forms of life and doctrine—it was in fundamental antagonism to the spirit of the coming century.

The intellectual features of the succeeding period have often been described. It was a time of awakening to the summons to a fuller understanding of physical, and of the more elementary impulses of human nature, as the foundation of everything else in the life of man. It was a time of awakening also to what was thought to be the only true *way* of understanding that nature. The old way was to start from ends and ideals, what things were for, what they were to be. The new way was to start with beginnings and with what things simply are. While synthesis may be said to have been the watchword of the old, analysis was that of the new. Analyse things into their elements, discover what these are and the laws by which they are governed, and you have the secret of their being. Once these are known, you have the clue to the nature of the aggregates of them which are the objects of ordinary experience. In Physics this meant atoms; or, if atoms meant as to Hobbes and Descartes units of spatial extension, then the union of this with time in motion.[1] In psychology it meant impressions and images and their union by association, which, as Hume explained, bears the same relation to these units of mind as gravitation bears to the units of matter. In Ethics it meant the primary instincts of self-preservation and self-interest weaving themselves into a general sense of utility. In Politics it meant that the State was an artificial creation of the individuals who compose it—the art consisting in the alchemy by which the sense of utility for the self is converted into the sense of what is useful for the aggregate of selves. In Religion, finally, it meant the evacuation from the idea of God of everything that could relate Him to man in the intimacy of spiritual communion. God became the name of the Great Being alternatively conceived pantheistically as the aggregate of beings, appearing in them "as full and perfect in a hair as heart," or theistically as the remote Creator and hidden mechanist of the cosmic order.[2] It is these features of the age which are indicated by the terms commonly applied to it as intellectualist, naturalistic, individualistic, and deistic. The words have acquired a certain dyslogistic meaning. But each stands for a piece of iconoclastic work that had to be carried through to the end, so that the implications of the principle from which the start was made might be brought fully into view, and an estimate formed of its adequacy to explain the concrete facts of experience. No one who does not realize this can begin to understand which this period of apparent negation stands for. No one who does realize it, and who also realizes how slowly and intricately the mills of God in philosophical matters grind, is likely to undervalue the "destructive" work of the eighteenth century. It concerns us here as explaining why it had to run its course, before there could be any real revival of a philosophy which started from presuppositions in every department of experience the precise opposite from those just described.

2. CARLYLE AS THE PROPHET OF REVOLT

In the book referred to in the Preface[3] I have indicated some of the

[1] Hobbes was a "motionalist" rather than a "materialist". See article by Z. Lubienski, *Journal of Philosophical Studies*, V. 18.
[2] John Toland (1680–1722), the earliest and in some respects the most representative of the eighteenth-century men in England, seems to have been the first to use the words "free-thinker" and "pantheist". See Erdmann's *History of Philosophy*, vol. iii. p. 153 (Eng. tr.).
[3] *Coleridge as Philosopher*, J. H. Muirhead, 1930, from which one or two of the sentences which follow are borrowed.

forms of experience which were forcing themselves upon the nation at the end of the eighteenth and the beginning of the nineteenth century, and which raised in an acute form the question of the adequacy of the dominant philosophy for their explanation, together with the circumstances that marked out Samuel Taylor Coleridge as the reviver of the Platonic tradition and the founder of nineteenth-century Idealism in England. I believe that much more may in this respect be claimed for the poet-philosopher than is usually conceded. Yet the more we dwell on this claim, the more remarkable it might seem that it was Carlyle and not Coleridge who was the accepted prophet of the immediately succeeding generation. "There are few middle-aged men of active intelligence", wrote H. D. Traill in 1889,[1] "who can avoid the confession of having 'taken' Carlylism in their youth; but no mental constitutions not predisposed to it could ever have caught Coleridgism at all." With even better opportunities of observation, E. Caird [2] speaks of Carlyle as for that generation "the author who exercised the most powerful charm upon young men who were beginning to think". The reason was doubtless partly to be found in the elder writer's failure to give effective expression to his ideas in published works; to a still greater degree, perhaps, in the impression which what he did publish produced of a certain timidity in applying his ideas to fundamental problems. Contrasted with these failures, we have Carlyle's incomparable success in the published expression of his thought and his equally incomparable courage in the application of it to the political and religious life of his time. But the main reason of this difference was in the time itself.

The best minds in Coleridge's generation, as John Stuart Mill saw, were already feeling the narrowness of the older philosophy, but the school to which Mill himself belonged was still in the heyday of its influence, and many of the younger men were still filled with the hope of what it might accomplish. By the time that Carlyle began to become known all this was changed. Disillusionment had set in: "The new generation," writes Traill, "was tired to death of the eighteenth-century tradition, and profoundly disgusted with the intellectual and spiritual patrimony which they had inherited from it. They were sick of its sandy Utilitarianism, its cast-iron economics, its uninspired and uninspiring theology, the flat and deadly prose

---

[1] *Coleridge* in the *English Men of Letters* Series, p. 206.
[2] *Essays on Literature*, "The Genius of Carlyle" (1892), p. 218.

of its theories of life. They were ripe, especially the younger of them, for rebellion against a system which, however eminently conformable to the practical reason, had no word of response to utter, no shred of satisfaction to offer to those two most important claimants in human and especially in youthful human nature—the energies and the emotions. The new generation were crying out for at least a religion of action if they could hold no longer by any religion of speculative belief. They wanted a politico-social creed which would find room for the new ideas and aspirations rejected or coldly viewed by the politicians of the old order. Above all, they passionately longed, as did the newly arisen Romanticists in France— for a presentment of human life in literature with all the wealth of colour and animation of movement that belonged to it in every age, and which they felt were not wanting to it in their own. They were unutterably weary of contemplating the world as a mere storehouse of facts and figures or as a mechanical creation of laws, forces, and formulæ; and they were eager to realize it once more as the scene of the endless drama of human action and passion of struggle and triumph and defeat."[1]

This was a notable change, and under other circumstances it might have been expected to stir the younger men to a more philosophical examination of the view of the world which had brought things to this pass. As a matter of fact, as Traill in the same passage notices, a distrust of all speculation was itself a part of the general reaction; and among the other sources of Carlyle's influence must be reckoned his own denunciations of the "transcendental moonshine" of his great predecessor.

This admission might seem fatal to looking in Carlyle for any important contribution to the development of idealistic philosophy in England, and, if the possibility of pointing to any sustained effort of metaphysical thought were all that was in question, it would be decisive. But there are other ways in which a man may contribute to philosophical progress. It is a mistake to regard philosophy as merely an intellectual exercise in the analysis of experience. Philosophy, like experience, is a house of many mansions. There is a place in it for everyone who by word or act gives typical expression to the deeper mind of the race in any one of the departments of its operation. A man may thus be of service to philosophy by the deepening of consciousness that

[1] Introduction to *Sartor Resartus*. (Centenary edition of *Works*, 1896.)

comes from speaking to his time from a level of experience more truly representative of that of his nation than others. There are departments of philosophy, notably in ethics and politics removed by a certain distance from metaphysics, in which he may have been able to lay hold of precisely those truths which are needed to give substance and direction to the new practical aspirations of his time. Before a *new* philosophy, moreover, can find a place in the mind of a time and a country (and this perhaps is particularly true of England), the inadequacy of the old must have become superabundantly plain. From this point of view effective criticism of systems which have ceased to represent any vital thought and merely cumber the ground is the very life-blood of philosophy. If added to this a writer can point effectively to new sources of philosophical inspiration, to however small an extent he may himself have followed them up, his services may be greater still. Finally, by the very defects of his own general method, particularly if he has exhibited it at its best and on the grandest scale and in just proportion to the importance of the truths he has sought to enforce by it, a writer may help to open men's eyes to its inadequacy and direct them to the necessity of substituting others more adequate to bear the strain put upon them.

In all these ways Carlyle exercised an influence in England and America that no other did upon the course of philosophical thought of his time, for the true understanding of which a more detailed reference to each of them may here be in place.

3. ESSENTIAL PURITANISM

Coleridge's primary and eminent qualification to speak as a philosopher was that he embodied, as none other, not even Wordsworth, did, the quintessence of the Romantic spirit which had been and still was the source of all that was best in English poetry, and that he was thus able in all that he said of the nature and foundations of the æsthetic and kindred forms of experience to speak as from their very soul.[1] To no less a degree than Coleridge embodied the Romantic spirit, Carlyle may be said to have been the living embodiment of the Puritanic spirit which had been the source of what was best in the history of England and Scotland, the British Colonies,

[1] On this see *Coleridge as Philosopher*, Introduction.

and the New England States. His most recent biographer [1] has enabled us to realize the extent to which the burden of his teaching had its roots in the kind of life he saw around him in his early years in the village of Ecclefechan: the loyalty to duty and the pride in efficient work of his mason father, the simple, but broad-minded piety of his mother, the noble Stoicism of his Uncle Tom, the visible continuity of family life in a village community, which led one instinctively to look beyond the individual and even the particular generation in estimating the issues of good and evil. "The greatest truth he had to teach, that Righteousness is a law of Nature, was a living tradition around him as a child." [2] He has been accused of inordinate family pride in an exaggerated and quite parochial estimate of the qualities of his own people. There may have been something of that in him, as in so many of his countrymen; but the real explanation is to be found in the singular good fortune of having been born and brought up in a corner of the country uncorrupted by false standards, in which his neighbour, Robert Burns, could see and say as patent fact

> The rank is but the guinea stamp,
> The man's the gowd for a' that.

It was by the power with which he was able to bring this and therewith what is deepest in moral and religious experience home to his contemporaries that Carlyle impressed them, as perhaps none other could have done, with the scope of the problem that a metaphysics which would do justice to it had to face and the essential inadequacy of any that failed.[3]

4. CRITICISM OF CURRENT ENGLISH PHILOSOPHY

Carlyle never fell as Coleridge did under the spell of the philosophies that were being expounded in his own country in his time. Dugald Stewart, the Professor of Moral Philosophy in Edinburgh University, was already old and failing. His colleague, Thomas Brown, with

[1] David Alec Wilson in *Carlyle Till Marriage*, 1923; *Carlyle to the French Revolution*, 1924; *Carlyle on Cromwell and Others*, 1925.
[2] Wilson, *Carlyle Till Marriage*, p. 47.
[3] On his first visit to Paris in 1824, "at the Theatre Français he saw Voltaire's *Œdipe*, Talma performing; and when Talma said: 'C'est nos craintes, qui ont forme les cieux', the audience rose up with a vehement shout of approval, which was a sign of the times. 'Unhappy France!' thought he, which was a sign of Carlyle". *Op. cit.*, vol. i. p. 350.

his "dissolving" empiricism and his rhetorical style, was not likely to impress Carlyle either by the matter or the manner of his lectures. On the other hand, the Nithsdale Calvinist was far more deeply steeped than was the young Cambridge Unitarian in the orthodoxies of traditional Christianity. For this reason one might have expected a far more troubled and less complete deliverance in his case than in Coleridge's. It was a proof at once of the depth of his moral and religious convictions and of his own clear-sighted outlook that it was quite otherwise. The trouble came later. Meantime it was only by a very gradual and gentle process that he realized that he could not enter the ministry as he had intended, and "put off his Christianity 'as when one layeth his worn-out robes away' ". Influenced chiefly by his reading of Gibbon in 1818, he tells us, he "first clearly saw that Christianity was not true".[1]

Christian theology had gone, but his faith in the moral order of the world remained steadfast, resting on deeper foundations than any which it or any system of philosophy could give. It was this that enabled him to look with a certain objectivity at the popular philosophies of the time. Hume's scepticism ran off him as the proverbial rain off the duck's back. "I intended to have said something of the bigoted scepticism of Hume," he writes to a friend in 1814, "but, as I am convinced you see through his specious sophisms and detect his blind prejudice in favour of infidelity, I shall defer it."[2] Little as Hume's philosophy impressed him, he found even less in the writings of its chief opponent at the time. "Dugald Stewart", he wrote in 1815, "has done me hurt. Perpetually talking about analysing perceptions, and retiring within oneself, and mighty improvements that we are to make—no one knows how— I believe he will generally leave the mind of his reader crowded with disjointed notions and nondescript ideas—which the sooner he gets rid of the better. Probably", he adds, anticipating a later conviction, "the fault is in the subject."

"When will there arise", he writes in the same year, "a man who will do for the science of mind what Newton did for that of matter— establish its fundamental laws on the firm basis of induction—and discard for ever those absurd theories that so many dreamers have devised?" ending with a similar note: "I believe this is a foolish

---

[1] Wilson, *op. cit.*, pp. 133 and 147.
[2] *Op. cit.*, p. 99. Next year, after closer acquaintance, he finds Hume's *Essays* "admirable both in matter and in manner", *ibid.*, pp. 109–110.

question, for its answer is—never."[1] Writing twelve years later, after his discovery of the Germans, he sums up his view of Stewart's writings as "not a philosophy, but a preparation for one", and more particularly as a preparation for what is to be found in Kant.[2]

It was for this reason, too, that, when the crisis, described in the well-known chapter in the "Everlasting No" in *Sartor Resartus*, actually came and his belief in the world as a moral order was for the time shaken, it was to nothing that he read in the philosophers that he owed his deliverance, but first to his own stalwart Puritan heart reasserting its manhood, and secondly to the aid that came to him from Goethe, who was the Great Heart who raised him out of the Slough of Despond.[3]

By 1829 he had discovered the source of the malady that afflicted the philosophy together with all the other elements in the life of the time. We have seen what that was.[4] From the time of Locke our metaphysics had been a physical and mechanical one. "It is not a philosophy of the mind: it is a mere discussion concerning the origin of consciousness of ideas, or whatever else they are called; a genetic history of what is in the mind. There is no word in it of the secret of our Freedom, of our mysterious relations to Time and Space, to God and the Universe." Even those who, like Reid in Scotland, had a dim notion of something wrong in a philosophy that could lead to conclusions such as Hume's, have themselves "taken a mechanical course, not seeing any other. They let loose Instinct, as an undiscriminating ban-dog, to guard them against these conclusions; they tugged lustily at the logical chain, by which Hume was so coldly towing them and the world into bottomless abysses of Atheism and Fatalism. But the chain somehow snapped between them, and the issue has been that nobody now cares about either—any more than about Hartley's, Darwin's,[5] or Priestley's contemporaneous doings in England".

This estimate of the value of Reid and the philosophy of Common Sense may not have been a wholly sympathetic or fair one. It might

[1] *Op. cit.*, pp. 110 and 117.
[2] *Miscellaneous Essays*, vol. i, "State of German Literature".
[3] "The Everlasting No" is not, as it has sometimes been taken to be, a sceptical philosophy, but the renunciation of the law of Righteousness. To deny the "everlasting No" was to affirm the "everlasting Yea".
[4] He himself described it in the early *Essay on Signs of the Times* (1829). See *Miscellaneous Essays*, vol. ii.
[5] Erasmus Darwin. Charles Darwin went as a student to Edinburgh in 1825.

be shown, as it has been by more sympathetic critics,[1] that Reid was quite aware of the distinction between what is common in the sense of "vulgar prejudices" and "what is common in the structure of all languages", because it is common to the structure of all thought; and that he is appealing, as Kant himself was, to the real unthinkableness of the conclusions to which Hume's premises led. But it is admitted even by his defenders that Reid himself makes no consistent effort "to distinguish the speculative from the practical aspect of philosophical questions", and "does not hesitate to make play for the unitiated with the results of the 'theory of ideas' ", in a way that no one who fully understood the real issues that were involved could have permitted himself to do. Carlyle is therefore essentially right, and shows his own philosophical insight in expressing the view (more fully stated in the well-known passage in Kant's Prolegomena on the same subject) that Reid's appeal to mere popular belief is "an act of suicide" on the part of philosophy, "the life and business of which, that of interpreting appearances, is hereby at an end".[2]

In the *Signs of the Times* he points to old days for men who were wise in the dynamic science to which he makes appeal, but he had learned already that there were extant in his own time men who were elsewhere recognized as exponents of it, and from whom British philosophy had much to learn.

5. German Metaphysics

Traill[3] speaks of Carlyle as "alike ignorant of philosophical systems and contemptuous of philosophical method". There is a certain truth in both of these accusations. He was never a systematic student of philosophy, and relied largely on his intuitions in his judgments in philosophical questions. But his reading was wide and his intuitions extraordinarily accurate. Similarly with regard to his general attitude to philosophical method the question is not so simple. There were different periods in his life when his attitude was different, and there were, in his view, differences in method.

There was a period, coinciding with that in which he was acquainted mainly with the philosophies of his own country, in

[1] *E.g.*, James Seth, *English Philosophies and Schools of Philosophy*, pp. 233 foll.
[2] *Miscellaneous Essays*, II, "Novalis", p. 275.   [3] *Loc. cit.*

which, as we have seen, he was inclined to attribute their failure to
the nature of the subject and the limitations of man's powers. It
was under this impression that we find him resenting the intrusion
of philosophy in his favourite authors. "One is tired to death", he
wrote in 1823, "with Schiller's and Goethe's palabra about the
nature of the fine arts. Did Shakespeare know aught of Æsthetics?
or Homer?"[1] Closer acquaintance with these writers opened his eyes
to the debt they owed to the work of the metaphysicians in their
own country, and led him into studies which considerably modified
his view.

Coleridge's introduction to the German language and literature
was a comparatively late addition to his education and more or less
of an accident. Carlyle's may be said to have come in the course
of the ordinary education of an Edinburgh student. Lockhart in
his *Life of Scott* tells us that "German had been in fashion (in
Scotland) for thirty years", and Carlyle's biographer has noticed
that: "The Scotch appreciation of modern languages was what then
distinguished their culture from the English."[2] In 1820 we find
him already "living riotously with Schiller, Goethe, and the rest",
and learning to appreciate them as "the greatest men". We have
already seen what Goethe was to him in the spiritual crisis which
took place in 1822. It was Goethe, he said in 1877, who "taught me
that the true things in Christianity survived and were eternally
true; pointed out to me the real nature of life and things".
And of the German writers as a whole he said in the Lectures of
1838: "I can only think of the revelation, for I can call it no other,
that these men made to me. It was to me like a rising of a light
in the darkness which lay around and threatened to swallow
me up".[3]

But it was his studies for his *Life of Schiller* (published in 1825)
that revealed to him the influence that the Kantian philosophy
had in the formation of the poet's mind, and convinced him that
what had led in him to new standards of criticism "could be no
merely crazy mysticism". "The philosophy of Kant", he there
writes, "is probably combined with errors to its very core, but
perhaps also this ponderous unmanageable dross may bear in it
the everlasting gold of truth! Mighty spirits have already laboured
in refining it: is it wise in us to take up with the base pewter of

[1] Wilson, *op. cit.*, p. 277.   [2] *Op. cit.*, pp. 276 and 280.
[3] *Ibid.*, *op. cit.*, p. 221. See *passim* and his own Essays on Goethe.

utility and renounce such projects altogether? We trust not"; and he asks in a note, "Are our hopes of Mr. Coleridge always to be fruitless?"[1]

Following on this, we find him in 1826 reading and "partially understanding" Kant's *Critique of the Pure Reason*, and "full of projects for instructing his benighted countrymen on the true merits of this sublime system at some more propitious season".[2] Meantime he was engaged on his Essay on the *State of German Literature*, his studies for which only helped to confirm him in his view of the importance of such an enterprise. In this Essay he quotes Wilhelm Schlegel's opinion with regard to the Kantian Philosophy to the effect that "in respect to its probable influence on the moral culture of Europe it stands on a line with the Reformation", and goes on:[3] "But the worth of Kant's philosophy is not to be gathered from votes alone. The noble system of morality, the purer theology, the lofty views of man's nature derived from it, nay, perhaps the very discussion of such matters, to which it gave so strong an impetus, have told with remarkable and beneficial influence on the whole spiritual character of Germany. . . . Such men as Goethe and Schiller cannot exist without effect in any literature or in any century; but if one circumstance more than another has contributed to forward their endeavours and introduce that higher tone into the literature of Germany, it has been this philosophical system; to which, in wisely believing its results, or even in wisely denying them, all that was lofty and pure in the genius of poetry, or the reason of man, so readily allied itself." The system he goes on to prophesy must become known in England as it already is over Europe. For himself he is only an inquirer. But he "permits himself to state" what has most struck him as characterising Kant's system.

After a criticism of the Scottish School, on the lines of that already quoted, as "a total abdication of Philosophy strictly so called", he goes on to indicate the central principle of Kant's philosophy as the distinction between reason and understanding. The passage has a particular interest for our present Study in that it slides without warning from Kant to "the Kantists", and instead of a first-hand statement of the doctrine in question gives us the modification of it, which we find in Coleridge, and that to a large

[1] *Life of Schiller* (New York, 1899), p. 114. See the whole passage of which the above is the conclusion.
[2] Wilson, *op. cit.*, p. 429.　　　[3] *Miscellaneous Essays*, vol. i. pp. 90 foll.

extent in the very words of Coleridge.[1] Whatever the passage may suggest as to the extent of Carlyle's own acquaintance with Kant, it witnesses to the seriousness with which at this time he took Coleridge's work, in the field of philosophy and the revolution which he thought it destined to make in the whole outlook of the time.

That up to this time he still harboured the idea of completing Coleridge's work seems to be indicated by such entries as we find in his notebook of March 1830: "I have now almost done with the Germans. Having seized their opinions, I must turn me to inquire how true they are? That truth is in them, no lover of Truth will doubt: but how much? After all, one needs an intellectual Scheme— or ground plan of the Universe drawn with one's own instruments."[2] Why did Carlyle make no serious attempt to carry out this excellent programme? The answer is doubtless partly that the opportunity which he sought on the vacation of the Moral Philosophy Chair in St. Andrews by Dr. Thomas Chalmers, and again on the foundation of a chair of Philosophy in the new London University, was denied him; but far more that ideas were forming themselves just at this time in his mind on the relation between thought and action which diverted him from any such task, while simultaneously he became inspired with the idea of putting what he already understood of the "ground plan" drawn by the instruments of others to a use of his own.

There is a sense in which British philosophy has been pragmatic from the first. Practice at the time of which we are speaking, was a dominant interest. To this bent the teaching of Kant and Fichte, so far as it was known, gave apparent confirmation. Coleridge had been repelled by the exaggeration of it in Fichte, but he had him-

[1] For a similar reproduction of Coleridge's ideas almost in his words see the Essay on "Characteristics" (1831) in *Miscellaneous Essays*, vol. iii. p. 343, where Carlyle speaks of every society as the "embodiment, tentative and more or less complete, of an Idea". And for a fine tribute to the hints of a philosophy in Coleridge's *Friend* and *Biographia Literaria* (*op. cit.*, vol. ii. p. 251 in the Essay on "Novalis", 1829), where they are compared to "living brooks, hidden for the present under mountains of froth and theatrical snow-paper", and which only "at a distant day, when these mountains shall have decomposed themselves into gas and earthy residuum, may roll forth in their true limpid shape to gladden the general eye with what beauty and everlasting freshness does reside in them". Later in the same Essay he characterizes Kantian Idealism as "the most serious in its purport of all philosophies propounded in these latter centuries" as having been taught by men of the loftiest and most earnest character, and as bearing "with a direct and highly comprehensive influence on the most vital interests of men".

[2] Wilson, *Carlyle and the French Revolution*, p. 132.

self, in his own way, been led to the assertion of the priority of the moral to the intellectual. Carlyle, with no such repulsion, but on the contrary an ardent admiration of Fichte,[1] may be said to have carried this teaching to its logical issue.

In his notes at the time of which we are speaking there is a growing emphasis on action: "What we have done is the only mirror of what we are." "One thing we see: the moral nature of man is deeper than his intellectual." History goes beyond philosophy. It is "philosophy teaching by experience". True, narrative is only "linear" while "action is solid", but narrative has at any rate the advantage of dealing with the solid: "history is the science of act and fact"; and he exhorts himself: "no longer eat your heart. Man *sollte greifen zu*".

Carlyle knew well enough that thought was itself a form of action, and might be for individuals or epochs the duty that lay nearest to them. He further held that the present was such an epoch when the sceptical philosophy of Hume had to be met with a new constructive or dogmatic metaphysic. But he had persuaded himself that that work had been already done by Kant, "the fire of doubt consuming doubt that so the Certain come to light and again be visible on the surface". "In that wide-spreading, deep-whirling vortex of Kantism, so soon metamorphosed into Fichteism, Schellingism, and then into Hegelism and Cousinism, perhaps finally evaporated, is not this issue," he asks, "visible enough that Pyrrhonism and Materialism, themselves necessary phenomena in European culture, have disappeared and a Faith in Religion has again become possible and inevitable for the scientific mind?"[2] Thought, indeed, there will still be, but it will be what it was intended to be, nothing but "the picture and inspiring symbol of action", in other words, "Poetry and Religion".[3]

Holding thus that speculative philosophy had for the time done its work, and that all that was required was the recognition of it in other countries besides Germany, it is not surprising that Carlyle should have been content to leave to others the task of expounding this work in detail in England, and turned himself to the more

[1] See his noble tribute to him in the Essay on the "State of German Literature" (1827), *Miscellaneous Essays*, vol. ii. p. 89.
[2] Essay on "Characteristics" (1831), *Miscellaneous Essays*, vol. iv. p. 37.
[3] An allusion probably to Novalis's view that "The division of philosopher and poet is only apparent and to the disadvantage of both. It is a sign of disease and of a sickly constitution." See Carlyle's own *Essay on Novalis* of 1829, p. 294.

congenial task of translating it into symbol, and using it as a clue to the interpretation of history and of the special needs of his own distressful time.

6. The Philosophy of Work

With what effect he performed the first of these tasks is known to the reader of *Sartor Resartus*, and particularly of the two great chapters on "Natural Supernaturalism" and "The Everlasting Yea", in which its teaching is condensed. In the former we have what W. D. Traill has described as "Perhaps the grandest and most awe-inspired exercise on the everlasting theme: O World, O Life, O Time, that exists in human language."[1] The same might be said of the exercise, in the chapter "The Everlasting Yea", on the theme "O Man, O Act, O Worth". If the present generation has outgrown the manner of both, the matter is of perennial interest.

Science has done its best to banish the miraculous. There is a "mechanism of the Heavens" which has marked out the courses of the stars, yet Nature remains as miraculous as before. "The course of Nature's phases, on this our little fraction of a Planet, is partially known by us: but who knows what deeper courses these depend on? what infinitely larger cycle (of causes) our little epicycle revolves on? To the minnow every cranny and pebble, and quality and accident of its little native creek may have become familiar: but does the minnow understand the Ocean Tides and periodic currents, the Tradewinds and Monsoons and Moon's Eclipses, by all which the condition of its little Creek is regulated, and may from time to time (unmiraculously enough) be quite overset and reversed? Such a Minnow is Man; his Creek this Planet Earth; his Ocean the immeasurable All; his Monsoons and periodic Currents the mysterious Course of Providence through Æons and Æons."

What hides all this from us is partly the veil which custom weaves between us and reality: "Innumerable are the elusions and legerdemain tricks of custom, but of all these perhaps the cleverest is her knack of persuading us that the miraculous by simple repetition ceases to be miraculous." Going deeper than custom are the two grand fundamental appearances of Space and Time which are woven for us from before birth to clothe us for dwelling here and yet to blind us to their relativity. Fortunatus's wishing-cap anni-

[1] *Loc. cit.*, p. xxii.

hilated space. We want another for time. Yet are not Memory and Hope just such another? mystic avenues through which we can summon up past, future, yesterday, and to-morrow, as what really *are*; parts of an Eternal into which we may thus glance? But more miraculous than these and of a fuller reality is the Me round which the temporal and material is gathered as the reality of which limbs, life-force, and passions are but the shadow form wherein "for some moments or years the Divine Essence is to be revealed in the Flesh". The great question for man is how this revelation is to be made, what is there in him to yield to the ghostly trend of the Spirit and take the imprint of its presence? This, which to Carlyle was the great question, is answered in the second of the chapters referred to.

Amid all that is uncertain, the one great certainty (Carlyle's grasp of it is the centre of his Idealism) is the presence of an Infinite in man, "which with all his cunning he cannot quite bury under the finite". Albeit the Temples that men have built to It in the past are all sunk to ruins, the altar and its lamp are still there. To hold to this conviction is Belief; all else is Opinion. But "conviction were it never so excellent is worthless till it convert itself into Conduct—properly is not possible till then. Only by a felt indubitable certainty of Experience does it find a centre to revolve round and so fashion itself into a system". But here too illusion awaits us. The very Infinite within us puts on the form of illusion, nad we seek to find it in mere limitless happiness. There can be no true peace till men cease from the love and pursuit of pleasure. "Love not pleasure; love God. This is the Everlasting Yea wherein all contradiction is solved: wherein whoso walks and works, it is well with him." If we still ask where is He to be found, the answer is here and now in the Duty of the moment. The Divine and the Ideal are the same, and the Ideal is nowhere but in the actual. "Yes; here in this poor, miserable, hampered, despicable actual wherein thou even now standest, here or nowhere is thy Ideal; work it out; and working, believe, live, be free."

In this teaching it is easy to see how profoundly Carlyle has been influenced by Kant and Fichte. But he is far from the exaggerated moralism of either. Teufelsdröckh's teaching is no mere Duty for Duty's sake. His own emancipation was not through any access of reverence for an abstract Imperative, but through the working of pity and love for his fellow-men: "With other eyes could

I now look upon my fellow-man: with an infinite Love and Pity. Man with his so mad Wants and so mean Endeavours had become the dearer to me; and even for his sufferings and his sins, I now first named him Brother."[1] Nor is the ideal, as it was to Kant, a mere "ought", merely a something "to be" entirely beyond the actual, but, as we have seen, the reality that lies veiled in the actual. What finally is achieved both for self and the world is no mere Stoic suppression of contending elements, but the organization and re-birth of them into a new form: "The mad primæval Discord is hushed; the rudely jumbled conflicting elements bind themselves into separate Firmaments; instead of a dark, wasteful chaos, we have a blooming, fertile, heaven-encompassed world."

In all this we may well be content to have parted with the form of philosophical "deduction" to regain touch with the matter of human life as experience actually shows it to be. What we have is an anticipation of the later idealistic ethics of Green and Bradley, especially as we find in the latter's well-known chapter of "My Station and its Duties."[2] If in Carlyle it reads too much like the unthinking acceptance of what is momentarily pressing to be done, and of things as they are to the neglect of the ideal element that looks beyond them, this is doubtless partly the result of his unphilo-sophical method. But here, as in other parts of his philosophy, we have to take one thing with another, and in his political teaching he makes amends by the vigour with which he insists on the as yet unrealized ideal of a truly human society.

7. SOCIAL APPLICATIONS

So taken, we can see it as merely a further development of his transcendentalism. Despise as he might the logic of the schools, it was the clearness with which, both in his life and his writings, he followed where the ideas of these chapters seemed to lead, that was the most excellent thing in Carlyle and made him so powerful a social influence in his time. They are the clue to his interpretation at once of the meaning of man's life as a social being, of the duty of statesmanship, and of his own work as a writer. The emphasis

[1] See the whole passage, perhaps the finest in all Carlyle's writings, and showing a side of the man which has had scant justice done it both by enemies and friends.
[2] *Ethical Studies.* Essay V. See below, p. 233.

which he laid upon Heroes and Hero Worship has given the impression that, in spite of his rejection of the individualism of his time, he remained himself an individualist to the end. The name is ambiguous, and as a term whether of praise or reproach has perhaps ceased to mean much. If we take it to mean that spirit must take shape in individual lives and move forward by its own strength to fuller, more personal form, Carlyle was an individualist, for this was the essence of his teaching. But to say that he held that the individual drew this strength from any source other than that which was supplied by his society taken in the widest sense of the word, or that there were objects that fell outside those that ministered to *its* perfection, is precisely the reverse of the truth. What surprises us rather is the conviction and force with which, in an age of the narrowest individualism, he expressed the opposite.

"To understand man," he wrote in 1831, "we must look beyond the individual man, his actions or interests, and view him in combination with his fellows. It is in Society that man first feels what he is, first becomes what he can be. In Society an altogether new set of spiritual activities are evolved in him and the old immeasurably quickened and strengthened. Society is the genial element wherein his nature first lives and grows; the solitary man were but a small portion of himself, and must continue for ever folded in, stunted, and only half alive. Such is Society, the vital articulation of many individuals into a new collective individual; greatly the most important of man's attainments on this earth; that in which and by virtue of which all his other attainments and attempts find their arena and have their value. Considered well, Society is the standing wonder of our existence; a true region of the Supernatural as it were, a second all-embracing Life, wherein our first individual Life becomes doubly and trebly alive, and whatever of Infinitude was in us bodies itself forth and becomes visible and active."[1] The reason is, as he had learned from Fichte, if not also from Coleridge, that "Every Society, every Polity, has a spiritual principle; is the embodiment, tentative and more or less complete, of an Idea: all its tendencies of endeavour, specialties of custom, its laws, politics, and whole procedure are prescribed by an Idea, and flow naturally from it as movements from the living source of motion. This Idea is ever a true Loyalty; has in it something of a religious, paramount, quite infinite character; and is properly the

[1] *Characteristics*, pp. 9-10.

soul of the State, its Life; mysterious as other forms of Life, and like these working secretly and in a depth beyond that of consciousness."[1]

Carlyle's political teaching came as a direct corollary. He saw social theory being debased and the very existence of Society threatened by the prevalent Utilitarianism and the doctrine of the supremacy of self-interest. This was one of the "Signs of the Times", and it had its work to do in clearing the ground for something better.[2] But its day was past. Men were living in a new world to which its maxims were no longer applicable. New portents, notably the Workhouses with their 1,200,000 occupants, were setting it new tasks, the chief of which was the organization of Labour. "Giant Labour" was stirring, beginning to claim its own. Under what sign was the work of its emancipation to go forward? Carlyle was clear it could not be *laissez-faire*. He was equally clear it could not be the "ballot-box" alone. Democracy truly had come, "everywhere the inexorable demand of these ages, swiftly fulfilling itself".[3] But representative Democracy was impotent of itself to make men free. It might only be a name concealing man's real slavery. "Mock me not with the name," exclaims Teufelsdröckh, "when you have but knit up my chains into ornamental festoons."[4] It might merely mean "despair of finding any Heroes to govern you, and contentedly putting up with the want of them".[5] More fatal still, it might mean the loss of all reverence for the heroic. "In these days men can do almost all things, only not obey. Yet whoso cannot obey cannot be free, still less bear rule; he that is the inferior of nothing can be the superior of nothing. What if the character of our so troublous Era lay even in this: that man has for ever cast away Fear which is the lower; but not yet risen into perennial Reverence which is the higher and the highest." But, though reverence was asleep, Carlyle did not believe that it was dead or ever could die, "so cunningly has Nature ordered it that whatsoever man ought to obey he cannot but obey". It was therefore in a true Hero Worship that he saw the "corner-stone of living rock", on which alone Politics could stand secure.

Holding all this as to the nature of our world and man's work in it, and as to the particular need of his own age, he seemed to have

---

[1] *Characteristics*, p. 12, condensed. *Cp.* the chapter called the Phœnix in *Sartor Resartus*.
[2] *Sartor Resartus*, iii. c. v.
[3] *Past and Present*, Bk. III. c. xiii.
[4] *Sartor Resartus*, c. vii.
[5] *Past and Present*, *loc. cit.*

a clear vision of his own mission. No one with his books before him can for a moment regret his choice. Besides the metaphysical poetry of *Sartor* and the direction of men's minds at a critical period of national life to the conditions of social well-being, we have in his histories an entirely new standard of authentic narrative and of the interpretation of the forces that underlie great events. But the choice was not without its price. If, as he himself held, the construction of "an intellectual scheme or ground-plan of the universe with one's own instruments" was indespensable to the thinker, how, in the absence of it, could there be any security in his work against gaps and misfits, joists at one place without support, at another running counter to one another? To say that Carlyle's building was a patchwork of this kind would be wholly untrue. What is undeniable is that a matter so fundamental could not with impunity be neglected, and that no literary brilliancy could make up for the want of firmly drawn, consistently developed philosophical principles. In the result his contempt of "metaphysic" took its revenge, on the one hand by surrounding his central teaching with an air of unsubstantiality, which made it an easy prey to cold positivist analysis, on the other in an exaggeration of half-truths, which went far to vitiate the effect of what was truest in it.

8. When Prophecy Shall Fail

We have seen the extent to which Carlyle owned obligation to the general results of German thought which he took as the last word of the philosophy of his time. But already there were those who, with at least no less a grasp of its methods, were prepared to regard it as given over to conjecture and formula, "the two vices which have corrupted human thought". With an equal detestation of the abstractions and impieties of Utilitarianism and Individualism, Positivist thinkers were carrying Carlyle's contempt for metaphysics to its full issue, and seeking to recall men's minds from the vain attempt "to grasp the formula of everything" to what they could really understand of the world that surrounded them. What this meant was brilliantly shown on the publication in 1863 of Taine's great *History of English Literature*.[1] The "vehement religious poetry charged with the memories of Milton and Shakespeare",

---

[1] English translation by H. van Laun, New York, 1876, from vol. iii, of which the (condensed) quotation that follows is taken.

which passes in Carlyle for philosophy, Taine wrote, "is but an English transcription of German ideas manufactured according to a fixed rule. First the world, as science reveals it, consisting merely of regular groups or series with a law of their own, next the law is converted into a force which is seized upon in the aggregate, made into a distinct existence situated beyond the reach of experience, conceived of as spiritual and as containing the principle and substance of concrete things. So far we are within the region of metaphysics, illegitimate as its method may be. But add one degree to imagination and enthusiasm, and we will say that this spirit is situated beyond time and space and is manifested through these. Add another, and we will declare it to be the only reality, that the rest is but appearance. By this scale of transformation the general idea becomes a poetical, then a philosophical, then a mystical existence, and German metaphysics concentrated and heated is changed into English Puritanism". At the time when Taine was writing, Positivism was exercising an enormous influence on the Continent. Freed from the vagaries of Comte's "Positive Polity", and combined with the practical enthusiasm of leaders like Frederic Harrison and John Henry Bridges for the cause of Trade Unionism and the improvement of social conditions, it is not surprising that it was proving a formidable rival to Carlyle's teaching in these years, or that, repelled by his growing dogmatism and the barrenness of his denunciations, "some of the shepherdless migrated to Comte".[1]

To-day, perhaps, no one out of France, and perhaps few in France, would imagine that Carlyle's general teaching has been disposed of by the satire of the brilliant Comtist or be willing to exchange its fire, as he would have us do, for the pale moonlight of Ernest Renan.[2] But if it has survived and shows to-day a new vitality, it is not because of any reasoned reply to Positivism that is to be found in his writings or that his method could have supplied. He and his followers were too like a battalion that, in the haste of advance, has lost touch with its base and is in danger of being left hanging in the air with flank and rear alike exposed to the attack of the enemy. If what was true in it was to be secured, and a safe advance rendered possible in the line which it indicated, it had to be by quite other methods than those which he had adopted.

[1] Richard Garnett's *Life of Thomas Carlyle*, London, 1886, p. 159.
[2] Taine, *op. cit.*, p. 319.

What saved it was that thinkers of quite a different kind, of how-ever inferior literary powers, were already grappling with the problem from which he had turned away and setting themselves to discover exactly how much of truth there was in the Kantian philosophy and the developments it had received from Fichte, Schelling, and Hegel. If their work was critical rather than dogmatic, academic rather than popular, this in the growing specialization of the work of the thinker and the scholar was only what was to be expected. At the worst it needed to be no more academic than that of Plato[1] and his Academy, which hitherto had been the chief source of inspiration of what was best in British Idealism.

There is a similar Nemesis in the perversity with which in his later years Carlyle seemed to be setting his face against all the great constructive ideals of the century: Democracy, Progress by Reform, Biological Evolution. I believe that the central truth of his teaching stands sure, and that the alleged contradictions can in the end be shown to be merely apparent. But there remains sufficient ground for the suspicion under which so much of it has fallen, and it is not difficult to-day to see the precise points at which, just because of the absence in him of the patience required for that "obstinate effort to understand", which is the soul of metaphysics, he allowed the violence of his prejudices (or was it merely the violence of his language?) to blind him to the real implications of his central doctrine. It is not without injury to Heaven when the violent take it by force.

(a) It is easy to show that, in the widest sense of the word, Carlyle's teaching was democratic to the core. Even more explicitly than Burns he taught that "every unit of the masses is a miraculous Man, struggling, with vision or with blindness, for his infinite Kingdom". No passage has been oftener or more rightly quoted from his works than the one in *Sartor*, beginning, "Two men I honour and no third."[2] Going along with this was his constant and consistent advocacy of that most democratic of all rights, the right to education: "That there should one Man die ignorant who had

---

[1] Carlyle's ignorance of Plato till Emerson called attention to him is interesting and illuminating. "Plato", wrote Emerson on the occasion of his visit to him at Craigenputtock in 1832, "he does not read, and he disparaged Socrates" (Cabot's *Memoirs of R. W. Emerson*, quoted by Wilson, *op. cit.*, vol. ii. p. 333). Still more interesting and characteristic is the fact that when he did discover him, what attracted him most, as he himself tells us, was the scorn Plato expressed for Athenian democracy.

[2] Book III. c. 4.

capacity for Knowledge, this I call a tragedy, were it to happen more than twenty times in the minute, as by some computations it does." But it was just the absence of this education in the mass of the voters and what he took to be the equation of "the vote of the Demerara negro to that of Chancellor Bacon, Judas Iscariot to Jesus Christ," that was the source of his fear and distrust of political democracy.

The state of public education before 1870 was indeed lamentable, but what more than the unreformed Parliament was responsible for this? And if a Parliamentary vote did not give knowledge, it was at least a stimulus to acquire it for oneself and a means of securing the diffusion of it to others. There was more wisdom in T. H. Green's demand for the working classes, "First untie their hands, and then see what they will do with them." What, as a matter of fact, those who in 1867 had their hands untied immediately set about doing was to pass the Education Act of 1870–71. Along with universal education in the coming years went the extension of freedom of industrial combination, which has probably done more than anything else to prepare the working classes for participation in political government. Many who were not philosophers, as well as some who like Green were, foresaw all this. What closed Carlyle's eyes to it, as by a kind of judicial blindness, was his failure to see the incompatibility of a philosophy which proclaimed the presence in every man of a soul "struggling for its infinite Kingdom" (in other words an ideal of self-direction to self-chosen Good), with the persistent denial to him of elementary civil rights. When traced to its source, this meant the survival in a philosophy, at best half-baked, of just that tendency to treat men as isolated, passive, present units, which was the vice of the philosophy he lost no opportunity of denouncing. He was fond of emphasizing the necessity of a "dynamical" as contrasted with the mechanical philosophy then in vogue. But he conceived of the "dynamics" far too much as something that had to be supplied from without in the person of the "Ablest discoverable Man". Granting that the "ablest man" were discovered and that he were as good as he was able, you would not have what you want if it meant simply acquiescence in a benevolent despotism. Man is a political as well as a social animal, and Carlyle at least might have learned from his idol Goethe that true liberty is something which nations, like individuals, can only possess on condition that they daily win it for themselves.

(*b*) There can be no doubt at all as to what Carlyle meant to teach as to Might and Right. Speaking of the view that identifies them, he said in his old age: "This is the very precise and absolute contrary to the truth I hold and have endeavoured to set forth, namely and simply, that Right makes Might. Well do I remember when in my younger days the force of this truth dawned on me. . . . It was a sort of Theodicy to me, a clue to many facts to which I have held on from that day to this. But it's little matter to me at this hour. I'll not undertake to set myself right now. If the truth is in my books, it will be found out in due time; and if it's not there, why then the sooner they utterly perish the better."[1]

It *is* in his books, but unfortunately there are other things in his books as well: his admiration of Napoleon Buonaparte whom he coupled with Goethe as one of the "two great men" of the time, whom he chose for one of his "Heroes as King", and of whom he once thought of writing a Life;[2] his actual choice of Frederick the Great instead of Luther as the subject of his later work; things he said about Bismarck and about the unerringness of Nature which his latest biographer by way of defence illustrates by quoting Pope:—

> One truth is clear, whatever is, is right.[3]

It is impossible, I think, to deny that Carlyle was attracted to these "Lords of the World" by their faculty to get things done instead of merely talking of them.[4] That he for the moment—perhaps for many moments—allowed himself to forget the infinite difference between the things that were done, was the result simply of his contempt for the supreme, if prosy, virtue of philosophical consistency. Inconsistency may be, as it has been called, the last infirmity of noble minds, but it is an infirmity that is dangerous in proportion to their nobility. That Carlyle sought to correct this particular one[5] was noble in him, but it ought not to have required correction, and a little more philosophy would have saved him from the necessity.

[1] Wilson, *op. cit.*, vol. i. p. 315. [2] *Ibid.*, vol. ii. pp. 277 and 343.
[3] *Ibid.*, vol. i. p. 316.
[4] "Say nothing, if one can do nothing", quoted from Napoleon, *On Heroes*, c. vi.
[5] *E.g.*, in distinguishing between Napoleon and Cromwell, *Heroes*, *ibid.* Yet if there is that in the former which "at last involves him and his work in ruin", why "a Hero"? So later, Frederick was admitted to be "to the last a questionable hero with nothing of a Luther in him". Why then choose him, as he did, in preference to Luther for his last great work?

K

(c) His hostility to the new biological doctrines he never lived to correct. But here also a more philosophical appreciation of the roots of his own teaching, not to speak of the example of Goethe, who was an evolutionist on his own account, would have saved him from the charge of obscurantism. It would have led him to see that the question of man's origin in time was one thing, that of the nature of the being who had thus arrived on the stage of the earth was quite another, and that it was the latter with which he was concerned and on which he had a word of quite indefinite and independent importance to say. It might have led him even further to see that, if his own doctrine of the Right as the fittest and the only fit to survive was the gospel truth he held it to be, Darwinism, properly interpreted, so far from being inconsistent with what he had himself been teaching from the beginning, was only a further illustration of it. That he failed to see all this and resorted instead to his old weapons of denunciation and ridicule was only another proof that, great as were his services, both direct and indirect to the cause of idealistic philosophy, something more thoroughgoing than the literary methods of poetry and prophecy was called for to meet the intellectual demands of the new time.

CHAPTER II

HOW HEGEL CAME TO ENGLAND

1. Hegel and the Modern Spirit

The stages of the post-Kantian development of thought in Germany are by this time familiar matter of history: first Fichte's Moralism with its emphasis on the Ego; next the reaction against it in the Natur-Philosophie of Schelling, with its emphasis on the Absolute as the neutral basis both of self and nature: the so-called Philosophy of Identity; lastly, Hegel's Absolute Idealism, which sought to establish Mind or Spirit as the principle that has been manifesting itself under the form of space and time in nature, of consciousness and the creations of science, art, morality, religion, that are the embodiments of its ideals in the life of man. What all these had in common with Kant and with one another was the proof, contained in Critiques of the Pure and the Practical Reason, of the impossibility of explaining either nature or human life except on the assumption of the presence of elements that are neither contained in sensitive data nor built up out of aggregates of them, but are ideal in the sense of transcending what is merely actual. Where they differed from Kant, but still agreed with one another, was in denying that the resulting forms of experience, owing to their supposed origin in the finite mind, make a division between it and an ultimate inapprehensible reality, and confine us to a knowledge of phenomena. Knowledge, morality, art, and religion are only explicable on the assumption that, so far as they go, reality is revealed, and not merely side-tracked by them. Where they differed from one another was in the comprehensiveness of the view they respectively took of the form of experience to which we have to look as containing the most direct revelation of the nature of the ultimate reality. While to Fichte it was the will and the consciousness of the "ought" to which we have first to look, to Schelling the "intuitions" of æsthetic experience, to Hegel these were only partial, and, taken in themselves, abstract forms of that concrete notion, grasp or Begriff, through which the Absolute or Spirit of the Whole manifests itself to us.

Coming at the end of a period of speculative activity, perhaps unexampled since the time of Socrates and Plato, seeming in many of its features and even in its language to recall the philosophy of Aristotle, in which Greek thought attained fullest expression, gathering into itself the aspirations of the new century and offering satisfaction as no other seemed to do to the claim of the modern spirit "to be free, to understand, to enjoy",[1] the Hegelian philosophy was assured of a hearing wherever this claim was making itself acutely felt. In England we might have expected at least as eager a one as elsewhere.

2. OBSTRUCTIONS TO RECOGNITION

Yet there were difficulties and obstructions that had to be overcome.

Hegel was born in 1770, and his name had been before the public in Germany since 1801, when he published his essay on *The Difference between Fichte and Schelling*. But it was long after this before we find him even mentioned in English philosophical literature, and longer still before any of his works appeared in English dress. When he did come to be mentioned by historians, it was only to be held up as an example of the extravagances to which "the intellect left to itself", and particularly the German rationalizing intellect, might lead its votaries. It was not until 1855, when an English translation of part of the Logic[2] was published, that any word of his was available to students ignorant of German. Thus it happened that before his work began to attract attention in England the whole movement of which it was an organic part had been disowned by its greatest living representative, Schelling, as having started from a negation and ended with an abstraction,[3] the school founded by him had been shattered into fragments,[4] and a violent reaction had set in against the whole attitude of mind which it represented. Two questions are thus suggested to the student of British Idealism: (1) Whence this belated arrival in England of the greatest thinker of his time? (2) How under the circumstances just mentioned did he arrive at all?

In attempting an answer to the former of these questions we have

---

[1] T. H. Green's phrase, *Works*, vol. iii. **p. 94.**

[2] *The Subjective Logic of Hegel*, translated by H. Sloman and J. Wallon·

[3] See Schelling's *Werke*, vol. iii, Bk. I. pp. 87 foll.

[4] "Since 1840", wrote Vaihinger in his essay on *The Jubilee of Kant's Critique of the Pure Reason*, "there has been hopeless philosophical anarchy in Germany." See the whole passage quoted by Max Müller in Preface to *Translation of the Critique of Pure Reason*, vol. i. p. xxiii.

to recall in the first place the singular insularity that, precisely at this time, as contrasted both with an earlier and a later period, was a conspicuous mark of such British philosophers as there were. While in political matters, in physical Science, and even in a sense in general literature, England was in close touch with Continental life, in the matter of philosophical speculation there was a singular want of interest in what was being thought and written on the other side of the Channel or the German Ocean. Writing in the 1829[1] edition of the *Abridgment of his History of Philosophy*, Tennemann could say with more than partial truth: "Speculative Philosophy has been altogether neglected by the English, and Practical treated principally with reference to general Politics. Their national pride has at all times inclined them to concern themselves little about the philosophical pursuits of other nations, and, with few exceptions, they have attempted nothing by the path of abstruse and painful research. In consequence they continue to know little of the labours of the philosophers of Germany, and are very imperfectly acquainted even with the system of Kant."[2]

In the same spirit the French Philosopher Cousin announced to his audience in 1828: "England, Gentlemen, is a very considerable island; in England everything is insular, everything stops at certain limits, nothing is developed on a grand scale. England is not destitute of inventions; but history declares that she does not possess that power of generalization and deduction which alone is able to push an idea or a principle to its entire development, and to draw from it all the consequences it encloses." "England", says the same author, in his *History*, "has, strictly speaking, for some time past, and I might almost say for the last half-century, not contributed her share to the philosophical researches of civilized Europe; no celebrated work on metaphysics has been published in England."[3] No better illustration of this insularity could be given than the philosopher whose recent death Cousin goes on to deplore.

In these years, if anyone had asked who was the leading British

[1] The first edition dates from 1812.

[2] *Op. cit.* Eng. Tr. by the Rev. Arthur Thomson, M.A., Late Fellow of Wadham College (Oxford, 1832). In the *Morning Chronicle*, in the course of a correspondence in 1814, Henry Richter (himself a pioneer in Kantian study) refers with surprise to "the appearance in your columns of so obsolete a character as an ENGLISH METAPHYSICIAN", which he attributes to the interest aroused by the publication of Madame de Staël's *Germany*.

[3] Introduction to the *History of Philosophy*, by Victor Cousin. Tr. by H. L. Linberg (Boston, 1832).

philosopher, he would probably have been told Dugald Stewart, whose *Dissertations on Metaphysical and Ethical Science* were written for the Supplement to the then edition of the *Encyclopædia Britannica*. Yet, as Stewart himself tells us in a note, he was totally ignorant of German. This, he adds, "would have prevented me from saying anything of the philosophy of Kant if the extraordinary pretensions with which it was first brought forward in this island, contrasted with the total oblivion into which it soon after very suddenly fell, had not seemed to demand some attention to so wonderful a phenomenon in the literary history of the eighteenth century". He proceeds to piece together such information as he can obtain from Kant's Latin *Dissertation*, and from French and English translators and commentators, in a long condemnatory article on "Kant and other Metaphysicians of the New German School".[1]

We can see, however, from these passages in Stewart that links were already being established between Germany and England.[2] By the 'twenties the cordon had been broken through, and more special causes than mere parochialness and self-complacency are required to account for the slowness with which the new thought made its way. These are to be found in the barriers, which both what might be called the official philosophies within the Universities and the unofficial outside of them had themselves erected against the new thought.

(*a*) In the older English Universities, pledged to theological orthodoxy and "revealed religion", short shrift might be expected for any philosophy that relied solely on the powers of reason and was committed to following its lead. Endless vagaries and vain disputations were the natural result of its impious claims. "Of these everlasting disputes", writes the translator of Tennemann's *History*, "what has been the result? How little has been gained by endless controversy. The inadequacy of Human Reason to satisfy its own

---

[1] *Dissertations* (Edinburgh, 1835), pp. 187 foll. The chief interest for the historian in the caricature of Kant here given is the claim which Stewart puts forward on behalf of Cudworth to have anticipated his central doctrine of the place of the mind in the constitution of the objective world, and "to be far superior to the German metaphysician, both in point of perspicacity and of precision". Needless to say, he does justice neither to the one nor the other in the version he gives of their respective teaching. The note he adds on Cudworth's *Eternal and Immutable Morality* is important as illustrating the interest which that work had aroused on the Continent after the publication in 1732 of Mosheim's Latin version.

[2] See below, pp. 154 foll.

requirements ought to incline the learned and the wise a little to mistrust the guide to which they are apt to commit themselves without hesitation. The most fantastical dreams of the wildest religious enthusiasts were never more repugnant to common sense than the Neo-platonism of Proclus, the Absolute Identity of Schelling, or the Ego and Non-Ego of Fichte."[1]

Substituting "Theism" and "belief in immortality" for "Revealed Religion", the same note of theological prejudice runs through the academic histories of the next two decades that bear the names of J. D. Morell[2] and Robert Blakey.[3]

We shall have to return to the measure that these writers provide of the state of British criticism at this time. Here we are concerned with the veil that theological prejudice drew over their eyes with regard to the significance of German Philosophy. Morell's criticism, otherwise contrasting with that of his contemporaries in containing a real attempt to find some meaning in the Hegelian paradoxes, ends with the total condemnation of the system on the ground that in it "Theism with all its mighty influence on the human mind is compromised. . . . This being the case, the hope of immortality likewise perishes. . . . Religion, if not destroyed by the Hegelian philosophy, is absorbed in it and *as religion* for ever disappears."[4] Blakey who, writing later, might have profited from the work of his predecessor is merely "filled with melancholy" at the thought of writers "whose lives are spent in playing one paradox against another, and in striving who shall promulgate the most startling and outrageous conceits". He "stands aghast in amazement at the audacity and folly which gives utterance to doctrines so denuded of every particle of scriptural authority and common sense".[5]

(b) Equally hostile to the whole spirit of German Philosophy was the Positivism that was the prevailing spirit of non-academic philosophy in England in the 'thirties and 'forties of the century. There was a singular irony in the fact that the leading historian of

[1] Translator's Preface to Tennemann, *op. cit.*, p. xi. After mentioning some trifling alterations which he has permitted himself, the translator goes on: "I am compelled to add that I have judged it better to omit altogether a few passages which appeared to militate against Revealed Religion rather than to alter or soften them." The reader is left wondering how so timid a defender of the faith could have summoned up courage to translate the history of so useless and dangerous a study.

[2] *Modern Philosophy* (London, 1846).

[3] *History of the Philosophy of Mind* (London, 1850).

[4] *Op. cit.*, vol. ii. p. 159.   [5] *Op. cit.*, vol. iv. p. 158.

philosophy at the time was a writer whose aim was to show "how
and why the interest in Philosophy has become purely historical",
and to whom it seemed the highest recommendation of his own
work that it was "written by one disbelieving in the possibility of
metaphysical certitude", and from the point of view of a science
that "teaches us to regard the unhesitating temerities of Plato and
Plotinus as we regard the efforts of a child to grasp the moon".[1]
Lewes, like his more orthodox contemporary, is only restrained
from laughter by the pain with which he contemplates the pretensions of German idealism in general and the "absurdities of the
Hegelian system" in particular.[2]

(c) Finally, there was Scotland, with its tradition of comparative
detachment from theological dogma and a metaphysical genius which
has always made it proof against the compromises of Positivism.
After the dead hand of Reid's Common-Sense Philosophy had been
removed by the death of Dugald Stewart, something better might
be expected from the great chairs of philosophy in Edinburgh and
Glasgow. There was at least vitality and movement in the work of
Sir William Hamilton, but here also the fates were against the
admission of post-Kantian German thought. Hamilton had identified
himself with an interpretation of Kant's work on precisely opposite
lines to those which the post-Kantian movement in Germany had
pursued. Kant was accepted as having raised an insuperable barrier
between the human mind and knowledge of the Absolute, and
Hamilton's efforts were directed to the task of entrenching himself
and his contemporaries in the resultant agnosticism. Again, also,
there was an irony in the occupation of the successor to Stewart's
seat with an interpretation of the syllogism that revived the worst
traditions of the old formal Logic and made him entirely incapable
not only of understanding the significance of Hegel's work in this
department, but of coming within sight of the meaning of its fundamental principle and method. His well-known essay "On the Philosophy of the Unconditioned, in reference to Cousin's Infinito-
Absolute", dates from 1829. In the new matter introduced on its
republication in 1852 there occurs a long note on Schelling and
Hegel in which the battle is joined:—

"If Hegel's Dialectic were (was?) logical, it was a logic outraging

[1] G. H. Lewes's *Biographical History of Philosophy* (Library Ed., 1857).
p. xxxi.
[2] *Op. cit.*, pp. 725 foll.

that science and the conditions of thought itself. Hegel's whole philosophy is indeed founded on two errors: on a mistake in logic and on a violation of logic. In his dream of disproving the law of excluded middle (between two Contradictories), he inconceivably mistakes Contraries for Contradictories; and in positing pure or absolute existence as a mental datum, immediate, intuitive, and above proof (though, in truth, this be palpably a mere relative gained by a process of abstraction), he not only mistakes the fact, but violates the logical law which prohibits us to assume the principle which it behoves us to prove. On these two fundamental errors rests Hegel's Dialectic; and Hegel's Dialectic is the ladder by which he attempts to scale the absolute."[1]

Whatever may be said of Hegel's use of the Dialectic as a whole (and Croce[2] has in our own day found much to say in criticism of his extension of it to what he calls "distincts", or "forms of the spirit" such as sensation and thought), there is a peculiar perversity in attributing to a doctrine, that depends from first to last on the validity of the law of non-contradiction, the design of undermining that law. Criticism has come full circle when the same modern author finds in Hegel's discovery of the union of opposites his chief permanent achievement in philosophy.

These historical influences would not, however, of themselves have been sufficient to explain the slow arrival in England of the Hegelian philosophy had it not been handicapped by its own inherent difficulty. In one respect Lewes was right, namely, that Hegel differs from Kant and Fichte in that, while these latter carry on a certain tradition of philosophical language and form of presentation, in Hegel the very language has to be learned. It is true that Hegel claimed for himself the intention of attempting "to teach philosophy to speak in German". But when used to denote philosophical ideas, ordinary German words and phrases were apt to break down under the weight of the meaning and leave one with nothing. As Wallace has put it, "In the atmosphere of Hegelian thought we feel very much as if we had been lifted into a vacuum where we cannot breathe, and which is a fit habitation for unrecognizable ghosts only."[3] Hence it came about that the ablest men of these years might be prepared to open their minds to the new

[1] Hamilton's *Discussions* (Edinburgh and London, 1866), p. 24 *n.*
[2] Croce in *What is Living and What is Dead in the Philosophy of Hegel*, tr .by Douglas Ainslie, 1915.
[3] *The Logic of Hegel*, p. xv.

philosophy if it would but open its mind to them, and yet might fall back defeated after the most strenuous effort. The experience of Ferrier,[1] writing in 1854, was probably typical of that of many.

After an interesting reference to the hopes that men were then placing in the octogenarian Schelling "to show that speculation was not all one 'barren heath' ", Ferrier goes on: "Hegel! But who has ever yet uttered one intelligible word about Hegel? Not any one of his country-men—not any foreigner—seldom even himself. With peaks here and there more lucent than the sun, his intervals are filled with a sea of darkness, unnavigable by the aid of any compass, and an atmosphere or rather vacuum in which no human intellect can breathe. Hegel had better not be meddled with just at present. Whatever truth there may be in Hegel, it is certain that his meaning cannot be wrung from him by any amount of mere reading, any more than the whisky which is in bread—so at least we have been informed—can be extracted by squeezing the loaf into a tumbler. He requires to be *distilled*, as all philosophers do, more or less—but Hegel to an extent which is unparalleled."[2]

Schelling died the next year. It was perhaps the failure of all hope in that direction that led Ferrier later to renew his attack on Hegel with somewhat better results. But that belongs to the next section of our story. Up to the middle of the 'fifties it may be said that no intelligible word had been spoken by British writers as to the place and significance of Hegel's work. What were the chief influences which brought about a change for the better and were to end in bringing Hegel to England?

3. New Influences

(1) The first place in these influences must be assigned to the steady flow into England, in face of indifference and prejudice, of translations and interpretations of Kant's works. For the more Kant was studied the more evident it became that his was not the final word, and that the powerful movement, which he set agoing, swept inevitably on to his successors, of whom Hegel in point of

---

[1] The brilliant St. Andrews Professor of Moral Philosophy and Political Economy between 1845 and 1864, the year of his death, author of *Institutes of Metaphysics* (1854), described by the writer of the article upon him in the Ninth Edition of the *Encyclopædia Britannica* as "perhaps the best propædeutic to the study of Metaphysics in the English language".

[2] J. F. Ferrier's *Institutes of Metaphysics*, Third Edition, pp. 95–96

his conclusions was the last. I know of no complete account of the progress of Kantian study in England. Any attempt to give one here would carry us too far from our present text. But the mention of a few of the earlier translations and commentaries may serve at once to illustrate and to mitigate the accusations of the insularity, directed against British thought which have been already quoted.

While, as compared with the three hundred books and articles on Kant's philosophy which are said to have appeared on the Continent within the first ten years after the publication of the *Critique of Pure Reason*[1], they make a sorry list, they yet show that from the middle of the 'nineties of the eighteenth century and already in Kant's lifetime there was a steady stream of translation, comment, and exposition upon his work.

In 1795 Professor F. A. Nitsch, who had attended Kant's lectures in Königsberg and was one of his favourite pupils, delivered public lectures in London on "The Analysis of the Mental Faculties as established in the Critique of Pure Reason", and in the following year published *A General and Introductory View of Professor Kant's Principles concerning Man, the World, and the Deity, submitted to the consideration of the learned.*

Two years afterwards appeared *The Principles of the Critical Philosophy selected from the Works of Emmanuel Kant,* by James Sig. Beck, translated from the German (London and Edinburgh, 1797); and, in the same year, an article by Henry Richter, another pupil of Kant, in a Supplementary Number of the *Monthly Magazine,* on "The Origin of the Idea of Cause", in which the writer earnestly urges the necessity of a candid examination of Kant's system.

In 1798 appeared *Elements of the Critical Philosophy,* by A. F. M. Willich, M.D., who explains in the Preface that he "had the good fortune to attend Professor Kant's lectures between the years 1778 and 1781 during my residence at the University of Königsberg, and on the occasion of a visit to my native country again heard several of his lectures in 1792". This book contains a chronological account of thirty of Kant's principal works, including the *Critique of Pure Reason,* and fourteen of his minor works, as also a *Synopsis of the Critical Philosophy,* which was translated from the German of John Schultze, Chaplain to the King of Prussia, as a College exercise, by no less a hand than that of Dr. Reid of Glasgow. It was to this and

[1] See Max Müller, *op. cit.,* p. xv.

Nitsch's book that Dugald Stewart seems to have owed a considerable part of his very imperfect knowledge of Kant.[1]

To the same period is to be referred the article on Kant in the fifth supplementary volume of the *Encyclopædia Britannica* by John Colquhoun, an Edinburgh advocate.

In 1814 occurred the correspondence in the *Morning Chronicle* already alluded to. In the course of this, on March 12th, appeared a long letter signed "A Friend to True Metaphysics" (in reality Henry Richter),[2] to direct its readers to a better source of information than the eloquence of Madame de Staël. Kant is described as "the *intellectual soul* that is beginning to dawn upon the long infancy of the world" and the central point of Kant's work is vigorously stated as the establishment of the constitutive function of the understanding, "whose business is to give an intelligible nature to the objects of knowledge, that is, to constitute them as such before any consciousness or logical classification can take place". The same writer published in 1817 a philosophical satire, *Day Light, a Recent Discovery in the Art of Painting; with Hints on the Philosophy of the Fine Arts and on that of the Human Mind as first dissected by Emanuel Kant,* in which the attempt to discover what the object of sense is, apart from the use of the intelligence, is compared to "the whimsical practice of christening the child before it is born" in order to enforce the Kantian doctrine that "the word used to express a quality of sense must also express some property of the Intellect".

It was not till 1819 that we have, so far as I can find, any actual translation of Kant's works. In that year John Richardson published in English *Prolegomena to Every Future Metaphysic which can appear as a Science* and Kant's posthumous work on *Logic,* each with a reproduction of Wernet's portrait of Kant at the age of seventy-one (probably the first to appear in England); the *Logic* with a biographical appendix.

An impulse was given to Kantian study by the publication in the *Encyclopædia Londonensis* of long articles on Logic, Metaphysics, and Moral Philosophy[3] on Kantian lines by Thomas Wirgman, as well as of *An Entirely New, Complete, and Permanent Science of Philosophy founded on Kant's Critique of Pure Reason,* which was issued from its press. The latter part of this work is occupied with

[1] See *Dissertation,* vol. i. p. 191.
[2] See Wirgman in work quoted below, p. 160a.
[3] These articles were printed separately with plates, 5s. coloured, 4s. plain.

an abridged translation of the *Critique*, undertaken, as the author tells us, with the object of introducing "to the notice of England that long dormant book which is the pride and the glory of Germany".[1]

By the 'thirties, through the influence of Coleridge, De Quincey, and Carlyle,[2] Kant's name had become familiar in circles far beyond the "learned". Henceforth it occupies a conspicuous place in the histories of philosophy.

By this time also Hegel's name begins to appear. In the translation of Tennemann's *Manual of the History of Philosophy*, already mentioned, Hegel is referred to in the section on "Partisans and Adversaries of the System of Schelling" as having seceded with Krause from the tenets of his master; and later in the section on "Most Recent Philosophical Systems" he is again named as "a professor at Berlin whose system is one of Absolute Idealism".

Within the next ten years on the Continent Schelling's name has been superseded by Hegel's as that which really counts in the post-Kantian movement. In England Hegel appears in Lewes's *History* (1841) as closing the Ninth Epoch, which is described as "Demonstration of the Subjectivity once more leading to Idealism". In spite of his contempt for German Philosophy as the pursuit of a shadow and for Hegel's as mere verbalism, Lewes is prepared to recognize the "high order of intelligences" to which its leading exponents belong. "Hegel especially impresses you with a sense of his wonderful power. His works we have always found very suggestive; his ideas, if repugnant to what we regard as the truth, are yet so coherent, systematically developed, so obviously coming from mature meditation, that we have always risen from the perusal with a sense of the author's greatness." His lectures on

[1] This book, with its long preface dated October 6, 1823, was also obtainable with plates, 5s. coloured, 4s. plain. The author makes the interesting prophecy that if England does not adopt transcendental Philosophy, "Germany will on speculative points soon be many centuries in advance. But should this system once strike root in Britain, I should not be surprised if, by her active powers, she were far to surpass, in application, all that has been effected at the birthplace of this divine system." Besides a complete translation of the *Critique*, he tells us he has himself in view an arrangement of the elements of Kant's philosophy for school use, "so susceptible is it of being conveyed into the tender mind of youth".

[2] On Coleridge's relation to Kant, see *Coleridge as Philosopher*. De Quincey's translation of Kant's Essay on "The Idea of a Universal History on a Cosmopolitical Plan" appeared in *The London Magazine*, October 1824. For his essay on Kant see *Miscellanies chiefly Narrative*, vol. iii. On Carlyle, see above, p. 131.

the *Philosophy of History* is even "one of the pleasantest books on the subject we ever read".[1]

In Morell's *Historical and Critical View of the Speculative Philosophy of Europe in the Nineteenth Century* (1846) the German School occupies a hundred and twenty pages in which Hegel's position is similarly recognized, and for the first time the attempt is made to find at least some sense in his paradoxes. The two principles of the Unity of Contradictions and the Identity of Being and Thought are singled out as the central ones and allowed to have "a *germ* of truth". The germ in the former is that "in every judgment two different things form a unity: subject and predicate are the differences", and that "as knowledge advances differences become more and more merged into higher principles". The germ in the latter (the identity of Being and Thought) is contained in the fact that the infinite essence which we must suppose to be the absolute ground of things "only exists as it is thought: Universal Being is a purely rational conception, a necessary idea" which "does not come to its full reality except in the human consciousness: the real and the ideal meet in one; the very essence of the former consisting really in the process of the latter".[2] For the rest Morell interprets Hegelianism in a sense that makes it an easy mark for the kind of criticism which for half a century was in fashion among its enemies: Hegel resolved everything in process of thought. But whence the process? Hegel begins with Nothing, and shows with logical precision how everything regularly proceeds from it by the law of the Dialectic. But is it not as easy to imagine an Infinite Being for the source of all things as an infinite law? Hegel makes the dialectic process everything: all nature, all mind, all history are but pulsations of this movement. But if this is so, what becomes of man's freedom? "His personality is sunk in the infinite," "the law of progress being fixed, man becomes irresponsible".[3]

I spoke in the last section of the bar of both theological and antitheological prejudice that obstructed the advent of Hegel. But a weakness that is conscious of itself is on the way to correct itself. Frederick Denison Maurice at the beginning of the 'sixties marked a new era in philosophical criticism when he declared that, while "he had felt as a theologian, thought as a theologian, written as a theologian", while "all other subjects in his mind were connected

[1] *Op. cit.*, pp. 726 and 734.   [2] *Op. cit.*, vol. ii. p. 156.
[3] *Op. cit.*, vol. ii. pp. 157 foll.

with theology and subordinate to it", if he had allowed this to warp his judgment of philosophers with whom he disagreed, "not my theology but the atheism which fights in me against my theology is answerable for that wrong". "So far as I confess God who is revealed in Christ I dare not misrepresent anyone; I dare not pass judgment upon him."[1] Similarly Maurice marked a new era in Kantian Criticism in England when he remarked upon the misfortune "for Kant's reputation in England that the epithet 'transcendental' had been much more associated with his philosophy than the epithet 'critical', and that the reasons which led him to adopt the former word had not been considered in the light of the latter". "The notion that Kant was in some sense reversing the decrees of Locke by bringing in *a priori* truths has blinded us to the fact that the German had even a greater horror than the Englishman of that 'ocean' which he forbade us to approach."[2] Equally from the side of the conception of Kant as the *Alles-zermalmende*, made current in England by De Quincey, he declares that "Kant's reputation as a destroyer even of the metaphysics and psychology of his predecessors has been greatly exaggerated".[3]

In Maurice also we have an end to the soul-destroying method which preceding historians had adopted of epitomizing (usually in a wholly unintelligent way) the philosophies of Kant's successors. These epitomes were merely tombstones to the philosophies they epitomized, and were indeed intended to be nothing more. In the short twenty pages devoted to him in the chapter entitled "Glimpse into the Nineteenth Century", Kant may be said at last to have come to his own in England in this Cambridge successor of Cudworth and Coleridge. Finally, in the still shorter account of Hegel as the completer of the movement begun by Kant, our interest is excited and the mind thrown forward by hearing of him as the bearer of the "watchwords Being and Not Being, Being and Becoming", which, "as in the days of Plato, will be rung in our ears", and as the reviver of the thought of a dialectic which "had dawned upon Plato" and which constituted the pulse at once of logic and history.

But in Maurice, as he himself confessed, the theological was still

---

[1] *Moral and Metaphysical Philosophy* (1882 edition). Preface, p. ix.
[2] *Op. cit.*, p. 620. *Cp.* p. 627. "The critical philosophy is born to be the scourge of dreamers, especially when their dreams assume the shape and air of philosophy, especially when they try to turn their dreams outward and apply them to the business of the world."
[3] *Ibid.*, p. 635.

the dominant interest, and while his catholic sympathy and his real power of philosophical interpretation may be said to have marked the end of blind opposition to German influences, he was not the man to lead in making them the starting-point of a new era of speculation. This was to come from men trained in another school.

(2) The curse of British philosophy in the first half of the century was the survival within the Universities of the theological bias, outside of them of the positivist Humean tradition, inherited, notwithstanding all that had been done in the direction of naturalizing Kant's work in England, from the pre-critical stage of thought. But as the result of the better understanding of that work, powerfully aided in these years by the teaching of Carlyle, Emerson, Matthew Arnold, Tennyson, and Browning, there was growing up in the younger men of the 'fifties and 'sixties, both within and without the Universities, a wholly new attitude at once to the orthodoxies of the Church and to the negations of the positivist creed. There was an increasing number of those who were prepared neither to sacrifice the reality of the experiences represented by morality, art, religion to what appeared to be the demand of positive science for a rigidly naturalistic view of the world, nor to allow that the vindication of that reality depended on the maintenance of doctrines resting on other foundations than the witness of the spirit of man itself. Kant was being studied as the enemy of dogmatism in all its forms. But was Kant rightly understood by his professed exponents?

Sir William Hamilton was a great power in the 'fifties, and Hamilton had succeeded in converting elements which were positive in Kant into mere negatives. Space, time, causality were expressions not of the constructive powers of thought, but of its impotence to grasp the Absolute. Here once more was the opportunity for the reassertion of dogma under the name of faith on the one hand, of a complete agnosticism on the other. Herbert Spencer joined hands with Dean Mansel in laying the foundations of a new form of reactionary metaphysics with the stones that Kantian Criticism seemed to have provided. But, if this interpretation was right, it might well be asked whether Kant had indeed gone beyond Hume.

The malady of the age of which Hume's philosophy was the completest expression was the separation of subject from object, the deal from the real, the individual from society, the finite from the infinite. What was needed was a rational philosophy that should reunite what reason had divided, reclothe what it had stripped bare, reconstruct what it had destroyed. Carlyle had felt all this—no one more vividly—and had stated the need with incomparable power. His literary method was adequate to that. He had even become convinced that Kant had supplied the needed principle, but he knew little in detail of Kant's work,[1] and still less of the work of his successor, Hegel, who had developed it in an entirely different direction from Hamilton.

Emerson's position in America was almost precisely parallel in this respect to Carlyle's in England. He saw what was needed. He prophesied of it, but he had to leave to others the philosophical vindication of the transcendentalism he preached. "For Emerson," writes Lewis Mumford,[2] "matter and spirit were not enemies in conflict: they were phases of man's experience: matter passed into spirit and became a symbol; spirit passed into matter and gave it a form; and symbols and forms were essences through which man lived and fulfilled his proper being." The writer adds: "To withold the name of philosopher from the man who saw and expressed this integral vision of life so clearly is to deny the central office of philosophy." This is true; but something more than vision and expression is needed if philosophy is to be justified of her children. Emerson himself knew this well enough, and sought it with tears in the technicalities of Hegel.[3]

It was to men who were deeply impressed with the need of a comprehensive vindication by philosophy of the great spiritual interests of mankind, who felt that the healing word remained with Kant, however much Kant had been misunderstood and misrepresented by the Hamiltonian philosophy, who believed that the clue to the real meaning of his work must be sought for in that of his German successors, and who were undismayed by the fate that had overtaken Hegelianism, under circumstances entirely different from their own, in the land of its birth—that we owe the first systematic attempt to understand and expound the bearing of Idealism on what they rightly regarded as the central problem of their time. In this attempt James Hutchison Stirling has the credit of being the leader. But there were skirmishers who went before and there were others who followed after him and completed his work. Of the former J. F. Ferrier deserves especial mention.

[1] See previous Study.   [2] In *The Golden Day*, p. 104.   [3] See below, p. 171.

4. Pioneers: Ferrier

Ferrier's account in the 'fifties of his abortive efforts to penetrate the secret of Hegel has been already referred to. But it was characteristic of the man, as perhaps of his nation, that he did not know when he was beaten. We learn from the articles in the *Imperial Dictionary of Universal Biography* on Schelling and Hegel that he was employed to the last in seeking to understand the meaning and the significance for contemporary thought of the philosophy of the Absolute. The articles are very short, and even so are mainly occupied with biography, but they contain what may be said to be the first sympathetic and therefore understanding word in English upon their subjects.

In the essay on Schelling he points to the fundamental distinction between Hamilton's Unconditioned and Schelling's Absolute. Carried to its logical conclusion, Hamilton's conception of the unconditioned, as that which lies beyond all relation, means that truth lies not only beyond the grasp of the human mind but beyond the grasp of Omniscience itself. To escape this absurdity we must abandon that conception and interpret the unconditioned or absolute truth, not as that which is out of relation to all intelligence, but as that which is in relation to intelligence simply ($\dot{a}\pi\lambda\hat{\omega}s$), or in itself, as contrasted with that which is merely in relation to *our* intelligence. Is there any such truth open to us? Schelling's whole theory of the "intellectual intuition", obscurely as it is worked out by himself, means the assertion of the reality of an element common to all intelligence, human or divine, actual or possible. It is the necessity of verifying this claim that leads Ferrier to the conclusion that "the philosophy of the unconditioned still calls for patient and impartial reconsideration".

In the article on Hegel he has himself advanced a step farther in such a reconsideration. He recognizes Hegel's whole philosophy as "nothing but an explanation of the Absolute". He repeats his own simplified interpretation of the meaning of "truth absolute", as truth for intellect considered simply as intellect, and goes on to illustrate it from the place of the categories of "being" and "unity", as contrasted with the sensational or relative element in all knowledge. He defends the Dialectic as the legitimate attempt to show how the categories from lowest to highest evolve themselves through a self-conversion into their opposites; as a work "replete at once with the profoundest truth and the most marvellous speculative sagacity"; finally as affording the solution of the "antinomies" by which Kant succeeded in bewildering the reason of his contemporaries. He goes on to accuse Hegel's critics in this country of totally misunderstanding the nature of the Absolute by taking it to refer to the *quantity* instead of the *quality*, or nature of knowledge. "The absolute has nothing to do with the extent but only with the constitution of cognition. Wherever knowledge or thought is, even in its narrowest manifestation, there 'the absolute' is known; because there is something apprehended by intellect which is intelligible to reason universally."

He admits the difficulties that have to be met in establishing "a philosophy of the absolute", more particularly the difficulties that attach to the conclusion that "rational self-consciousness is the only ultimate and all-comprehensive reality". But he insists that this conclusion cannot be disposed of (*pro* or *con*) by any inquiry into the limitations of the human faculties, but only by a thoroughgoing analysis which shall distinguish between the relative and absolute elements in our cognitions. It was precisely here, he thought, that Kant, by making the absolute elements into something merely relative, and thus denying that intelligence has any nature or essence, had failed. "Hegel made the attempt in a far better and truer spirit", however labyrinthine the mazes in which he has involved himself and his readers. Finally he sets aside the heterodox opinions of some of Hegel's followers as deductions for which "neither the system itself nor its author are in any way responsible".[1]

Ferrier's account of what Hegel meant by the Absolute is far from adequate. His own contribution to the development of Idealism was his insistence on the mutual implication in all experience of subject and object—the place we might say of the idea of the self both in knowledge and practice. But he never got beyond a merely formal interpretation of the self as a polar opposite of sense and passion, realizing itself by the negation of them. The self as a principle of organization in the data of experience, theoretic or practical, was never clearly apprehended by him. It is for this reason that the Absolute is for him little more than a universal element side by side with the particulars (what Hegel would have called an "abstract" universal), instead of the identity of principle that manifests itself in them and constitutes their substance. Notwith-

[1] *Philosophical Remains*, pp. 567–568.

standing this failure, we might say of Ferrier in contrast to his British contemporaries what Aristotle says of Anaxagoras, in a similar connection, that he was "as a sober man speaking among babblers".

5. HUTCHISON STIRLING

James Hutchison Stirling has the merit of being the first clearly to perceive that there was nothing really constructive to be looked for from British philosophy, until it had put itself to school in the German idealist movement. In leading the way to this school, he conceived himself as only giving expression to a widespread conviction of his own generation of students. "There appears", he wrote in explaining the source of his own inspiration, "to be no wish nearer to the hearts of all honest students nowadays than that Hegel (and with him Kant is usually united) should be made permeable. Even the general public carries in its heart a strange secret conviction, and seems even to its own self to wait on them with a dumb fixed expectation of infinite and essential result."[1] This faith he believed to be founded on the true intuition that first in Hegel emancipation had been won from the tyranny, the "thin negative," as he believed it to be, of the abstracting intelligence, that was responsible for the deplorable separation of man from what he called his "substance" in nature, society, and God.

Born in Glasgow in 1820, he was trained for the medical profession in the old University in High Street, taking the diploma of Surgeon in 1842.[2] But he had other interests besides medicine. Like so many of the younger generation, he had been powerfully stirred by *Sartor Resartus*, and had already opened a correspondence with Carlyle, in which he described his works as "the most important element in his being". Forty years later he wrote of Carlyle's extraordinary influence at this time: "He was every literary young man's idol, almost the God he prayed to. Even a morsel of white paper with the

---

[1] *Secret of Hegel*, Preface to First Edition, pp. xxv–xxvi.
[2] The relation between modern medicine and idealistic philosophy in Great Britain would make an interesting study. In Stirling's case his medical training gave him, as it gave to Joseph Henry Green, the author of *Spiritual Philosophy* (posthumously published 1865), an eye for biological illustrations of the idealistic principle. "The very cell," he afterwards wrote, "which is Virchow's first, and beyond which there is in that sphere no other, is quite Hegelian. Seyn, Daseyn, Fürsichseyn repeat themselves in the cell of Virchow, the membrane, the distinguishable involution of the membrane, the apex or the functioning and individual *one*." *Secret of Hegel*, Preface, p. xxii.

name of Carlyle upon it would have been picked up from the street as a veritable amulet."[1] But it was still literature rather than philosophy that he thought of as an alternative profession, and when, on the death of his father, he came into a small competency, which enabled him to give up medicine, it was to France and not to Germany that he went to pursue his studies in the eventful year of Napoleon III's *coup d'état*. It was not till 1856 that with a view to learning German he settled in Heidelberg.

Before going to Germany he had seen the name of Hegel in a Review, and had been attracted by it as a young Athenian might have been attracted by the name of Heraclitus, the "dark philosopher". Now, as he tells us, he had his interest reawakened and deepened by two fellow students who talked of Hegel as the deepest, if also the darkest, of all philosophers. "It was understood that he had not only completed philosophy, but above all reconciled to philosophy Christianity itself." "*That*," he adds characteristically, "struck."[2] He turned to his works only to find them "utterly refractory". He has vividly described the sensations of the student who approached Hegel for himself in these days: "One approaches Hegel for the first time—such is the voice of rumour and such the subjects he involves—as one might approach some enchanted palace of Arabian story. New powers—imagination is assured (were but the entrance gained)—await one there—secrets—as it were the ring of Solomon and the passkeys of the universe. But, very truly, if thus magical is the promise, no less magical is the difficulty; and one wanders round the book—as Aboulfaouaris round the palace—*irrito*, without success, but not without a sufficiency of vexation. Book—palace—is absolutely inaccessible, for the *known* can show no bridge to it; or if accessible, then it is absolutely impenetrable, for it begins *not*, it enters *not*, what seems the doorway received but to reject, and every attempt at a window is baffled by a fall. This is the *universal* experience; and one is almost justified to add that—whether in England or in France or in Germany—this the experience of the beginning is also—all but equally universally—the experience of the end."[3]

Light, he tells us,[4] went up in his own case when he perceived that Hegel was only the end of a movement of which Kant was the

---

[1] *James Hutchison Stirling, His Life and Work*, by Amelia Hutchison Stirling, p. 48.
[2] *Op. cit.*, p. 115.   [3] *Secret of Hegel*, vol. i. p. 1.   [4] *Ibid.*, p. 118.

beginning, and that if we would understand him we also must begin with Kant. Yet to English students Kant was still an enigma. Most of the translations of him "were to be regarded but as psychological curiosities". Hegel was in far worse plight. Labels and summaries were almost[1] all that was available, and these were worse than useless. "Summaries only propagate ignorance, when used independently and not merely as useful synopses and reminders to those who have already mastered the whole subject." If this was true of summaries by masters like Schwegler,[2] it was tenfold more true of the kind of summary to which we have already referred.

Stirling returned to England in 1857, convinced that a thorough first-hand study of Kant and Hegel and of the relation between them was the clue to the whole philosophical situation, and determined to place that clue in the hands of his fellow-countrymen so far as was in his power. After three years in London, he settled in Portobello near Edinburgh, and for the next eight years devoted himself (as he afterwards explained to John Stuart Mill) "most laboriously—rather with positive agony and often for twelve hours a day" to his self-imposed task.

The fruit of this long wrestle was *The Secret of Hegel, being the Hegelian-System in Origin, Principle, Form, and Matter*, in two volumes (London, 1865).

If it is the merit of other writers, even in philosophy, to conceal the "labour of the file", the main interest, if not the merit, of Stirling's book is that no attempt is made to do so.[3] It is the account of his mind's pilgrimage, and owes the place it has in the history of British and American Philosophy to this rather than to any literary form or finality of statement. Our concern here is neither with the personal element nor with the details of the treatment,

---

[1] Besides the fragment of the *Logic* translated and published by H. Sloman and J. Wallon in 1855, there was only Sibree's translation of the *Lectures on the Philosophy of History* (London, 1857) available in English.

[2] Whose *Handbook of Philosophy* was translated with Supplementary Notes in 1867 by Stirling himself from the fifth German edition. It was already in its third edition in 1871, and in the undergraduate days of the present writer was a very present help in time of trouble.

[3] It is a somewhat amorphous work consisting of a long Preface; Section I, Prolegomena. The Struggle to Hegel; Section II, A translation from the complete Logic of the whole first Section, *Quality*; Section III, A Comment on the previous translation; Section IV, Extracts from the account of Quality in the Encyclopædia; Section V, A Summary or translation commented and interpreted by the Second Section of the complete Logic *Quality*; followed by a long section on Hegel's Commentators and a Conclusion.

but with the general terms in which Hegel for the first time received
r ecognition in England and in which his main teaching is expounded.

The sections to which the reader will turn for the succinctest
statements as to the place claimed for German Philosophy in general
and Hegel in particular are the Preface and the earlier written but
more detailed statement in Chapter III of the First Part, "Notes
of the Struggle Continued. The Secret of Hegel". The Preface is a
vigorous defence of German Philosophy against the charges *first*
that it is obsolete, and *second* that it is bad; the former founded
chiefly on the repudiation by its last representative, Schelling,
of his own philosophy, and Hegel's which followed it, as "a mere
poem"; the latter founded on the attacks upon historical Christianity by Strauss and his English followers, who hailed from the
Hegelian camp. To deny the former of these charges, it would seem,
was "to prefer yourself to Schelling"; to deny the second was to
"justify Scepticism". Stirling's answer to the first is that Schelling's
sentence had not as a matter of fact been accepted, but had been
"set aside by the mere progress of time". His answer to the second
is to show that, so far from making for scepticism, German Philosophy in general and Hegel's in particular is just what is required
to supply the counteractive not only to the negative movement in
theology as represented by Strauss and Colenso, but to the materialistic interpretation of history in such writers as Buckle, and to the
contempt of first principles represented by Macaulay's jeering question: "Who are wisest and best, and whose opinion is to decide?"
—all of them in Stirling's view retrogressive reflections of the
eighteenth-century "Illumination", and springing from the over-
emphasis on the rights of private judgment, of which the idealist
philosophy was the conclusive corrective.

As contrasted with this reaction, which places the accent on
private and leads to self-will, Idealism places the accent on *judgment*,
and therewith on the truth that is a common possession: the thought,
will, purpose that belongs to man as man. It stands for "the rights
of the object as something above the rights of the subject". Put in
another way, it stands for thought in a sense of which we in England
know little or nothing. We mistake vivid picturing for thinking—
"intensely vivid picturing almost constitutes Mr. Carlyle"; or, if
we get beyond pictures to conceptions, it is only to get caught in
the abstractions of the understanding, which, like the god Horos,
is the principle and agent of the definite everywhere. As contrasted

with all this, what is wanted is synthetic principles in every department, theoretic, practical, æsthetic. Just to supply these is the sole object of the three great works of Kant. If we would sum up Kant's teaching in a word, it would be in the word Freedom—"When this word was articulated by the lips of Kant the Illumination was at an end." But Kant was himself a child of the Illumination, and was never able wholly to free himself from its spell. Freedom was still opposed to necessity, reality to appearance, the self to the world. What Hegel did was to perceive and make clear that "the conditions of a concrete, and of every concrete, are two opposites: in other words Hegel came to see that there exists no concrete which consists not of two antagonistic characters, where at the same time, strangely, somehow the one is not only through the other but actually is the other." This union Hegel called the Concrete Notion, and the "concrete notion is the secret of Hegel". It is in this way that Hegel completes the compromise of the understanding by the "complement of the reason".

"The secret of Hegel is the secret of Kant", and can be put in a nutshell. Kant in his doctrine of the *a priori* forms of the sensory and the categories of the understanding had shown that thought enters into the constitution of the world of objects that we know. "Here lies the germ of the thought of Hegel that initiated his whole system. The universe is but a materialization, but an externalization, but a heterization of certain thoughts." His difference from Kant is that, while Kant conceives of these materializing thoughts as subjective and as hiding a beyond or thing-in-itself, which thus escapes our knowledge, Hegel conceives of them objectively as the absolute universal principles on which the all or whole is fashioned—the diamond net which by its invisible meshes encloses, not the veil that conceals, the real world. "Why crave a Jenseits, a Beyond to what we have? Why should not that be the all? Why not conceive an absolute Now and Here? We see the universe—we find the eternal principles on which it rests, which constitute it; why then go farther? Why feign more—a Jenseits, an unknown that is simply a Jenseits and an unknown, an unreachable, an unexistent? No, let us but *think* the universe truly and we shall have truly entered into the possession of the universal life and of a world that needs no Indian tortoise for its pedestal and support." The Absolute, so far from being the unthinkable, is the object of all thought. "Thought when it asked why an apple fell sought the

Absolute and found it—at least so far as outer matter is concerned. Thought, when, in Socrates, it interrogated many particular virtues for the one universal virtue, sought the Absolute. Thought in Hume when it asked the reason of our ascription of effects to causes sought the Absolute, and, if he did not find it, he put others on the way to find it. What since the beginning of time, what in any corner of the earth has philosophy, has thinking ever considered but the Absolute?"[1] The claim to think the absolute is not to be countered by "schoolboys' puzzle-boxes of Time and Space," with their "infantile dilemmas". Thought can think the infinite because it is itself infinite, and the infinite is thought. "Where is the difficulty? Is it not thought to thought?"—that which is seeking interconnection, wholeness in things, to the Whole which actually is, however far *we* may be from seeing that Whole in its completeness?

It is in this development of the arrested Idealism of Kant that we are to find the essence of Hegel. He did not accomplish it unaided. Fichte and Schelling furnished the intermediate stages. Hegel merely took the last step and completed the movement. Both Fichte and Schelling had renounced Kant's unknowable Absolute. Fichte had found the ultimate reality in the Ego in its clear-cut separation from the Non-Ego; Schelling in the obscurity of a substance which is neither subject nor object, neither thought nor thing; Hegel found it in the Thought or Reason which is the essence of the thing, that of which all things from those of sense upwards are but the "types, symbols, and metaphors".

From this it followed that, if all the forms of thought could be found and shown in their organic connection with one another, we should have the scheme of that "self-supported, self-maintained, self-moved life which is the All of things, the ultimate principle, the Absolute". It is this task that Hegel has attempted, as none had done before, in the *Logic*, which has proved the main stumbling-block and rock of offence to his critics. It has been assumed that he is offering this bloodless scheme for the rich life of concrete nature, and he has been asked to show how the one can pass into the other. This is sheer misapprehension. Hegel starts from the world of nature and man on the one hand, thought or reason on the other, and asks what is the relation between them. His answer is that they are one in their otherness, but reason is the prior not in the sense of cause to effect ("mundane succession" had no place here), but in

[1] *Secret*, vol. i. pp. 139–140, condensed.

the sense that it is reason that gives its unity to nature and that in the end "will resume it into itself", thus manifesting itself as Spirit, the final expression in Hegel for the Absolute.

After quoting the passage from the Introduction to the *Philosophy of History*, in which perhaps more clearly than anywhere else the Hegelian doctrine that it is "Reason that rules the world", that reason is "the substance as well as the infinite power of all natural and spiritual life", is stated, Stirling ends:—

"Such we believe to be the secret origin and constitution of the system of Hegel. We do not say, Hegel does not say, that it is complete and that no joining gapes. On the contrary, in the execution of the details, there will be much that will give pause. Still, in this execution—we may say as much as this on our own account—all the great interests of mankind have been kindled into new lights by the touch of this master-hand, and surely the general idea is one of the hugest that ever curdled in the thought of man. Hegel, indeed, so far as abstract thought is concerned, and so far as one can see at this moment, seems to have closed an era, and has named the all of things in such terms of thought as will perhaps remain essentially the same for the next thousand years. To all present appearance at least, what Aristotle was to ancient Greece Hegel is to modern Europe."

The *Secret of Hegel* was at once recognized both in the Universities and beyond them as marking a new departure in British philosophy. T. H. Green, who was among those who held that without a knowledge of German philosophy "a writer was outside the main stream of human thought", said of it, as an exposition of Hegelianism, that it "contrasted with everything else that had been published as sense with nonsense". A few years later Jowett wrote to the author: "You have made the general idea of Hegelianism more plain than it has been made before in England." Carlyle supported the author for a chair of philosophy as "the one man in Britain capable of bringing metaphysical philosophy in the ultimate, German or European, and highest actual form of it distinctly home to the understanding of British men". In America Emerson hailed the *Secret* as "the most competent and compulsive of modern British books on metaphysics", and paid it the tribute of carrying the two volumes with him on a prolonged journey. In Germany the historian Erdmann wrote to Stirling, as to one whose knowledge of Hegel was deeper than his own. Rosenkranz, Hegel's disciple, later spoke of the *Secret* as "ein wahrhafterstaunliches Phänomenon"; Arnold Ruge said that it marked "ein grosser Fortschritt in der Englischen Philosophischen Literatur", "a book which had truly assimilated Hegel's philosophy".[1]

6. HEGEL IN ENGLISH

With this Hegel may be said to have arrived, and Stirling's credit for so crucial an event in the history of contemporary Anglo-Saxon thought is unchallengeable. It has been generously recognized by the only other man who would have the least claim to challenge it. "To English readers", wrote Edward Caird in 1883, "Hegel was first introduced in the powerful statement of his principles by Dr. Hutchison Stirling."[2] But there was still much to be done to make these principles in Stirling's own phrase "permeable". Stirling was a path-finder, and his work bore the impress of the pioneer. It reminds one of the forts and shacks built by the early settlers in California to secure the rivers and mines they had won by their enterprise. The country itself had still to be won for civilization.

He was perhaps too near the subject of his long study and too deeply imbued with Hegel's terminology to be able to shake himself free from the letter and become the exponent of the spirit of the Hegelian system. The *Secret of Hegel* showed an entire absence of method with the result, as an otherwise sympathetic writer, the late Professor Seth, says, that it was "almost as difficult as the original which it is intended to illuminate".[3] As it was wittily put at the time, "if Mr. Hutchison Stirling knew the secret of Hegel he had managed to keep it to himself". Even his style, vigorous and redolent of the Scottish soil from which it had sprung as it was, had little to commend it to English readers. Though, therefore, he had brought Hegel to England, he can hardly be said to have naturalized him there. At the date of the publication of the *Secret* he was, indeed, still a comparatively young man, and he lived to be an old one. There was therefore ample time for him, had he been less of a rebel against ordinary standards of composition and pos- sessed less of the "manner" he attributes to his hero Hegel,[4] further

[1] For these and other references to recognitions by Continental writers, see *Secret*, Second Edition (Edinburgh and London, 1898).
[2] *Hegel* (Blackwood), p. vi.
[3] *English Philosophers and Schools of Philosophy* (1912), p. 342.
[4] Lectures on the *Philosophy of Law*, etc. (1873), p. 103.

to have befriended him in this respect. As a matter of fact, in the remaining work of his life he added little that was of significance for the understanding of Hegel,[1] and left much to be done not only in the exposition of Hegel, but in the even more difficult task of the exposition of Kant, which he rightly saw must precede it. The textbook on Kant which he published in 1881, in spite of what had been done in the interval,[2] merely reprints what he had written in 1862, twenty years before, containing an interpretation of the relation of the Categories of the Understanding to sense-perception which, it is not too much to say, is now merely a curiosity of Kantian literature.[3]

It would have been well had he been content to ignore the work of the younger men. Unfortunately for himself he made a long article on "Schopenhauer in relation to Kant", in the thirteenth volume of the *Journal of Speculative Philosophy*, the occasion for an intemperate attack on philosophy as represented by "the younger strengths", both in the English and the Scottish Universities, in general, and on Edward Caird's work on Kant in particular. Caird's devastating reply in the same volume and his restatement of his own essentially Platonic position in the following one are models at once of philosophical controversy at its best, and of the spirit that was necessary to domesticate the dry Hegelianism of the *Secret* in the softer and more humid atmosphere of British thought.

Before Hegel could be thoroughly naturalized, translations had to be made of the encyclopædic series of works in which his central conceptions were applied to every department of human thought and experience; commentaries had to be written; his ideas had to gain access to university class and common rooms. It was because there were in these years men in Scotland and Oxford who, equally convinced with Stirling of the importance of these ideas, were gifted with a quite unusual power of lucid exposition and even

---

[1] An exception to this statement should be made in favour of the brilliant chapter on Hegel in his book on *What is Thought?* (1900), in which he reiterated and tried to drive home his view of Hegel's attitude to Theism and Christianity.
[2] E. Caird's *Philosophy of Kant* had appeared in 1877.
[3] "Hutchison Stirling's criticisms of Kant in his *Textbook to Kant* are vitiated by a failure to recognize the completely uncritical character of the occasional passages in which Kant admits a distinction between judgments of perception and 'judgments of experience'." N. Kemp Smith's *Commentary to Kant's Critique of the Pure Reason*, p. 366 n. Professor Kemp Smith's new translation of this *Critique* (1930) is a notable addition to this work of interpretation.

literary expression, and who were prepared to devote themselves to these tasks with the additional advantage of the classical training, to which Hegel himself owed so much, that in the course of the next decades Hegel became a household word with the younger generation of students of philosophy. Among these teachers and writers the names that stand out are those of Edward and John Caird in Glasgow, William Wallace, T. H. Green, and (in his earliest book, *Ethical Studies*) F. H. Bradley in Oxford, somewhat later Bernard Bosanquet in London. If, as Bradley afterwards maintained, some of these with their followers "insisted too incautiously on the great claims of Kant and Hegel", this was perhaps inevitable. Before there can be intelligent criticism there must be thorough appropriation, and if some were led to give their hearts as well as their heads in a kind of *amor intellectualis* to the new ideas, no great harm perhaps was done. It merely added a touch of romance to the movement by which the stone that the builders had rejected in Germany was made in these years the head of the corner in England and Scotland.

NOTE.—The order of the chief translations of Hegel's works after the publication of the *Secret of Hegel* was as follows:—

The *Logic of Hegel*, translated from the *Encyclopædia of the Philosophical Sciences with Prolegomena*, by William Wallace (Oxford, 1874).
The *Philosophy of Art*, by W. Hastie (1886).
Lectures on the History of Philosophy, by E. S. Haldane (1892–1894).
The *Philosophy of Mind*, by William Wallace (1894).
The *Philosophy of Religion*, by E. B. Spiers (1895).
The *History of Philosophy*, by R. B. Haldane (1896).
The *Philosophy of Right*, by S. W. Dyde (1896).
The *Phænomenology*, by J. B. Baillie (1910).
The *Science of Logic*, by Johnston and Struthers (1929).

CHAPTER III

HEGELIANISM IN BEING

1. Essays in Philosophical Criticism

By the end of the 'seventies the results of the Kantian and post-Kantian criticism were familiar to students of philosophy in England, and were the rallying-ground of the movement generally known as Neo-Kantian. Its recognized leaders were Hutchison Stirling in Edinburgh, Edward Caird in Glasgow, Green and Bradley in Oxford.[1] At the beginning of the 'eighties a group of the younger men, mainly Scots, felt themselves united and strong enough to issue a volume of Essays which more than anything else since the publication of Mill's *Logic*, perhaps even of Cudworth's *Intellectual System*, had the appearance of a philosophical manifesto.[2] Published in 1883, it was contemporaneous with two other epoch-making books: Green's *Prolegomena to Ethics* and Bradley's *Principles of Logic*. As the book is now out of print, fuller references to its contents than would otherwise be permissible may be excused by students who themselves have access to it and may find such a résumé tedious.

It is dedicated to the memory of T. H. Green, who had died in March of the previous year. Edward Caird writes a Preface, in which he explains that "The writers of this volume agree in believing that the line of investigation which philosophy must follow, or in which it may be expected to make most important contributions to the intellectual life of man, is that which was opened up by Kant, and for the successful prosecution of which no one has done so much as Hegel. . . . It will serve the purpose of its writers if it shows in some degree how the principles of an idealistic philosophy may be brought to bear on the various problems of science, of ethics, and of religion which are now pressing upon us."

[1] On Stirling's work see above. Green's Introductions to Hume's *Treatise of Human Nature* were published in 1874, Caird's *Critical Account of the Philosophy of Kant* in 1877. Between these dates appeared Bradley's *Ethical Studies*, the first constructive application of the new thought in England.
[2] Professor Pringle-Pattison reminds me in a letter that the first idea was not a volume of Essays but a new Journal in which Metaphysics should play a greater part than in the *Mind* of that time, and which should be edited by Mr. A. J. (afterwards) Lord Balfour. It was only after the failure of this proposal that the Essays were determined upon.

It was the breadth with which this programme is carried out that gave particular impressiveness to the book, and rallied the more thoughtful of the younger generation to its standard. It is written with a freshness and vigour, almost an inspiration, that could only come from the sense of being alive and young at the beginning of a new era in the thought of their country.

2. Philosophy as Criticism of Categories

The first essay by Andrew Seth,[1] one of the editors, contains what is, perhaps, to this day the clearest succinct statement of the theory of knowledge from which the Neo-Kantian philosophy took its departure. As a matter of history it has the further interest of being the work of the writer who, four years later, was to come forward as the leader of the revolt from the metaphysical conclusions which his colleagues sought to found upon that theory.

The keynote of the essay and of the whole movement is struck at the outset, where it is explained that the important thing is to discover what notions Kant destroyed, so that we may know on what ground we stand. When we know this, "we are in a position to work for the needs of our own time, taking help where it is to be found, but without entangling ourselves in the details of any post-Kantian development". The notion which Kant had destroyed was that any secure metaphysical structure could be reared on an uncriticized basis of dogma. This held equally of system-builders like Wolff, who appealed to *a priori* principles, and of would-be empiricists like Locke, who rested his proof of the existence of God on ideas of time and causality, without inquiring into the availability of these ideas beyond the context of sense-experience. True, Hume had already shown how empty these speculations were, but in the general discredit that he had thrown upon human faculties, Hume had involved much of the knowledge of the natural world, which no one disputes, but which it is impossible to vindicate on Hume's own uncriticized assumption of the nature of experience. If we are to have knowledge of nature at all, based on universal and necessary judgments, and if, as Hume rightly saw, these were not derivable from the atomic data of sense, we must look elsewhere for their source.

---

[1] Afterwards Andrew Seth Pringle-Pattison. In the previous year Seth had published his *Hibbert Lectures* on the *Development from Kant to Hegel*, of the first chapter of which this Essay is an expansion.

Kant's answer was that Hume had overlooked the factor of unity or synthesis of the given manifold, which all knowledge involved. If we say that this element is not given in experience, then we must say that it is supplied by the mind itself, or, at least, that what we call experience is the product of an interaction between the mind and things. This is what Kant meant by his Copernican revolution. "If there is no necessity to be got by waiting on the world of things, let us try what success attends us if objects are made to wait upon us for their most general determinations." The form or ground-plan of experience which Kant discovers in following out this idea consists in categories, conceptions, or methods of combination, according to which the matter of sense is arranged in the perceptions or imaginative spectra of space and time, the process of arrangement being ultimately guided by ideals of intellectual completeness, and being referable at every point to the unity of the self. Unfortunately, in such a statement there is an ambiguity which has given rise to two entirely different interpretations of Kant's work as a whole.

Does Kant mean to separate the world of things and the mind that faces it, assigning one element in experience to each of them severally? Is the mind the seat of concepts so far as they imply universality and necessity, and the world a jumble of particulars on which these are superimposed? Or does he mean merely that these elements are indissolubly linked together in experience; that the given is not pure matter, but matter already formed, particulars already universalized, in other words related to one another and characterized by these relations? In the former case, say what we will, the world of objects which we know must appear as the creation of the relating mind, and there looms up behind it another reality from the apprehension of which our mind, by the very forms it uses, is excluded. Only in the latter case can knowledge be what we always assume it to be, the reading off and laboriously bringing to light of what is there in some sense complete before us.

There is, unfortunately, too much in Kant that justifies the former interpretation and that spells in the end his failure to reply to the subjectivism of Hume. Fortunately, also, it is possible to show that there is a deeper side to Kant's work, and that the apparent ambiguity is the result of his failure to carry out his own critical principle to the bitter end by applying it to the distinctions his own analysis had brought into evidence; chief among them the distinctions between subject and object, the contingent and the necessary, the world of space-time substances with their interactions and the world of organic life and mind.

In regard to the first of these distinctions, severe as is Kant's criticism of empirical psychology as an instrument of truth, he himself carries on the distinction between the subjective and the objective, which, for its own purposes that science arbitrarily makes, assigning to the one the matter, to the other the conceptual framework of the world of experience. This is to ignore the obvious implication of his own teaching that "from the standpoint of a theory of knowledge it will be found that the mind and the world are convertible terms. We may talk indifferently of the one or of the other; the content of our notion remains the same".

It is the same with the distinction between the contingent and the necessary. By making his argument centre round the appeal to the universality and necessity of certain judgments, as compared with the conditionedness and contingency of others, Kant lays himself open to the retort that these qualities are nowhere discoverable, not even in the propositions of geometry, and that, if he insists upon them, he brings us back to the ding-dong, now of the dogmatic assertion and now of the denial of "intuitions", which it was the aim of the critical philosophy to supersede. "No one who has learned Kant's lesson so as to profit by it should have any hesitation in finding Mill's hypothetical theory of demonstration to be truer in conception than any theory which insists on a difference of kind between the necessity of geometrical and that of any other propositions." The special necessity and universality, which seems to belong to geometry, come from the rudimentariness of the elements or conditions of experience with which it deals, and hold merely for experience in general only in so far as it depends on these conditions. "There is in a word no abstract opposition between the necessary and the contingent such as Kant presents us with; the difference is not one of kind, but of degree."

Connected with this mistaken view of necessity as a "mystic quality", attaching, or attached by the mind to the world of space-time appearances, is the quite arbitrary limitation of the word "experience" to this field, and of the table of the categories to those that are applicable to it—ending in the treatment of the categories of life, of beauty, and of morality as appendices of a more or less uncertain character. Again, the distinction has its source in Kant's habit of isolating different spheres of experience for the purposes

M

of his analysis and failing afterwards to bring them together, and exhibit them in their organic relation to one another, as his own deeper thought required. When in the Preface to the *Critique of Pure Reason* he speaks of the idea of freedom as the "topstone of the whole edifice of a system of pure reason speculative as well as practical", he passes condemnation on any attempt to treat this idea as beyond the pale of our rational apprehension.

If with these clues we return to Kant's distinction between phenomenal and noumenal, a new meaning for it begins to emerge. The world of space and time, not only as it appears to ordinary sense-perception, but as it appears to science, is indeed phenomenal, but judgment is passed upon it not because of the contrast in which it stands to a transcendental thing-in-itself, but because of the contrast which the externality of its parts to one another offers to the internal relations of higher forms of being such as we meet with in life and mind. At its own level the world of interacting material forces is as real as any other in so far as it reflects the ideal of an interrelated whole. Its phenomenality only emerges when it is compared (or when, as in materialism, it enters into competition for the prize of objective reality) with forms which like that of organism reflect this ideal more completely. Applied to the attempt to treat mechanism as more objectively real than organism we can see the tables turned upon it. "So far from mechanism being objective and the notion of organism subjective, we should be compelled, if we were in the way of talking in this strain, to reverse the relation."

If the categories of physical experience fail us in speaking of the living body, still less do they serve us when we come to treat of conscious individuals. It is in the *self*-consciousness which these embody that we first begin to see realized that complete inter-relation of elements which is the criterion of the completely real. It is in this way that we are led back to Descartes' "I think" as the clue to the real. But in contrast to Descartes' abstraction of the "I" from the world, "it is only in relation to the world or as the synthesis of intelligible elements that the self exists or can have a meaning". "The self and the world are only two sides of the same reality; they are the same intelligible world looked at from two oppo-site points of view. The transcendental self, as the implicate of all experience, is for a theory of knowledge simply the necessary point of view from which the universe can be unified, that is from which it becomes a universe."

It is in this way that the opposition between phenomenal and noumenal worlds is replaced by that between more abstract and more concrete points of view, and that our view becomes more concrete as it approaches the ideal which our own self-consciousness supplies, and to which it most nearly approximates.

This is the real Copernican change which Kant effected or at least puts us in the way of effecting. It is quite fundamental, seeing that it reverses the whole notion of reality on which the old metaphysics was founded. Once see that the "phenomenal" is a permissible phrase only when taken to mean something in which reason cannot rest, and that the ultimate reality is to be found in self-consciousness, and the unapproachable reality of which that metaphysics speaks, and which Spencer and others had uncritically taken over from it, is seen to be entirely a fiction of the mind. "The centre of the world lies in our own nature as self-conscious beings, and in that life with our fellows which in different aspects constitutes alike the secular and the divine community." So far then from supporting the view that metaphysics consists in the elaboration of transcendent entities like an extraneous Deity or Spencer's Unknowable, Kant's theory of knowledge teaches us that all such constructions in the void have their origin in the belief that the substance is something different from all its qualities, or that the cause is something different from the sum of its effects. "To be delivered from (all such) bad metaphysics is the first step and most important one towards the true conception of the science. True metaphysics lies in that criticism of experience which aims at developing out of the material of science and of life the completed notion of experience itself."

3. PHILOSOPHY AND SCIENCE

The second essay by the brothers R. B. and J. S. Haldane is the first clear statement of the view of the relation of philosophy to science in general and of the categories of the particular sciences to one another, which may almost be said to be identified in our own time with their names.[1]

Returning in the earlier part to the foundation which Kant had laid, the writers show this to consist: (1) In the discovery that while knowledge or thought can never as such become the object of

[1] See especially Lord Haldane's *Pathway to Reality* (1903), Dr. J. S. Haldane's *Philosophy and the Sciences* (1929).

experience, it yet can be seen to be that which enters into experience as a synthetic principle in the constitution of all objects; and (2) in the perception that the principles space, time, substance, cause, reciprocity, however adequate they may be as synthetic principles in the experience of the physical world, are wholly inadequate to the interpretation of the forms of being we meet with in organized bodies or in the creations distinctive of human life. We can no more express the properties of a body, *qua* organized, in terms of the categories of mechanism than we can express the properties of a stone in terms of the categories of moral judgment. Kant's mistake was to treat of the higher relations that appear in these latter fields as merely subjective, while those of mathematics and physics are regarded as constituting objective nature. In reality no object can be treated of as merely consisting of mechanical relations. Apart from their æsthetic and teleological aspects, objects are not objects at all, but mere abstractions. Nor can the æsthetic and teleological aspects be treated as existing merely in the percipient mind, if, as Kant held, the mind can perceive only under the conditions which thought (as itself the principle of objectivity in things) supplies. "The fundamental fact beyond which we cannot get is the fact of self-consciousness"; and this fact contains within it elements (the subjective and the objective) which, while distinguishable in thought, are inseparable in existence.

What then different categories represent is not any insuperable distinction between kinds of knowledge as Kant thought, but "from the relations of pure mathematics up to those of self-consciousness, a chain of aspects of Nature not one of which is reducible to another, but which are yet inseparably united together in thought", and represent a scale of degrees of comprehensiveness and completeness. This does not mean that we can have a philosophical classification of the sciences corresponding to those degrees. "The sciences are defined quite as much by convenience as by the categories which they employ, and it constantly happens that one science employs several distinct sorts of categories and overlaps the sphere of another."

After illustrating the inadequacy of mechanical categories for the explanation of the phenomena of life from those of self-preservation, adaptation, and development, the writers conclude with the prophecy, which present-day developments may be said to be in the act of fulfilling, "that the work of philosophy in the near future must pass into the hands of specialists in science, who are at the same time masters of philosophical criticism. . . . For such a class the mastery of the critical investigations of Kant and Hegel, or at least of conceptions, which have been profoundly influenced by these writers, will be absolutely essential".

4. LOGIC AS THE SCIENCE OF KNOWLEDGE

In what he modestly calls a "purely narrative paper", Bernard Bosanquet, then like the others an unknown name in philosophy, sketches the place that Logic, as widened but imperfectly related to metaphysics by Lotze, Sigwart, Mill, and Jevons, must in future occupy in the theory of knowledge and reality. The first part is occupied with a criticism, of the attempt to separate it as "the science of thought as knowledge" from metaphysics as "the science of reality as such", hereby anticipating later attempts to undermine the Neo-Kantian position just by such a separation. The distinction cannot be that logic deals with the intellect and metaphysic with something beyond or external to the intellect. There are no forms of thought unrelated and indifferent to its matter. On the other hand, there is no world of reality unrelated to mind, and the outcome of its search for what is really real. Similarly it is idle, if not impossible, to separate logic from metaphysics as the exhibition of a process from the exhibition of its results. "In science there is no such thing as a net result. . . . To exhibit results apart from processes, except for the mere purpose of abbreviation, is not to construct a science but to arrange a vocabulary." The writer draws the conclusion thus early, which may be said to have been the text of all his subsequent work in philosophy, that "the general science of reality cannot be distinguished from the science of knowledge. Reality is the connection with the whole, and logic is the science of this connection in general, as direct science is in particular".

In view of this conclusion, he proceeds to rule out what he calls "the alternative method of a direct or uncritical metaphysic", by which he means "any method which seizes on this or that element of experience as representing reality, guided only by some conviction as to the source (in or out of the intellect) or the character (universality, necessity, or the like) of the required element". That such science is no better than a castle in the air is a proposition he thinks amply justified in theory but no less justified in practice. "The tree is known by its fruit", and "what strikes an observer in theories of this class is the absence of growth and development". Bosanquet afterwards confessed that the claim he here put forward for logic as forming the main content of philosophy was too exclusive,[1] but he never wavered from the critical position that "reality is the connection of the whole", and that any attempt to approach it by a dogmatic insistence on the supreme and ultimate reality of a part was bound to fail. The rest of the essay consists of a first sketch of what was to appear five years later in the writer's two volumes on *Logic or the Morphology of Thought*, to which there could be no better introduction than this early essay.

5. PHILOSOPHY OF HISTORY

(a) Work for the new principle lay to the hand of anyone who should put the question of the place of the historical method in the field of law and morality. The historical treatment of social phenomena since the time of Montesquieu had gone from victory to victory. In jurisprudence, Savigny and Maine; in ethics, Spencer and Leslie Stephen[2] were carrying all before them. Was the method wielded by these and other writers, even when supplemented by Darwinian principles, sufficient for the task they set before themselves? or were there questions with which it was, by its very nature as confined to chronological sequence, inadequate to deal, and which could only be answered from the point of view of a philosophy of consciousness as the underlying assumption of anything that could be called history? It is this question that W. R. Sorley attacks in an essay on "The Historical Method", which, like so many of those in this book, gives us the first condensed sketch of the lines on which the writer's own subsequent contribution to philosophy was to be built.

The principle from which he starts is merely the application to the social sciences of that which had been elaborated by the Haldanes in connection with the physical and biological, namely, "that the method suitable to one class of questions may imply a constant *petitio principii* if applied to others, which yet stand in close relation with the former". In law it is shown that, granted the great value of generalizations such as Savigny's as to "the organic connection of law with the being and character of a people", or Maine's as to

[1] See the posthumous volume *Science and Philosophy* (1927), p. 20.
[2] Spencer's *Data of Ethics* was published in 1879; by 1888 it had gone through four editions. Leslie Stephen's *Science of Ethics* had been published in 1882.

the course of development "from status to contract", there comes a time in developed and civilized communities when men have learned the lesson of reflection upon that being and character, and when conduct comes to be guided by a definite conception of its end, instead of by a vague belief in what is usual. It is for this reason that the analysis of the process whereby these conceptions or ideals are formed must always be one of the main problems in the philosophical treatment of social life, and must set a limit to the sufficiency of historical realism.

Similarly in psychology and morals. Anthropology may show how the present mental and moral condition of mankind is the result of historical evolution, but "are not cognitive categories, however crudely held and ill-applied, pre-supposed in the germinal knowledge of man? are not ethical ideals, however indistinctly conceived and blindly followed, implied in the rudimentary moral activity of the lowest races?" and does not the question thus come to be "whether the historical method, which exhibits the development of knowledge and morality, can also account for their existence"?

While it is true that it lies within its power to trace the growth of altruistic and other moral feelings, there are two questions which it fails to touch, or at any rate to decide. One is that of the difference between moral or consciously determined action and action which is merely natural or determined by conditions independent of consciousness..This may be said to be the *fundamental* question of ethics. The other, which may be called the *final* question, is that of the principle which guides our choice between various moral ends (as we should now say the criterion of the *value* of ends). A metaphysic of morals, which with an eye to the actual world of social experience and social values seeks to answer these questions, escapes the censure of being merely what L. Stephen calls "a transfigured bit of logic", while it, at the same time, is a necessary supplement to a method that implies categories of which it can trace the historical manifestation but with whose logical position and nature it is powerless to deal.

(*b*) While Neo-Kantianism has its main root in a reinterpretation of Kant's theory of knowledge which should make possible a positive theory of reality, it had also another root in a reinterpretation of his theory of morals which should make possible a positive theory of the place of reason in individual life and history. Here also it could be shown that Kant had himself furnished the means of correcting his own abstraction, not only in his *Metaphysic of Ethics*, in the conception of the Kingdom of Ends, but in the comparatively neglected essay on the *Idea of a Universal History on a Cosmopolitical Plan*, where he gave the first outline of the view of history as the progressive realization of freedom that was more fully worked out in Hegel's *Philosophy of History*. This was one of the earliest translated of Hegel's works, and was singled out by Lewes in his *Biographical History of Philosophy* for special praise.[1] But in the reaction against supposed *a priori* and teleological constructions of history in general and against Hegel's, with its arbitrary treatment of particular phases of evolution and its Teutonic and anti-democratic bias, in particular, the whole idea had fallen under suspicion.

David G. Ritchie was the only one of the contributors to the Essays who lived to fulfil only part of the promise shown in this volume.[2] His essay here on "The Rationality of History" has a special interest as a courageous and particularly brilliant defence of the possibility of a philosophy of history, if not precisely as Hegel conceived it, yet on similar lines.

Some philosophy of history is necessary, not only that philosophy may show itself equal to its task, but that history may realize its own end as an interpretation of the meaning of the events in its chosen period. While the "scientific historian" is right in occasionally ignoring final causes in order to avoid prejudgment, neither the ordinary thoughtful man nor the statesman believes that history moves without a purpose or that this is wholly inscrutable by man. Even Metternich, if he were now living, would admit that Italy is more than "a geographical expression". The only consistent unbelievers in a purpose in history are the defenders of anarchy or despotism. Can the belief that "history is the work of reason" be justified?

Objection cannot be taken to it either on the ground of the piety that holds that "God's ways are not as our ways": "An intelligent Providence can hardly be an unintelligible Providence"; or on the ground that history is the sphere of human freedom. To the philosopher freedom means something other than unaccountable caprice, and individuality more than unlimited unlikeness. Freedom means

---

[1] See above, p. 157.
[2] See his *Natural Rights* (Library of Philosophy, 1885), now in its third edition.

the escape from the tyranny of nature, and history is just man's constant struggle to rise above merely natural influences. He may not always know it as such. Only a few in the time of Milton knew, like him, that they were really fighting the battle of liberty. Nor is it a valid objection that such a history directs attention to results and is apt to slide into the view that might is right. In the end it is true that the permanence of any counsel or work is the best test that it is "of God"; but what remains permanent is never material conquest. What conquered the East was not Alexander's armies, but the civilization which came from Hellas, and especially from the conquered Athens. Nor finally is its selectiveness any real objection. History necessarily selects peoples and times, and individuals within them that have fulfilled their mission by realizing their portion of the potentialities of the human spirit, and are in this sense *representative*. Neither time nor space nor the order in either is the proper measure of value here. One day may count for a thousand years, and one spot in the depths of space for a spiritual universe.

While there is no magic in the number three, as compared with theories of chance, of special Providence, of cycles, or of continuous intellectual "progress", there is a logical basis for the movement of progress by thesis, antithesis, and their union.[1] People have a suspicion of all such formulæ, as ignoring or perverting fact. But this need not be so, if they remember, first, that formulæ of some kind are necessary if we are going to find any meaning at all in our material; and secondly, that the best of formulæ, where the material is complex, must be employed in more than one way, if we are to include all the facts; just as the spirit of a people or an epoch realizes itself more freely through having many channels of expression (*e.g.*, the Ionic and the Doric in the Hellenic world).

If this is true of the interpretation of the remote past, it is true *a fortiori* of our own time. Neither Hegel's errors in the application of his general idea, nor the different interpretations that others have put on it, are a disproof of its essential value at a time when we are all agreed that the principal end must be reconstruction in ethics, economics, the relation of Church and State, and of States to one another. Taken with the admitted qualifications, that idea will serve to remind us, first that, while there is no going back either

---

[1] On Coleridge's use of this principle see *Coleridge as Philosopher*. In America at the same time as these *Essays* were written the logician Charles Peirce was advocating what he called a "triadic" philosophy. See Pt. III, Chap. III, below.

to the pre-critical or the merely critical stage, the third or reconciling stage must take up the truth of both; and secondly (surely
wisely here in view of Teutonic or other pretensions), that the
civilization of the world is not now entrusted as of old to one keeper
only, and that no nation has the right to say "Surely we are the
people, and wisdom will die with us."

6. PHILOSOPHY OF ART

If it is true, as Bosanquet tells us, that "in Germany the historical
led up to the æsthetic synthesis",[1] there is an appropriateness in
the order of the next essay on "The Philosophy of Art". When the
same writer adds that " in England æsthetic insight has had a
remarkable influence on historical research", we may find an illustration of it in the subsequent life-work of W. P. Ker, the scholar
who wrote it.

From the side of idealistic philosophy nothing had been written,
scarcely anything from the side of any philosophy, upon æsthetic
theory since the time of Coleridge. True Ruskin and Morris were
giving new life to the appreciation of beauty in fine art. In Ruskin
we might be said to have in essence the same problem as Kant
discusses under the title of genius; in the work of Morris the corro-
boration and completion of "the theories both of the great idealists
and the exact æstheticians".[2] But Ruskin cared but little for system
or formula, and Morris cared still less. Both spoke more as prophets
and preachers than as philosophers at a time which, as we have seen,
imperatively demanded something more. When we ask what there
was in contemporary English philosophy to supply this want or to
point to the direction in which it might be looked for, it is difficult
to find an answer. The writer of the article "Æsthetics" in the ninth
edition of the *Encyclopædia Britannica* refers contemptuously to
Schelling's "curious system of transcendental idealism", and to the
work "of the Hegelians to construct what they call the dialectic of
æsthetics" as "among the most curious products of metaphysical
thought". It was this state of mind which gave particular significance
to William Paton Ker's essay in this volume, in that it directed
attention anew to the content and meaning of art as one of the main
ways in which reality reveals itself to us.

Starting from Plato's allusion to "the ancient quarrel between

[1] *History of Æsthetic* (London, 1892), p. 454.
[2] Bosanquet, *op. cit.*, pp. 453 and 457.

poetry and philosophy" and his settlement of it in favour of the latter, the writer agrees that the beauty of sensible things is in some way the image of an unseen beauty, and that there may be a progress from the half-conscious life of the child among beautiful things to the awakened life of reason. But he holds that the view that art is an education does not help to make art easier to understand. The problem of the philosophy of art for us is not, as to Plato, the relation of scientific knowledge to the blind impulse of creation, but the kind of object which the artist attains, and the relation of works of art to the mind.

Equally with science, art is a mode of making things clear to the intelligence. But whereas in science the particular object is important only so far as it is an illustration of a universal, and tends always to be resolved into relations with other particular objects, for art the particular thing exists with a being of its own, and as something whose relations to other things, whether as causes or effects, is an altogether subordinate matter. Art makes new things, which are self-explanatory in a way in which nothing is so to science. These things are in the world and partly subject to its laws, but they are not of it. Their only necessary relation is to the mind, which apprehends them as things which have no other nature than to be apprehended. With this is connected the further distinction that science is an endless process, in which we are always carried on to new relations in the effort to understand; art is the first attempt to find a cure for this unrest. It is a return of the mind to itself from seeking fact after fact, law after law, in the objective world—a recognition that the mind is an end to itself and its own law.

Morality seems to differ from science and to be allied to art in that it is concerned with the particular act, and therein is the denial of the necessity which belongs to nature. But the moral act differs from the creation of art in that it has again to lose itself in the objective world. It attains only an inward permanence in the character of the agent, whereas the freedom gained in the work of art is universal, and remains to be beheld by all men. Moreover, in morality, as in science, we have an endless pursuit of an ever unattained ideal. While therefore, like both science and morality, art stands for a conquest over nature, it differs from them first in uniting reality and appearance in a way these fail to do, and secondly in escaping from the contradictions of an endless process.

But this does not mean that art stands for any finality, or that it is left untroubled in its kingdom. The work of art, indeed, has a certain infinity in that it is free from the darkness and incomprehensibility, which is the curse of finite things considered in themselves. But it remains finite in that it is not the highest way in which the mind reveals itself to itself, and in the end is subject to the mind's criticism. It is for this reason that, at any one period or in any one form, it is only a partial revelation both of the mind and of the world, and has always to yield to some successor. In Greece, for example, tragedy succeeds sculpture, since it is an effort to solve the conflict in which sculpture is involved, between Olympian power and Olympian weakness. So comedy succeeds tragedy when attention begins sentimentally to concentrate on the inner life and the sorrows of the hero. Comedy cannot bring back the old simple manner of regarding things, but "it can show that there are other things in the world besides weeping heroes; it will show a new heaven with the clouds in it and the deathless race of birds, and a new earth with cool, green places in it, and the voice of frogs to reprove the faint-hearted".

So, too, in Christian art we have a new level of apprehension. In Greek art image and reality are one. In Christian art they are incommensurate from the first. Hence Christian religion could not pass away into art. But the progress in Christian, as in Greek art, is towards a completer conquest of the universe—to find beauty not in gods and heroes only, but in all levels of existence. In the effort to do this modern art has ceased to be merely the interpreter of Christian tradition; but it does not cease to express in its own way the essential idea of Christianity, "the idea that it is the individual subject which is of infinite value". "The Music", the writer adds, "which is the creation of the modern world expresses that which is inexpressible in all other arts—the mind's freedom from the contingency of the outward world and obedience to its own law."

7. SOCIAL PHILOSOPHY

In no field was new light more needed than in the study of Society. Green had already signalized the change in English Liberalism from a purely negative to a positive conception of freedom in his Lecture on "Liberal Legislation and Freedom of Contract".[1] F. H.

[1] Oxford, 1881.

Bradley, in the chapter in *Ethical Studies* on "My Station and Its Duties", had applied Hegelian ideas to the relation of the individual to Society with brilliant effect. But there was much that still required to be done, and all the more necessity to do it as the sociology of the day, whether that of Comte or of Spencer, was prepared in its own way to prophesy in the name of German philosophy. Comte had declared that, had he known of Kant's work earlier, he would have been spared much of his labour,[1] and Spencer was appealing to the German conception of Naturrecht in support of his own individualistic theory of natural rights. Both Comte and Spencer had used the conception of the Social Organism, but both also with qualifications that tended to obscure its real significance. By Comte it was made to lead up to the idea of a human society which, however organic in itself, had no demonstrable organic relation with its cosmic environment. Even within the organism of humanity Comte went far to deny any real place for the rights of the individual. With Spencer the social organism was little more that a biological metaphor which failed just at the crucial point, seeing that human society was without a common sensorium, not to speak of a common intelligence.

It was these defects in the social philosophies of the time, together with the very real difficulty of adjusting Darwinian ideas on the struggle for existence with an idealistic theory of human progress, that gave significance to the two essays which follow by Henry (afterwards Sir Henry) Jones and James Bonar,—the biographer and critic of Malthus.

(a) There was no one at that time better equipped to be an exponent of Hegelianism than the first of these writers. He had imbibed the pure milk of its word in the writings and verbal teaching of Edward Caird, whom he afterwards succeeded in the chair of Moral Philosophy in Glasgow. He had seized its essential spirit and conceived of the endeavour to carry it into every field, theoretical or practical, into which his versatile genius led him, as the mission of his life. But it was in the bearing of the doctrine on the conception of citizenship that his chief interest lay, and nowhere did he succeed in expressing himself upon it with greater clearness and force than in this early essay.

Modern speculation, he holds, is essentially synthetic. Particularly in theories of society we have a growing emphasis on the *relations*

[1] Letter to M. d'Eichthal, 1824, quoted Max Müller's translation of the *Critique of Pure Reason* (2nd ed., 1907), p. xlii.

of the individual as organic to his own constitution and inner life. While English practice and philosophy reflects this general movement, some of the most popular writers are still dominated by the presuppositions of an older individualism. "Like the servants of the wounded Ahab, they stay their master in his chariot till the eve." This is notably so in Spencer's exposition of the social organism. United with the attempt to conceive of society as more than an aggregate of individuals, we have in it survivals of an individualistic psychology and ethics. Under the influence of biological ideas Spencer draws out the points of resemblance between society and the natural organism, but immediately becomes conscious of the equally significant differences. The result is that, when he abandons, or is abandoned by the idea of the "living body" which he has taken as his guide, he at once stumbles into individualism. Society becomes merely a means by which the welfare of individuals is secured. And seeing that to each individual it exists only as the collection of other individuals, these also become merely the means to his private welfare. Must we then give up the idea of the organic nature of society? Or may it not be shown that the unlikeness which wrecks Spencer's analogy comes from the fact that Society is more organic and not less so than the living body?

In the individual animal or man, what gives its primary unity to the organism is not its material parts and their functions, but sensation. It is by sensation that these are retracted out of their externality and become organs. It is in this, so long as it lasts, that organs and organism become one. But sensations are fleeting. They overcome the outwardness of space, but are themselves overcome by the discreteness of time. It is only (and this is the central teaching of Kant) when sensations are related to a self, when they are known as in a "me" and as "mine", that they attain fixity and permanence. Only in such a consciousness does the unity of the organism become a permanent fact; only so does the thought, which exists first in the form of sensation, come to itself. This is why, while the life of the animal suggests a meaning, and an end, the end is nature's and not the animal's own, and, so far, it fails to be organic. In man it is different. The meaning of a man's life is within his own grasp. He shows it by his power of stamping his environment with his own meaning, and raising the natural to the level of the spiritual. "Man is self-conscious; man is free." This to the Alpha and Omega of ethics. But if every individual is thus a complete organism with his meaning in himself, we have only Spencer's "discreteness" in a deeper form: individuals are not only "not in contact", but they are ethically isolated, each is his own end. If society is organic it must conquer difference in a stronger citadel than Spencer has in mind, and conquer it by ethical means. For this freedom has been bought at too great a price to be lightly bartered away. Society has gone out into difference. Can it gather itself back?

It is here that Kant has again led the way in giving the quietus to any merely negative or subjective conceptions of freedom. Freedom from all limit and restraint from without is freedom *in vacuo*, motiveless, inactive. To be active there must be a motive, and motive must come from beyond a man's isolated momentary self. Where can such be found? Individualism has sought to save itself by finding it in pleasure variously interpreted. But however interpreted, pleasure can afford no ideal. It is necessarily the pleasure of the present self, and so far is attained; but it passes away in the act of attainment. The writer had F. H. Bradley's conclusive criticism of hedonism before him, and could afford to be brief in proving that it levels all actions and deprives the moral life of its whole *nisus*. Even briefer is his treatment of the ideal of "duty for duty's sake". There is no point on which Neo-Kantianism was more convincing than in its criticism of the categorical imperative. As hedonism equates the ideal with the present self, Kant's rigorism offers the ideal of a self which can never be present. The true ethical ideal is a self as well as a not-self. It must not only be itself real, but it must be that which makes the individual real. The universal must be also particular, and live in its own detail. If we ask where such an ideal is to be found, there can be no other answer than in the social organism, or rather the moral order which is embodied in the various forms of society. This gives a law, an *ideal* to the individual; on the other hand, the order of society is an *actual* fact. The task of a man's life is to answer the demands made upon him by it. It is in this way that the individual finds his freedom in society, and society is possible only because its members are free. It is an organism not because it is like an animal, but because the individual realizes himself as an ethical being in society, and society realizes itself in the individual.

This solves the difficulty of the antinomy of egoism and altruism. They are counter-abstractions. "Rousseau would not wash the feet of his neighbour. Comte would wash 'not his feet only, but his hands and his head', and drown himself in addition." It solves, too, Spencer's difficulty about the dispersal of consciousness in society. There exists no such thing as a merely individual self-consciousness. The individual is conscious of himself only as he distinguishes himself from his environment as not-self, but it is *his* not-self, and that means that he relates himself to it. Although there is no social pineal gland or sensorium, yet society is conscious in each of its members. Just as we can say either that the artist finds meaning in the picture or that the picture reveals itself to the artist, or again, that the scientific man discovers the thoughts of nature, or that the thoughts of nature reveal themselves to him, so we can say either that the individual finds the meaning of society, or that society finds its meaning in him. The social organism is an organism of organisms, in that it repeats itself in every part. By the same sign it is a kingdom, in which all are kings because all are subjects.

New problems have risen since this Essay was written. The conflict may be said to have passed from that between individual and society to one between social groups within society. A new individualism has developed in which separate and independent rights are claimed for the separate groups. But the same principle contains the solution. The assertion of the rights of the individual groups is a real advance as against the conception of an all-absorbing or all-dominating State. But the assertion of the rights of individual groups to the neglect or denial of the Kantian idea of a "kingdom of ends", to which these contribute, not as means or merely as means, but as conscious sharers, is the denial of the essentially social nature of man, or, which is the same thing, the essentially human nature of society.

(*b*) It was a sign of the force and comprehensiveness of the Hegelian movement that it made itself felt not only in the reconstruction of the more strictly philosophical sciences, but in the more philosophical spirit it introduced into British scholarship in other fields. In earlier writers, notably in Adam Smith and John Stuart Mill, political economy was a part of a general philosophy of life, but specialization had recently set in, and that just at a time when the incursion of Darwinian ideas into politics and the spread of Socialism, which may be said to have been a reaction against these ideas as commonly interpreted, were raising new problems which seemed to require the wider outlook. Under these circumstances the essay on "The Struggle for Existence—Hints for a Philosophy of Economics", by James Bonar, a writer who early united a training in philosophy and economics,[1] was a particularly timely reminder of the broader issues for life and politics that were involved in that study, and of the point of view from which, in accordance with the newer philosophy, they could most hopefully be faced.

The philosopher, Bonar explains, has a distinct task in relation to economic facts, beginning earlier and ending later than the economist. He has to take these up from the side of their roots in national life, and he has to follow them to the point where they pass into cosmopolitan politics. True he is regarded with suspicion, especially when he appears in idealistic garb. "Darwin may steal a horse, while idealists may not look over a hedge." But, taking economists as they are and philosophers as they might be, there is no great presumption in overlooking these suspicions, and in considering what light they throw on each other.

Of economic facts that reach beyond economy, and are a crucial problem for a philosophy of man, "the struggle for existence" is a conspicuous example. What part does this play in civilization as a whole? Is it a necessary feature of modern society and the modern State? Granted, it has a place in the origin and perfectionment of society, must it go on after perfection has been reached?

The first thing to make clear is that the phrase is ambiguous. It is distinctive of human life that the struggle is no longer for bare existence, but for an improved form of existence—in other words for an ideal. It is this and not the drive of hunger that is the source of progress. It is a commonplace of poor-law administration that those nearest to pauperism take the least pains to avoid it. Granted that starvation has played a rôle in the history of races, it has at best only driven them to seek more convenient dwelling-places. Progress begins with the greater convenience and the leisure which it makes possible. The history of civilized nations illustrates the same truth. So far as there was struggle in the Greek States leading to progress, it was not of destitute slaves against wealthy possessors, but of one idle class against a still idler. So with the French Revolution and the American War of Independence. In modern States there is certainly a new factor, "the liberty of the individual", which was ignored in the ancient. Our ideal State

---

[1] Subsequently used with effect in his *Philosophy and Political Economy* (First Edition 1893, Fourth Edition 1927) and his recent volume on *Moral Sense*.

must provide that free scope for individuality which is the most modern feature of modern politics. A good State is like a true theory.[1] As that theory is truest which explains most difficulties, and that truest of all which seems to increase in its powers of explanation the more widely it is applied, so the best State is that which develops the greatest number of the best qualities of its people. This cannot, however, be taken to mean in politics any more than in education the uniform development of all the faculties. This would be to try to follow all roads at once. "We cannot, therefore we ought not" to do that. Faculties always imply objects, and objects differ. "The man who devotes himself to those of the things needful for his time and country, which he can do best, is not far from the chief end of man."

It is this that the modern State must continually have in view. It involves that the weak as well as the strong should be cared for, that they may have their chance of really choosing their work. "The struggle for mere being would from childhood exclude them from the struggle for well-being. Not only would the weakest go to the wall, but many who might have been strong would be kept weak." Modern society is beginning to recognize this new view of liberty, and, instead of letting the struggle for existence rage itself out in the lower strata, takes every pains to end it. "Where Darwinism was wont to rule absolutely, it may not now rule at all."

Yet, granting this, the problem remains of the place of liberty in the more negative sense of freedom from interference. Is it true that in all circles except the lowest the rule must be "hands off"? Is this "a postulate of the modern notion of liberty"? It is here that we wake up the "old quarrel" between the economists and philanthropists. Economic changes, leading on the whole to progress, have gone along with hard dealing, suffering, public indignation, philanthropic (mainly useless) remedies. The average Englishman is a philanthropist in his words and an economist in his deeds. "The American", says Bryce, "throws himself at one moment into politics as if the State were all in all to him, and the next moment devotes himself to his private business as if he were alone in the world." Is the Englishman generous in theory and selfish in practice (in other words a hypocrite)? Is the American quite social and quite selfish by turns? or are the completely generous and the completely selfish,

[1] An analogy which Idealism in the hands of Bosanquet was to develop into a whole political philosophy.

the economic man and philanthropic man, both alike fictions of the
magazine writer, whose place will know them no more, if truth is
to conquer fiction?

From the side of the economists, it is to Adam Smith, not to
Ricardo, that every scientific doctrine of *laissez-faire* must trace its
genealogy, and Adam Smith is far from believing in the power of
individualism to cure its own wounds. " 'Natural liberty', as conceived by him, is rather the positive power to use powers than the
negative absence of restraint; it is not without law, still less without
society." The competitors are fellow-citizens; they have not only
the laws but (witness his book on the *Moral Sentiments*) the feelings
of citizenship to diminish the friction of their competition. Even
the *laissez-faire* of the Manchester School is on the whole in harmony
with this view of the State. Their "bargain" is not a bargain *in vacuo*
but under the conditions of English law. The true solution of the
apparent conflict between the moral sentiments and economic
competition is to be found in the training in the family and its
expansions, which ought to precede that competitive action in the
market and in the wider world, which is necessary if we would have
the whole nature of a man drawn out and all his powers tested.

The impossibility of separating self and society is confirmed by
the psychology which shows that the desire to better one's condition
is not selfish in the invidious sense of the word. Such ambition
courts the opposition of others, without which it is nothing. Moreover,
it seeks success for the sake of friends, who are a great part of its
own life. Men are threads whether of warp or woof; they cannot
unweave themselves. "A man", in fact, "is an abstraction, and
there is nothing real but humanity." The industrial counterpart of
this psychological fact is division of labour, and the co-operation
that is necessary, if there is to be anything accomplished at all.
"Division of labour made perfect by co-operation is the key to the
greatest movements of industrial civilization"; and "industrial union
fastens another fetter on the competition of selfish atoms". Doubtless mutual dependence is not the same thing as consciousness of
it, but they both bear out the impossibility of an absolute selfishness. Men only differ in the extent to which the self includes other
selves. "Even the worst men have something social in their notion
of self; and the good men have more than a little—they have all
the social interests which make life valuable."

Applied to the love of money and commercial ambition, this means that these are not the universal motor force of modern society, but only at best the engine through which other forces work. Restrained and modified by these, and interpreted as the struggle to maintain a high standard of social necessaries, so far from being evil they may even be said to be the chief redeeming feature of our civilization. It is right to protest against the mere increase of material goods and the luxurious tastes it may engender, but "it is difficult to believe the arrest of material progress to be compatible with the continuation of spiritual". Here as elsewhere progress comes from ideas; and "ideas of well-being have far more influence on industry than any other cause whatever".

The "Objective Idealism" of Germany, if it has done nothing else, has loosened the belief in the separateness of things distinguishable, and in the possibility of describing the living thing by any category which does not share in the living thing's complexity. "The civil society in which men first become truly human owed some of its materials, but none of its distinctive attributes, to the merely animal instincts of struggling men." In society, again, we may distinguish the sum-total of competing individuals and their associations from the State. But the two are inseparable. "If the parts depend on society for their character, they depend on the State for their career. To make the State all in all with Bismarck, or the individual all in all with Spencer, is to fall into equally false speculation and equally dangerous policy."

The writer ends these "social prolegomena" with a warning against taking them for prophecy; but he himself prophesied better than he knew. He did not, perhaps, fully estimate the power which "commercial ambition", when it takes hold of whole nations or becomes concentrated in great national or world-wide undertakings, might come to acquire, nor foresee the fatal influence it might exert on foreign and domestic politics. As a result, he speaks perhaps too lightly of the dangers that go with the extension of the acquisitive spirit in society. But he saw the dangers of the Bismarckian State. And for the rest, within the limits of the horizon of the 'eighties, his essay contains in condensed form a sufficiency of fertile ideas to revolutionize political economy in the direction, which on the whole it has since taken, and which it is likely more and more to take, as the science, not of a dismal struggle for existence, but of a hopeful and considerate progress in the materials of civilization.

8. Philosophy of Religion

British Idealism from the first has been in essence a philosophy of religion. At each stage in its development it has recognized, as the final test of its truth, its power of explaining without explaining away man's religious consciousness. Nowhere was the failure of eighteenth-century individualism more apparent than in this field. Kant's criticism here, as elsewhere, contained the promise of something better. His own moral argument for the being of God was founded on the necessity of providing a link between the life of Man and of Nature, between virtue and happiness, which his own general philosophy had ended in separating. From such a point of view religion could only appear to be something external—the direction of men's minds to a Being who could secure to the individual a harmony and satisfaction which his own nature denied him. But this doctrine was in sheer opposition to the essential spirit of Christianity. It was opposed to the conception of nature and history as a growing revelation of the divine element in a world groaning and travailing with it until now. It was opposed to the idea of the Church as a society in which men combine their forces against evil, and support one another not merely in the pursuit of happiness, as Kant supposed, but in their allegiance to a common spiritual good. Finally, it was opposed to any idea of reconciliation or atonement, which is only possible if we conceive of it as an actual fact every day accomplished in the soul of the believer through its self-surrender to the spirit of the whole which the Fourth Gospel calls love.

Kant was far too deeply imbued with the spirit of Christianity to fail to be conscious of the problem that his own philosophy thus raised with regard to it, and in his Treatise on *Religion within the Bounds of Mere Reason* goes a long way to reinterpret his own moral individualism so as to bring it into harmony with that spirit. The Neo-Kantian philosophy of religion consisted in developing the deeper principle involved in his general teaching to the point of the elimination of the remaining opposition. The Essay by T. B. Kilpatrick, afterwards Professor of Divinity in Knox College and in Emanuel College, Toronto, which comes at the end of this representative volume, aims at stating in condensed form the principle on which this reconstruction must be based.[1]

[1] John Caird's book on the *Philosophy of Religion* had appeared in 1880, and marked an epoch in religious thought. The writer of it was too deeply steeped in Hegelian ideas and even terminology to be entirely satisfying to

The writer sees that the possibility of such a reconstruction centres round the problem of Evil. Just as, granted an individualistic theory of knowledge, there was nothing that could save philosophy from the scepticism of Hume, and just as, granted a like theory of society, there was nothing that could save it from the anarchism[1] of Spencer, so, on the basis of any view that isolated man with his infinite claim upon his environment in nature and society, there was nothing to save us from the pessimism of Schopenhauer and von Hartmann. But equally with scepticism and anarchism, the presence of pessimism in modern thought meant the demand for reconstruction. The world that pessimism describes is a world of fragments. On the other hand, History proves that men have realized their identity with a principle supreme throughout their world, leaving no element in it in isolation, but leading all to the unity of one result. Can the faith in such an identity be vindicated? Is a principle of synthesis discoverable that can build the world up again before our eyes?

Comte had attempted such a synthesis. But it was a relative and incomplete one.[2] Man and his *milieu* in nature were left without organic connection. True the individual was not left without a Helper in Humanity. But the struggle, with the certainty of being beaten, to which pessimism reduces life, becomes only the more fearful when on the one side of the conflict there is ranged the whole race of man in the unity of a single personality. The reason of Comte's failure was that he had not gone deep enough into the nature of individuality, and that he healed the division between individual and universal too lightly. If our object is to find our way out of the individualism which disintegrates experience, and makes pessimism inevitable, we must discover first what it is that makes the claim for the individual against the world possible, and secondly in what sense the principle that makes it possible is compatible with any absolute division between these two: does it really shut the individual up within himself?

Starting from the position that the complete realization of individuality is only to be found in a conscious being with the power of concentrating upon himself, in what we call *self*-consciousness, the

the men of the younger generation. All the more it made them feel the necessity of a freer rendering of these ideas.

[1] "Anarchy plus the police constable", as Huxley called it.

[2] Edward Caird's article on Comte in the *Encyclopædia Britannica* (subsequently reprinted in a volume) appeared in 1875.

writer proceeds to develop the Neo-Kantian interpretation of this as necessarily involving a consciousness of what, as object, is beyond the self conceived of as mere subject. Underlying, therefore, the consciousness of the self and the world as separate, there is the consciousness of a principle which unites them. Following Kant and Hegel, the author calls the principle that effects this synthesis "thought", but it is more than the formal and subjective activity usually meant by the word. It is the universally determining principle of both our knowledge and its objects, and so the principle of the explanation of our world. The advance of knowledge is the deliverance of thought from the subjectivity and formality of its first contrast with the world, the exposition of it as it relates itself to and manifests itself in the manifold forms of the life of the world.

It is the same in conduct. The merely sensuous consciousness of animal life is still merged in nature. The "tragedy of copse and hedge-row" rouses no rebellion and raises no problem. *Self*-consciousness means the possibility of breaking the bond with outward nature and withdrawing into self-isolation from it. But this has a positive as well as a negative side. The world we set over against ourselves is also conceived of as the sphere of our self-realization— a realization that goes beyond the pursuit of the objects presented by casual desires. To self-conscious beings these objects only appear and have meaning as part of a "moral organism". What makes morality, with its distinction of selfish and unselfish action, possible is the consciousness of the difference between objects in their capacity to secure the completion of the moral self. Pessimism itself, which means the despair of any such completeness and sense of the satisfying, can only reach its conclusions through the recognition of this distinction and the universal self-transcending principle on which it is founded.

From the point of view which these facts force upon us, just as moral good consists in the identification of the self with the principle which enables it to be a self at all, and may be said to constitute its inner being, so moral evil is the consequence of the self-made division of a man's nature against itself. The extreme of this division "gathering all evil into a first iniquity" is concentration on the extreme point of individuality, acting in defiance of the very principle which makes this concentration possible. As the opposition and its pain lie wholly within the self, so the conquest of the self-contradiction lies within the self. But as in both cases the self is not individual

merely, but extends outwards to the world, and may even be said
to be the principle which constitutes and explains the world, "its
reconciliation with itself involves the harmony of the world".

Such a solution of the problem of evil is doubtless full of difficulty, more particularly with regard to individual responsibility for
inherited evil tendencies or social environment, and with regard to
the existence of natural evil. But in the case of the former, if we hold
both to the fact that evil is evil only to a being who can recognize
it as something that can influence his will, and therefore as more
than "a death-working object in nature", and to the fact of man's
organic relation to his whole environment, physical and social, we
can see that inherited and social evil mean not the narrowing but
the broadening of his responsibility. "His wrong is his, but since
he is no isolated individual it extends to all with whom his life is
bound up." And with regard to natural evil, seeing that it is impossible to give a complete account of a natural object apart from the
principle through which for us it is an object of knowledge or a
sphere of action, "our conception of nature's evil is filled with the
consciousness of our own". Only thus is it a "world-pain". And if
this is so, it may very well be that evil in us is the key to evil
in nature, evil in nature only the "illustrated catalogue" of evil in
us, and that our sympathy with it and our condemnation of it as
evil necessarily partake in the quality of repentance.

The error of pessimism is the same as that of empiricism. It
regards the world as a collection of disconnected phenomena. From
this point of view it must always be strong owing to the prevalence
of evil and pain. On the other hand it is answered, as empiricism is
answered, when we descend into the depths of the problem and
inquire into the ground of its own possibility and the conclusions
founded upon it.[1] This is why it may be said that "Pessimism in
this century has spoken its last word. From it we have learned the
anarchy of the world, but this is from the other side the problem of
its reconstruction."

The writer does not follow the argument to show how a religious
reconstruction is possible on the basis of it, but he indicates in a note
the correction of Kant's view that it entails. If, as he has argued, the
reality to which our moral self-consciousness points is not that of a

[1] While British Neo-Kantianism was thus seeking for the foundations of
truth and goodness in the depths of our judgment of evil, its supporters in
America in the same years were seeking for them in the depths of our judgment
of error. (See below, pp. 363 foll.) The argument was in both cases the same.

separate individuality, but that with which we unite ourselves when we surrender this individuality, this surrender and the reconciliation it brings with it are not anything which is merely subjective, an interminable warfare (as Kant would have it) with an unknown antagonist. However imperfectly realized, it is always being realized in actually "accomplished good". And this, so far as it is conceived of as a state or condition, constitutes the Kingdom of God, "the eternal", as Hegel expressed it, "which is the home of the spirit— an actuality in which God rules".

The essay comes appropriately at the end of the volume. Beginning in a modest claim to be a reconstruction of Kant's theory of knowledge, the new philosophy seemed to be carried by its own logic into all departments of life, and to end in what meant nothing less than a reconstruction of our world. It was in this sense that it was taken by most of the writers and made the basis, by themselves and by those who gathered to their standard, of the work of the next quarter of a century. But this extension of its programme was not to go unchallenged. There were those who, however they might admit inconsistencies in Kant's theory of knowledge, were so deeply imbued with Kant's critical spirit that they hesitated to depart so widely from it as to break down the division which he had raised between theory of knowledge and theory of being. Their suspicions, moreover, were deepened by the subordinate place which seemed to be assigned to human personality in a philosophy in which, whatever the place assigned to self-consciousness, the self of which we are conscious seemed to lose all real individuality in the life of the Absolute. What gave this criticism a special interest at the time was that it was first powerfully stated by the writer who had come forward as the leader of the pioneer group, and that it could not be taken as the result of any failure to have understood what Hegelianism meant from the inside. As the reaction it initiated was to grow in power both in England and America, and to take form under the name of Personalism, and as the book that better than any other on either continent gives credibility to its claim to represent a truer type of Idealism is out of print, a fuller study of it in an historical retrospect like the present may not be out of place. It will at least serve the purpose of bringing into clearer perspective through contrast what British Idealism stood for in this phase of its development.

CHAPTER IV

HESITATION AND ARREST

1. SEEDS OF REACTION

What in post-Kantian philosophy attracted the generation, for which the *Essays in Philosophical Criticism* spoke, was the freedom it seemed to bring from the limitations with which Kant had sought to surround the application of his principles. The first blow in the assertion of this freedom had been struck by Fichte in the identification of the Ego or Self, revealed in the analysis of knowledge, with the reality of the world. Speaking for himself as well as others of what Fichteism had meant to it, Andrew Seth wrote: "Probably no one who has really lived in this phase of thought can fail to remember the thrill with which the meaning of the new principle first flashed upon him and the light which it seemed to throw on old difficulties. . . . The universal consciousness seemed to rise upon us as a creative power which was not without us but within—which did not create a world of objects and leave it in dead independence, but perpetually unrolled, as it were, in each of us the universal spectacle of the world. . . . We had a new and better Berkeleianism, for God in this system (as it seemed) was not an unknown Spirit, hidden, as it were, behind the screen of phenomena. Here too we had a principle which seemed to satisfy, as well as Pantheism, the imperative need of unity, but did so without sacrificing the claims of self-consciousness."[1]

To the Fichtean doctrine of knowledge and conduct Schelling and Hegel had added a philosophy of Nature, as partly obscuring but also partly revealing in herself the characters of mind. The detailed dialectic of the *Logic* of Hegel was repulsive to British modes of thought. But once the general meaning of it was grasped, it seemed to give the clue to the contradictions involved in the one-sided views with which the history of philosophy was thickly strewn. To the theologically minded (and theology, affirmative or negative, was still a part of the mind of the time) came the additional attraction of a view of the Trinity which linked it with Neo-Platonic conceptions and seemed to retrieve cosmic significance for it. It was not surprising under the circumstances that for the moment at least

[1] *Hegelianism and Personality* (1887, long out of print), p. 59, quoted below as *H. and P.*

"Hegelianism" held the field, all the more effectively from the access of strength it received in 1883 from the publication of Green's posthumous *Prolegomena to Ethics*.

But it was not to go unchallenged. There were those who, like A. J. Balfour, had never bent the knee even to Kant, and who sought characteristically to cool the rising temperature of British thought with a cold douche of philosophic doubt.[1] If this might be discounted on the ground of an imperfect understanding of Kant and the work of his German successors, there were other influences coming from some of these successors themselves which could not be so easily set aside.

Lotze's works were by this time becoming known in England. A translation of his *System of Philosophy* (1874–79), designed and partly executed by T. H. Green, was completed and published under Bosanquet's editorship in 1884. A translation of his *Microcosmos* appeared in 1887. Lotze's main thesis may be said to have been the necessity of separating between reality and the work of thought as merely mirroring it in human consciousness. To sensation and perception thought owes the material on which it works, as the builder owes his stones to the quarryman. Its function is merely external and formal, ending in the production of a world of ideas which are not things. The reasons that are the mortar and plaster of such a world are not to be confused with the causes that constitute the real connections. Do what thought will, it fails to grasp what always must constitute the heart of reality in the individual thing. From this point of view the Hegelian system stood condemned as an attempt to deduce reality from the abstractions of logical thought.

Outside the Neo-Kantian school Lotze may be said to have been the dominating influence among thinkers with a leaning to idealism of some kind, but who hesitated to accept it in Hegelian form. Even within the Hegelian pale his work was not without effect. Bradley's *Principles of Logic*,[2] as contrasted with his *Ethical Studies*; Seth's *Balfour Lectures*, as contrasted with his contribution to the *Essays in Philosophical Criticism*, showed unmistakable signs of its influence. The difference between these two writers was that, while the contradictions, to which the attempt to adhere to Lotze's view of thought led, roused Bradley to suspect its adequacy, and in the end to substitute another for it much more allied to Hegel's Absolutism,

[1] His book *A Defence of Philosophic Doubt* had been published in 1879. In an article in *Mind* of 1884 he attacked Green's Metaphysics of Knowledge in the interest of Theism.
[2] See on this below.

Seth was borne by the Lotzean reaction to suspect the whole idea of the Absolute as a menace to individual reality in general and human personality in particular.

2. HEGELIANISM AND PERSONALITY

By the year 1887 the latter had become convinced that the advance represented by the *Essays*, his own included, had been too incautious and endangered positions, which, with A. J. Balfour, he believed must at all hazards be defended. He was thus prepared to sound a retreat, and, in the second series of his Balfour Lectures, published under the above title the book, which at once became the rallying point of the opposition to the Neo-Kantian movement. It was a powerful summons, not to go back from Kant's theory of knowledge, but to go back *to* it and take it for what Kant meant it to be—a theory positive as to knowledge of phenomena, but negative as to knowledge of the reality behind them. The error of the Neo-Kantians was that they had departed from the spirit of the *Critique* in turning what was only known as a condition of ordinary experience of the world of phenomena into a metaphysical entity. Green's *Prolegomena* had brought this clearly into view. The "eternal self" at which he had arrived is no more than "a *focus imaginarius* into which the multiplex relations which constitute the intelligible world return". So far from being countenanced by Kant's argument, this would have been denounced by him in the words he uses of the psychologists of his time: "The logical exposition of thought in general is mistaken for a metaphysical determination of the object."[1] Far truer to the spirit of Kant, in fact "the most clear-sighted and thoroughgoing application of the Kantian method", was Shadworth Hodgson's *Philosophy of Reflection*, which jealously maintains the "immanent nature of the inquiry" and resolutely rejects the "causal-entity view" as just that from which the critical theory of knowledge has set us free. What had misled the successors of Kant was his description of the Self as "the highest principle of the exercise of the understanding", and as "the vehicle of all conceptions whatever". This description holds of it as a principle of knowledge. But to exalt it into a principle of being was to commit the opposite fallacy to that of Hume and present us with an abstract and empty universal in place of his abstract particular.[2]

[1] *H. and P.*, p. 26.   [2] *Ibid.*, pp. 16 foll.

This criticism of Green is illustrated by the difficulties in which he involves himself in respect to the relation of sensation to the relating intelligence which is conceived of by him as the source both of knowledge and being. If intelligible relations are that which constitute the world of reality, it would seem that, to a perfectly intelligent subject, what to us appears as sensation must have an entirely different character. Feeling and sensation, in fact, drop out of reality altogether. Green, it is admitted, hints at another solution when he tells us that "feeling and thought are inseparable and mutually dependent in a consciousness for which the world of experience exists". A more sympathetic critic might have found in this the natural interpretation of Green's teaching, involving no more than the assertion that, as feeling and thought, particular and universal, subjective and objective, are inseparable elements in our experience, they must be conceived of as equally inseparable in an all-embracing experience. But the author will have none of it; it carries us into "abysses our line is too short to fathom".

All this, however, is only introductory. Green and his friends, while leaving much of Hegel on one side, are really reproducing Hegel's fundamental positions. For the complete exposure, therefore, of their fallacies we have to go deeper and attack them at their source in Hegel himself.

The chapters that follow may be said to contain the first informed criticism of Hegelianism that had appeared in England, and still occupy a place as one of the few founded on exhaustive first-hand knowledge. Most of the points attacked, the relation between the abstractions of the *Logic* and concrete reality, the idea of the Contingent, and the being of God, had been mentioned by the writer in his article in *Mind* of 1882. But while they had there been met sympathetically by showing what Hegel might be supposed really to have meant, they are here taken *in sensum deteriorem* and directed to the conclusion that in a system like his "the universe will tend to shrink together into a logical process, in which individuals, whose existence is after all the only reality, are merely the *foci*".

Hegel is indeed still given credit for a great advance. In finding the principle of all nature and history in the idea of End, he represents what is profoundest and best in modern philosophy. As compared with Kant, he has the credit of having rectified and completed the table of the categories and of having thus given us for the first time a systematic grammar of thought. Especially has he shown that the higher categories of life and mind, instead of being an illegitimate importation of our own into the only intellectually valid ones of the physical sciences, are in reality a more adequate rendering of the nature of things. "Pre-eminently is this the case with the category or notion to which all the rest lead up, the notion of self-consciousness. Instead of being dealt with as an unexplained excrescence upon the universe, the self-conscious knower is the ultimate fact to which all other facts are relative, and in which they find their explanation. Instead of shrinking from Anthropomorphism, Hegel accepts this ultimate category of thought as the only one we can use in seeking to give an adequate account of the great fact of existence." "Here", the author adds, "it seems to me that Hegel is unquestionably correct. Nothing can be more certain than that all philosophical explanation must be explanation of the lower by the higher, and not *vice versâ*; and if self-consciousness is the highest fact we know, then we are justified in using the conception of self-consciousness as our best key to the ultimate nature of existence as a whole."[1]

But in spite of these merits, Hegel's method is entirely misleading on account of the "air" he succeeds in giving his philosophy of starting without presuppositions and deducing reality from the forms of thought by which we determine it, in other words producing it out of nothing. As a matter of fact, it is pointed out with truth, he cannot move a step without presupposing an experience, which already contains all that he makes appear to be reached independently of it. This appearance of "letting down the ladder only in order to mount again by it to his original starting-point" might be excused as a part of a standing characteristic of Hegel's thought, "namely, that the order of exposition always reverses the real order of thought by which the results were arrived at", and as doing no harm except to Hegel himself by creating a prejudice against his philosophy. But the error goes deeper, for it leads to the delusion of supposing that not only is the end of the process to be conceived of as the ideal of perfected knowledge or as an eternally complete self-consciousness, but as something actually realized in Hegel's own philosophical system. "It is one thing to assert the metaphysical

[1] *H. and P.*, p. 39 (condensed). The writer does not explain how Hegel could be "unquestionably correct" in advancing from Kant's idea of the self as the condition of knowledge to self-consciousness as "our best key to the ultimate nature of existence as a whole", while Green is as unquestionably wrong in taking the same step.

necessity of an Absolute Self-consciousness, another to assert the present realization of absolute knowledge in a philosophical system."[1]

We thus come back to "what has long been regarded as the *mauvais pas* of the Hegelian system", the transition from abstractions of logic to the concrete life of nature. Instead of being content with an analysis of the concept of nature as part of our given world, Hegel seemed to aim at a deduction whereby nature itself is shown to have emerged from the Idea by a kind of relaxation of inner tension. It was possible even here, as the author had previously shown,[2] to put a more sympathetic interpretation upon Hegel's meaning, according to which both nature and the universals of logic are abstractions existing relatively to or within the life of the universe as reflected in mind. What forces us beyond both of them is not anything in either taken separately but the experienced fact itself. It is because we are minds, in touch from the first with the world of concrete fact in its wholeness, that we cannot rest either in the abstractions of logic or in the quasi-reality of nature as merely given, but have to unite them in a system of interrelated elements. But further reflection had convinced the author that criticism was not to be side-tracked in this way. In so far as Hegel offers us an absolute philosophy, he is committed to show that everything proceeds by a necessity of thought, and thus to repeat "the extraordinary but apparently fascinating attempt to construct the world out of abstract thought or mere universals".

If further proof that this is the true interpretation is wanted, we may find it in the scorn which Hegel habitually pours on existence or being. Being is not everything, but we must touch reality somewhere, otherwise our whole construction is in the air. Our concepts and categories have meaning only if we assume as somehow given a real world to which they refer: "Even an atom is more than a category". Thought, in fact, demands or postulates existence rather than supplies it. As Bradley had put it in his recently published *Principles of Logic*[3]: "The real is inaccessible by way of ideas. We escape from ideas and mere universals by a reference to the real which appears in perception."

Disingenuous on the part of Hegel as this turning the tables in reality seems to his critic to be, still more disingenuous is his treatment of the contingent—the mere collocation of parts, to which we must at last come in nature, as the result of an impotence in her.

[1] P. 100. [2] In the 1882 article above quoted. [3] Pp. 63 and 69.

The result of this can only be that the End (which it is Hegel's merit to have emphasized) will be the realization of some abstract idea, without regard to the individuals for whom alone it can be realized and whose existence is after all the only reality.[1]

It is vain to hope that out of these ambiguities there can emerge any adequate idea of the existence and nature of God. The German language itself, in which *"the* absolute Spirit" does not necessarily mean an individual spirit but merely spirit in general, favours equivocation here. Hegel doubtless intended to find in this idea, as a "concrete universal", the uniting principle between God and man; but there is no real unity. "If we scrutinize the system narrowly, we find Spirit or the Absolute, doing duty at one time for God, at another time for man; but when we have hold of the divine end we have lost grasp of the human, and *vice versâ.*"[2]

The same holds of the relation between the temporal and the eternal in general. Hegel talks of "development", but he has in mind logical implication, to which time is irrelevant. But "if we give up time we move out of reality altogether". On the other hand, admit time, and the eternally perfect recedes into the background.

Finally, it is not difficult to see what becomes of personal survival in such a philosophy. Immortality takes its place beside the eternity of the "active reason" of Aristotle, and the *"pars eterna nostri"* of Spinoza, which is just *not* our personality. No philosophy is able to demonstrate the immortality of the soul; but one that makes for the denial of it "seems so much at variance with our notions of the moral reasonableness of the world that it must ultimately act as a corrosive scepticism upon morality itself".[3]

3. THE ISSUES RAISED

The book marks as no other does the beginning of the reaction, within the lines of a general acceptance of Kant's work, against the Neo-Kantian interpretation of its meaning. In bringing together the difficulties, which any close attachment to Hegel seemed to involve and which would have to be met if there was to be any real advance, it performed undoubted service. Even its severest critics were ready to testify to "the value and suggestiveness of every page".[4] There

[1] P. 140.
[2] P. 156 (*cp.* 162–169). Hegel's reply to the last clause would have been "so much the worse for us".
[3] P. 228.   [4] D. G. Ritchie in *Mind*, vol. xiii. p. 263.

was much, moreover, in the latter part of it with which Green himself would have been in agreement. Green believed that a philosophy of the Absolute was one thing, an absolute philosophy quite another. "When we have satisfied ourselves", he had written in 1880, "that the world in its truth or full reality is spiritual because on no other supposition is its unity explicable, we may still have to confess that a knowledge of it in its spiritual reality—such a knowledge of it as would be a knowledge of God—is impossible to us."[1] In the same article he had criticized the Hegelian doctrine of the identity of thought and reality. "A well-grounded conviction has made men refuse to believe that any dialectic of the discursive intelligence would instruct them in the reality of the world, or that this reality could consist in thought in any sense in which thought can be identified with such an intellectual process." Green goes on to state what he took to be the essence of Hegelianism in the sense in which it could hope to gain acceptance "among serious and scientific" men as the view "that there is one spiritual self-conscious being of which all that is real is the activity and the expression; that we are related to this spiritual being not merely as parts of the world which is its expression, but as partakers in some inchoate measure of the self-consciousness through which it at once constitutes and distinguishes itself from the world;" finally "that this participation is the source of morality and religion".

But the criticism under review went farther, and sought not only to purify Idealism of doubtful Hegelian elements and to remind it of the problems still awaiting it, but to remove the whole basis on which it stood as a development of the Platonic tradition on English soil, which should assimilate while going beyond the work of Kant. It is therefore with the criticism of British Neo-Kantianism in the first part of the book rather than with the strictures on Hegel in the second part that we are here concerned.

The issue that was raised went far beyond the merits and defects of the particular form which the proposed advance took in Green. What was challenged through him was a doctrine which was the common basis of all the great European philosophies from Plato downwards, and the abandonment of which would mean in the end a complete scepticism as to the possibility of any philosophy. It is this wider challenge that makes it worth while to go in more detail

[1] Review of John Caird's *Introduction to the Philosophy of Religion*. See *Works*, vol. iii. p. 145.

into the question of the ground from which it was issued and the method of attack.

4. The Method of Speculative Philosophy

With regard to the method, it was with some justice that, as indicated in the title of the book and largely followed in the text, this struck its critics as in fundamental contradiction to the true spirit of speculative philosophy.

From Plato's time genuine philosophy has claimed to be "synoptic", pledged, that is, to the view that it contemplates "all time and all existence". Its spirit is what Bosanquet called the "spirit of totality". This means, as that writer had insisted in his essay in the 1883 volume, an "indirect" as contrasted with a "direct or uncritical" method of metaphysics. There is no direct route to truth through the selection of any one of the contents of experience, however important, and the subordination of everything else to it. Nothing has such prerogative right except the Whole. Everything else has its right to a place, lower or higher, in proportion as it reflects ("represents", as the older English Platonists called it), the nature of the Whole. It was therefore not without reason that *Hegelianism and Personality* was suspected of a method which seemed to consist in taking its stand on the uncriticized pronouncements of consciousness as to personality and the "requirements" of a particular form of theology, and in pressing these against results which, however still mixed with baser elements, had been passed through the crucible of the best available, including the Kantian, criticism. It was right to insist on the claims of personality. Modern civilization meant nothing less. Rousseau, and after him Kant, had based their ethics upon it. Hegel had announced that modern philosophy had advanced from substance to *subject*, and had paraphrased Kant's moral imperative in his own formula "be a person and treat others as persons". Green had even gone so far as to assert that "the only reality is persons and for persons". But personality is a complex idea. Its nature can only be discovered after analysis of the different elements that enter into it and estimation of the place it occupies in a scale of reality, the measure of which is not any isolated pronouncement of consciousness, but the most comprehensive and therefore the deepest experience which the soul is capable of receiving.

What is true of personality in man is still more true of it in God. The question is not to be settled off-hand by the "requirements" of a particular form of theology. "Persons who proclaim themselves Theists", wrote an acute critic of the book, at the time, more in harmony with the spirit both of Plato and of Kant, "may so formulate their requirements that no philosophy can or ought to satisfy them".[1] It would hardly be worth while dwelling on so obvious a point were it not for the illustration it offers of a method which was, perhaps still is, apt to have a peculiar attraction to British thinkers,[2] and which in the present case is peculiarly capable of different applications and leads to results agreeing with those of this book in nothing but their intolerance of Neo-Kantian idealism.[3]

5. KNOWLEDGE AND REALITY

Leaving for the present the theory of Personality that underlies the criticism of the book and coming to the substance of the criticism itself, in spite of the inconsistency already mentioned,[4] it centres in the denial of the right to pass from the implications of knowledge to assertions about reality. Kant had proved that certain ideas, more particularly the idea of a permanent self, were implied in the fact of knowledge. But he had sought to prove also that this gave no warrant for the passage from conditions of knowledge to the nature of reality. The issue thus raised was of the utmost importance for all who were concerned with the advance of philosophy in the line at once of the idealistic tradition and of the Kantian contribution to it. There was the question of the teaching of Idealism on the possibility of separating theory of knowledge—epistemology as it was beginning to be called—from ontology or the theory of being, and there was the question of the bearing of Kant's criticism upon that teaching. The answer to the first of these questions could not be doubtful. Right or wrong as to the second, the Neo-Kantians were in essential harmony with the central idealistic tradition.

i. Plato's Ideas were not forms superinduced by our minds upon

[1] D G. Ritchie in *Mind*, vol. xiii. p. 258.

[2] *Cp.* what Bradley wrote in 1863 of the "prejudice" with which he found English philosophy "choked" (Preface to *Principles of Logic*, p. vi).

[3] See, *e.g.*, the interesting *Essays in Personal Idealism*, edited by H. Sturt (1902), by a group of writers actuated by different motives, starting from different points of view, and leading to results often entirely contradictory of one another.

[4] See p. 206 *n*. above.

reality, but were determinate forms of reality itself. It was true that there was an ambiguity in Aristotle's οὐσία or substance, of which he sometimes speaks as though it were something separable from the universals by which it was known. But his main criticism of the "Platonists" was precisely that they made this separation; and his own central doctrine of the supreme reality as νόησις νοήσεως meant the ultimate unity of thought and reality. To mediæval philosophy the *ens realissimum* was the Holy Grail of philosophical search. To reach it an act of faith was required, but it was faith in man's own intelligence as well as in the existence of the object: it was *fides intellectum quærens*. It was a faith, moreover, the sheet-anchor of which was the ontological argument, hinging on the ultimate identity of idea and reality. If Descartes' *cogito ergo sum*, as an appeal to the mere fact of thinking and not to the contents of thought, gave doubtful support, his doctrine of clearness and distinctness of ideas as the test of truth to reality asserted this identity in another form. To English Platonists Cudworth's "Intellectual System" and Norris's "Ideal World" were different names for the ultimate reality as revealed to thought. In New England Jonathan Edwards had spoken the first word of a true speculative philosophy in his doctrine that knowledge was of value only as it led to that "consentience with being" in which all "felicity" consists. In all of these the validity of knowledge is the ποῦ στῶ of philosophy. To all of them knowledge has value (in modern phrase), *is* a value, because it is real knowledge, and real knowledge is knowledge of reality.

ii. Did Kant in reality break this great tradition? And have all attempts by his successors to rehabilitate it been an anachronism? It was a crucial question, and it was well to have it raised in the clearest form. Partly as the result of the challenge of this book, Kantian writers were deeply intrigued with it in the decade we are speaking of,[1] and answered it in a way that has since found general acceptance, and by this time is familiar matter of history.

Put shortly, the answer they gave consisted in showing that while Kant seemed to himself to be proving one thing, he was in reality proving quite another. He seemed to himself to be proving that all knowledge is merely of appearances; the reality of which these are

[1] Royce's *Religious Aspect of Philosophy*, the book which in America more than any other corresponded to Green's *Prolegomena to Ethics*, was published in 1885; his *Spirit of Modern Philosophy* in 1892. Caird's *Critical Philosophy of Kant* appeared midway between them in 1889.

appearances, the thing itself, for ever escapes the net of the forms
by which we seek to enclose it. What he was really proving was first
that subject and object are necessary components of all knowledge;
any attempt to resolve it into either alone must end in failure;
secondly, that when we follow out what we mean by the *object* as it
is in reality, we are forced to bring in a reference to a form of experience, which goes beyond that of any individual mind, in harmony
with which the validity or true objectivity of our *judgments*
depends.[1] Having thus made provision for objectivity, both in the
ordinary and the deeper sense of the word, within the field of experience, there was no longer any place for the idea of an object falling
wholly outside of all experience. In vain could it be said that knowledge proceeds on the assumption of the distinction between what
things appear to be and what they are, and that, whatever our
advance, what they are always recedes before us—Science merely
"setting a new limit to our ignorance". This is true, but it is equally
true that knowledge proceeds on the assumption that it is reality
that appears, and that we could not condemn anything as mere
appearance unless we had some means of contrasting it with what
is more than appearance and would turn appearance into reality:
in other words, unless we knew wherein reality must consist.

What the acceptance of this as the real meaning of the "revolution" that Kant had effected involved can hardly be said to have
been as yet clear, and critics of Neo-Kantianism were within their
right in complaining that Green had left both the line of his advance
and the position which he had reached in some obscurity. He
accepted self-conscious experience in knowledge and conduct, as the
best clue to the nature of the ultimate reality. But, as we have seen,
he was too keenly aware of the limits within which knowledge and
will in man move to be willing to identify these with what we must
hold to be attributes of a divine self-consciousness. For this reason
he was content to speak somewhat vaguely of this as the "spiritual
principle", which communicates itself to our consciousness in knowledge and goodness. It was part of Caird's more wholehearted
"Hegelianism" not only to hold that self-consciousness is the type
of all-embrace because all-relating experience, but to identify

[1] Kant indeed thought to escape giving objectivity to this experience by
speaking of it as a merely "possible" experience, but he had himself shown
that it was impossible to separate possibility from actuality. It was to the
exposure of this subterfuge that Royce directed his criticism of Kant in the
books above mentioned. See below, Part III, Chap. III.

them in essence. To know the self in its essential features, as revealed in its highest experience, is to know the Absolute.[1]

Which of these views, or whether either of them, was to be endorsed by the younger men yet lay in the future. What was matter of common agreement among them at the time was the proved necessity of advancing beyond Shadworth Hodgson's "Philosophy of Reflection", if there was to be any advance at all. If the judgment court of philosophy (as, according to Schiller, the judgment court of the world in general) is its history, this was about to prove how essentially right they were. Where the Philosophy of Reflection may be said to have left an empty page, Neo-Kantian Philosophy was about to write one of the most brilliant chapters in the history of English thought.[2] It is safe to say that, if it had listened at this time to the counsels of its critics, there would, at any rate in England, have been a gap with little or nothing of speculative value to fill it for a whole generation.

6. THE PROBLEM OF PERSONALITY

The point, as we have seen, which the writer who had come forward as the leader of revolt had seized upon was the rights of personality. This was the test he proposed to apply to the Neo-Kantian movement. Had Hegel succeeded, where Spinoza had failed, in saving the reality of the individual in its citadel of human personality? It was disquieting, to say the least of it, to be told that "the Notion" (that apotheosis of the universal) was "the very heart of the mind and the ego". Hegel's habitual mode of treating space and time existence, on which individuality in any form in the end depended, was moreover not reassuring. Green indeed had committed himself to the statement that "the only reality was persons and for persons". But this might itself be merely a personal aperçu, a return to the sanity of common-sense philosophy, which a more logical development of his fundamental doctrine was bound to repudiate. The real spirit of that doctrine was in a wholly contrary direction. For it the only reality was, and must more and more be seen to be, the "impersonal and for the impersonal". The issue was again clearly a fundamental one, and credit must be given to the writer of *Hegelianism and Per-*

[1] See his review of the *Prolegomena to Ethics* in *Mind*, 1883, and for his own view, *Life and Philosophy of Edward Caird*.
[2] To include at a later stage sections, it should be added, not less brilliant than the rest, by the writer of *Hegelianism and Personality*.

sonality for being one of the first to raise it in clear form. Idealistic writers both in England and America were to find themselves more and more concerned with this also, and to produce some of their best work in the attempt to meet it. But the wide scope of the problem and the lines on which alone a solution of it was possible ought to have been already sufficiently plain. Ten years before Bradley had called attention to the problem of individuality as one of fundamental importance. "A discussion", he had written in *Ethical Studies*,[1] "that would go to the bottom of the question, what is an individual? is certainly wanted. It would certainly be desirable, showing first what an individual is, to show then that 'individualism' has not apprehended that but taken an abstraction for reality."

i. On the question of the meaning of individuality in general, it ought to have been clear to any follower of Kant that, while, if we take "notion" in its ordinary sense of a general idea, individuality escapes its net, the mere particular, as here and now experienced, fails to give us what we want. While it is true that, if we give up space and time existence, we move out of reality altogether, it is equally true that, if we take the here and the now as all, we cut ourselves off from anything that can be called individual and real.

Kant's best interpreters, including the author of *Hegelianism and Personality*, were by this time agreed that the only consistent interpretation of Kant's aphorism, that conception without perception is empty, perception without conception is blind, is that both the particularity of sense and the universality of thought, taken apart from each other, are mere abstractions. If Hegel sometimes seemed to forget this and to "snort" at the element of particularity, it could only be because of the vogue in popular philosophy of the fallacy that mere presence to sense, inner or outer, could give us individuals or anything that has significance for minds. Neo-Kantian logic was founded on the necessity of the marriage of the "that" and the "what" in anything we are to know as individual. Whether and in what form in the Universal Mind the distinction between sense and understanding, the given and the thought-determined, would survive, was a further question. It was an old tradition of idealistic philosophy that there was a form of experience, foreshadowed in the more elementary consciousness of feeling, and, to a degree, realized in some of the higher phases of human experience, which carries us beyond all such distinctions. Kant was himself

[1] P. 150.

haunted by the idea of an intuitive, which would at the same time be a creative, intelligence, and there were Hegelians who were prepared to interpret this to mean that thought and knowledge, carried to completion, would *be* the thing.[1] Be the answer to this question what it may, in reading criticisms like that which has been before us in this chapter, dealing with the analysis of ordinary human experience, it is impossible to avoid the suspicion that they rest just on the confusion between particularity and individuality which Kant's analysis had undermined.

ii. What has been said of individuality in things in general as objects of knowledge holds of the individuality in persons we call personality in like case. It is only through the universals of place, time, activity, etc., that we apprehend them. In the case of others than our own selves it is difficult to see how otherwise we could have any knowledge of them at all, seeing that we are excluded from the organic feeling which is their outgoing centre. But it may be said to be different with regard to the personality of each for himself, and that it is just on the exclusiveness of feeling that the doctrine of the imperviousness of selves and their claim to be ultimate realities is founded. To this the reply must be: If the hereness and nowness of the body-soul organism, as given to internal sense, is the foundation of all personal life, it is only the beginning of it. Even as immediate feeling it always comes to us with the sense of belonging to a wider world whose life we share. It is in and through interaction with this world that we come first to be and then to know ourselves as separate persons, and this interaction would be impossible unless in a literal sense we shared one another's thoughts and emotions: "lent our minds out" and received the minds of others on loan in return.

Even so personality in the merely psychological sense may be the emptiest of human attributes.[2] Personality as something of value comes only in proportion as a man enters more fully into the life about him by his expanding interests, and brings these into har-

---

[1] "It may very well be held", wrote D. G. Ritchie *a propos* of the present subject, "that a *complete* knowledge of anything in the whole infinity of its relations (including that to our sensitive nature) would mean the making of that thing. Can we really think of omniscience apart from omnipotence? If I knew another individual person through and through, I should be that person." *Mind*, vol. xiii. p. 260. For Bradley's application of this idea in *Appearance and Reality* see below.

[2] Mary Graham, according to Mr. Pecksniff, is not a young lady, but merely a "person, young person". Quoted by C. J. Webb, *Divine Personality and Human Life*, p. 24.

mony with one another. On the other hand, the division of personality we hear of in morbid psychology has its analogue in the incoherent lives we see about us and experience in ourselves, and means the loss of anything that we can call personality in this truer sense. If we do not actually become things, yet we sink to a state in which things live in us rather than we in things.

All this the writer of *Hegelianism and Personality* is ready to recognize. "We may safely say," he writes, "that the mere individual is a fiction of philosophic thought". And his ground is the ontological one of the necessary relation of whole and part: "There could be no interaction between individuals unless they were all embraced within one reality; still less could there be any knowledge of one individual by others, if they did not all form parts of one system of things." It is all the more difficult to understand how in the same passage we find the individual self described as "in its nature perfectly impervious to other selves in a fashion of which the impenetrability of matter is a faint analogy".

Putting aside the doubtfulness of the support to the doctrine of the imperviousness of minds that is to be derived from modern theory as to the impenetrability of matter, it seems clear that in such a statement we have not only passed far beyond the limits of Kantian epistemology to which the writer would confine us, but we have committed ourselves to a doctrine that makes it impossible to understand how there can be any real interaction, not to speak of inter-communication, appreciation, and understanding between individuals. If minds appear to start from a basis of incommunicable feeling which separates them, it separates only that they may unite, and they unite in virtue of their power, through imagination and sympathy, of entering, as participants, a world of common meanings, affections, purposes, apart from their use of which all true individuality is lost.

Returning to Kant, just as his best English interpreters took their departure in their theory of knowledge from the hint that he gave of a new criterion of objective reality, so in their theory of conduct they took their departure from the hint he gave of a new criterion of personality. As the criterion of the truth of knowledge must consist, not in correspondence of our thought with what is altogether beyond it and must be taken merely as an unknown X, but in the degree in which the "idea of the reason", in other words rational interconnection, is established between the elements given to experience; so the criterion of personality is not to be sought in anything merely given, but in the degree in which each is able, through the exercise of reason, to bring unity into his life (to free it as Kant would say from self-contradiction) by making himself a true member in a kingdom of ends.

Again, as we look back it would be safe to say that in no respect would the form of arrested Idealism, represented by this reaction, be more reactionary than by seeming to lend countenance to the individualism from which in every department of thought and action the age was struggling to escape. British philosophy was fortunate in having in those days men who were determined to feel the ground secure beneath them in any advance they proposed to make—to prove all things and hold fast only that which was good. But it was fortunate also in having others, who, where all perhaps at best was adventure, were prepared to put these hesitations aside and go forward from what they took to be a new insight to new enterprises in construction. Criticism of past endeavours is a necessary part of the work of the philosopher, but it is only a part. As one of the most enterprising of the younger leaders wrote in criticism of Lotze's attempt to turn the flank of the Neo-Kantian advance: "The philosopher who is satisfied with exposing the abstraction and inconclusiveness of earlier systems may effectively point out the labour that remains to be achieved by others, but he does not perform it himself."[1]

In the conviction that so far its critics were right in insisting that individuality in some sense is identical with reality, Idealism was by and by to face, in a far fuller way than there has here been space to indicate, the problem that was thus raised. But it faced it with all the greater confidence and all the greater chance of finding a comprehensive solution because of the apprenticeship it was for the moment content to serve to the wide-reaching principles which it borrowed from the workshop of its latest masters and which it had already found so fertile.

[1] Henry Jones in *The Philosophy of Lotze* (1895), p. 14.

CHAPTER V

FORWARD FROM HEGEL

BRADLEY (i). EARLY ESSAYS

A. THE PRESUPPOSITIONS OF CRITICAL HISTORY

1. GENERAL SPIRIT OF BRADLEY'S WORK

F. H. Bradley's name, more than any other, stands for the effort to deliver British philosophy from the spell that Kant and Hegel had cast upon it. If we are to believe his own account, it was his failure completely to understand the latter and the dissatisfaction he felt with so much of him as he did understand that urged him on to attempt a restatement of idealist principles. "For Hegel himself", he wrote in the Preface to the first edition of the *Principles of Logic*,[1] "assuredly I think him a great philosopher, but I never could have called myself an Hegelian, partly because I cannot say that I have mastered his system, and partly because I could not accept what seems his main principle, or at least part of that principle." What roused his suspicions, needless to say, was not any threat to orthodox theology, but, as in the case of Green,[2] the place that seemed to be claimed for thought, as not merely apprehensive but, in some exclusive sense, constitutive of reality. It was this not less than the prejudices, theological and other, which still "choked" English philosophy at its source, that convinced him that what for the moment was required was not a new system, whether home-grown or imported, but a new and more thoroughgoing criticism of first principles. The first thing was to clear the ground, and the ground could not be cleared without what he called "a critical, or, if you like, a sceptical study" of accepted notions. Such a study, he held, could only be the result of education and labour, including a training in other schools than our own. On the other hand, given such a discipline, he saw no reason why the English mind should not in his own

---

[1] London: First Edition, 1883; Second Edition, Revised with Commentary and Terminal Essays, 1922. Quoted below as *Logic*.
[2] He would have agreed with Green's restatement of Hegel's central teaching already quoted(p. 209). If we take this along with the doctrine of the concrete universal, which was a corollary from it, as Hegel's "main principle", no one had mastered it more thoroughly than Bradley; if he carried it a step farther than the Hegelians of his own time, this may have been because he understood it not worse but better than they.

day produce a rational system which it could call its own.[1] Sceptical though the study must be at the outset, it could never end in mere scepticism as to the *existence* of first principles, if for no other reason than that any philosophy which denied this must appeal to first principles of its own; to repudiate these was to stand outside not only philosophy but all intelligent discourse.

While he had thus no doubt about the reality of metaphysical truth, he was under no delusion as to the limits within which it was attainable. The secret, I believe, of the singular attraction that his writings have had for friends and enemies alike, was his readiness to confess that "if you push me far enough I end in doubts and perplexities".[2] He believed that, in a philosophy like his own, these perplexities were far less than in any other. But it was not in any results, positive or negative, practical or theoretical, that he found the ultimate justification of metaphysical study, but in the need to find a contact with something beyond the world of sense. Like poetry, art, and religion, metaphysics had its justification in itself. "All of us", he wrote, "are led more or less beyond the region of ordinary facts, and some in one way, some in another, seem to touch and have communion with what is beyond the visible world. In various manners we find something higher, which both supports and humbles, both chastens and transports us. And with certain persons, the intellectual effort to understand the universe is a principal way of thus experiencing the Deity. No one, probably, who has not felt this, however differently he might describe it, has ever cared much for metaphysics. And, wherever it has been felt strongly, it has been its own justification."[3]

It was these two characteristics: the conviction first, that if there was to be a truly British philosophy, realistic, idealistic, or both, it must take its start from a more thoroughgoing examination of first principles; and secondly, that metaphysical study, even though it was, in his own notebook phrase, the "finding of bad reasons for what we believe upon instinct", satisfied a need of the human mind as fundamental as that of art, religion, social life, or science itself, that mark Bradley's work as epoch-making in the history of British philosophy. If towards the end of a long life he could write, "There has been, I think, a rise in the general level of English philosophical thought such as fifty years ago might well have seemed incredible,"[4]

---

[1] Preface to *Appearance and Reality*.   [2] *Logic*, p. vii.
[3] *A. and R.*, p. 5.   [4] Preface to *Essays on Truth and Reality* (1914).

it was to his work more than to that of any other individual that it was due.

The aim of the present Study is (1) to trace the development in his own mind of the form of idealistic philosophy with which his name more than that of any other is likely in the future to be associated; (2) to try to form some provisional estimate of the value of his contribution to the great tradition he sought through a long life of undivided devotion to philosophy to carry forward.

2. THE PRESUPPOSITIONS OF CRITICAL HISTORY

While it may be said that there was no "precritical period" in Bradley's published work, it is possible to trace certain definite phases in the development of the ideas which were peculiarly his own, corresponding in general to the date of the publication of his chief books.

The essay with the above title [1] is not one of these, but it has a general interest as an application (so far as I know the first in England) of idealistic principles to the study, which perhaps at the time had deeper roots in Oxford than in any other place in the English-speaking world. It has also a particular interest for us here as Bradley's first contribution to philosophy and the first indication of the spirit he was bringing to a study which even more than history had found its home in that University.

The religious motive, which is obvious in the book, while characteristic of idealistic philosophy in general, is characteristic also of the time and place. Orthodox Christian tradition had recently received a shock from the higher criticism of Germany, which to many sincere minds had diffused an air of doubt over the whole historical basis of Christianity, and the choice seemed offered between allegiance to scientific method or blind adherence to theological dogma. The first "Oxford Movement" led by John Henry Newman may be said to have chosen the latter. To Bradley, who was to become one of the leaders in the second and deeper movement, there could be no doubt on which side philosophy must take its stand, though there might very well be doubt as to the consequences for religion of the acceptance of the results of criticism. "I

---

[1] Oxford, 1875; long out of print and even out of reach in second-hand-book stores. For this reason I have permitted myself longer quotations than would otherwise be allowable.

cannot help it", he writes, "if anyone thinks that the conclusions of this essay are reconcilable with only one belief or disbelief. I can only say beforehand that such a man's opinion is not mine. These conclusions I think are negative only of a breach between the worlds of the present and the past; and to point out where such a breach exists was not my business, still less my business to express an opinion on the relative truth and falsehood of existing religious beliefs. . . . The extent and generally the nature of the influence which a modification of history must exercise in religious belief is a subject on which it is remarkably easy to come to a conclusion and extremely hard to come to a right one. . . . After all, alas! the result may be that of the figures of one, whom we most wish to see as he was, we can accept not one as the likeness; and after the removal of vicious distortions there is left some feeble and colourless outline of him, in whose soul the world's 'broken heart', it may be, was born again."

Leaving this question, what seemed clear to him was that a wider problem than the truth of recorded events in the history of the Church was here involved, and that the whole question of the possibility of any kind of history was one on which the time had come for a rational decision. He believed that only from the standpoint of idealistic philosophy could a rational answer be found, and it is the indication which he gives of what he regarded at this time as its main contention that constitutes the special interest for us here in the remainder of the essay.

Hegel's name is not mentioned, but Bradley tells us in the Preface that the essay was suggested to him by reading C. F. Baur's *Epochen der Christlichen Geschichtebeschreibung*, and it is not difficult to discover in that essentially Hegelian work outlines of the philosophical principle on which its argument is based.[1]

3. The Argument

Starting from the actuality of history as a record of fact, we have two sides to consider: the *objective* of the events in time, and the *subjective* of the re-collection of them. "That history as a whole has been so made," Bradley writes before Italian Idealists had com-

---

[1] Baur's opening words, "The method of historical writing has hitherto received too little attention as a subject of special investigation", may well have suggested to Bradley the form of his essay.

mitted themselves to something very like the theory he here sweeps aside, "that in it we have nothing but a series of projections of present consciousness in the form of a story of past events from time to time gathered up or abolished in a larger and more inclusive projection—this has, so far as I know, been upheld by no sober-minded man, nor could be." How then are these two sides to be reconciled?

We have one kind of answer in the "simple theory" that all that the historian has to do is to reflect the *fact* in unadulterated form. But how can this be? For in the first place there is no such unadulterated fact anywhere discoverable. In the second place, owing to "the ceaseless passion of the mind to be at home in its object", there are always new aspects of the fact coming into view. This "simple theory" is merely a reflection of the uncritical view of knowledge in general as consisting in the reception of sensory impressions, representing fact, by a mind whose main duty is passivity.

To controvert this view as it had infected British philosophy from Locke to Spencer was the chief work in these days of T. H. Green. Bradley's refutation of it is interesting as an early example of the dialectic in which he afterwards became so supreme a master, and, dead though the theory may be, is worth quoting in condensed form. "The proof or even the assertion of this doctrine is a sheer self-contradiction. An assertion, and more so, a proof is intellectual; it is a judgment which implies the exercise of the understanding, and the terms invited by the judgment therefore fall within the sphere of the understanding. They must be objects for the intellect, and so, in a sense more or less entire, relative to the intellect; in a word intelligible. But the essence of mere sensation is the entire absence of the intellectual, and hence to make one single affirmation with respect to sensation as sensation is to treat as relative to the understanding that which is supposed to exclude the understanding, and this is a contradiction. To pursue with the reason an object which when found is to be irrational, to think the opposite of thought while fixed as opposite, to comprehend the incomprehensible yet without transforming it, such is the task of that which calls itself 'the philosophy of experience'. It is the pursuit of a phantom for ever doomed to fade in our embraces, a mocking shadow beyond the horizon of our grasp known to us as the unreality of all that we can hold and whose existence must perish at the threshold of human possession."

Bradley does not further pursue this "metaphor hardened into dogma", but before the end of the essay he gives a sufficiently clear indication of what was to form his own main contribution to the theory of knowledge, though still tinged with the colour of the Neo-Kantianism which this in the end was intended to supersede. If we are to understand the nature of knowledge and the process by which it grows from less to more, we must make our start neither with Hume from the theoretical entities we call *sensa*, nor with Kant from the combination of these with *intellecta*, but from the confused mass that constitutes the world of every mind at the first, and conceive of the growth of knowledge as the gradual permeation of it with the idea of systematic order supplied by self-conscious mind.

Leaving meantime the question of what makes fact for knowledge in general, Bradley turns to the errors as to the writing of history to which the "simple theory" gives rise. Here at any rate the appeal to *sensa* is senseless. Contact with the actual data is irrevocably lost, and there is no direct way to the recovery of it. Our only resource is intellectual construction of some kind. Just as rightly to observe in the narrow sense is "not to receive a series of chaotic impressions, but to grasp the course of events as a connected whole"; just as "our memories are certain only because they are corrigible", so in the case of the extended observation we call history. What we have to do is not to renounce judgment and inference (that leads nowhere), but to improve them. "There is no such thing as history without prejudication; the real distinction is between the writer who has his prejudications without knowing what they are, and whose prejudications, may be, are false, and the writer who consciously orders and creates from the known foundation of that which for him is the truth." And Bradley proceeds to sum up what he describes as the main thought of the essay. "The canon of history is the historian. . . . The historian, as he is, is the real criterion; the ideal criterion (if such an antithesis can be pardoned) is the historian as he ought to be. And the historian who is true to the present is the historian as he ought to be."

Arrived at this conclusion, it might seem that the objective side has disappeared, and we have capitulated to subjectivity and therewith to a complete relativism. The historian has indeed to be true to the present; but as the present of every historian is different and as each historian himself varies with his present, to be true to the present means to have different histories: in other words to have no history at all. But this is to forget the presupposition which history shares with common sense and science, namely, that "the world is one, and that in that world history exists and has but to demonstrate the existence of itself". And the principle on which the demonstration proceeds is that: "Testimony goes beyond individual experience, but not beyond our experience." Bradley makes as little allusion to Kant as to Hegel, but in the apparent paradox with which this section of the argument ends it is not difficult to recognize the Kantian distinction between the experience of the individual and "experience in general", and the removal of the criterion of validity from the one to the other, which is a characteristic mark of Neo-Kantian thought.

While History is one with science in sharing this fundamental presupposition, there is an important difference, which the remainder of the essay is occupied in defining. This cannot consist in the fact that history has to take account of freedom of the will, if this means that the life of man is subject to no law, for in this case again history disappears. "If we cannot count on human nature, our hold on tradition is gone." As little can it consist in the novelty or strangeness of the events in history. As in science, so in history, the appeal must always be to analogy. The real difference is partly in the subject-matter, partly in the character of our interest, partly, rising out of this, in the extent to which probability reigns in each. History moves in the field of human tradition. Facts for it are not mere illustrations but embodiments. "For the universal *as such* the historical writer cares not at all; at most it concerns him to see it embodied in a single person or the spirit of a nation." Similarly with the interest. "The interest of the historian is to breathe the life of the present into the death of the past and re-collect into this Pantheon of the mind the temporal existences which once seemed mortal. When this interest fails, as it does when we encounter an alien element, the hope and purpose which inspired us dies." It is for this reason that we never can have the same certainty in history as in science. We can never have the assurance of the complete integrity and accuracy of the witness, nor of having entered completely into his mind. In science, seeing that it abstracts, it is possible to reconstruct the observers and their conditions so as to possess ourselves of their faculties and use them as our own. In history this is never so. Borrowing a metaphor and stating a view that was growingly to dominate his whole philosophy, Bradley writes: "If the bud were

P

self-conscious, it would know of itself, but not in the way that the blossom knows it, still less as the fruit knows it, and as failing of the truth its knowledge must be said to be false."

It is for these reasons that it is vain to talk of a science of history or a scientific historian. Statistics merely give us at best the relations which the elements of particular societies bear to one another. It is quite another thing to find eternal laws which shall "explain the changes in an unending evolution, which is for us only in so far as it has made itself, and each stage of which is the qualitative new-birth of an organic amd more than an organic unity which resumes its lower developments in a fresh integration and informs its elements with its own distinctive nature. . . . In this way to seize 'the red strand of necessity' in progress is simply impossible, and 'science of tendencies' is an amiable phrase which sounds not much better than 'science of intentions' ".

While on this showing much remains unknown (a reproach which history and philosophy may well be content to share with science), to assert unknowability is an entirely different thing. Meantime (here again striking a ground-note of his future work) criticism must go its own way. "However humble the sphere of her rule, yet at least, while within that sphere, criticism is subject to no intrusion and oppressed by no authority. She moves on her path unheedful of the clamours of that which beyond her realm may be, or may call itself, religion and philosophy: her philosophy and her religion are the realization and the fruition of herself, and her faith is this, that while true to herself, she can never find an enemy in the truth."

4. The Reality of Progress

The "Notes" are occupied with illustration and defence of the doctrine of the essay against the charge of self-contradiction. If there is no progress, there is no history; yet if all experience is personal, and if all personal experience is inevitably coloured by the accepted mass,[1] in fact is a subsumption under it, how is progress possible? The mass grows, but its presuppositions remain the same: as a whole it admits no change. Bradley was to be attacked on the ground that in the "block universe", of which he was supposed to be the exponent, there was no place for progress. All the more interesting is the answer he here gives to the difficulty as thus stated.

[1] The phrase is Baur's.

The objection rests on the same fallacy as the mechanical theory of knowledge: the idea, namely, that progress is by accretion instead of by the discovery of contradiction in the world of experience as it has been accepted. With the growth of experience and reflection a new world is set in the process of formation, gradually diverging from the old, and so "contradicting the unity of consciousness", which is the basis of all personal experience. The new formation may be accelerated or retarded, the discovery of the contradiction may be the result of reflection or forced upon the mind by accident, but sooner or later it is inevitable. If we ask why it is inevitable, the answer is the same. From the first our world is no mere accumulation, but "bears the character of the self, the personality, to which it is relative and without which for us it is as good as nothing". True the mind or self is actually limited. It can never succeed in fixing more than a part. But on the other hand it is "virtually unlimited" and in possession of a "potential whole" with which its part so far as fixed is in necessary contradiction and with which it can only be brought into harmony by a never-ending process of expansion and systematization.

It is this constant expansion and systematization that constitutes what we call progress, and that is the subject-matter of history. The mind, of whose work history is the record, moves forward, everywhere seeking to remove what is in contradiction to its ideal; but it is no more in contradiction with itself than with the logic which is the motive power within it. Bradley does not here raise the question of the reality of time which is bound up with that of progress, but he makes clear the kind of reality that must be assigned to progress within the world of time.

5. Philosophical Significance of the Essay

The significance of the essay in the history of English Idealism has already been referred to.[1] It is surprising that so little notice was taken of it at the time, and that it has since been left in obscurity. Negatively it meant the emancipation of philosophical criticism from subservience to apologetics, on the one hand, and from the dogmas of empiricism, on the other. Positively it meant an original

[1] "It gives the best account known to me", wrote Bosanquet in *Knowledge and Reality* (1885), "of the process by which *all* the parts of a whole can be criticized and adjusted *on the basis* of each other."

application of Kantian principles to the interpretation of the work of the mind. Bradley was to separate himself by and by from the Neo-Kantian doctrine of the supremacy of self-consciousness as the supreme principle for the interpretation of reality. But in the present essay his argument moves on the orthodox lines. While insisting on the ideal of totality as the fundamental principle of movement in the life of the mind, he as yet sees no contradiction between it and the idea of the self. This to him as containing the idea of a potential whole of experience is still the supreme category. For the rest, what has here to be noted is the early indication of the two features we have already noticed as characteristic of his thought: the determination first not to linger over the past, but, having seized the new clue, to get forward by whatever means in his power; and secondly, to test every step of his own thought by the same constant criticism that he applied to that of others, prepared to insist on what he clearly saw but ready to admit the limitations under which he saw it.

B. ETHICAL STUDIES [1]

I. An Epoch-making Book

Bosanquet has spoken of the publication of this book as "an epoch-making event",[2] not merely because of the re-statement and conclusion of the long controversy with Hedonism, but because of the wider philosophical significance of the suggestion it contained for restoring to the idea of the *noumenon* "its true Platonic meaning of that which is most fully and determinedly experienced, and superseding the ridiculous usage in which 'what is understood' has become equivalent to 'what cannot be known' ".

Moral philosophy in England was still divided between a utilitarianism that failed to do justice to the moral consciousness and a dogmatism prepared to find whatever it wanted in uncriticized "intuitions". What was required was, *first*, to carry over into ethics the revised form of Kant's theory of knowledge which by this time, thanks to Stirling, Green, and Caird in Great Britain, to Harris and his coadjutors in America, was beginning to make its way in the English-speaking world, by a fresh analysis of desire

---

[1] First Edition, 1876, Second (posthumous) Edition, 1927; quoted in notes as *E. S.*

[2] *Contemporary British Philosophy*, vol. i. p. 58. Elsewhere he tells us of a plan which he had himself entertained in these same years of writing a book on ethics, but which was "blown to the winds" by the appearance of Bradley's.

and will; *secondly*, to get beyond the dualism, which finds in the moral life nothing but the endless struggle of the individual will with recalcitrant elements in itself and the world, by showing the place of social habit and institution in the creation and maintenance of the moral order in individuals and communities; *thirdly*, as against both the Moralism to which religion consisted in devotion to an unattainable ideal supplied by the abstract reason and the Positivism which sought for a visible object of religious devotion in the idea of a collective Humanity, to vindicate the reality of a perfection, by identifying himself with which, through faith, the individual could find himself justified and at peace. It was the brilliant and detailed way in which Bradley's book met these requirements of the time that give it a place in the great line of English Moral Philosophy, and make it to this day what the *Encyclopædia Britannica* calls it, "the most readable extant book upon the subject". Unfortunately it was out of print for the last thirty years of the author's life, owing to his disinclination to republish without rewriting it.[1] Partly to this cause we may attribute the failure of a whole generation of philosophical students to assimilate and carry along with them the theory developed in it in all its depth and range. Though, owing to the recent reissue of the book, there is less reason for a detailed analysis, this lacuna and the misunderstanding it has caused of the essential features of Bradley's doctrine in his critics[2] and in some even of his would-be followers,[3] seem to justify a statement of the argument, freed from the detail with which the author was apt to overburden it.

2. SELF-REALIZATION AS THE OBJECT OF WILL

Conscious that the fundamental problem of ethics is the nature of freedom, the writer leads up to the main discussion by showing that "what we call freedom is both positive and negative. There are two questions: What am I to be free to assert? What am I

[1] This unwillingness seemed to some of his contemporaries to indicate a departure from some fundamental parts of its teaching. It is all the more interesting to find in the notes, on which he was engaged at the time of his death in view of a new edition, so little alteration in what is vital to it.

[2] *E.g.*, C. D. Broad in *Five Types of Ethical Theory*, pp. 99 and 180, who takes it as a form of Egoism.

[3] *E.g.* (I cannot but think) A. E. Taylor in his early book *The Problem of Conduct* (1901).

to be free from? And these are answered by the answer to one question—What is my true self?" To prepare the way for his own answer to this last, he gives in the second essay an analysis of desire that cuts across current theories, necessitarian and libertarian alike.[1]

While it is not true that the object of desire is always a state of the self, it is true that it must always be something with which the self is identified in idea. Desire is in fact "the feeling of our affirmation in the idea of something not ourself, felt against the feeling of ourself, as, without the object, void and negative. Action is the result of the tension of this relation which produces motion". Further, seeing that the self is not a mere collection, stream, series, or aggregate of states, but that the whole self is present in its states as the unity of them, it follows that in the idea of the object of desire there is always a reference to this totality. In a word, what we seek in desire to realize is the self, and to realize self is always to realize a whole which is not the sum of its parts, nor yet some other particular beside them.[2] For assurance of this we do not require to go to psychology or metaphysics. Take "the normal, decent, serious man", when he has been long enough in the world to know what he wants, and you will find that he has a notion of happiness, which, when examined, is seen to be "not something straggling and discontinuous, but is brought before the mind as a unity; and, if imagined more in detail, is a system where particulars subserve one whole".

But this still leaves us with the question, *What* whole? Here Kant had led the way, but Bradley, as usual, is more concerned with what he sees for himself than of his relation to Kant. What he sees is that from the side of its *form* the "will" stands to the "act", *when each is taken separately*, as the general or "abstract universal" to the abstract particular. When they are taken, as they

[1] Green was at the time developing a similar thesis in his college lectures (see *Prolegomena to Ethics*, Bk. II). The difference was that while to Green this was overtly part of a metaphysical theory of man's relation to nature, in Bradley metaphysics was as yet in abeyance, "chafing" though he already was at the restrictions imposed by his subject. See Editor's Preface to the Second Edition of *E. S.* It ought, however, to be added that the crucial pages 50–85 were left without a note. The reader may draw his own inferences. I do not myself believe that it meant that he was completely satisfied with the theory of desire as it stood, but that he was reserving it for a more complete overhauling. See below, p. 232.

[2] P. 69.

must be, together, they give the individual whole, which he had learned from Hegel to call the "concrete universal"—the whole which from one side is act, from the other will. But this only brings us back to "wholeness" of some kind as that to which we are pledged "by the nature of our own mind". To get forward, we have to return to what, as a matter of fact, we are always doing both in theory and practice. What we aim at in both of these is to find and possess our world as a whole. Science rests on the assumption that the object or not-ourself is intelligible: what it does is to alter and alter a view till it sees it as consistent, not only with itself, but with the facts. A doctrine that claims to be true "must not only hold together, but it must hold the facts together".[1] When we have got this we rest, "because we have found the nature of our own mind and the truth of facts in one". It is the same in practice *mutatis mutandis*. Here also we start with an assumption.

As in science I take for granted that the world is intelligible, so in practice "an instinct of my nature tells me that the world is mine". As in science I alter and alter my views till they are to my mind, so in practice "I alter and alter the sensuous facts till I find in them nothing but myself carried out. Then I possess my world, and I do not possess it until I find my will in it; and I do not find that until what I have is a harmony or a whole in system".

Finally, this harmony, like that of theory, is impossible unless we include all the facts: all our wants and the interests which are developed from them. "We have no right first to find out just what we happen to be and then to contract our wants to that limit. We cannot do it if we would, and morality calls to us that, if we try to do it, we are false to ourselves. Against the sensuous facts around us we must for ever attempt to widen our empire." It is in this way that we arrive at the full scope of our formula. To the injunction "to realize yourself" we have to add "realize yourself as a whole", and to that again "realize yourself as an *infinite* whole".

Bradley is aware of the trouble that awaits him with readers

[1] P. 73. The passage is particularly interesting as containing the earliest statement of what was to become the central principle of his whole philosophy, the twofold criterion of comprehensiveness and consistency. He has also begun to see that these two are really one, for he adds in a note: "I leave out of sight the important question whether any partial whole *can* be consistent. If (which seems the better view) this cannot be, we shall not need to say 'systematize and widen', but the second will be included in the first."

who here refuse "to enter the region of nonsense". But with the
clue of the Hegelian distinction of the true and false infinite in
his hands, he is prepared to show that the self is both finite and
infinite: it is finite, but it knows its finitude, and is, so far, beyond
it. It is by reason of this double essence that morality is possible,
though possible only as a perpetual progress. But he agrees that
this is a merely formal statement and does not meet the material
problem of how the self is to be completely "homogeneous and
self-contained and at the same time completely specified"[1] in the
external relation represented by our wants and interests: how I
can be so extended as to take in all my apparently external relations? The problem here raised was to recur later at a deeper level.
Meantime it is postponed by the discovery that the whole is to be
looked for, not in the private, exclusive self, but in the organism
of which the individual may become in a true sense a member,
and thereby partake of a larger and completer life—at once specifying himself in the details of his functions and remaining homogeneous with himself.

Looking back on this analysis, it is easy to see that it may be
said in some respects to have been superseded by recent developments in psychology which have emphasized on the one hand the
place in the moral life of instinct, in contrast to anything that
can rightly be called desire, and on the other hand the self-realizing
power of ideas in which, again, desire in the strict sense of the
word is absent. Bradley was himself to make ample amends on the
latter point in his own later contributions to the psychology of
conation and will,[2] in which we might say that the self-realization
of the idea of an object has taken the place of the realization of
the idea of the self in an object as the essence of will.[3] I have
already suggested that this development of his view may have
been responsible for his leaving this whole section in the preparation of the new edition without cursory notes. Be this as it may,
the change would not have affected its main teaching as to the

[1] Bradley quotes these expressions for the different sides of the ideal as
from Kant. So late as 1914 he uses the same terms for the two aspects which
are both essential in truth. See *Essays on Truth and Reality*, p. 114 *n*.
[2] See the series of articles on this subject in *Mind*, N.S., vols. x–xiii, which
deserve to be published in a separate volume.
[3] "The presence or absence of myself as an element contained in the idea",
he was to write, "can hardly be vital"; and again, on the question whether
a change in the not-self must be qualified in the idea as a change of myself,
"I cannot maintain the affirmative here" (*Mind*, N.S., vol. xii. pp. 161 and 164).

end and criterion of action. The end of moral action is always some kind of whole, corresponding to the nature of mind, and the criterion is the most comprehensive and harmonious whole that, under the conditions, is achievable.

3. SOLIDARITY OF SELF AND SOCIETY

Returning to the text, with the idea of the life that comes to a man by the specification of his functions, we come to the second of the above-mentioned tasks. Bradley prepares the way for it, at the same time confirming his results by settling accounts on the basis of it with the opposing theories of "pleasure for pleasure's" and "duty for duty's sake". Each in its own way, the one by taking the particular apart from the universal and proposing a mere sum or aggregate of pleasure as the end, the other by taking the universal apart from the particular and giving us a mere formal law, offends against the idea of the concrete whole that has to be realized in conduct. Their futility is shown by the contradiction they both are found in the end to conceal. On the pleasure theory, happiness is always and everywhere realized, and yet is shown never to be realizable. So with duty: if no particular act is prescribed, any particular act may be interpreted as duty, and the ideal is *every-where* realized; on the other hand, if to do one's duty is to obey a merely abstract law, this can never be done, and the ideal is *nowhere* realized. Yet the latter theory has the immense advantage of recognizing the reality of the universal, and it is in the correction of the abstract way in which this is conceived by Kant rather than in the total rejection of it that the true theory emerges. Bradley's chapter on "My Station and its Duties" is the most classical part of a classical book. If anything it suffers (as Bosanquet complains of the whole) from "the excess of thought and experience" which it contains,[1] and is all the more difficult on that account to condense.

We are in search of the real self not in any metaphysical sense of the term—he leaves metaphysics to the theorist who sets up

[1] If the student is in search of Bradleiana, he could easily collect a score of them in its forty pages of the type of: "what we have to do is not so much better than the world that we cannot do it", "marriage is a contract to pass out of the sphere of contract", "our private ideal, because an abstraction, is all the better fitted for our heads and all the worse fitted for actual existence".

the idol of an individual (not even an economic) man, and who
"has no right to refutation"—but in the sense of the self that
actually is. We find this in a being immeshed in relations to his
antecedents and contemporaries. "If we suppose the world of
relations, in which he was born and bred, never to have been,
then we suppose the very essence of him not to be, . . . he is what
he is, in brief, so far as he is what others also are." It is no use
replying, "Like, even exactly like, but not the same". Likeness is
for the person contemplating. *Objects* disown it. "We do not hang
one man because he is 'exactly like' another, or at least we do
not wish to do so." Nor can we say that the individual is this
individual because he is *exclusive*. If we deduct from him what he
includes, he loses the characteristics which make him himself; and
if we take what he includes, we find this to be what others also
include. He is indeed a particularization or specification, but what
he specifies or particularizes is that which is common, which is
the same amid diversity, and without which the "individual"
would be so much another than he is that we could not call him
the same.[1] Nor, lastly, can we say that this subordination to the
life without him is something to be resisted in the interest of
individuality as the "advanced thinker" would have it. What
happens to a man in the progress from childhood is, in the first
place, conversion by the discipline of mere wilfulness into the
social will, and, secondly, the widening of his world until he
apprehends through successive spheres the whole in which he lives.

If then we turn from what the individual is to what he has to
do and realize, this is not something for which he has to search
within him in any subjective ideal. It is there facing him in his
different spheres or stations, each with its duties. Even when he
seems to make his own sphere, as when he marries, he "brings
himself under a unity, which is superior to the particular person
and the impulses that belong to his single existence, and which
makes him fully as much as he makes it".

The whole passage reminds us of Carlyle's teaching on the same
head.[2] It was, indeed, just what was wanted to turn Teufelsdröckh's
prophesyings into the philosophy he wished them to be; and the
main point, as in the detailed comparison with Kant that follows,
is that the imperative of duty is "objective", not only in the
sense of being independent of this or that person, but in the sense

[1] P. 171. [2] P. 139 above.

of having outer existence in so far as it has already carried itself out and embodied itself in social institutions and traditions from the family to the nation and beyond it. What I have to do is thus not something I have "to force on a recalcitrant world", but something which in a sense the world may be said to do through me, making between us "a solid reality which is both mine and its"—something, therefore, in which my whole heart may be. I might have a better heart, and it might be a better world, but if I live up to the requirements that are awaiting me in it (including its and my own betterment) I may be "at peace with reality". If all this seems to make morality relative to situations and therefore everywhere different, we have to remember that "*unless* morality varied there could be no morality", and yet that "all morality is 'absolute' because at every stage the essence of man *is* realized, however imperfectly".

Since this essay was written the idea of the social organism has perhaps come to be overworked. Apart from this, there is much here that, owing to advances in social philosophy, would have to be stated differently. Society is a much more complicated structure than the division which Bradley, following Hegel, makes of it into family, social position, the State and a wider community would imply. It is, moreover, a mistake to suggest that personal morality consists in identification of the will with the actual moral world. Bradley himself, in a note to the second edition, warns us against taking this as more than a provisional statement.[1] But, even so, his own conservatism led him unduly to belittle the essential *unreality* of much that seems consecrated by social and economic tradition, and to quote with too little reserve Hegel's identification of "wisdom and virtue" with "living agreeably to the ethos of one's people". Unless "ethos" is understood in a deeper sense than either Hegel or Bradley had in view, and be taken to mean what is best in its own past, to live agreeably to it, however agreeable to oneself, may be the reverse of ethical.[2]

Yet, with these reservations, the main contention of this section must continue to stand as against any pluralistic (ultimately pessimistic) attempt to treat society as a mere aggregate, whether

[1] *Op. cit.*, p. 179.
[2] I may perhaps be allowed to refer to my own *German Philosophy in Relation to the War* (1915). I would merely add that what is there said of Germany is true to a large extent of the rest of the Western world. The existing ethos had been allowed to fall below the level of its own best tradition.

of individuals or of groups. The human spirit is itself a unity, and seeks to find itself, and to a large extent has already found itself, in a society which, however imperfectly it does so at present, is bound more and more to reflect that unity.

4. The Ideal Self. Religion as the Completion of Morality

Arrived at the conclusion that the true and desirable self is the social self, we might seem to have arrived at the limits of morality. In a sense we have. We are familiar with attempts both before and since to identify it with altruism in the sense of regard for the well-being of the Social Whole. Idealism, though leading the way and itself going far along this line, has never been quite satisfied with it as a definition of the full scope of the good life. There are other selves besides the social. There is that of the artist and of the inquirer. It is a man's moral duty if he has either of these in him (and who has not some portion of both?) to realize it, a moral offence to fail, and any attempt to resolve this into a duty to society seems to put an unwarrantable strain upon the facts. Bradley, at any rate, will have none of it. In the pursuit of art or science a man is social, but he is more. There may even be a conflict between a man's duty to either and to society, scarcely to be solved by the appeal to a wider or a future society, or perhaps on any universal principle, "except, of course, the universal law to do the best we can in the circumstances".[1] Be this as it may, it is not the point that Bradley aims at establishing in the rest of the book, but something that goes deeper still, seeing that it is involved in the very form of morality whatever its content.

In spite of what has been said of the actuality of the good in the world, we have in the end to recognize that neither individual nor society is a perfectly harmonious whole. "The ideal self in the world and in us realizes itself against itself." The good in it is never made wholly real, the bad wholly unreal, and morality lives in the conflict between them. To end this would be to end itself. "Morality", in a word, "aims at the cessation of that which makes it possible; it is the effort after non-morality, and it presses forward beyond itself to a super-moral sphere where it ceases as such to

---

[1] Cursory note on p. 157, in connection with the general problem of conflicting imperatives. Even this would not be quite satisfactory in the present case as a final law. We still ask the best for what?

exist."[1] The reader familiar with Bradley's later work knows the fate that awaits everything, however exalted, which can be shown to harbour such a contradiction in its heart. The difference between the doctrine here already in germ and the fully developed form it afterwards assumed is the measure of the distance he had travelled in the interval.

After a chapter and a half of ἀπορίαι packed with suggestion, he returns to the problem here set, and meets it with an appeal to the Hegelian principle that to feel a contradiction is, *ipso facto*, to be beyond it. "Unless man was and divined himself to be a whole, he could not feel the contradiction, still less feel pain in it, and reject it as foreign to his real nature." But so to reject it is one thing, to escape from it is another. Yet this also is possible owing to his power to unite himself in thought and will (he must do both) with the whole which in morality he fain would but cannot be. Such a union we have in religion, which is just this sense of oneness with a whole or perfection which both is not and which *is* ourselves. In this way religion gives us what morality cannot give in the consciousness that "God and man are identical in a subject". It is this atonement or reconciliation to which we must come if we mean to follow the facts of religious consciousness. It involves faith in a sense in which the social consciousness does not. In social ethics there is what might be called sight. To religion the reality of the ideal is out of sight. But it is no mere intellectual belief. "In faith we do not rise to an idea and leave our will somewhere else behind. If will has ceased, faith has ceased." Nor is it "the desperate leap of a moment", but something which works continually in us and with which we work.[2] Nor, finally, has religion anything different for its content. "For religion and morality the content of the will is the same, though the knowledge and the spirit are widely different."[3]

[1] P. 235. He was afterwards to apply this to the whole field of practice which he conceives of as straining to identify itself with theoretic and æsthetic perfection and therein ceasing to be itself. See *A. and R.*, p. 160. In the note to the second edition upon the above quoted passage he goes so far as to admit that "in and through morality" this ideal is "to some extent realized in the goodness that has become a 'natural instinct' and is admired more than the strictly 'moral'"—an instance of the more positive bent of his thought in the period succeeding *A. and R.*
[2] P. 341.
[3] He was to write more fully on the nature of Faith in the *Essays on Truth and Reality*.

C. MR. SIDGWICK'S HEDONISM [1]

I. THE METHODS OF ETHICS

In *Ethical Studies* Bradley had attacked hedonism, while the popular textbook of the doctrine was still Mill's *Utilitarianism*, written fifteen years before.[2] He had urged that it was irreconcilable with morality; that the conception of pleasure as an end was illusory; that the Good must be a whole, and that this a sum of pleasures cannot be; that "my pleasure" gives no rule of life, while the pleasure of all is impossible of realization; that Mill's distinction of higher and lower pleasures has no meaning unless we go outside pleasure and bring in forms of life: *i.e.*, unless we give up the doctrine; with the conclusion that "hedonism is bankrupt". But even while Bradley was writing its doom, Professor Henry Sidgwick was preparing to publish his *Methods of Ethics*,[3] in which it was treated not only as a going concern, but as the only concern that had any chance of going, if there was to be a Science of Ethics at all.

The author was one of the acutest minds that the University of Cambridge had produced for a generation, and by his scholarship, the singular attractiveness of his character, and his power as a thinker, was already beginning to exercise a dominating influence over the younger men. His courage was equal to his learning, and showed itself in his readiness to subject the prejudices and pre-suppositions of current orthodoxies to unsparing criticism. But his own training had been in the methods of British empiricism, with its leaning to pluralism in metaphysics, utilitarianism in ethics, and individualism in politics. What he sought, therefore, in this book to do was not to revolutionize the method of his predecessors in this line of thought, but, by contrasting it with other methods and freeing previous applications of it from obscurity and error, to give it more accurate formulation. While accepting, therefore, the main principles of Mill's essay, he sought to fortify them, first, by recognizing, in the spirit of Butler and Clarke, a faculty of reason which informs us of what is intrinsically good and desirable, while leaving us free to choose or reject it; secondly, by correcting Mill's errors in supposing that pleasure was the only possible object

[1] *An Examination of the Main Argument of the Methods of Ethics*, London, 1877; the length of the time it has been out of print may perhaps excuse the length of this reference to it.
[2] For *Fraser's Magazine*; reprinted as a separate volume 1863.
[3] London, 1874.

of desire, and that there may be different qualities in pleasure; finally, by indicating the view as to the moral government of the world as pledged to the reward of virtue and the punishment of evil that seemed to be required in order that there may be a reconciliation between the apparently equally rational principles of egoism and altruism.

Although Bradley's essay in *Ethical Studies* upon "Pleasure for Pleasure's Sake" had been written, as he tells us, before the appearance of *The Methods of Ethics*, it was not yet in print. The reputation that Sidgwick's book[1] had meantime acquired impressed him with the necessity of an immediate reply, and he added the long note at the end of the essay to prove that, in spite of the opinion of many, Sidgwick "had left the question exactly where he had found it. . . . Ostensibly critical, the work goes throughout upon presuppositions, which are not only not discussed but which are not even made explicit": first and foremost the presupposition that there is such a thing as a mere individual, as shown in the appeal to a hypothetical "single sentient conscious being" inhabiting the universe in solitude in proof of the doctrine that pleasure is the only thing intrinsically desirable. To set up an unimaginable and inhuman predicament, so far from being, as the author supposes, good common sense, is simply bad metaphysics. It is to effect the conversion and suppress the egoist in this supposititious being that he introduces the further supposition of a desire for the right and reasonable as such; but to the egoist who knows his case these are mere words. To him there is no distinction between what he actually desires and what is desirable, and if he allows himself to be suppressed by iteration of the words, he deserves his fate. But Bradley felt himself hampered on what seemed to him so vital a matter by want of space, and in the following year published the small book which bears the above title.

After a tribute to Sidgwick's book as one that had done more "to stimulate ethical speculation among us and in more senses than one to point to a reform in our moral philosophy" than any that had been published for years, he notes its failure to take account of "the views most opposed to traditional English doctrine" —in other words, those for which Green, himself, and others stood. He believes that this failure has been "at least one cause of the

[1] A second edition appeared the next year; by 1901 it had reached its sixth edition.

uncertain handling of leading conceptions and the confusion of the result",[1] and devotes himself to bringing out the depth of this confusion. If Sidgwick's main argument is a ruin to-day,[2] it is to this little book more than to any other that we must go for the logic that has sapped its foundations. Having served its purpose, it might perhaps be allowed to sink into the oblivion that has overtaken it but for the further light it throws on this phase of Bradley's own philosophical development. For those who like polemics it has the additional interest of showing better than any of Bradley's writings—indeed, alone among them—what these could be in his hands.

2. BRADLEY'S POLEMIC

In the first section, which is concerned with "Definitions", it is pointed out that "the audacious *petitio principii* which commended itself to Mr. Mill" whereby "desirable" is taken indifferently to mean "what I like" and "what I ought to like" remains uncorrected, if more veiled, in Sidgwick. On the other hand, his proposed correction of Mill's doctrine of differences in the quality of pleasure involves him in the deeper error of supposing that feeling as feeling can be taken in abstraction from its object and its pleasantness from the other characters of feeling. This enables him, doubtless, to return to the idea of a quantitative measurement, but only to involve himself in the difficulties with which the idea of "the greatest possible sum of happiness" is beset, as pressed by his critic in *Ethical Studies*.[3]

In the second section, on "The Argument", Bradley shows that it is the difficulties raised by what he has already said on the futility of appealing against the egoist to the "rules of equity and benevolence" that drive Sidgwick in the end to admit that egoism itself is reasonable. Seeing that selfishness therefore requires to be somehow reconciled with morality, Sidgwick is at his wit's end for the means of performing this miracle.

Leaving this for discussion under the head of "The Final Difficulty", the writer goes on in the third section to criticize Sidgwick's view of Ethical Science as a "complete method of determining

[1] *Op. cit.*, p. 59.
[2] As even his greatest admirers admit. See Broad, *op. cit.*, Chap. VI.
[3] P. 89 and note.

right conduct", bearing the same relation to common-sense morality as the technical methods of science bear to ordinary practice.[1] Here he is content to let the ironical logic of this attempt to rehabilitate casuistry in the tattered garment of utilitarianism develop itself in the author's own words.

There is to be a "code", and this has to be made as complete as possible by the inclusion not only of the circumstances of the act, but of the natures and characters of individual agents. Nevertheless, it will not be possible to exclude exceptional cases, where a man may claim to judge for himself and to disregard the code in the belief that his action is not likely to be widely imitated. But if he acts openly, he can never be sure that he will not be setting a bad example. His best resource will, therefore, be secrecy. Hence Utilitarian principles must be ready to admit that "an act may be right if it can be done with perfect secrecy, otherwise not".[2] But as this opinion is manifestly at issue with common sense (for the very notion of the latter involves the repudiation of an esoteric morality), the utilitarian conclusion, carefully stated, would seem to be this: that the opinion that secrecy may render an action right, which would not otherwise be so, should itself be kept comparatively secret; and similarly it seems expedient that the doctrine that esoteric morality is expedient should itself be kept esoteric. It is in this way we are brought to the discovery that "The Romanist view of the 'economy' to be observed in the distribution of truth seems to be strictly in harmony with Utilitarian principles".

Sidgwick holds, indeed, that in an ideal community of enlightened utilitarians this swarm of puzzles and paradoxes would vanish, and if he really believes that a time is coming when the community will be so enlightened as not merely to have and to have mastered this complete code, but to be able by private judgment to bring each action under the fitting clause, Bradley is prepared to withdraw his objections. But he leaves it to the reader in that case to judge "whether argument is any longer possible; whether we are not in the realm of fiction and apocalyptic literature; whether, after having enptied the contents of each human being into this monstrous code, Mr. Sidgwick has not been forced to postulate something like omniscience in 'the individuality of

[1] See *Methods of Ethics*, First Edition, pp. 217 and 396. With what follows should be compared the onslaught on Casuistry in *Principles of Logic*, pp. 247-8, First Edition.
[2] *Op. cit.*, p. 452.

the individuals' which is left to execute it".[1] If, on the other hand, this is not his view, and he holds that the relative distinction of the "enlightened" and the "vulgar" may or must continue, then "is it not moral for anyone who likes to call himself a moralist to use and act upon his private judgment as to the means that will produce the maximum of pleasure in any and every case in which he chooses to do so? And has not the result proved mere individualism and the 'objective' criterion turned out subjective?"

Bradley has no objections to a hedonistic art of life as it may be used by a man of practical good sense, but he will not be responsible for what is likely to happen "if men with no sense nor hold on real life but gifted with a logical faculty" begin to make deductions from this "slippery principle".[2]

Having arrived at the conclusion that it is reasonable to seek both one's own maximum pleasure and that of the whole creation, if the Universe is not to be judged fundamentally irrational and morally chaotic, it becomes a matter of life and death to Sidgwick's Practical Reason to show that morality is the only true selfishness. But this cannot be shown from the internal nature of either. What then remains? We turn to the last few pages of the *Methods of Ethics*: "Surely, surely it is our old friend the *Deus ex machina*, and anxiously we sit awaiting him: the crisis is at hand, the actors are at a deadlock, and we on the stretch. Vain expectation, for the days of Paley are gone by. The machine has grown old, and the God will not come to the front, and the stage is in confusion, and the curtain falls hurriedly in the middle of the fifth act."

3. THE REAL PROBLEM RAISED BY SIDGWICK AND BRADLEY'S ANSWER TO IT

Yet Bradley admits that there is a real problem raised by the fact that man is not happy according as he is virtuous, and that he

[1] P. 46.

[2] Still less does he deny that deductions may be usefully made from a less slippery principle. All that he contends is that it is not the business of Ethics to make them. For him the question of Ethics is not how to turn rules into practice, still less to alter the facts of morality to suit abstract rules, but "solely: Is moral science true? Has it or has it not succeeded in understanding the facts of morality?" (*Ethical Studies*, First Edition, p. 143.) This view is therefore untouched by Rashdall's attempt to rehabilitate Casuistry in *Theory of Good and Evil*, vol. ii. pp. 421 foll.

ought to be so, because he deserves to be so; and in one of those passages which, in Bosanquet's phrase, seem overweighted with thought, he goes on to give his own suggestion for an answer. It is that the law, if it is a law, that virtue should be rewarded and wickedness punished cannot be the highest. There is only one supreme law: "Realize the greatest amount not of pleasure, but of Good." If there is a law in society to reward virtue and punish wickedness, this is justified only on the ground that in this way the greatest good will be furthered. But no rational society tries to go by an absolute law of rewards and punishments. All communities, for instance, exercise the right of pardon, and they do so because they rightly believe that justice is not the highest moral law. He does not quote *summum jus summa injuria*, but he is prepared to argue that not only in inflicting punishment but in conferring rewards more harm than good may be done. Even although the law were more absolute in society than it anywhere is, the analogy would not necessarily hold for the Universe. Here we do not know the conditions, and we have no means of judging. Yet we can put a question: "Supposing that in all cases the self-realization of each man as such were proportionate to the identification of his will with the will of the whole, would the will of the whole system be more intensely realized in fuller individuals?" Bradley answers: "I do not see how any man is to say Yes. The merely moral consciousness cannot pronounce here". But if we bring in religion, we may get some light. For "it does seem that the notion of claiming reward for our merits and standing on our rights with God is a pre-Christian point of view. I had almost said an anachronism".

While the essay gave a new idea of the power of the Neo-Kantian principle of self-realization as an instrument of criticism, "a new, sharp, threshing instrument with teeth",[1] it did not add materially to the teaching of the *Ethical Studies* on this head. The only difference is that while, in the latter, the abstractness of the "mere moral consciousness" is brought home from the side of the conflict between the ideal and the actual in the individual life, here it is brought home from the conflict between social justice and what we have to suppose the higher law holding in the scheme of the

[1] Isaiah xli. 15.

universe.[1] In both religion, with the deeper self-consciousness on which it rests, is appealed to as containing the solution. In neither is there as yet any hint that religion also may be founded on abstraction and fail of the truth.

SUMMARY OF FIRST PHASE OF BRADLEY'S THOUGHT

Taking these three early essays together, they may be said, as Bradley himself put it,[2] to have contained nothing that had not been before the world for years and been calling either for admission or refutation. Some things, indeed, were left obscure. Besides the points already mentioned, there is in reference to the central doctrine of the social organism a certain hesitation and consequent ambiguity in the treatment of the idea of Humanity. In more than one passage[3] this is taken to stand for a mere collection—an abstract universal lying outside the "spheres" with which morality has to do, at best as a possibility of the future ("humanity may *become* an organic whole"). On the other hand, it seems to be demanded by Bradley's own view of the relation between ideal and reality that in some sense at least the ideal is already realized. But the general agreement with Neo-Kantian ideas is clear. Together with the *Essays in Philosophical Criticism*, Green's *Prolegomena to Ethics*, and Wallace's translations from Hegel, these essays went to form the foundation of the idealist literature that was to follow. At the time it may be said that no one suspected Bradley's book of containing any other leaven. Yet for us, looking back with his later work before us, it is possible to see the beginning of the cleavage. We can see his own thought beginning to work into clearness both as to the nature and as to the implications of what he conceived of as the fundamental principle of a true idealism.

With all the great philosophers from Plato to Hegel, Bradley had come to the conviction that the world is a hierarchy of higher and lower forms of reality and value. Further, while "into the definition of perfection mere size does not enter at all", yet, if quantity is not to be considered at all, "why", he asks, "is the

---

[1] The hint given as to the subordinate place of distributive justice in that scheme was by and by to be developed by Bosanquet in the well-known chapter in his Gifford Lectures on the *Value and Destiny of the Individual*, entitled "The World of Claims and Counterclaims".

[2] *Ethical Studies*, p. 323 n.   [3] See, *e.g.*, *Ethical Studies*, pp. 232 and 343.

more inclusive position the higher?"[1] And he proceeds to give an answer to the problem thus raised into which it is possible to read the whole of his later thought. "I know of no answer but this, that the perfect is that in which we can rest without contradiction, that the lower is such because it contradicts itself, and so is forced to advance beyond itself to another stage, which is the solution of the contradiction that existed in the lower and so a relative perfection. . . . And this is the reason why the advance consists in greater specification and more intense homogeneity, and therefore to a certain extent may be measured by quantity. On this view, the higher is above the lower, not because it contains a larger number of units, but because it is the harmony of those elements which in the lower were a standing contradiction." This conclusion he asks the reader to take not as a positive doctrine, but merely as a matter for his reflection.

That he was himself beginning to reflect upon it and upon its bearing on the fundamental question of the relation of subject and object in self-conscious experience is plain from the note[2] in which he calls attention to the present "position of our philosophy" with regard to it. He traces the steps by which the ordinary dualism of subject and object advances by its own logic, *first*, to the attempt to unite them in a third, which is neither, but an unknowable Beyond; *next*, to the recognition of an Identity of the two which yet is not mind; *finally*, to the question how, "if it is in and for mind, it can be a whole which is not mind and in which the mind is only a part or element? . . . If we know the whole, it can only be because the whole knows itself in us, because the whole is self or mind, which is and knows, knows and is, the identity and correlation and subject and object".

English thought, Bradley holds, had been unwillingly forced on from the admission of identity of outer and inner to consider the claim of "mind or self in some sense" to be this identity, and "it is time that this conclusion should be admitted or refuted". He has hitherto himself shown no sign of any desire to refute it. But he is clearly beginning to have doubts, and he ends the note enigmatically: "Perhaps not that; but if not that, then I think we must begin on a fresh basis, or else give up the attempt to have any theory of first principles."

It is in this passage, even more than the one to which the Editor

[1] *Op. cit.*, p. 249.   [2] P. 323 (First Edition).

of the Second Edition refers in his Preface, that makes one feel, as he says, that Bradley is "already chafing at the limits imposed by his subject". But, as though he was as yet uncertain as to his ground, it is logic and not metaphysics to which for the present he turns. It is only when similar doubts are forced upon him by a reconsideration, in the light of recent advances, of the first principles of thought that he finds himself driven "to be in earnest with metaphysics" and to give himself up to it.[1]

[1] *A. and R.*, p. 452.

CHAPTER VI

BRADLEY (ii). REORIENTATION

1. THE PRINCIPLES OF LOGIC[1]

On the place of Bradley's second important book in the development of logical doctrine in England there can be no question. British contributions to the science in the nineteenth century, as represented especially by Mill and Jevons, make a notable chapter in its history, the value of which does not diminish with time. But in these years the principles on which they were founded had been sapped by the general advance of thought and called loudly for revision. In Mill's inference from "particulars" there was the attempt to work on a basis of mere similarity without sameness; in Jevons's "logic of identity" the attempt to work with mere sameness without difference. In the one case all inference is analogy, in the other it is tautology. Lotze and Sigwart, on the Continent, had led the way to a revision, and by this time, as Bradley put it, the whole subject was in motion. He himself expresses his debt to both, and especially to Lotze. But the work of these writers was only beginning to be known in England,[2] and, in logic as in ethics, Bradley found himself "confronted with a mass of prejudice",[3] to succeed in shaking which by "bringing uneasiness to one self-satisfied reader" seemed to him to be a service. As a matter of fact, his work, as in the case of the *Ethical Studies*, had significance, not only as putting an end to old controversies,[4] but as raising a fundamental issue in philosophy and containing the first hint of the direction in which he himself was to seek for a decision upon it.

It is this wider issue with which we are here chiefly concerned. Its nature, and the particular way in which it came to be raised, will best be seen if, neglecting as far as possible the details of his logical analysis, we try to follow the movement of his thought with regard to the adequacy of the principle which in the main had hitherto guided him. We shall ask, *first*, whether in general there is any conscious movement away from that principle;

[1] See above p. 219; referred to below as *P. of L.*
[2] See p. 181 above. The translation of Sigwart's *Logic* (Helen Dendy, afterwards Bosanquet) did not appear till 1895.
[3] *Op. cit.*, Preface, p. x.
[4] See especially Bk. II. Pt. II. ch. i., "The Theory of Association of Ideas" •

secondly, what it was that, in spite of a general adhesion to it, seems to have roused Bradley's suspicions with regard to current applications of it; *thirdly*, whether there are hints of something deeper than was at the time suspected by his critics working towards a new orientation of his thought.

2. THE TWO VOICES

The principle that had hitherto guided him was, as we have seen, the implication in human knowledge and conduct of the idea of a perfected wholeness or individuality of content which mind and will seek by consistent effort to appropriate.[1] With this it seems clear Bradley had no intention of breaking. Wherever in the course of his logical analysis he allows his thought to play round the central principle that guides him, it is to this that he returns. "There has come to us here," he writes,[2] "shut up within these poor logical confines and pondering on the union of two abstract functions, a vision of absolute consummation. In this identity of analysis and synthesis we recognize an appearance of our soul's ideal, which in other shapes and other spheres has perplexed and gladdened us; but which, however it appear in Metaphysics, or Ethics or Religion, or Æsthetics, is at bottom the notion of a perfected individuality." As in conduct self-realization means a process motived by the ideal of a completely unified system of relations driving the will "by all means to enlarge its domain", so, in knowledge, "The striving for perfection, the desire of the mind for an infinite totality, is the impulse which moves our intellect to appropriate everything which it is not forced off."[3] In the face of a suggestion coming from experience for the extension of our knowledge, we have a process "which does not seem to fall under any previous process, but, on the contrary, to be at the root of all our reasoning. On the negative side, you may give it the form of 'I must because I cannot otherwise', and you may reduce every form of inference to this form. But on its positive side, and that is the truest, you may state it as 'I must *so*, because I will *somehow*' ".[4]

It is in this way, as he elsewhere expresses it (in contrast to the

[1] See what Bosanquet says of this principle as it appears in *The Presuppositions* (p. 227 *n*. above). He notes in the same passage how the same principle reappears in *E. S.*
[2] *P. of L.*, Bk. III. Pt. I. ch. vi. § 30.   [3] *Ibid.*
[4] *Loc. cit.*, § 31.

theory that would reduce inference to association of ideas founded on habit, and brings in the content from a world without), that the content appears as "that natural outcome of our inmost constitution, which satisfies us because it is our own selves".[1] He goes on to identify this movement with the Dialectical Method, which, while acknowledging the "most fruitful results" that it produced in Hegel's hands, he proceeds to state in a "simpler" form in order to avoid the difficulties, which, as implying the identity of opposites, it there seemed to involve.[2] Whatever be the truth as to the interpretation he here puts on Hegel's use of the method,[3] it is clear that he has no intention of breaking with the central tradition of idealism or with the principle that underlies the Hegelian form of it.

On such a view we should have expected to find the emphasis throughout on the concrete nature of thought as the process whereby the defects of what is merely given in perception are supplemented in the more comprehensive and unified idea of the underlying reality which the impulse to self-completion demands. It is true that thought moves to its end through a division between subject and predicate, being or reality and the characters it possesses, and that hypothesis or ideal experiment is a necessary part of the process. But neither in the division (the *Urtheil*) of judgment nor in the adventure of hypothesis does thought ever move away from its concrete basis in fact. In the copula judgment asserts this basis; hypothesis, as contrasted with mere guess or supposal, is never in the air, but moves on the solid ground of existing conditions; it comes out of the facts and returns to them. Even error is never wholly without its basis in fact, never *sheer* error. All this, with its general corollary that reality is *for us* such as our judgments have made, and as they sustain it,[4] we might have expected from the book, and we are not wholly disappointed. We get a great deal more of it than from any previous English writer on logic. In its central doctrine that reality cannot be a

---

[1] Bk. III. Pt. I. ch. ii. § 19.

[2] His own statement represents both the given reality and the supplement "forefelt in the mind", which is necessary to complete it, as *positive*.

[3] In a note in the second edition he refers to McTaggart's work and the possibility of another interpretation.

[4] See Bosanquet's *Knowledge and Reality, A Criticism of Mr. F. H. Bradley's Principles of Logic* (1885), p. 47. The italics are mine, but the qualification as it stands in Bradley ought to have been taken as an early warning against the common misunderstanding that idealism teaches the dependence of reality on our judgments.

predicate because it is the subject of all judgment (emphasized probably, as Bosanquet suggests, as a criticism of Lotze's view that "real" is an adjectival or predicative conception), we might seem to have the whole thing in a nutshell. The idea in the predicate —not of course as a psychological entity but as a logical meaning— is in the very act of judgment affirmed to *be* fact.

It is all the more surprising to find the opposite view more and more coming to the front as the analysis proceeds. Concreteness seems more and more to fall to the side of that which is given in immediate perception, and the forms of thought to fade into abstractions and artificial constructions of the mind. We try in judgment to get right down to fact, but we are always left with an artificial extract, a fragment, got by mutilating facts. Categorical judgments, which are defined as those which affirm existence of the subject, may be an exception, but in hypothetical judgments (and all truly universal judgments are hypothetical) we are left with abstractions. What is true of judgment is, *a fortiori*, true of inference: "Begotten of falsehood, it cannot so far be misbegotten as to show us in the end the features of fact."[1]

The eloquence with which Bradley develops this thesis, and the fury, with which in the light of it he sweeps aside not only the Hegelian doctrine of the identity of thought and reality, but the Platonic suggestion that "our sensuous presentation may be mis-representation that cannot give fact", are well known from the passage which is perhaps the most frequently quoted in modern idealistic literature. "That the glory of this world in the end is appearance, leaves the world more glorious, if we feel it is a show of some fuller glory; but the sensuous curtain is a deception and a cheat, if it hides some colourless movement of atoms, some spectral woof of impalpable abstractions, or unearthly ballet of bloodless categories. Though dragged to such conclusions, we cannot embrace them. Our principles may be true, but they are not reality. They no more *make* that Whole which commands our devotion than some shredded dissection of human tatters *is* that warm and breathing beauty of flesh which our hearts found delightful."

3. WHENCE DO THEY COME?

What does this seeming change of front mean? Where does it come

---

[1] Bk. III. Pt. II. ch. iv. §§ 7 foll.

from? To what is it leading him? It is not surprising that even the most sympathetic and understanding of his readers were puzzled at the apparent backsliding. "If I have read Mr. Bradley right", Bosanquet wrote,[1] "he joins a thorough understanding of the ideal of knowledge to a peculiar impatience of something, I do not quite know what, in the ordinary doctrine of relativity." It was only natural that the critic should suspect the author of playing fast and loose with a double standard—on the one hand, that of a stable intellectual construction; on the other, that of correspondence with sense-given fact: "It was well done, in my judgment, to invest Perception with the pre-eminent importance of being the one point in which we have direct contact with reality, and to give this contact with reality the decisive position in the activity of judgment. It is one thing, however, to recognize the actual differences of elements in a whole; another to establish two centres for the world of reality. You cannot at once treat reality as ideal construction, and demand from it characteristics approaching to those of presence in the sensible series."[2] Bosanquet attributes the apparent vacillation to Bradley's having attached himself to a perplexing extent to the "writers of the German reaction",[3] and goes on in a passage which, though less familiar than the corresponding passage in Bradley, is hardly less eloquent: "The dream of the intellectual world as a land of shadows now below and now above, now more obscure and now more brilliant than reality, a dream which the unwisdom of ages has ascribed to Plato, seems never to lose its maleficent spell. There have been some who have hoped that the labour of centuries had in part overcome this baleful enchantment, and attained the lesson that reality alike for feeling and for intellect is the world in which we live; a world which is sustained and transformed by the patient labour of the intellect and will, but can only be maimed and degraded by the impatience which splits it into a shadow on the one hand, and on the other hand a substance

---

[1] *Op. cit.*, p. 332. *Cp. Mind* of the same date, p. 257. "I am unable to decide whether the bitter words 'mutilation', 'garbled extract', 'not the fact', which are hurled at scientific truth, are ascribed with savage irony to the supposed believer in sense-presentation as the only fact, or at times sincerely come from the author's heart."
[2] *Op. cit.*, p. 17. The Neo-Kantian position could not be more clearly stated.
[3] He elsewhere speaks of Lotze as having gone as far in the right direction as was possible to one "who had not the root of the matter in him". The fact that this book is out of print and difficult to come by will perhaps excuse the length of these quotations from it.

more shadowy still. Surely the more glorious reality is that which our vision and our will can make of the world in which we are; and the certain frustration of all such achievement is to relax the grasp which holds real and ideal in one."[1] Bosanquet's book is a detailed criticism of the logical doctrines of the *Principles*. Its own principle is developed in the first chapter, which attacks Bradley's attempt to draw a hard and fast distinction between categorical and hypothetical judgments on the ground that the former attributes present reality to the subject. Vital as Bosanquet's criticism on this head is, there is the less need of dwelling on it here, as it was wholeheartedly accepted in after days by Bradley. "These distinctions", he writes in the second edition of the *Principles*,[2] "are all in the end untenable. See Bosanquet, *Knowledge and Reality*, Chapter I. All judgments are without exception conditional." What here concerns us is the question whether Bosanquet's intervention was to draw Bradley back into the orthodox Neo-Kantian fold, or whether there was something already in his mind, some "lingering scruple", as he himself expresses it, that still deterred him, and if so, what it was.

4. HINTS OF NEW DEPARTURE

With Bradley's later work before him, the present-day reader will find little difficulty in finding the answer to this question. But *Appearance and Reality* had not yet been written, and it was by no means so easy in those days to perceive the inner drift of his thought. Even Bosanquet seems to have failed to catch it. In the one allusion in his book to the place which is assigned by Bradley to *feeling* he seems only to find in it one of the motives driving him in the direction of " dualism".[3]

To us, looking back, it is possible to see more in it than this. Yet the passage which is decisive upon the whole matter is not without its difficulty, due, as so often in Bradley, to the weight of thought with which it is loaded, and both on this ground and

---

[1] *Op. cit.*, pp. 19 and 20. [2] Vol. i. p. 208.
[3] *Op. cit.*, p. 18. "The author has true and just sympathy for the claims of feeling as contrasted with intellect, or at least not identical with intellect, and therefore cherishes a deep discontent with any effort to resolve reality into an intellectual movement. Only a rich man may wear a bad coat, and only a philosopher of Mr. Bradley's force could escape suspicion of a crude dualistic realism."

because it gives us the first word of the real direction in which his
thought at this time was moving may be worth dwelling upon.

He puts the problem in the form of a dilemma. On the one hand
we seem to have an instinct which tells us that there is a correspondence of truth with fact; on the other hand we have discovered that truth is the work of the intellect, and that this leaves
us with abstractions, which are merely "an essence distilled from
our senses' abundance", and remote from fact. Can we give up
either? At the stage at which we have arrived we cannot give up
the latter without stultifying our whole argument. But perhaps
the former may be more amenable. True, it appeals to an instinct;
but instincts, if they cannot err, may be misinterpreted, and this
in the present case, in spite of the subtle philosophical attempts
that have been made to justify the interpretation in question,
Bradley suggests may have happened. He doubts "whether truth,
if that stands for the work of the intellect, is ever *precisely* identical
with fact, or claims in the end to possess such identity".[1] True,
reason may urge that what is not intelligible is nothing, and to
this it might be difficult to find an intelligible reply. But "perhaps
it may stand with the philosopher's reason as it stood with the
sculptor who moulded the lion. When in the reason's philosophy
the rational appears dominant and sole possessor of the world, we
can only wonder what place would be left to it if the element
excluded might break through the charm of the magic circle and,
without growing rational, could find expression. Such an idea may
be senseless, and such a thought may contradict itself, but it serves
to give voice to an obstinate instinct. Unless thought stands for
something that falls beyond mere intelligence, if 'thinking' is not
used with some strange implication that never was part of the
meaning of the word, a lingering scruple still forbids us to believe
that reality can be purely rational". It is in the further development of this idea that the more famous passage above quoted
occurs. Taken in its context, and still more in the larger context
of Bradley's philosophy as a whole, it points clearly enough to one
or two things with regard to the stage his thought had here reached.

First, diverted though he likely enough had been by the "Germans
of the reaction" from the lines of the Neo-Kantian theory of
inference, this was rather the psychological origin in his mind than

---

[1] P. 590. The italics are not in the text, but we gather from the 1922 note
(vol. ii. p. 595) that Bradley wishes they had been.

the logical ground of the doubt as to the identity of truth and reality. The doubt had a deeper source in the suspicion that truth as revealed to the reason and expressed in its terms, *real* truth though it might be, could not be the *whole* of reality. *Secondly*, and going deeper, this *whole*, if it were to "break through"—in other words, if it were experienced—might have the effect, to say the least of it, of making the reason and its results look foolish. *Thirdly*, this conclusion, while doing justice to the real claims of instinct and common sense, is not intended to support a double standard. Sense-perception may be as provisional a resting-place as rational thought. What may break through, to use his own simile, is not the raw material of the artist's lion, but a life which is deeper than both matter of perception and form of thought. *Finally*, it is more than likely that the full bearing of this suggestion was still very imperfectly realized by Bradley himself. What the difficulties, in which his logical theory had involved him, were already beginning to make clear to him, was the impossibility at the same time of being in earnest about logic and playing fast and loose with meta-physical assumptions; of accepting from common sense an uncritical theory of reality and trying upon the basis of it to work out any-thing that could satisfy the demands of logical theory. On these lines there was imminent danger that common sense would be robbed of its conviction that to think was to come to closer grips with reality; while logical theory would be robbed of its belief in the validity of the process it spent its life-blood in analysing. Whether in trying to amend this defect he would be led back to the foundations on which he had worked in his earlier books or forward from them to something else, was perhaps not yet clear to himself. What was beginning to be clear, and what Bosanquet's intervention must have made clearer still, was that the attempt must be made.

Meantime, and in justification of Neo-Kantian criticisms of the book like that of Bosanquet, even when it is read in the light of the above explanation, it is permissible to suspect the tone of

[1] In a note to Chapter IV (Second Edition, p. 591), Bradley frankly admits that "the attempt made at times in this work for the sake of convenience to identify reality with the series of facts, and truth with copying", was misjudged, and calls attention to a number of passages in which he gave the reader sufficient warning that he did not accept this view. None of them perhaps is very convincing, and readers, being what they are, could hardly be expected to read *between* his lines when there was so much to read *in* them.

depreciation of the work of thought into which Bradley had allowed himself to be betrayed. Granted that there are phases of reality that lie outside the relational system represented by our thought, and are liable to break through the limits of thought's "magic circle", it is still a part of that magic that, while it starts from the sense-datum as the controlling centre of its radii, these radii with the circumference they demark are ever-extending lines, and, if they cannot be said to create the world of sense, feeling, and action that come within them, are able to mould it to ever truer forms. If, as Bradley was afterwards to insist, there are degrees of reality in the forms of experience, where but in the degree of inner order and harmony whose name is reason or λόγος is the criterion to be sought?

5. Dioscuri

Besides marking the first stage of his divergence from the Neo-Kantian tradition, the publication of the *Logic* was significant as the first meeting in print of two writers, whose work henceforth was so to dovetail the one into the other that they "might almost be regarded as one person",[1] and who between them were to give a new stamp to the idealist philosophy of the time. It is interesting that the first contact was more like a clash, which through the more fundamental agreement and the generosity of both was turned into an enduring partnership. Notable and unique though this partnership was, the contrast both between the circumstances of their lives and their philosophical personalities was not less notable: The elder already more or less of a recluse to those outside his own family and his college; haunted by visions of unattainable perfections, with an ear to "promptings" coming from regions deeper than his "instincts", "obstinate questionings" that refuse to be content with any "cheap and easy monism"; determined to swear by the words of no master or formula, of whose meaning he was not perfectly assured by seeing it carried out in satisfying detail; hence sceptical on principle, inquiring and exploring to the end, not as to what people about him were thinking, but as to where his own deeper thought was leading him; declaring the relativity of all that others took for absolute, the absoluteness of what they took for relative; setting out his argument in a style

[1] J. S. Mackenzie in *Mind*, April 1928, p. 235.

which, while it often leaves his reader in doubt as to whether he is speaking of his own actual thought or merely experimenting with a possible thought, yet sentence by sentence is crystal clear. The younger, mixing freely with all sorts and conditions of men both in town and country, leaving college life in Oxford early for the larger life of London; distrusting instincts and intuitions, as too often the promptings of one's own inertia, and believing in "the patient labour of the intellect and will" as the best guides, which "Nature or Deity" has provided, to lead us into all truth about ourselves and the world; equally with the other determined to think for himself, but with a loyal desire to found himself on the deeper insights of the older masters, Plato, Hegel, Green, Bradley himself; and carry them on with him as guides in dealing with new problems; believing in progress, but believing also that it was possible only on the basis of actually assured results; a believer also, not less than Bradley, in the Absolute, but refusing to think of it as an unknown, incomprehensible Beyond, instead of as that which is in reality the most known, and the touchstone of all that was best in ourselves, the expanding, uniting, harmonizing, redeeming force in human life; ready therefore, if not to preach (though even this was not all foolishness to Bosanquet), yet to carry such light as seemed to be given him into every field: art, morals, private charity, social propaganda, politics, the Church of the future, and everywhere to challenge the abstractions of current practice and theory; to the end willing to learn from those with whom he was in least agreement, lest he should fall behind the progressive spirit of his time; with a style somewhat involved and jerky, which made him difficult to his readers, but exceptionally straightforward, and leaving them in the end without any doubt, which was not the result of their own inattention, as to his meaning. Now that we have the work of both before us in all the fullness of its content,[1] we may perhaps see in it the best illustration of their own central doctrine of the self-differentiating, self-enriching power of any single valid principle—the unity of sameness and difference.

[1] Bosanquet died in 1923, Bradley in 1924. In death they were little divided.

CHAPTER VII

BRADLEY (iii). APPEARANCE AND REALITY

1. INTERVENING STUDIES

While at the end both of the *Ethical Studies* and the *Principles of Logic* we find Bradley straining at the limitations imposed by these subjects, the articles which he published in the years immediately following the appearance of the latter show him engaged with psychological rather than metaphysical problems. Yet they have an important bearing on what was to follow.

The later 'seventies and early 'eighties were a time of intensified psychological study. Alexander Bain was still trying to rally the scattered forces of psychological atomism. James Ward was developing, under Wundt's influence, a psychology more or less Kantian, based on the idea of the activity of the self. William James was laying the foundations of his "radical empiricism" in the idea of an undifferentiated continuum, a "buzzing confusion", as the embryonic beginning of our conscious experience. In one of the few autobiographical passages in his works[1] Bradley tells us that already, in 1879 and before James's articles in *Mind* of that year had appeared, he had learned from Hegel[2] the doctrine of "feeling as a vague *continuum* below relations" and grasped its vital importance. In his account of "the nature of the primitive mind" in the *Logic* he had spoken of this as a "blurred and confused totality"[3] in which differences, though present, are present merely as something felt.

This was the idea which was to prove revolutionary both in psychology and in metaphysics. It clearly cut away the root, not only of the old associationism, but of any attempt to start with an active self as something primarily given along with a confused objective content into which it brings order, and Bradley's articles in *Mind* of these years, more particularly the crucial one on "Association and Thought" in 1887, show us his own thought

[1] *Logic*, Second Edition, pp. 515–516.
[2] See *Encyklop.*, §§ 399 foll. Recent critics have pointed out his debt to Herbart for this and other features of his metaphysics. Bradley would probably have gladly acknowledged it, but he would have resented the suggestion that it was a case of borrowing.
[3] Bk. III. Pt. I. ch. vii. § 2, on "The Beginnings of Inference".

R

rapidly developing in this direction. "Is there anything at the start", he asks, "beyond mere presentation with the distinctions of quality, quantity, and 'tone' which *we* abstract from one another, but which at first come within one blurred whole which merely *is*?" And he replies: "I am convinced that there is nothing." "In the beginning there is nothing beyond what is presented, what is and is felt, or rather felt simply." "All is feeling in the sense not of pleasure and pain, but of a whole given without relations."[1]

In these articles he was engaged in developing the psychological aspect of this doctrine, and particularly in the attempt to show how thought may rise out of this menstruum and be related to it. But he is aware that problems are raised also as to the relation both of it and of thought to reality, for the answer to which, as he says at the end of the article just quoted, "we must go else-where". If he had been asked where in British or American philosophy we could go, he would have had to reply, "Nowhere"; but he was already himself preparing to supply the want.

2. THE METAPHYSICAL PROBLEM

Our study of the movement of his thought in the *Logic* brought out that, while there was clearly a conflict in his mind between the natural instinct to regard truth and reality as identical, and the proved abstractness of thought, and while he was sometimes tempted to sacrifice the one to the other, this "prompting" was checked by the trenchant criticism of Bosanquet's book, the text of which[2] was the union of those principles which in Bradley seemed to be falling apart. Henceforth there could be no question of a double standard; but this did not prove that the reality which appears in the constructions of thought is *all* that there is of it.

It did not need philosophy to teach us that there are elements in our experience of reality which are not included in the system of relations to which thought leads. There is the whole world of pleasure and pain, there is æsthetic feeling, there is striving and willing. Even in the world of knowledge there is immediate intuition below the world scarred with intellectual distinctions. But to point to these was not enough. They might be irrelevant adjuncts, as some, or imperfect forms of the life of reason, as others have held.

[1] *Mind*, vol. xii. pp. 363 foll.
[2] As also of the *Logic or Morphology of Knowledge*, which followed three years later.

Even Bradley's own metaphor[1] was unconvincing, and might be read in another sense. If the lion break out of the marble, it may go badly with the artist, but the *form* of the lion remains the essential thing. All that is proved is that his art has united with the reality in a way he did not expect. Unless there can be shown to be some inherent contradiction in the form itself—something that forbids us to take it for "the real thing"—our argument is incomplete. In order to complete it, it will be necessary to face anew the whole question of the criterion or standard of reality. If this standard, as Bradley now believed, is neither immediately given fact nor yet logical rationality, what is it?

It is in some such form as this that we must conceive of the problem which presented itself to him in those years, and to which *Appearance and Reality*[2] was intended to give the answer. More than any of his books it carries out the programme of the criticism of first principles which he still thought was the most pressing need of the time. True, there was no longer "the same dense body of stupid tradition and ancestral prejudice" as he had found fifteen years before; but there had been a certain incaution in the advance that had been made on the borrowed lines of Kant and Hegel, and there was a fair field for anyone who had anything to say in criticism of this also.[3]

It is this that explains the otherwise puzzling and in the end misleading form of the book. Instead of beginning with the positive statement of the guiding principle, the criterion of reality, which he was himself prepared to accept, proceeding thence to the criticism of the intellectual, moral, and æsthetic standards, and ending with an examination of the more common abstractions of space and time, substance, primary attributes, relations, activity, things-in-themselves, this order is more or less inverted. Without orientation or guidance the reader is plunged into a vortex of dialectic, directed to the loosening of every anchor by which he may have hitherto attached himself to the real world, by having it labelled "appearance", which in the context is naturally taken to mean illusion. It is only in the second part that the situation begins to clear up, first by the statement of the criterion, secondly by the translation of "appearance" into "degree of reality", finally by the reinstate-

[1] See p. 253 above.
[2] First Edition, 1893; Second Edition, 1897; referred to in notes as *A. and R.*
[3] See Preface, p. xiii.

ment of the discarded principles in a hierarchy of being, which it
might or might not be worth the while of a future metaphysic to
elaborate in detail. Bradley himself became keenly conscious of
this inversion and of the mistakes it had caused as to his true
meaning, and, in more than one passage in the Appendix to the
Second Edition, tries to make amends by stating the real order
of his thought. As it is with this order, and not with the details
of the book, that we are here concerned, we may avail ourselves of
the assistance these later statements afford in trying to follow the
author's methods and main result.

3. THE METHOD OF IDEALISTIC METAPHYSIC

The commonest criticism of idealistic metaphysics, which was
promptly applied to Bradley's form of it, is that it starts from
unproved assumptions of which it is itself unconscious. True,
Bradley replies,[1] therein speaking for Idealism in general, he does
make an assumption, or rather two assumptions. He assumes, in
the first place, that truth has to satisfy the intellect, and that
what does not do this is neither true nor real. But this is an
assumption which can only by the sceptic be challenged in its own
name as itself failing to give intellectual satisfaction, and such a
scepticism destroys itself. In the second place, he assumes that we are
from the beginning in presence of *being*—something experienced,
which is "at once positive and ultimate". But from this he does
not go on, as he is accused of doing, to assume that being is simple
and self-contained. On the contrary, he finds certain things offered
as ultimate facts or truths which fail to satisfy the intellect, and
when he asks why they so fail, he finds the reason to lie in the
fact that they contain elements or diversities which are merely
there *together*, but from one of which to the other there is no path
which the intellect can follow or "repeat in its own way", in other
words, can understand. "My intellect may for certain purposes
swallow mysteries unchewed, but unchewed it is unable in the end
to stomach and digest them." It is no use appealing to "intuition".
Intellect has no such sensuous intuition to fall back upon. It is
essentially discursive. It goes from point to point, and to be satisfied
it must go by a movement which satisfies its own nature. This is
as much as to say that in going from one point in a causal or other
complex, say from A to B, it must take A with it, and not drop it

[1] Pp. 569 foll.

by the way, simply *finding* B. It is not sufficient to offer their conjunction as matter of fact. "For my intellect that is no more than another external element", equally unsatisfying, therefore for my intellect untrue, and, in the form in which it is offered, not for it the real thing. The claim is made that there is an underlying identity, but this claim is not made good, and this is what we call self-contradiction.

It is on the ground of these failures, and not as a mere assumption, that it is maintained that, to be real in the sense of something that satisfies the intellect, what is offered must be self-contained and self-consistent. A cheap and easy way out of the difficulty would be to deny the reality of the diversity. But this is impossible, seeing that diversities exist and must somehow be real. If, then, we are to find reality, it must be in a whole of parts which are united in the way that the intellect requires, namely, by their own nature from within. Whether the intellect by itself is ever equal to the task of finding such reality, whether it can ever be satisfied, is a subsequent question. Meantime, what seems to be clear is that to be accepted as real "the diversity must fall within and be subordinate to a self-determined whole, an individual system, and any other determination is incompatible with reality".

4. THE STANDARD OF REALITY

Read in the light of the clue here given, unsystematic as are the detailed criticisms of Book I of *Appearance and Reality*, we can see how they are intended, in the first place, to bring out that reality, as distinguished from mere being or existence, is what in modern phrase would be called a "value", and from the side of philosophy as truth-seeking, an intellectual value; and in the second place, to lead up to the fuller consideration of the standard or criterion of such a value. What has emerged with reference to the first of these points is that, if it is an assumption, it is one that is universally made by anyone who takes philosophy seriously; and, with reference to the second, that the standard is consistency. The only question that remains is as to the more precise meaning of this last.

Consistency cannot mean the mere exclusion of discord. A kind of harmony may be secured by merely abstracting elements that happen to be inconsistent, leaving everything else outside. We may say reality excludes discord, but we may not say that whatever by abstraction can be made to exclude discord is real. How, then, extend and amend the definition? Anything for which we claim reality in an ultimate sense must be not only self-*consistent*, it must be self-*subsistent*. There must be nothing outside of it on which it depends for its existence and character, and this, when we understand fully what we mean by the word, is equivalent to saying that it must be *individual*. There must be nothing within itself to divide it, and there must be nothing outside of it that threatens to break into it. These two—security, we might say, from within and from without—may ultimately be one (it was a fundamental part of Bradley's doctrine that the one involved the other); anyway, both are required in anything that is to satisfy the intellect and be accepted from its point of view as real.

With this distinction between individuality in its ordinary or relative and in its eminent or absolute sense we have Bradley's whole philosophy in a nutshell. Tested by this criterion, it is at once clear that there is nothing in the world of which we can say that, taken by itself, it is thus individual and real except the World itself. The general doctrine was indeed a part of the idealistic tradition. What is new in Bradley is the fierce fire of dialectic which he applies to the different forms of finite reality, including even the highest for which a certain ultimacy had been claimed, and which are now made to dissolve before it. It was hardly to be wondered at that the first impression produced even among idealists was that they had before them a new form of Spinozism. "The Absolute", wrote Caird, on first reading the book,[1] "is to be all the attributes and yet *none* of them like Spinoza's. We might perhaps say that his theory is a new Spinozism."

By the order he had adopted, Bradley was himself largely responsible for this suspicion. But, as Spinoza sought to meet it by his doctrine of degrees of reality, so in the second part of his book Bradley appeals to the same principle to reinstate finite things each with its quota of reality in proportion to the level of inclusiveness and self-consistency which is achieved by it. The difference is that while the admission was forced from Spinoza as

---

[1] *Life and Philosophy of Edward Caird*, p. 193. Caird's impression of the Spinozistic tendency in Bradley's thought deepened with closer acquaintance. His own position has already been referred to (p. 172) as nearer to Plato in asserting the reality of universals and of Mind as "the place of universals". See also p. 433 *n*. 3 below.

a gloss on his philosophy in reply to a critic,[1] it was an integral part of Bradley's view from the first. What remains, nevertheless, as a fundamental ambiguity in his general statement is his apparent readiness to treat the most substantial of finite entities, including human personality, as mere attributes or "adjectives" of the Absolute. To fail of entire self-consistency and independence, it might still be replied to him, is one thing, to sacrifice all self-respect by the admission of adjectivalness to something else, even though it be the Highest, is quite another. A sound idealism is committed to the doctrine that no finite thing is wholly self-contained and self-consistent—none, therefore, wholly individual and self-subsistent; but it is also bound to hold that the category of substance and attribute is wholly inadequate to express the spirit of a philosophy which claimed to have passed from the frozen heights of substance to the living stream of subject minds and wills. Whatever more the Absolute may be than a unity or society of persons, it cannot be less. To return to a mode of thought allied to, if not derived from, the grammatical division between subject and predicate, whose finality Bradley himself denies, is to do justice neither to the Absolute nor to the Relatives in which its nature is expressed.[2]

5. THE MATTER OF REALITY

So far Bradley has been speaking of reality from the side of its form and in the abstract. What can be said of it from the side of its matter and in the concrete? It is here that the doctrine which meanwhile he had been developing from the psychological side begins to acquire metaphysical import. The passage in which he gives the preliminary answer,[3] with its uncompromising identification of reality with "experience", has attracted probably more attention and raised more questioning than any other part of the book. It is too long and too familiar to quote in full. The argument is an old one in the history of idealism, and rests for its force on experiment.[4]

---

[1] See especially Letter to van Bleyenberg of date March 13, 1665.
[2] See the interesting discussion of this point by Bosanquet and others in the *Proceedings* of the Aristotelian Society, 1918, and the reference to it by the present writer in *Mind*, N.S., vol. xxxii. No. 128, p. 406. There is nothing in which A. N. Whitehead's "philosophy of organism" is in more fundamental agreement with idealistic metaphysics than in his insistence on the long-drawn-out consequences of this error.
[3] *A. and R.*, pp. 145-146.
[4] See, *e.g.*, Ferrier's *Institutes of Metaphysics*, pp. 381 and 510; *Remains*, p. 305.

Try to think of anything that can be called fact or that may be said to have being, and then judge if you can continue to think of it when all perception and feeling have been removed. As this is impossible, we are driven to the conclusion that for us "experience is the same as reality . . . to be real is to be indissolubly one thing with sentience. It is to be something which comes as a feature and aspect within one whole of feeling, something which, except as an integral element of such sentience, has no meaning at all".

To realists pledged to the existence of a reality wholly independent of experience in any form, such a doctrine was frankly foolishness. But it came at the time as something of a surprise to idealists also. They were familiar with the experimental argument to prove the inconceivability of any reality that was entirely independent of an experiencing subject, whether as sensitive or reflective, and on the ground of it to hear that all reality was "spiritual". But Bradley seemed to be saying something more than this. Reality is not merely to be *as* and only *as* it is to experience of some sort, but it is to *be* experience, and, further, experience not in the sense of thinking experience, but of *feeling and sentience*. Both of these claims raised serious questions. From the side of the first, how can there be experience without an experiencing self? and, if we are thus shut up for our real world within the self, how can we escape from a thoroughgoing subjectivism? Bradley seemed to have escaped the Charybdis of Spinozism only to fall on the Scylla of Solipsism. It is, again, not surprising that the leader of orthodox Hegelianism at the time should have come to the conclusion that the whole passage "really involves that Berkeley is right. Bradley has great difficulty with Solipsism".[1] Equally serious seemed the difficulties raised by the emphasis on sentience. In the *Logic* he had roused the suspicion of having in thought and perception a double standard. Is this the heresy of the *Logic* come to its own by a surrender to the latter?

Yet to anyone who had followed the development of his thought, as we have here tried to do, the doctrine ought not at any rate to have caused any surprise, and, as to the difficulties it raises, Bradley himself is keenly aware of them. Anticipating those just mentioned, he proceeds to set aside a "serious mistake" as to the meaning of his doctrine. It does not mean that he proposes to

[1] Caird in *op. cit.*, p. 194.

separate the percipient subject from the universe, or to contend that this subject can never transcend its own states, and thus to make the whole of reality into experience in the sense of an adjective of that subject. This to him seems "indefensible". But what he holds to be not less indefensible is to set up an object in entire independence of a sentient experience and with a content untranslatable into the matter of such experience. "If, seeking reality, we go to experience, what we certainly do *not* find is a subject or an object, or indeed any other thing whatever, standing separate and on its own bottom. What we discover rather is a whole in which distinctions can be made, but in which divisions do not exist." What he must be understood to be repudiating is, therefore, not an object which carries us beyond the states of the subject, but "the separation of feeling from the felt or of the desired from desire, or of what is thought from thinking, or the division of anything from anything else".

It might still be replied that this answer only emphasizes the difficulty raised by "sentient" experience. Why, if we are to abide by the *whole*, does Bradley himself insist on speaking of what is merely an element in experience as though it were the whole, and on identifying experience with sentience? And why, if reality *is* sentient experience, does he go on to include it *in* sentient experience as only a "feature" or "element" of it? Either the reality he is speaking of as sentience is something different from that, the general nature of which he is here trying to define, or, if it is the same, he is inverting the true order. Ought not experience rather to be defined as an element or feature of reality? And if the latter is the true view, have we not again as our alternatives either a realism to which experience is the inexplicable outcome of a non-spiritual process, or an idealism to which it is the content of an encompassing mind?

I do not think that the passage as it stands is wholly free from ambiguity, but taken along with what is elsewhere said, and particularly with what we have at the end of the same chapter, I believe that the meaning is fairly clear. Bradley is pledged to the view that the relational aspect of the world cannot be the ultimate one. Relations have already been shown *if taken by themselves*[1] to

---

[1] It is essential to remember this qualification. Not so taken, relations have their own peculiar form of reality, and Cook Wilson is within his right (*Statement and Inference*, vol. ii. p. 692) in criticizing the argument by which

be in the end self-contradictory and therefore "appearance"; and he is going on to apply the same measure to thought as involving them. But he is long past the danger of supposing that this can mean that we have to fall back on "things" or "qualities" as given to sense-perception for our "real world". What he means is that these also have been condemned as abstractions and, when taken as ultimates, as leading to self-contradiction. The experience to which we can attribute reality in the full sense of the word, while it can be found neither in the relational system nor in any immediately given object of sense, must be conceived of as an immediately present whole, in which all relations, among them those of subject and object, sense and thought, are contained. What he is contending for is not the identity of reality with any given feeling of ours, but the givenness to feeling as an inexpugnable element in the real. While reality cannot be less than any experience of ours, whether feeling or thinking, and "no feeling or thought can fall outside its limits", it may well be more. In his own words, "If it is more than any feeling or thought which we know, it must still remain more of the same nature. It cannot pass into another region beyond what falls under the general head of sentience."

He had spoken in the *Logic*[1] of the view that "our sensuous presentment" may "be misrepresentation that cannot give fact", as an "old dream" of the "deepest philosophies", only to reject it. But it was also an old dream of theirs that there may be an intuitive reason or a rational intuition beyond the distinctions and divisions of both sense and discursive thought. With this Bradley was in essential agreement. "We might have", he writes in a later note on the above passage,[2] "a fundamental identity underlying both sides (both the sensuously given reality and discursive thought), and a demand on each side for the complete and explicit realization of this identity". The present text is his way of giving expression, from the side of sentience, to this ancient doctrine. The question that remains is that of the sense in which this higher form of experience can be said to enter into our own; in other words, in what sense we can be said to know the Absolute. It is this which he discusses in the short but crucial passage at the end

Bradley tries to show their unreality by conveniently forgetting their nature as relations. On Bradley's real view see below, pp. 283 foll. and p. 393.
[1] *P. of L.*, p. 589.   [2] *Ibid.*, p. 595.

of the chapter, and to which we must go for the true understanding of its general teaching.[1]

6. OUR KNOWLEDGE OF THE ABSOLUTE

The question of our knowledge of the *real* world was crucial for Neo-Kantianism. This was "new" chiefly in respect to its rejection of Kant's unknown thing-in-itself. Its main argument from the formal side consisted in proving that thought could only affirm a limit to its own scope if in some sense it was already beyond that limit. To say that something is not known is to say that we know, not only that it exists, but that it possesses some feature on the ground of which we assert that what we do know is not the whole. But Neo-Kantianism went beyond this formal argument. It appealed to the concrete nature of *self-conscious* experience as not only, so far as it was the union of sense and thought, inseparably one with its object, but as the supreme type of what reality must be. Reality must be *that* completely which *we* are as yet incompletely but seek completely to become. And what we seek completely to become is a *self*, in which subject and object are completely at one, the self realized in its object, and the object penetrated with the ideal nature of the subject. Short of this transparent unity, in which both we and our world are known as we are, and are as we are known, we cannot rest. How far does Bradley go with Neo-Kantianism in all this? Can he fall short of it without involving himself in a new form of mysticism, not to say agnosticism? These questions were asked at the time, and are crucial for the understanding of his relation to idealism in the more generally accepted form.

He had already dealt with the theory of things-in-themselves in the chapter with that title, where he reproduces the familiar Neo-Kantian argument against it: " If reality were not knowable, we

---

[1] The interval is occupied with a discussion of the place of feeling in the sense of pain and pleasure in Reality. It goes without saying that, while neither is illusory, each taken by itself is only appearance. The existence of a balance of pleasure (though this is not the only possibility) is supported partly by an appeal to experience, "though it is difficult to estimate and easy to exaggerate the amount of the balance", but chiefly by an appeal to his general principle of the nature of reality as completely harmonious and at rest within itself. For his fuller doctrine upon feeling in this sense what he here says has to be taken along with the long note in the Second Edition, pp. 609 foll.

could not know that such a thing even existed. It would be much as if we said, 'Since all my faculties are totally confined to my garden, I cannot tell if the roses next door are in bloom'. And this seems inconsistent." But he proposes to take another line which he thinks may be "plainer".

To begin with, it cannot be a question of *things* in themselves, the diversity and relations of which merely bring us back to the difficulties we are seeking to solve. We must talk henceforward of the *thing* in itself. To this appearances must either be related or not. If they are related, they are so as adjectives, and so qualifying the reality. But, we ask, how related? and we have the whole problem again on our hands, not to speak of the fact that the Thing is no longer by itself. If they are unrelated, the Thing in itself drifts away into a nonentity as being without qualities, and serves only "as a poor and irrelevant excuse for neglecting our own concerns" and taking no pains about what are only phenomena.[1]

So far he may be said to be only developing the Neo-Kantian argument in his own way. But beyond this it seemed impossible for him to follow it. He devotes two of the longest chapters of the book to a destructive criticism of the idea of the Self as one in which we can rest as ultimate reality. He was convinced that it was impossible to leave the self or subject out of reality, but he was equally convinced that it was only possible to bring it in as the clue to all reality by a failure to complete the work of criticism. "Of those who take their principle of understanding from the self", he wrote at the end of his own examination,[2] "how few subject that principle to an impartial scrutiny. It is easy to argue from a foregone alternative, to disprove any theory which loses sight of the self, and then to offer what remains as the secret of the universe—whether what remains is thinkable or is a complex which refuses to be understood. And it is easy to survey the world which is selfless and find this vanity and illusion, and then to return to one's self into congenial darkness, and the equivocal consolation of some psychological monster. But if the object is

---

[1] P. 130. The passage here condensed has a special interest in view of pragmatist criticisms of Bradley's own Absolute on precisely those grounds of uselessness and irrelevance. The essence of Bradley's theory is that, while there is no "other world" to provide us with an excuse for neglecting our business in this, there is another aspect of this world, which it is part of the business of all of us, the *chief* business of the philosopher, to try to understand.
[2] P. 120.

to understand, there can be only one thing which we have to consider . . . for metaphysics a principle, if it is to stand at all, must stand absolutely by itself." And this the self fails to do.

We shall have to return to the whole question of the ground and the fairness of this criticism so far as it applied to the Neo-Kantian position. Meantime we are concerned with its bearing on the question of the sources of our knowledge of Reality. Seeing that none of the forms in which the self appears as a factor can be accepted as real until they shall have undergone an unknown amount of transformation, we seem to be cut off from any appeal to the contents of finite experience as such a source, and I believe that if we take Bradley at his word, and lay the stress upon the "unknown amount", it might be difficult to avoid this confession.

But he found it still possible to hold that, while the *details* of the transformed result are unknown, the *direction* of it is an open secret, and that, if there are phases of experience which clearly point in that direction, these may be enough to add at least something to our knowledge. Such phases he found both below and above the level of ordinary consciousness. What ruined consciousness at its ordinary level was, on the one hand, the relational element, and therewith the element of unsolved contradiction it contained, and, on the other hand, its partialness. But below that level there was immediate presentation and feeling in which all the elements were present, albeit as yet in an undeveloped form. True, this is something which "we hardly possess as more than that which we are in the act of losing". Yet it serves to suggest to us a total experience in which subject and object, and therewith will and thought and feeling, "may be once more at one". Likewise, at the other end, and reaching beyond relational consciousness, we have hints of what we seek—"a kind of hostility" to exclusive relations, which leads theory to seek to merge itself in practice, practice in theory; and in this way the relational form may be said itself to point to a "substantial totality beyond relations and above them, a whole endeavouring without success to realize itself in their detail".

Thankful though the reader may be for these admissions, what is apt to strike him is the exceptionalness of the elements appealed to, and the apparent failure to take account of such very ordinary experiences as that of beauty (*e.g.*, in a landscape or a face), which

are in a quite definite sense inclusive and supra-relational. To the
end it is the unreal element rather than the real that Bradley
emphasizes.[1] Even in the matter of the "substantial totality beyond
relations and above them" it is possible to point to the consciousness of this as something which, so far from hardly possessing "as
more than that which we are in the act of losing", we continually
cherish as the securest of all our possessions and the source of all
that is of any value in us. It was because he realized this other
side of the matter that Bosanquet felt himself free to throw
aside Bradley's reserves and boldly claim that "we experience
the Absolute" not as a fleeting shadow but "better than we
experience anything else".[2] How far the recognition of it would
have brought Bradley back into line with the philosophy of
self-consciousness is another question. For the present he was
more interested in widening the division by bringing the view
he had thus reached to bear on the main problem as he had
left it at the end of the *Logic*, that of the relation of thought
to reality.

7. THOUGHT AND REALITY

The chapter with this title contains, Bradley tells us, "the main
thesis of this work".[3] By the time it was written it had become
clear to him (if it ever had been doubted) that no solution of the
problem was to be found by a return to the idea that the standard
of truth was to be found in anything merely given to perception,
whether inner or outer, still less in any thing-in-itself that was
beyond our knowledge. But he was equally convinced that it was
impossible to accept the products of thought as equivalent to
reality. True, we are to hear no more from him of the externality
and artificiality of thought and idea, as something imported into
or imposed upon facts: "as if facts when let alone were in no sense
ideal".[4] He had learned (not, we may suppose, without aid from

---

[1] On beauty see especially pp. 463 foll.
[2] *Principle of Individuality and Value*, p. 27. The whole passage might be
taken as a comment on Bradley's view as here stated.
[3] P. 555.
[4] In 1907, referring to the view that "the given facts are not the whole of
reality, while truth cannot be understood except in reference to this whole",
he wrote: "This is the main thesis which was urged in my *Principles of Logic*.
It did not occur to me that I should be taken there or anywhere else to be
advocating the copy theory of truth." *Essays on Truth and Reality*, p. 109 *n*.

Bosanquet[1]) that "facts which are not idea and which show no looseness of content from existence seem hardly actual", and that this "ideality of the given" is not manufactured by thought, but "thought itself in its development and product". "The essential nature of the finite is that everywhere, as it presents itself, its character should slide beyond the limits of its existence." There is, as it were, a "disease" in things, and thought, with its product truth, "is the effort to heal this disease homœopathically". But to assert the naturalness and intrinsicness of this effort is one thing, it is quite another to assert its complete success; and by this time Bradley had come to see the reason why, as he thought, the cure could never be complete.

In the first place, the thought that counts in judgment and inference lives in the distinction between the concrete reality, the "that" and the abstract character, the "what". Doubtless the "what" is a content, in modern phrase a "meaning". Doubtless, too, thought restores to the concrete basis the element it has separated off from it. But, however rich the meaning, it can never be rich enough to contain the whole existing reality. "This basis is of necessity richer than the mere element of itself." It is this stubborn ideality of thought and its incommensurability with reality that sets it on the road of indefinite expansion, where it is dogged with the dilemma *either* of failing to reach its goal *or* (if it were to succeed, "if its adjectives could be at once self-consistent and re-welded to existence") of ceasing to be truth any longer, and of passing "into another and higher reality".

In the second place, even although *per impossible* thought were to escape this dilemma, and emerge safely beyond the dualism of subject and predicate, we should still find it impossible to take any "system of ideal contents united by relations and reflecting itself in self-conscious harmony" as the whole of reality. There would remain outside of it the whole life of feeling and emotion, "the delights and pains of the flesh, the agonies and raptures of the soul". Can these burning experiences, Bradley asks, be "mere fragments fallen from thought's Heaven? . . . Feeling belongs to perfect thought or it does not. If it does not, there is at once a side of existence beyond thought. But if it does belong, then

1 See *Knowledge and Reality*, p. 45, where "fact" is defined as "a middle term between Thing or reality and the knowledge which is in our heads", so that " 'existing fact' is almost a contradiction in terms".

thought is different from thought discursive and relational. It must have been absorbed in a fuller experience". You may still call it thought, but if anyone prefers another name, such as feeling or will, he will be equally within his right. It may (perhaps it must) be that the complete satisfaction of thought would be the complete satisfaction of will and feeling. But we cannot *know* this, and in any case it would be equally true of these others.

Yet a difficulty remained. Neo-Kantian idealism was deeply entrenched behind the Hegelian doctrine that, in order to be able to assign a limit to our thought, we must *in thought* be in some sense beyond that limit, and in this sense thought must encompass reality. Bradley's own doctrine of our knowledge of a standard of reality, by which particular claimants are judged, seemed itself to imply the acceptance of this principle. If, accepting it, he still urges that there is to thought (and it was to thought he was there appealing) a reality beyond the reach of thought, is he not attempting to hold together two contradictory propositions and leaving us in the cleft stick of scepticism?

Bradley is too deeply pledged to the Hegelian doctrine of the "Other", that thought sets up, to propose to solve the difficulty by renouncing it. He agrees that, if reality were quite beyond intellectual apprehension, it would be self-contradictory to assert that thought fails to reach it. But he goes on to explain that this is not his contention. What he contends is that thought consists in the endeavour to compass through predication that completely individual thing which the reality, as given in simple apprehension, is necessarily taken to be but is not yet. It is thought's constant failure to attain its ideal within itself that drives it on and is the source of progress. But this movement is possible because thought already possesses in incomplete form what it seeks to complete, and, though this must always have a certain air of paradox, it is not self-contradiction. Progress is only another name for self-transcendence, and what makes self-transcendence possible is that, while "mere thought" fails to apprehend a reality above relations, yet there is working in it an "underlying identity" which the relational form is an attempt to grasp. It is *this completion of thought beyond thought which remains for ever an Other*.[1]

The passage which follows may be said to be the main one

[1] Pp. 181-182.

in the chapter which contains "the main thesis" of the book. The gist of it is that, while the entire reality will be merely "the object thought out", yet it will be thought out in such a way that "mere thinking will be absorbed". Moreover, it will be equally describable as volition willed out or as feeling that is completely satisfied; but, again, it will be a volition or a feeling which, as so completed, is absorbed in something higher, something "not too poor but too rich for division of its elements".

Here at last was Bradley's solution of the problem that had been vaguely present to him in the *Ethical Studies* as dissatisfaction with the Neo-Kantian principle of self-consciousness, and had taken definite form in the *Logic* as that of the relation of thought to reality. The dualism involved in all thought, and the recognition of will and feeling as essential features of the real world, made it impossible to assign any privileged position to the merely rational. The real must be rational, but it must be a great deal more. To say that thought was a *sine qua non* of any real world was not to say that it was the same altogether with reality, with no difference between them. A like criticism disposes of the objection that "the thought here spoken of is not perfect: Where thought is perfect there is no discrepancy between subject and predicate. A harmonious system of content predicating itself, a subject self-conscious in that system of content, this is what thought should mean. And here the division of existence and character is quite healed up. If such a completion is not actual, it is possible, and the possibility is enough".[1] Such completion of thought, he replies, is unmeaning, and therefore impossible. If there is no difference, there is no judgment; and if there is no judgment, there is no thought. On the other hand, if there is a difference, then the subject is beyond the predicated content.

8. THE ISSUE RAISED FOR IDEALISM BY APPEARANCE AND REALITY

How far this reply is convincing is part of the issue, perhaps the chief part, raised by a book the appearance of which was an event of first-rate importance in the history of Anglo-Saxon philosophy in general, and of Anglo-Saxon Idealism in particular. The book vindicated a place for original metaphysical study untrammelled

[1] P. 170.

either by consideration for orthodox dogma[1] or by over-reverence
for dominating, perhaps tyrannous, German ideas. Nothing like it
had appeared since Hume's *Treatise*. Like Hume's work, it roused
men of all schools from their dogmatic slumbers. Unlike Hume's,
ending as that did in the celebrated "Appendix" to the *Treatise*
with the statement of an unsolved contradiction and a problem
for the future, it offered a principle in which Hume's and all similar
problems might find their solution. Bradley was as far as Hume
from claiming any finality for his conclusions in detail. He was as
convinced as Hume was of the narrowness of the field within which
metaphysical theory moved and of its failure to cover the whole
of life. But within that field he believed that his principle of the
ultimate unity of all experience and the impossibility of explaining
the whole from any arbitrarily selected element in it could be
sufficiently established to save philosophy from anything that
could be described as mere scepticism.

Few at the time, and perhaps fewer to-day, might be willing to
accept his conclusions as they stand. But, if a philosophy is to be
judged not by the number of its adherents but by the largeness
of its view, the fertility of its suggestions and the power of the
reactions it set in operation, there was no book that came out in
these years that was at all comparable to Bradley's. As contrasted with the narrowness of current realism, with its too exclusive
occupation with questions of perceptual experience, the view it
expounded showed how impossible it was to rest in any so-called
sense-data as real except in the most elementary and subordinate
sense. Whatever the reality, even the "independent" reality, that
might be claimed for the world of sense-perception, it was but
a small part of the world of knowledge, and a still smaller part
of the wider world which includes feeling and will, society and
religion, and which stretches beyond and overlaps what is expressible
as truth in the theoretic sense of the word. *Vice versa*, as contrasted
with the theory that, through William James's influence, was
spreading both in America and England, and that sought to treat
the world of will with its practical values as the supreme, if not
the only, reality, Bradley's book was a vindication of the real and
independent, though still partial, validity of ideals of truth and

[1] Its treatment of religion (pp. 438 foll.) as the attempt to express the complete reality of goodness through every aspect of our being, sympathetic
and profound as it may seem to-day, was probably the chief cause of the
refusal of the book by the Oxford Press of the time.

beauty, which could only be identified with practice by a falsification of human nature and of their own essential quality. Henceforth the question was not of the reality and relative independence of these overlapping worlds, but of their relation to the whole of which they were aspects, and through that to one another. But it is the relation of the teaching of the book to the current form of idealism with which we are here chiefly concerned. That it raised an important issue seemed clear. What was not so clear, owing to the subtlety and many-sidedness of Bradley's thought, was the precise nature of the issue.[1]

With regard to some of the aspects of experience to which Bradley sought to do more justice than had hitherto been done, there could in the end be nothing but agreement with him. Too zealous Hegelians might have overemphasized the place of thought and reason to the neglect of feeling and will. But this was no part of their idealistic inheritance. Nineteenth-century idealism in England had its origin largely in the attempt to vindicate the reality of the will and feeling,[2] and in its later teaching had found itself particularly at home in the interpretation of social and political life. Royce in America claimed for Hegel that his strength lay in the exposition of the logic of passion, and he was himself working out a view that sought to do more justice to will.[3] What the older idealism here stood for was not the denial of the reality of these elements in experience, but the doctrine it had inherited from Plato, Spinoza, and Hegel, that the form these took differed in value according to the rationality, which was also the substantiality, of their contents. In all of them there was a *logic* which, while it might not be expressible in intellectual terms, was subject to the same law of inclusiveness and internal harmony. Even in the field proper to logic, Idealism had never dentified itself with the view that there could be an equation between discursive

---

[1] "I am trying to yield myself to Bradley," wrote Caird, "but though I think there is a fundamental incoherence, I can't quite satisfy myself as to his error; for he so oddly brings in, in a secondary way, the points one would allege against him" (*Life and Philosophy of Edward Caird*, p. 192). "Elusiveness of this sort", wrote one of the most understanding of his American critics at a later date, "is inherent in the nature of the system. A subtlety less in degree than Mr. Bradley's is bound to flounder in a philosophy which balances so nicely the conflicting motives of absolutism and relativism" (*Philosophical Review*, vol. xxiii, p. 550).

[2] See the present writer's *Coleridge as Philosopher*, pp. 102 foll.

[3] See below, pp. 366 foll.

thought as commonly interpreted and the kind of thought to which could be ascribed the apprehension, not to speak of the creation, of real essences. It had inherited from Plato the distinction between "understanding" and intuitional "reason", and if recently it had been chary of employing it, this had been partly because of Kant's use of it in an almost diametrically opposite sense by assigning to reason a merely "regulative" function, partly because of the supposed abuse of it by writers who, like Coleridge, were credited with employing it as a smoke-screen to cover a gap in their philosophy. Equally little ground was there to take exception to the doctrine of the fundamental place of immediacy in experience. The doctrine, as Bradley claimed, is staring us in the face in Hegel. All that he did was to recall attention to it. It certainly raised new problems both for psychology and metaphysics, as Bradley was himself more and more to find; but it was indispensable to any sound idealism. To deny it on the ground of the priority of the Kantian or the Fichtean Ego was a backward step.

What thinkers of the older school found difficult and doubtful in the book was the subtle way in which the criterion, which we derive from experience at the level of self-consciousness, seemed to be turned against the validity of that consciousness itself. The sections of the first of the two chapters, devoted to showing the impossibility of giving a coherent account from the side of psychology of what is meant by the self, were a veritable Seven against the Self. But as a criticism of the Neo-Kantian doctrine such an argument was bound to seem irrelevant. What this had in view was not a psychological definition of the subject or self, but the fact that the division between subject and object itself only comes before us as a difference in a presupposed whole of meaning. To be thus distinguished and related meant to be held together in a unity which went deeper than the empirically distinguished subject and object, and manifested itself in the power of making an object of either of them. It was this deeper level of selfhood to which Kant's transcendental Ego pointed. But, as explained by him, it was open to the objection that in calling it Ego he was transferring to a noumenal entity ideas derived from and only applicable to phenomenal appearances. As thing-in-itself there was no more reason for calling it ego than non-ego, or, indeed, for calling it anything at all. It was to correct this error that the

Neo-Kantians[1] refused to recognize any abstract form of selfhood distinct from that which manifested itself in the apprehension and organization of the matter of experience into a world. It is its power of victorious self-affirmation in what appears as its object or other (whether taken as external or internal) that was the warrant for ascribing to the self a share in the absoluteness of ultimate reality. To ask that *this* self should be given as the object of intuition in a time-series, with ordinary empiricism, or to reduce it to the emaciated ego of Kant's *Critique*, is equally to lose hold of its real being.

Instead, therefore, of the failure of the different psychological accounts of the empirical self to satisfy criticism being a proof that there is no such unifying principle, it might be argued that the fact that we can look for such an account at all is itself the proof of its existence, for it is only to a being involving such a principle that there can be any psychological question. To ask to have its features set forth as those of a given object is like asking for a candle to see the sun.

Not less when Bradley comes to what he calls the "main thesis" of the book in the chapter upon "Thought and Reality", something seemed to be ignored that was fundamental to a sound idealism. His account of the ideality in all judgment, the separation in it of existence from character, when freed from the ambiguities of the *Logic*, was all to the good. But to emphasize this separation on the ground of the psychological difference between the concreteness of the given particular and the abstractness of the idea seemed again irrelevant. What Neo-Kantianism stood for was the impossibility of having this separation except on the basis of an underlying union, apart from which both the particular and the universal of psychology were abstractions. Bradley had declared[2]: "If there is no difference, there is no judgment; and if there is no judgment, there is no thought." But the reply was obvious: "Also, if there is no sameness, there is no judgment. And the sameness falls as much within the judgment as the difference." To treat the element of identity as falling outside the judgment, or, again, when taken as within it, as something wholly inexplicable, was to open the door to just that scepticism on the exclusion of which Bradley's

[1] Following Hegel. See *Science of Logic*, Eng. Tr., pp. 418 foll., which may be said to contain the whole Neo-Kantian doctrine.
[2] *A. and R.*, p. 127.

whole scheme depended. What was puzzling was how on such a view there could be claimed for thought even the limited validity of "compromise". In compromise something is yielded by both sides. But here there is nothing to be put to the credit of thought. It fails to take up the fact—in other words, to be valid at all; and no multiplication of in-valids can make up one validity. As well try to make up unity by a multiplication of ciphers. It will be vain in reply to lay emphasis on the ideal to which our thought commits us as that of a consistent and inclusive whole. What we have at best on this showing is a more or less consistent system of *ideas* which never *ex hypothesi* can give us the *thing*. Granted that we are bound to move forward in the direction in which thought by its own nature drives us, unless we can carry with us the assurance that it is reality itself that is thinking in us, we shall be bound to believe on such a view that we have dropped reality by the way. *With* that assurance we may rest in the faith that thought can as little be false to us as to itself. Does Bradley's own theory imply this assurance? and will he in the end be prepared to give it to us, and thus leave room to hope for a reconciliation between the old and the new doctrine? *Or* will the more negative side of his teaching develop its own consequences? and will the enemies of Idealism see in these consequences a proof that Absolutism has over-reached itself and only opened the door to a new form of Relativism? It is with such questions as these that the reader turns to Bradley's later work.

CHAPTER VIII

BRADLEY (iv). ESSAYS ON TRUTH AND REALITY

1. THE NEW PHILOSOPHICAL ATMOSPHERE

The years that followed the publication of *Appearance and Reality* were a time of hitherto unexampled philosophical activity in England and America. "It is a satisfaction to me", wrote Bradley in 1914, "when approaching the end of my own career to note (whatever school or tendency may be in fashion) the increasing devotion amongst us to philosophical inquiry. There has been, I think, a rise in the general level of English philosophical thought such as fifty years ago might have seemed incredible."[1] To this result no one had contributed more than he himself had done, not only by the new currents which he set moving within the lines of idealistic thought, but even more by the stimulus he gave to writers coming to philosophy from other points of view.

There was much in the temper of the time that favoured reaction. Idealism had had a long innings, owing partly to the great ability of the group of thinkers who had initiated the movement on both sides of the Atlantic and the inherent weakness of the form of empiricism which in those days was its chief opponent; partly to its success in vindicating, amid a general dissolution of traditional beliefs, the reality of the objects from which what was best in religion, art, ethics, and politics drew their nourishment. But new forces were at work. It was not only that old beliefs were undermined, but men were ceasing to be interested in the background of experience on which they rested. New interests concerned with the science and art of human life filled the horizon. Even in the physical sciences, where the mind in search of the permanent had seemed to find this in atoms and the laws of their interactions, a revolution was taking place which seemed to involve everything in movement and relativity. Under these circumstances it was not surprising that philosophy, weary of grappling with metaphysical conceptions of an Absolute, which seemed not only remote from the actual everyday world, but to have been invested by writers like Bradley with a certain ghostliness, should have been tempted to turn to methods more in harmony with the "modernism" of the time. This movement in the

[1] *Essays on Truth and Reality*, Oxford, 1914, quoted below as *Essays*.

'nineties was as yet in its beginnings, but in men like Bertrand Russell and William James it had leaders exceptionally well equipped and gifted with a persuasiveness of speech and personality that was new in their several departments.

Yet in estimating the new philosophical currents it would be a mistake to regard them all as in essence hostile to a philosophy whose chief successes had been in the interpretation of the ideal standards which form the background of human experience in all departments of life. In a world determined at all hazards to keep in touch with fact, it was not likely that in the end the fact of the existence of what Royce called "the world of appreciation" should escape observation. The extravagance with which Nietzsche, himself the high priest of Modernism, seemed to be asserting mere power to be the ultimate criterion of value, was itself sufficient to redirect men's minds to the whole question of the true nature and standard of human good and to the as yet comparatively uninvestigated problem of its mode of operation in the human mind.[1] Here was a field which traditional idealism from Plato to Hegel might be said to have made its own, and in which, freed from what was merely traditional, it might come to its own again.

All these influences are clearly reflected in the articles which Bradley contributed chiefly to *Mind* in the twenty years between 1894 and 1914, and it was these articles which, with one or two additions,[2] he published in the *Essays*. Those which were not merely fuller statements of doctrines already familiar to his readers were partly controversial, directed to a criticism of the central doctrines of Pragmatism as represented by William James and John Dewey and of the Logical Realism of Mr. Russell, but partly also aimed at the solution of new problems raised, but, as he thought, left unsolved by these writers. Our purpose here will be best served if, neglecting those in which we have chiefly restatements of old doctrines, we confine ourselves to the other groups as more likely to contain indications of change of emphasis in his own positive teaching.

[1] Nietzsche may be said to have been for a later generation what Carlyle in a different way was to an earlier. See Professor Urban's recent book on *The Intelligible World*, where his name constantly recurs.

[2] Of the additions, the first chapter beginning "Every aspect of life may in the end be subordinated to the good" was written in 1906 as an introduction to a book he had at that time in contemplation. Important as is the collection of critical and expository essays we have instead, it is impossible not to regret the loss to the Philosophy of Value of the direct treatment of the whole subject which this introduction seemed to promise.

2. Idealism v. Pragmatism and Radical Empiricism

Bradley apologizes in the Preface for the space devoted to pragmatism, but deprecates the idea that it occupied a corresponding place in his mind. From the point of view of a philosophy like his, any attempt to isolate one side of the Good, understood in the wider sense as that in which the mind seeks satisfaction, and to assign an exclusive and absolute value to it, was self-condemned. What he missed in current pragmatism as represented by James and Dewey was, in the first place, any clear and unambiguous statement of what was meant by "practical" as opposed to other forms of activity, and, in the second place, any thoroughgoing analysis of what was involved in proposing to ourselves and following out any purpose whatever, whether practical or theoretical. An explicit statement on either point would, he believed, be the end of pragmatism as a tenable philosophy. In one of the last passages which we have from his pen he sums up, perhaps better than in any other, the spirit which he opposes to that expressed in this form of doctrine. In opposition to the charge of abstractness levelled by its supporters against himself he retaliates: "An existing world of mere events with an activity that means no more than their change is surely itself an abstraction, most paltry and unreal. And if practice is to bring nothing from a higher world into this region of what happens, then, however much it may *do*, its activity and its result will have no practical sense or value. . . . Everything that is worth our having is (you may say) our own doing, and exists only in so far as produced by ourselves. But you must add that, in the whole region of human value, there is nothing that has not come down to us from another world—nothing which fails still to owe its proper being and reality to that which lives and works beyond the level of mere time and existence."[1]

But while Bradley found nothing but ambiguity and error in William James's pragmatism, there was much in his "radical empiricism" which fell into line with his own doctrine that "there is no reality but experience, and that what falls outside of what is experienced is not real". He was in fundamental agreement with what, in spite of manifold ambiguity, he took to be James's meaning, namely, that "given experience is non-relational, an unbroken fluid totality in one 'now', an undivided lapse". What he objected to

[1] *Principles of Logic*, Second Edition (1922), p. 724.

was James's assumption that this doctrine was inconsistent with idealism and his consequent failure to accept the answer, laid by it ready to his hand, to the problem which the doctrine raised. That the teaching of idealism should here have been ignored by him only showed "that Professor James, like his public, failed to realize the wealth, the variety, and the radical differences which are to be found in that outburst of German philosophy which came after Kant".

The problem was how from present, actual, non-relational experience to pass to the familiar world of interrelated actual and non-actual or ideal elements—to the world, for instance, in which we have an existent present united with a non-existent past and future, or, more generally, to the world of objects and ideas. The clue to the answer was just what had been before the world for a century in the Hegelian doctrine of the identity of the universe or world of reality with what is given in immediate experience. Let these be taken as different and separate, and the problem of their union becomes insoluble. Let them, on the other hand, be taken together: let it be taken to be *reality* that lives and moves in experience, and, when experience expands into past, present, and future, or again into objects and ideas, let it be taken to be reality that is its content and that is qualified by these distinctions, and the road at least to a solution is open. But James and his followers, by committing themselves to the assumption, that reality is *no more* than our immediate experience or a succession of such experiences, had closed their eyes to this, with the result that knowledge to them is essentially a temporal process of facts—the mere series of experienced events, beginning with the idea and ending with the object. It was to commend this paradox that James had used all his great persuasive power. He had indeed succeeded in investing it with a certain plausibility, but only by covertly and inconsistently bringing in the symbolical character of ideas and the self-transcendence which his own doctrine denied. To be consistent, radical empiricism must remain true to its primary assumption, that reality is from the first a mere flux, diversified by sensible selection and emphasis, and that beyond these (which must include its own philosophical assertions) there is at no stage anything, even in appearance, which is ideal. To develop the doctrine, as thus consistently interpreted, Bradley held, would be a work of the greatest philosophical interest, but it had not as yet been anywhere attempted. When it had been so developed in an authoritative form, it would be time enough to consider its claims.

Seeing that radical empiricism has its *rationale* in the endeavour to escape the net of a logical system, and would fain include logic itself in the fluidity of the flux, it is perhaps not likely to take up Bradley's challenge. But in refusing, it can hardly resent being treated, if not as a negligible quantity, as at best giving us only half-measure, by a writer who like Bradley believed in Logic—not indeed as everything, but as supreme in its own field of speculative truth.

3. Idealism v. Logical Realism

As contrasted with pragmatism, the form of realism advocated by Bertrand Russell, in spite of his fundamental difference with it, had a singular attraction for Bradley. "The general tendency which Mr. Russell so ably represents", he wrote in 1909, "has long been as good as unadvocated among us, and there has thus been, I agree, a very serious defect in the main body of our speculation."[1] One of the most drastic chapters in *Appearance and Reality*, giving the key-note of all his subsequent criticism, was that in which he sought to prove the ultimate unreality of relations.[2] While this contained a challenge to idealistic philosophies like Green's, which tended to rest upon relations as something ultimate, it was also and much more a challenge to the form of realism which was then shaping itself both in America and England, founded on the attempt to atomize reality into relations and their terms.

To a monistic philosophy like Bradley's, there could be no question of relations which were extrinsic to their terms, any more than terms extrinsic to their relations, and in the Appendix to the Second Edition of *Appearance and Reality* he went on to attack the doctrine of extrinsic relations at its strongest point in the supposed externality of the relations of position in space. As against this, he maintained that a space consisting of merely external relations is an inconsistent abstraction. "Without qualitative differences there are no distinctions in space at all, there is neither position nor change of position, neither shape nor bodies nor motion."[3] "The merely external", he

[1] *Essays*, p. 237 *n*. He adds: "Whatever the result, Mr. Russell's inquiries should do a service to philosophy which, I imagine, it would not be easy to overestimate."
[2] On this see above, p. 265.
[3] *A. and R.*, p. 577. This was written before the physical doctrine of relativity had appeared. "Relativity" does not establish idealism, and has probably less

concluded, "is in short our ignorance set up as reality." In the present volume, coming to the question from the side of his renewed emphasis on forms of experience, which could by no possibility be resolved into terms and their relations, Bradley found in the realism that based itself upon this plurality the opposite defect to that which he found in radical empiricism.

While the latter had rightly taken its starting-point from immediate experience, it had failed to explain the origin and place of the relational system involved in all knowledge which is based on ideal construction. Russell's logical atomism[1] had sought in its starting-point to do justice to mathematical and logical entities, but had failed to find a place for forms of reality which were either infra-relational or supra-relational. This central failure was reflected in his recently developed theory of judgment,[2] according to which (1) judging is a relation between the judging mind and what it asserts or believes; (2) what it asserts or believes is never anything single, but involves a "multiple relation"; (3) the only whole or complex is that formed by the judging mind and the manifold of objects to which it is related. Professor Stout had already criticized this doctrine on the ground that the items to which the mind is related in judgment must have a unity of their own, if, as the theory holds, one of them is a relation. If it is insisted that the unity comes from the act of judging, this is to move from the position of an uncompromising realism in the direction of a thoroughgoing idealism.[3] Bradley accepts this criticism so far as it goes, but uses the opportunity to give the argument a broader sweep by attacking the root fallacy of "multiple relations", and at the same time showing what a "thoroughgoing idealism" would really mean.

What he and the idealism for which he stood meant, was not the denial that there is any unity except that made by the judgment. This might have been accepted by overzealous disciples of Kant, according to whom "every particular relation found in the object appears to have been thrown out by an impartial, not to say casual, eruption from the synthetic Ego". But it has no place in the revised

philosophical significance than has been claimed for it, but it does seem to go a long way to disestablish the view that spatial relations and qualitative differences are separable from each other.

[1] He had not yet given his philosophy the title he afterwards adopted in his essay in *Contemporary British Philosophy*, vol. ii.

[2] *Proceedings of the Aristotelian Society* (1910–12).

[3] *Ibid.*, 1910–11, p. 205.

doctrine that has come to us from Hegel. It puts the cart before the horse, and turns everything the wrong way. Idealism, truly interpreted, stands as solidly as any realism for the objective order as forming the content of experience. What it rejects as false in a realism like Russell's, is the attempt to treat the elements of the objective order as not only distinguishable, but as separable and independent entities.

Starting from relations and terms, and adopting the method of ideal experiment, we find it impossible to have the one in entire independence of the other. Remove the terms, and the idea of relation is forthwith destroyed. "The terms may be to the last degree vague and schematic, but once attempt to abstract them and you find that they are there." Relations, moreover, are only one kind of universal, and Bradley carries his criticism a step farther by attacking the whole idea that you can have bare universals without any reference to the aspect of particularity. This aspect may be difficult to observe, and, as in the case of terms, may be highly schematic—necessarily so, seeing that we are treating it as momentarily irrelevant, in fact as a negative element in the situation; but it is as certainly present as negation is present in all affirmation.

It only remained to show that the idea of "multiple relations" was wholly untenable. It is of no use in showing how relations, of themselves, can make a unity. A relation is one thing, a relational whole is another. The fact (to take Russell's example) of jealousy has a unity from which any analysis of it must start, and which can never be made up again out of the elements, into which you analyse it, taken by themselves. In a word, the idea of multiple relations is without foundation. It is "merely something which has to be postulated because the theory requires it".

Again, as in the case of radical empiricism, Bradley sketches the outline of a philosophy which, if it were ever filled in, would have to be taken seriously, but to which he does not think that Russell would be prepared to commit himself. Relational realism, consistently interpreted, still remains, and is likely to remain, a programme.

These critical passages in the book have an interest for us as an illustration of Bradley's resource in the application of the principles he had sought to establish in *Appearance and Reality*. Absolutism shows itself in them anything but a dead lion. But our special concern is with the indications they contain of the operation of the logic of these principles in his own thought. What here forces itself upon our attention is that, in both the above criticisms, the emphasis is laid on a factor which, if not denied, was held in the background in the former work. In the criticism of radical empiricism the argument rests on the presence of reality in the forward movement from fact to idea, from the immediate to the mediate—a movement which involves the presence, whether in latent or developed form, of each in the other. Similarly, in the criticism of relational realism the point of the argument is the mutual implication of terms and relations, more generally of particular and universal. What the reader finds it difficult to understand is how the wholeheartedness with which the writer seems here to accept this unity in both cases, is compatible with the rejection of it as in neither case "intelligible". Granted that each of the elements is only intelligible in virtue of an underlying totality, of which it is merely one aspect, granted also that it is legitimate to ask why this totality expresses itself in these particular differences or in any differences at all, is it anything more than what Bradley would call a "bare possibility" that such an ultimate unintelligibility can invalidate what we have found when we have obeyed his injunction to "realize what we are doing and cease to ignore and forget"?

As a matter of fact, when we turn from these critical essays to those which seek to deal constructively with the problem of the relation between the undifferentiated and the differentiated forms of experience, what the writer is himself aiming at is the extension of the bounds of intelligibility with regard to it.

4. THE PSYCHOLOGY OF VALUE

We have already noted the new emphasis on the idea of value in the opening chapter of the *Essays*, and remarked on the promise it contained. The promise was not fulfilled, but the existence of the world of appreciation and judgment raised problems both in psychology and metaphysics which could not be longer postponed. How on the basis of the doctrine of immediate experience, which Bradley shared with the leading psychologist of the time, could the rise of such a world be rendered intelligible? How could we avoid the recognition with William James of "Many Worlds",[1] ruled by

[1] See *Principles of Psychology*, vol. ii. p. 290.

apparently different principles of valuation, and therewith of the problem of their relation to one another, finally that of the relation of these various principles to the one on which his own philosophy was founded? It is these questions that are attacked in the chapters which form the second of the main groups of Essays above mentioned, and mark a further stage in the progress of his thought.[1]

Already in *Appearance and Reality* Bradley had indicated that there were problems in reference to the doctrine of immediate experience awaiting solution.[2] In discussing the process by which a portion of the "internal mass of feeling" could become an interchange between self and non-self, he had raised the question first of how the existence of this surrounding nebula could be observed at all, and secondly of how we can become aware of a discrepancy between this felt whole and any object that may be separated off from it. But he had put aside the detailed answer as belonging rather to psychology than to metaphysics. It is to this primarily psychological question that he now returns in the chapter "On our Knowledge of Immediate Experience".[3]

He begins by trying to make it clear that, while what he is speaking of is a form of consciousness, as contrasted with the unconscious or "subliminal", it excludes anything that can be called consciousness of self in opposition to object. To hold to the existence of this form is vital both for psychology and metaphysics. With it "the road is open to the solution of ultimate problems, without it there is none". But while opening the road it does not bring us there, and he proceeds to deal with two of the principal difficulties: How can immediate experience ever serve as a criterion of value? How can that which *ex hypothesi* is not an object become itself an object, as it must needs be if we are to know and speak of it at all? It is impossible here to follow in detail his answer to either question. He is dealing himself in condensed form with admittedly a very difficult subject, and his treatment of it is not made easier by a certain hesitation to come to grips with it. It must be sufficient to state what seems to be the main point in regard to each.

[1] The most important are that "On Our Knowledge of Immediate Experience", "On Floating Ideas and the Imaginary", and "On My Real World".
[2] *A. and R.*, p. 93 *n.*; *cp.* p. 110.
[3] In the short analysis that follows I have had the advantage not only of James Ward's critical article on "Bradley's Doctrine of Experience" in *Mind*, N.S., vol. xxxiv. No. 133, but of manuscript notes in Ward's own copy of the *Essays* in the possession of the University of Birmingham.

(a) It is important to realize that the first of these questions is not the metaphysical one of the reason *why* any object satisfies feeling. Objects, the writer insists (thereby cutting away the ground of theories which would resolve valuation into the satisfaction of subjective feeling or "interest"), satisfy feeling because they are of a particular nature; we do not assign them a particular nature as good, real, true, beautiful, because they satisfy immediate feeling. What we can see as a matter of fact is that our satisfaction *may* be an element in all sense of value, and may itself, in certain cases, be the criterion; and our question is *how* this can come about. His answer is that it can only come about by the object itself becoming qualified by that which before "was merely felt within" us. In his criticism of this passage Ward asks whether this means that, when we are pleased with anything, we transfer our feeling of pleasure to the object. Clearly this is not what Bradley means by the transference of the felt. Emotional tone enters into the situation, but it is the toned *quality* that is felt, and it is this, as the situation develops, that comes to qualify the object.[1] To take his own example, we are instinctively repelled or attracted, or perhaps both repelled and attracted, by a person or thing. There is something in our psychic content which has not yet been recognized as a quality of the object or perhaps of our own feeling about it. But let the object be allowed to develop itself (by redintegration or what not), and we come to see things in it we had previously only felt. We know what it was that affected us in it, and what the affection in ourselves was, with the result that "the object may be said to be judged in accordance with and from the content of immediate experience".

(b) With this answer to the first of the two questions before us, we can attempt the answer to the second. What is wanted here is not a proof that immediate experience can be made an object. The fact Bradley takes to be incontestable,[2] in the sense not only that a part of the content can be separated off and made an object, but that we can know the general character of this phase of experi-

[1] Speaking of the relation of these two, Whitehead insists on the priority of emotional tone to sensation: "We prehend other actual entities more primitively by direct mediation of emotional tone and only secondarily and waveringly by direct mediation of sense" (*Process and Reality*, p. 197). There need be no contradiction between this view and Bradley's so long as it is admitted that sense must be there in some degree and must become prominent "as the situation develops".

[2] Herein again agreeing with what I understand Whitehead to hold as against Santayana (*ibid.*, p. 199).

ence as a "many in one", which can be contrasted with what has become a manifold of related elements. What is wanted is an intelligible account of *how we come to know it*. Given the suggestion of the idea of it, the proof of the idea will be that of all other ideas, its success as a working hypothesis.

Starting from what he has already said of immediate experience as a criterion, Bradley rests his case upon the difference we feel when the object before us, which is accompanied with a sense of unrest or dissatisfaction, gains definiteness of character by some addition coming from without the object, or from some previously undistinguished element in it, or again (when it seems to come from within ourselves), from something which we ourselves previously felt. The instance he gives is the familiar case in which "the beautiful reality" seems to say for us what we always wanted to say but never could express, and gives us a "positive sense of expansion and accord", which in the other case is absent, its place being taken by a feeling of mere novelty or otherness. Reflecting upon this difference and the impossibility of explaining the source of the new matter as coming either from a non-perceived object-world outside our particular object, or from any non-relational "nebula" within it, we get the idea of an experience neither objective nor relational, but immediate. Once there, and so far accepted as real, we can go on to test it by its "working".

It is characteristic of the writer that at the end of his exposition he is ready to admit that it may contain logical flaws, and that the real origin of the idea may have escaped him. He is even prepared to say that in the idea of immediate experience at all we run up against something inexplicable. All that in the end he claims is that it is an idea necessary both for psychology and metaphysics, and that, granted its existence, its mode of operation is not unintelligible.

Even with the additional light which the chapter throws upon this central point in Bradley's philosophy, the reader might still fail to find in it complete assurance that he has escaped the snare of solipsism, and that the feeling appealed to as the source of the criterion of the completeness of the object is not something merely subjective.[1] But in this book, on account of its form, more than

[1] On the sentence at the beginning of the last paragraph: "Nothing in the end is real but what is felt, and for me nothing in the end is real but that which I feel", after underlining the last three words Ward remarks, "here is B. still building on his πρῶτον ψεῦδος" (MS. note).

elsewhere we have to take one passage with another in order to get the writer's complete meaning, and in a later Essay, where the present passage is referred to, he adds the all-important point that the reason why the object before the mind can be experienced as defective, in contrast to the fuller content present in feeling, is that "The universe is one with my mind", and that "not only is this so, but the Universe is actually now experienced by me as beyond the object". Whereas, therefore, the essence of solipsism is that the universe is experienced on the hither or subjective side of the object, according to Bradley, "with the object there is present something already beyond it, something that is capable both of demanding and furnishing ideal suggestions and accepting or rejecting the suggestions made".[1]

So explained, there is nothing in the doctrine of immediate experience with which Neo-Kantian Idealism need have any quarrel. It was indeed a step farther away from Kant's intellectualistic interpretation of the unity of apperception, but it was all the nearer to a true interpretation of what Hegel had done in bringing the movement in our mind into integral connection with the movement of reality. Where Bradley would differ from Hegel is, as he tells us in the passage above quoted, that he hesitates to say that the defective object *itself* suggests its own completion, or to call the process Dialectic. The defect in the object must be felt, though not necessarily as such, and it can be felt because, along with the object, there is also felt the presence of something that goes beyond not only the object but mere feeling. The "dialectic", such as it is, is the movement initiated in our minds by the sense of discrepancy between the object and the totality which is present to feeling: the "wonder", as Plato would put it, in which all philosophy begins. If anything deserves the name of "direct realism" it must be something like this.

The real question that is raised by the doctrine, as thus filled out, is not of its consistency with Hegelian Idealism, but of its consistency with that which is no less fundamental in Bradley's philosophy, namely, the severance he found in his *Logic* between idea and existence at the point where relational thought emerges. If, as is here clearly taught, the universe is one and continuous with the mind in feeling, and if it is itself the source of the movement forward from mere feeling to reflective recognition, why at the point where

[1] P. 225.

this discernment begins must we suppose that the umbilical cord between the Universe and the work of the mind is severed, and ideas go forward in a way of their own, which is not the way of the Universe? Putting it otherwise, why, if *feeling* as such survives the process of being transcended in *thought*, should thought be doomed to proceed with a halter round its neck? and why, when *it* is transcended in some higher manifestation of reality, should the rope have to be tightened and thought be no more?

Again, it seems as though the logic of Bradley's system is here leading him to a reorientation of his mind on the whole subject of the relation between the factual and the ideal world, and it is with all the more interest that the reader turns to the chapters "On Floating Ideas and the Imaginary", and "On my Real World".

5. THE MANY WORLDS

In the *Logic* Bradley had seemed to be committed to the existence of "floating ideas" in the sense of ideas "divorced" from existing reality. Bosanquet's criticism in *Knowledge and Reality* had cut away the ground beneath this doctrine, and by the beginning of the 'nineties the question of the existence of ideal worlds of various shades had passed into psychology. In his brilliant chapter on "The Perception of Reality",[1] William James had called attention to these "sub-universes" as something to which it was the task of "the complete philosopher" to assign a place in "the total world which *is*". In the first of the above chapters in the *Essays*, dating from 1906, we find Bradley prepared to revise his doctrine on the whole subject. There can, he now insists, be no idea, however remote from the world of ordinary sense-perception (defined as that which is "continuous with the felt, waking body"), whether in imagination, dream, even madness and error, which is a mere wanderer without a local habitation and a name in some kind of world. We may still use the notion of "floating ideas" for certain purposes; for other purposes it is useless. As implying the possibility of a clean cut between idea and existence, such a notion "gets into trouble at once" with past and future and with universals: "and to say that when confronted with the facts of the spiritual world, with art and science, morality and religion, it proves inadequate, is to use a weak expression".

[1] *Principles of Psychology* (1890), vol. ii. pp. 291 foll.

So far there is nothing which is not in James's dissertation on the text "The Many Worlds". In the sentences just quoted it might seem that Bradley was adopting the pragmatic test of utility as the criterion of truth. But while James is mainly interested in the psychological question of degrees of *belief*, Bradley's concern is with the metaphysical question of the reality of these various worlds. He wishes to show that any hard and fast division between them "will have to give way to degree and to differences in value"—"human value" if you will, so long as "human" is not understood as "merely human".[1] He is accordingly prepared to turn these admissions *against* pragmatism by showing, as a corollary from them, that what moves and is (unaware) insisted on by the "will" is "the reality in another world of that idea which it brings here into fact". "The star that I desire does not wander outcast and naked in the void. My heart is drawn to it because it inhabits that heaven which is felt at once to be its own and mine."[2] Other important corollaries follow with regard to hypotheses, suppositions, the place inhabited by rejected ideas in predication, and by self-contradictory ideas. Finally, we have a statement which ought to be taken along with his much criticized doctrine that the subject of all judgment is "reality as a whole": "The subject in a judgment is never Reality in the fullest sense. It is reality taken or meant to be taken under certain conditions and limitations. It is reality understood in a special sense."[3]

In the short, till then unpublished, chapter on "My Real World" he follows up what is here said of the world of dreams, with speculations which open up mystical vistas somewhat foreign to Bradley's usual contempt for "mere possibilities", in which it is unnecessary to follow him.

In all this the student of Bradley will be apt to find a notable contrast not only to James's psychological treatment of the same subject, but to the order of his own argument in *Appearance and Reality*. There we had the different claimants for reality, taken mostly from the world of common sense, first criticized and rejected

---

[1] P. 64 *n.*

[2] P. 35. *Cp.* the last of the "Terminal Essays" in *Logic*, Second Edition.

[3] P. 32. *Cp.* 41 *n.* and *Logic*, Second Edition, p. 626, where these passages are referred to. There is, of course, no necessary contradiction here. In all judgment there is an implicit reference to the whole world of reality with which the explicit subject is continuous.

as appearance, and then readmitted, with flags struck or drooping, to subordinate places, as after all more than *mere* appearance. Here the order is reversed. First we have an insistent claim for the reality of whole areas, which are commonly chevied out of the actual world, but are here raised to honour, though only in the end to be relegated to inferior places as failing of the order and system that marks our normal waking world of fact. For this change of emphasis, and for the service here done to Idealism by bringing it into line with that larger spirit of hospitality both to the subworlds and the superworlds overlooked by the incomplete philosopher, which was so marked a feature of the better thought of the time, Bradley's readers could have nothing but gratitude. They found in it one among other signs of a certain mitigation of the severity meted out in the earlier work to what they commonly called their "real world". As Ward put it, "there is no further mention of sundry suicides, those frequent tragedies of the earlier work. . . . There is here more about God and 'my real World', and less about an unmitigated Absolute with its *nulla vestigia retrorsum*, or the ultimate disappearance of appearances".[1] Everything, in fact, is justified in its own sphere and degree.[2] What sympathetic readers are apt to feel is that the proper complement of the teaching of these particular chapters, in which the emphasis is laid on "the degree of order and system possessed and effected" by any idea or universe of ideas as the criterion of its reality or value, is a fuller recognition than they anywhere find of the place of reason and the world it inhabits as the principle at once of the being and of the knowledge of that "order and system". How, with these concessions as to the reality of the ideal side of our world, could the writer continue to insist, as he does even more emphatically in this volume, that the demand for theoretical consistency may lead us away from reality and so "in the end to practical discord and sterility"?[3] Will the Terminal Essays explain?

[1] *Mind*, art., January 1925, pp. 38 and 36.   [2] *Essays*, p. 470.
[3] *Ibid.*, p. 432.

CHAPTER IX

BRADLEY (v). TERMINAL ESSAYS

1. INGATHERINGS

The "Terminal Essays", published along with a Commentary on the text in the Second Edition of the *Principles of Logic* in 1922, are a fitting conclusion to what Bradley wished to leave in book form.[1] "After Last returns the First." In these he comes back to logic, and offers us in this way succinct material for a comparison of his later with his earlier views, and a measure of the distance he has travelled in the interval.

We have already said enough of the ambiguities of the *Logic*: as to the *starting-point*, whether this is something immediate and undifferentiated, or something already containing qualitative distinctions and relational elements; as to *judgment*, whether there are unmediated judgments, or whether all judgment is not in the end mediated; as to *ideas*, whether these may float independent of existence; as to the *real subject*, whether it was reality in general or some selected aspect of it; as to *thought in general*, whether it did not contain an element of arbitrariness and subjectivity which invalidated it; finally, as to the *criterion of truth*, whether this was to be sought outside of the field of thought in immediately given fact or within it in the form of thought itself. By the time of which we are speaking Bradley had long ago reached a point of view from which all these questions might be regarded in a new light.

He had come to realize more fully: (1) That judgment in the explicit sense was not the starting-point, but emerges from a basis of immediate experience, in which, while there is no overt separation between the *what* and the *that*, yet there may be selection and abstraction, and so far something "ideal". (2) That what he had shown to be true of judgment in relation to ideas is true of judgment proper in relation to inference. All judgments, even the simplest and most apparently direct, have a ground or a "because", and may, when this is brought into evidence, develop into inference. (3) That floating ideas are a myth; that there is no idea, however aerial and fragile, that is not attached to some kind of reality, and which does not by this attach-

---

[1] On being approached by the present writer on the subject, he was unwilling to reprint the articles in *Mind*, N.S., vol. x foll., on "Conation", etc.

ment qualify it: if in the air, ideas still qualify that air.[1] (4) That, though it is true that "judgment asserts really of the Whole Universe",[2] "a total affirmation of the mere whole would itself be nothing". Judgment by its very nature is bound to distinguish and select, and there is therefore in it an element of arbitrariness and subjectivity: the world appears, as a matter of fact, to a psychical centre in my mind; but once the selection is made, all choice, so far as thought is concerned, is at an end: we give ourselves up to the object: judgment and inference are "the self-development of the object" in us. It is true that *we* are still active, but to say this is not to say that ours is the only activity. Reality is active also, and our activity is in fact its activity in us. (5) Most important of all he had come to a clear understanding as to the true and only criterion. In an interesting passage in the first of the "Terminal Essays" he dismisses the idea, that there is any touchstone by which a proposition isolated and by itself can be tested, as a mere superstition, and goes on to insist that "the true and real criterion is the idea of reality and truth as a system. Our actual criterion is the body of our knowledge made both as wide and as coherent as is possible, and so expressing more and more the genuine nature of reality. And the measure of the truth and importance of any one judgment or conclusion lies in its contribution to and its place in our intelligible system".[3] He adds that, though he had failed in the *Logic* to insist on it, this was the doctrine which he had "inherited and had always held", and he ends by referring the reader to Bosanquet's "consistent and invaluable" advocacy of it in his writings.

2. The Question Raised by Them

In view of these developments, in the interval we might have expected when we turn to these terminal essays to find them reflected in a change of his attitude to the general question of the relation of judgment to reality. We might have expected to hear less of the inherent defect of ideas and of the failure of truth to express the real nature of the world than we find in his earlier work. In certain respects we are not disappointed. We hear no more of the "divorce"

[1] *Essays*, p. 35.   [2] *Logic*, Second Edition, p. 632.
[3] *Cp. Essays*, p. 440. "Humanity has progressed so far as it has progressed by life and work in the daylight. And to seek for truth and satisfaction elsewhere I take to be the essence of superstition."

of the "what" from the "that". In the single place,[1] where so far as I know there is mention of this aspect of ideas, it appears as merely a "loosening" and a "transference". In the passage above quoted he not only refers in generous language to Bosanquet's constructive work, but conveys into his own statement some of the fine spirit of moderation that marks Bosanquet's writings throughout. Knowledge does succeed in "expressing more and more of the genuine nature of reality". The measure, moreover, of this success is not any unintelligible Absolute, but "*our* intelligible system". The ultimate test of a truth is not its power to enclose an unenclosable whole, but its necessity, if our own intellectual world is to stand. As Bosanquet puts it, the principle of verification is "This or nothing".[2]

But as his thought moved from emphasis on the defect of ideas and judgment as a prescinding of character from existence, it was only brought to lay the stress instead upon the limit imposed upon them by the unknown conditions which they failed to include. Similarly, as he became clear that the element of arbitrariness fell to the side of the psychical aspect of thought, as taking place in a soul-centre, and did not affect its logical aspect, this insight only seemed to reveal more clearly from another side the inherent defect of logic. Take it as you will, the psychical aspect is one of which logic by reason of its abstractness is unable to take account, and, so far as it fails, leaves us in the air.[3] Even in the matter of the criterion, after repeating in the second essay what he had said about it in the first in the statement that "the growth of our knowledge consists in a widening and in an increase of systematic mediation", he turns to lay emphasis on the inclusion of conditions, and warns the reader that "a system of knowledge where all judgment and inference would at once be the other and be perfect is in detail unattainable.

---

[1] *Logic*, Second Edition, p. 640.
[2] Probably his little book on *Linear Inference* is the best extant statement of this point of view. Bradley alludes to it in his Preface as coming too late to be used in his book. If it had come in time, one cannot help thinking that it would have had a still further moderating influence on many of his statements. Bosanquet's own view is little more than an application of Aristotle's celebrated account of the way in which truths get established like a wavering unit in an army by joining in the general rally. On such a view there is an appeal to an Absolute, but this is not something outside and altogether beyond the general system of knowledge, as the "Destiny" of Greek mythology is beyond the counsels of Gods and men, but rather is the redeeming, stabilizing spirit that moves and works in it, like the Deity whose nature is love in the Platonic and Christian theology.
[3] Pp. 616–617.

It remains an ideal, genuine and to be realized actually more and more, but never completely".[1]

It would of course be possible to understand this warning as merely a confession, which Idealism must share with every other philosophy, of the limits within which human knowledge necessarily moves—omniscience being no more a part of the idealist than of any other sane philosophy. But that it is more than this to Bradley is evident from his devoting the main part of the first and most important of these essays, in an otherwise illuminating review of the main types of inference, to proving it in detail. What concerns us here is the contrast between the note which is struck by writers, who, like Bosanquet, were devoting themselves to a positive view of the relation of thought to reality, and the critical and sceptical tone which continued to the end to dominate Bradley's treatment of the same subject. Is this contrast merely a difference of emphasis? or is there something more that requires to be taken into account, if we are to form a proper estimate of the relation of Bradley's work to the central line of idealistic thought?

3. BRADLEY'S "SCEPTICISM"

That there is a difference in emphasis has perhaps been made sufficiently plain. It was due in part to the essentially critical bent of Bradley's own mind, in part to what he conceived of as the main need of the time at which he began his work. He set out on his philosophical travels under the profound conviction that what was chiefly wanted was a criticism of principles, which had been too incautiously accepted from the past. He seemed himself to require the stimulus of opposition to prevailing complaisances to bring his powers into full operation. Some of the best chapters in his works are those in which he is congenially occupied in tearing to shreds popular "superstitions" in ethics, logic, psychology, and metaphysics. Idealism itself was not spared in so far as it seemed to him over-confident of the finality of its principles. By the time he came to write *Appearance and Reality* dialectical criticism may be said to have become a habit and to have given a permanent list to his thought on the sceptical side. In spite of a growing tolerance in his later work of different points of view, it was, as we have seen, the inevitable failures rather than the achievements, not only of other extant philosophies, but of his own and of any philosophy,

[1] P. 639.

that came more and more to be the prevailing note. But the question recurs whether this is more than a matter of emphasis or whether it does not represent a weakness in some of the principles in which he himself relied.

It must always be with the greatest diffidence that the student who is familiar with the subtlety and many-sidedness of his thought ventures to differ from Bradley upon fundamental points. Yet I believe that there are two assumptions[1] closely allied to each other, which, in spite of his constant self-criticism and his claim to rest his conclusions on experiment alone, he permitted himself to make and never afterwards fully renounced. The first was that *when we leave what he rightly held to be concrete particular fact as given in immediate experience and idealize in any form*, whether in that of the initial ideality that comes with the selection and abstraction of an object from its concrete background, or in the explicit ideality of the universals, by which in judgment we seek to characterize and individualize what has been thus selected, *we necessarily have dropped out the element of particularity and actual existence*. Logic as commonly interpreted, and as he himself interprets it, may not concern itself with this element. It may, like other sciences, be in this respect abstract. But the *science* of thought so taken is one thing, *thought itself* is another, and in the larger conception of logic which Hegel, following Plato, sought to vindicate, in spite of the stock criticism of its abstractness, there is no point which is more constantly insisted upon than that thought moves and only can move within the circle of Being, and that in the Notion there can be no severance of the ideal and the actual, the universal and the particular.

It was this point that was seized upon by one of the acutest and sanest of his critics, who probably would have himself repudiated "Hegelianism", so early as 1902 as the central ambiguity in Bradley's system. "It is one thing to say", wrote Professor Stout,[2] "that my judgment always qualifies something other than my immediate experience. It is quite another to say that it does not qualify my immediate experience at all. The position for which I contend is that any complete judgment does both coincidently." "Prescinding", "divorcing", "cutting loose", Stout goes on to say, are merely metaphors for what we more appropriately call discerning or distinguishing. "But what we discern or distinguish never does or can

---

[1] In addition to those he acknowledged. See above, pp. 260 foll.
[2] *Aristotelian Society Proceedings*, 1902-3. *Cp.* his article on "Bradley on Truth and Falsity" in *Mind* of July 1925.

lose connection for our thought with that from which or within which it is discerned or distinguished." The criticism ends with an appeal to the idealist principle to which Bradley is himself committed, that "to distinguish is to unite".

It is useless in reply to such an argument to appeal to the generality of the idea in the predicate. You not only never can have a universal without some reference implicit or explicit to particular instances, but in the predication of a universal of any particular subject there is a mutual qualification of the one by the other, which never permits the subject to escape into mere particularity or the predicate into mere generality. Once grant this central principle of idealistic philosophy, and there are whole sections of Bradley's work which would require to be rewritten so as to bring them into harmony with it.

The second of the assumptions referred to is the same in another form and is open to the same criticism. We have seen the emphasis shifting from the necessary abstractness of all ideas to the necessary conditionality of all judgment and inference, from the impossibility of including the "that" in the "what" to the impossibility of including all the conditions in any judgment or inference. In this case as in the other we are supposed to leave the security of immediate experience, and by our abstractions from it to commit ourselves to unknown conditions which may require a quite indefinite amount of qualification in what is judged or inferred. Like ideas, inferences live by compromise, but so far as their creditor is concerned it is an altogether unpromising compromise. The debt they have contracted can never be repaid, and in the end threatens any credit they may have accumulated. Leaving metaphor, the assumption here made is that it *is impossible to determine the relatively unknown from the nature of what is already known, and that what we regard ourselves as knowing is wholly at the mercy of a relatively unknown which is entirely merciless.*[1] So long as we are at all ignorant, all our judgments not only may but must be false. Press this conclusion (as Bradley was bound to press it, and as we have seen he does press it in the "Terminal Essays"), and it is difficult to see how we can escape from what we can only regard as an uncompromising scepticism.

Against any such conclusion we are surely justified in appealing to what Bradley himself so powerfully urged in *Appearance and Reality* as to our knowledge of the criterion as inclusiveness and coherence of content. The presence within us of this criterion is sufficient

[1] The phrase is Stout's, *loc. cit.*, p. 25 *n.*

guarantee that what we now hold in this form can never be wholly put to shame. It embodies a form which will be preserved to the end. *More* truth there may well be, changing the interpretation of the matter of present truth, but it will be *more of the same.* Bradley has himself urged this with respect to immediate experience.[1] Why should it be different with regard to mediate experience? If in the one there is a true sense in which we know not only the nature of what is, but the nature also of what shall be, why should it be otherwise in the other?

But this criticism does not make an end of Bradley's case, and it may still be urged that, be the implication of particularity in ideas what it may, the ideal of the ideas is the inclusion of existence in their network, and this can never happen except by their ceasing to be ideas and becoming one with fact. Similarly with judgment and inference, be our knowledge of the unconditioned what it may, they can never include all the conditions without ceasing to be themselves. But this is only to state the above assumptions in another form. The ideal of judgment is never the abstract identity of subject and predicate, thought with thing. Its ideal is to hold reality in the form of the unity of thought and thing. The idea moves forward *with* reality into distinction and difference *within a whole and a unity* of which it never loses hold. To deny this is to treat all discrimination as falsification and all plurality as illusion. Similarly with regard to inference. Its ideal is never the inclusion within itself of all the grounds and conditions in such a way that it ceases to be inference as we know it. Inference is not come to destroy but to fulfil. The goal towards which the spirit as intelligence presses is not a unity in which one of its elements passes into the other in such a way as to be the euthanasia of both, but a unity of differences each of which maintains its own relative independence. In the present case, to ask for a ground why there should be this difference between ground and consequent is equivalent to asking why the nature of things should be what it is. Like the question of why there should be reality and appearance (of which it is only another form), it points to an ultimate unintelligibility; but perhaps it is the question itself that is unintelligible, not to say worse.

4. SUMMARY OF ADVANCE

So much has already been said of the points at which Bradley sought to get forward from the current statements of idealist

[1] See p. 266 above.

doctrine, so much also of the ambiguity which attaches to some of his results, that a brief summary of what he seems to the present writer to have achieved may here suffice.

That he started from a general acceptance of Hegel's teaching and sought to remain true to it throughout, is sufficiently plain from the record of his own writings. His earliest work reflected it in the fields of history and ethics. If his *Logic* represented a momentary hesitation as to some aspects of it, this was more apparent than real. In *Appearance and Reality* it reasserted its influence. Over and over again in this and his later writings he refers deferentially to Hegel as to no one else. In a controversial article in 1894[1] he seems even to regret that he had not followed him more closely. It is in terms finally borrowed from Hegel that he sums up the teaching of his chief work to the effect that "Outside of spirit there is not, and there cannot be any reality, and the more that anything is spiritual so much the more is it veritably real".

Where Bradley sought to get forward from this basis was in the direction of freeing Hegelian Idealism, as it had taken root in England, first, from certain defects of method with a corresponding narrowness of outlook; secondly, from a certain obscurity as to the true standard or criterion of the supreme value which we call reality; and thirdly, from a certain arrogance as to the claims of philosophy which it had taken over from what was more questionable in Hegel.

1. We have seen how from the 'eighties Bradley was in revolt against the intellectualism, with which a too exclusive occupation with Kantian knowledge-theory and the logical aspect of things had infected current idealism. One of his chief services to it was to break away from this narrowness of outlook by bringing it into line with recent developments in psychology and metaphysics. This did not mean to him, as it did to some contemporary idealistic writers,[2] merely setting up feeling and will alongside of, still less in opposition to thought, as something more fundamental. If everything might in a sense be said to depend upon the will to good, good was something more than the will directed to results in the moral world, whether in the Kantian or the pragmatist sense. An

[1] *Mind*, N.S., vol. iii. p. 236. "If I had been able to keep closer to a great master like Hegel, I doubt if after all perhaps I might not have kept nearer the truth."

[2] Royce, for example, at one stage of his development (see *infra*, Pt. III. Chap. V. foll.), not to speak of less "absolute" pragmatists.

essential element in the good is *theoria* or vision of this and all other worlds in their connection with one another and "under the form of eternity". Delivery from the limitations of an overstrained rationalism was to be sought for, primarily, in another way by the revival of a neglected element in Hegel's own teaching: the existence, namely, of an immediate form of experience, in which the different elements of thought, feeling, and will, and the distinctions and relations which each involves, have not yet developed their separate powers, and in which psychic centres are directly in touch and continuous with reality and through it with one another. He felt, as keenly as his critics, the difficulty of this idea, and showed his usual courage in facing the problems which were raised by it both for psychology and metaphysics. But he also felt that on his view the difficulty was less than on any theory which ignored or denied the reality of this phase of experience; and, once he had formulated it, he never wavered as to its fundamental importance.[1]

2. But there was another way in which he sought to counteract the rationalistic bias of current idealism, bringing us to the second of the above-mentioned points. The reformed Kantian doctrine, for which that philosophy stood, had always been powerful in its insistence that the standard of truth must be sought, not in agreement of idea with a given object, but primarily in the systematic completeness of the ideas to which adherence to the teaching of experience leads. But, beyond the question of the criterion of truth, there was that of the criterion of a reality of which truth was only one of the manifestations, and which expressed itself equally in goodness or the identity of our wills with the will of God, and in beauty or the felt harmonies of nature and art. It was to define this criterion that Bradley bent himself in the two central chapters of *Appearance and Reality*. They were in effect an attempt to give a more adequate interpretation of the meaning of Individuality than had yet been given, and were the starting-point of much that was most significant in the work of his contemporaries, notably of

[1] I do not think that Ward's suggestion to the contrary in his article on "Bradley's Doctrine of Experience" (*Mind*, N.S., vol. xxxiv. No. 133) can be substantiated. What Bradley was willing to treat as an open question, was not the existence of such immediacy as a phase of developed experience to which we all perhaps at moments sink back, but whether there ever was or is in the development of the race and individual a stage in which experience is merely immediate. See *Essays*, pp. 173-174. His general view found confirmation both in what William James taught and in what he failed to teach with regard to this immediacy.

Bosanquet in his *Gifford Lectures* on that subject. Here also he was as fully aware as any of his critics of the difficulties which his account involved, constantly anticipating them and endeavouring with more or less success to meet them. More particularly in the last chapter of *Appearance and Reality*, in "Ultimate Doubts", and in the subsequent *Essays*, he points to the difficulty that Metaphysics itself (seeing that it is a form of knowledge) must inevitably fail to give us the truth about a whole of reality which goes beyond knowledge and truth. Yet he was convinced that, "apart from this foundation in the end we are left without a solid criterion of worth of truth and reality". On the other hand, *with* it, as something "owned by the universe" and knowable by us as so owned, we have a right to say "higher, truer, more beautiful, better, and more real—these on the whole count in the universe as they count for us".[1] Even the central difficulty just mentioned he sought to turn to profit as an appeal to that wholesome form of scepticism "which feels in its heart that science is a poor thing if measured by the wealth of the real universe", and justifies "the natural wonder which delights to stray beyond our daylight world and to follow paths that lead into half-known, half-unknowable regions".[2]

3. To-day this element of "mysticism" will hardly be regarded as a defect in a presentation of idealist doctrine. There are passages in Hegel in which a place is claimed for philosophy above the highest that any other experience, even religious experience, can give, and unwary disciples have been too apt to follow him in this. Bradley was aware that philosophy might be made and had often been made a religion. Perhaps he would have admitted that it cannot be true to itself, any more than art or science can be, unless it so far forgets itself and becomes to its devotee his "principal way of experiencing Deity". But he was aware too of the danger it thus ran of turning differences between philosophies into "the practical antagonisms of conflicting creeds", which it was just the function of philosophy to avoid.[3] Philosophy had indeed to find a place for all forms of experience and vindicate the reality of their objects. "A true philosophy", as he puts it, "must accept and must justify every side of human nature including itself."[4] And for those engaged in it this cannot be done without result in the form that moral, æsthetic, or religious beliefs take, which might cause distress and

---

[1] *A. and R.*, pp. 550–551.
[2] *Ibid.*, p. 519.
[3] *Essays*, p. 31.
[4] *Ibid.*, p. 14.

heart-searching in view of what was felt to be practically essential.

In view of the admitted limits of metaphysics, a man might well be justified in holding to these essentials. "If a man is assured on the part of philosophy that his religious belief is false, he is warranted at least formally in replying that this is so much the worse for philosophy."[1] This and similar passages in his later work have been taken as a surrender to pragmatism. This is wholly to misunderstand him. It is one thing to renounce a theoretic for a pragmatic justification, it is quite another to turn practical working into theoretic proof. Morality and religion may prescribe to a man whether and to what extent he may engage in philosophy. Once he has committed himself to philosophy, it is his master; and morality and religion themselves demand that he should give it his heart, in the confidence that, if it cannot lead him to *all* truth, yet it cannot fail of *truth*.

In all these respects I believe that Bradley's work is epoch-making in the history of Anglo-Saxon Idealism, and that he may with justice be called its fourth founder.[2] In all future advance account must be taken of what he has done in broadening and deepening its foundations, freeing it from the taint of a subjectivist epistemology on the one hand, and of a narrow logicalism on the other. That he has not lost sight of something, which was essential to the older doctrine and to a sound idealism of the kind he aimed himself at establishing, cannot, I believe, be affirmed; and the recognition of this must make anyone who tries to follow him in the main lines of his advance as loth to call himself a Bradleian as he was to call himself a Hegelian. If what has been said in this study by way of criticism should be of aid in the recovery of the missing link, it may have done something to point the way to a still surer advance. That there are things new and old still to be drawn from a line of thought which has been so fruitful in the past, can only be doubted by one who has lost faith in the inexhaustible richness of that world of reality of which thought, in spite of its limits, is one of the highest expressions.

[1] *Loc. cit.*, with which may be compared the caustic remarks on confusing philosophy with practical edification. *A. and R.*, p. 450.
[2] Professor Robert Macintosh's phrase; he does not tell us who the other three were. He probably had in mind Hutchison Stirling, Green, and Caird.

PART III

IDEALISM IN AMERICA

CHAPTER I

TRANSATLANTIC ECHOES OF EARLIER MOVEMENTS

1. THE FIRST WORDS OF IDEALISTIC PHILOSOPHY IN NEW ENGLAND

While there was nothing in New England corresponding to the Cambridge Platonism of the seventeenth century, there were already at the beginning of the eighteenth minds that reflected the same speculative interest in the foundations of religious consciousness and the same openness to the larger movements of thought that were taking place on the continent of Europe and in England. It might seem paradoxical to claim any such openness for the great Calvinistic preacher, Jonathan Edwards, and the present writer can remember his surprise on coming upon his early Notes on Being which have the merit of containing what Woodbridge Riley[1] calls the first words of idealistic philosophy on that continent. Whence they derived their inspiration is matter of interesting conjecture. What seems most likely is that it came rather from a subtle air wafted across the Atlantic from the Malebranchean mysticism of which his English contemporaries John Norris and Arthur Collier had drunk so deeply than from what he found in any individual writer. When at a date probably subsequent to the Notes, but still in his undergraduate days, Edwards tells of the pleasure with which he read Locke's Essay on the Human Understanding, "far higher than the most greedy miser finds when gathering up handfuls of silver and gold from some newly discovered treasure", we feel what American philosophy lost by the life-long imprisonment of his powerful mind in a particularly narrow form of Calvinistic theology, that was to follow.[2]

Less tantalizing, but with hardly more influence on the immediately subsequent thought of his own century, was the echo of Berkeley's philosophy in the writings of Samuel Johnson, the first President of King's College, afterwards Columbia University, in New York. Berkeley's connection with America even at that time went deeper than his temporary residence in Rhode Island in the years 1729 and 1731. Johnson found in his teaching a refuge at once from the fiery Calvinism of New England theology and the

[1] Author of *American Thought.*
[2] Yet his treatise in the *Freedom of the Will* (1754) is the first and one of the greatest landmarks in that new field.

cold Deism that was the natural outcome of the Lockean philosophy. As we know from his correspondence with Berkeley, he was no slavish follower, but sought to combine what he learned from him as to the nature of God with the Platonic doctrine of archetypes which he found in Norris and others.[1]

But apart from the political turmoil into which the American Colonies were about to be plunged, the same influences as checked the Platonizing spirit in England there made themselves felt, and as in the old, so in the New England this early dawn of idealistic philosophy was overcast for wellnigh a century.

There is a further interesting parallel between the circumstances under which at the coming of a better day thought reverted to the older line in the two countries. While it is true that Coleridge's influence as a philosopher was more definitely felt in America than in England, it was insufficient to direct men's efforts to a thorough-going revision of philosophical principles, and there, as here, the first reviving influence came rather from the side of what might be called "literary idealism" than from any first-hand study of the sources from which light was coming. There also it was only when the failure of literary prophecy to satisfy either the speculative or the practical needs of the time came to be obvious that men were roused to the deeper search.

2. THE TRANSCENDENTALISTS

The introduction of German influences into American philosophy is traceable to the second decade of the nineteenth century, when, following the example of Coleridge in 1798, a group of New England students[2] paid a visit to Germany and returned with authentic news of the new movements in thought that were there taking place. Their visit was to bear fruit later in translations from German writers of the Romantic movement in Frederick H. Hedge's *German Prose Writers*[3]—the American equivalent to Carlyle's early work in

[1] We have now for the first time a full account of the work, philosophical and other, of this interesting namesake of our own more famous Dr. Samuel Johnson, in the four memorial volumes on his *Career and Writings*, edited by Herbert and Carol Schneider in 1929, with a foreword by President Murray Butler. In the "autobiography" here published for the first time (vol. i) we have a record of his intercourse with Berkeley, and in vol. ii. pp. 263 foll. the correspondence above alluded to, Berkeley's part in which is of special interest as containing his reply to the difficulties of a particularly acute mind.

[2] George Bancroft, Edward Everett, and George Tickner.

[3] First Edition, 1849; Second Edition, 1870.

this field. The immediate effect which they produced was to turn the minds of some of the younger Unitarian ministers of Boston from the arid Deism to which a too slavish adherence to the Lockean tradition had brought the theology of their Church, to something that was more in harmony with genuine religious feeling. Unitarianism at this time was itself defined by an able contemporary as "the result of the attempt to explain Christianity by the sensual philosophy instigated by a desire to get rid of mystery and to make everything clear and simple".[1] It was in this way that Christianity was gradually emptied not only of all appeal to miracle, but of the elements of the great Platonic tradition which was of its very essence. In emptying the bath the reformers had emptied out the baby. For this reason the same writer could say "Unitarianism was sound, sober, good sense. But the moment a preacher rose to eloquence he rose out of his system." It was therefore not surprising that the younger men turned with relief to the philosophy of immanence which was to form the speculative basis, so far as it had one, of the Transcendentalist movement.

The school took its name from Kant, whether directly, or indirectly through Carlyle, who undoubtedly exercised a powerful influence on Emerson its founder and in the early days its chief hierarch.[2] But its very use of the word to indicate truths which transcended ordinary time and space experience, and its claim on behalf of the human reason to possess an intuitive apprehension of such truth show how little justification there is for attributing to its members any more accurate knowledge of the teaching of Kant than Carlyle himself possessed. So far as the movement owned any German prophet, it was not Kant but Schelling, whose ideas were being made familiar on the other side of the Atlantic by the publication of American editions of Coleridge's works.[3] But here also the school as a whole was too content to get its metaphysics from second-hand sources. Its members were for the most part ministers, teachers, men of letters, who, as Woodbridge Riley puts it, "cared more for free

[1] Article on the Unitarian Movement in New England in *The Dial*, vol. i. p. 431.
[2] D. A. Wilson quotes Carlyle to the effect that "Emerson took his system out of *Sartor*, and my other writings in the first instance, but he worked it out in a way of his own" (*Carlyle at His Zenith*, p. 138).
[3] The *Biographia Literaria* as early as 1817; *Aids to Reflection*, with Preliminary Essay and Additional Notes by James Marsh in 1829; *The Friend* in 1831. The movement of thought from Kant to Schelling and Coleridge's relation to it were sketched by an able writer (The Editor?) in the *Christian Examiner* in 1833.

thinking than for precise thinking". Hence it is that, while the historian of Transcendentalism[1] has chapters on "The Seer", "The Mystic", "The Critic", "The Preacher", "The Man of Letters", and the "Minor Prophets", he has none on "The Philosopher".

Yet some of them were keenly conscious of this limitation, and made intermittent, sometimes pathetic, attempts to remedy it. Theodore Parker lamented that he "was meant for a philosopher, and the times called for a stump orator". Margaret Fuller wrote: "When I was in Cambridge I got Fichte and Jacobi. I was much interrupted, but some time and earnest thought I devoted. Fichte I could not understand at all, though the treatise I read was intended to be popular and one which he says must compel to conviction. Jacobi I could understand in details but not in system. It seemed to me that his mind must have been moulded by some other mind with which I ought to be acquainted in order to know him well—perhaps Spinoza's. Since I came home I have been consulting Buhle's and Tennemann's histories of philosophy and dipping into Brown, Stewart, and that class of books."[2]

Repelled by these difficulties, which Coleridge's published or reported expositions did little to lessen, they betook themselves to a writer as lucid as Coleridge was confused, in whom they seemed to find all they wanted for their work as preachers and propagandists. Linberg's translation of Victor Cousin's *Introduction to the History of Philosophy* appeared in 1832, and its readers were encouraged to content themselves with what they there found by George Ripley the transcendentalist "Man of Letters" and editor of *Specimens of Foreign Standard Literature.*[3] In the Introductory Notice to the long extracts from Cousin that occupy the main portion of the first volume of the Specimens Ripley wrote: "The objects at which Mr. Coleridge aims, it seems to me, are in a great measure accomplished by the philosophy of Cousin. This philosophy demolishes, by one of the most beautiful specimens of scientific analysis that is anywhere to be met with, the system of sensation, against which Mr. Coleridge utters such eloquent and pathetic denunciations. It establishes on a rock the truth of the everlasting sentiments of the human heart. . . . Such a philosophy, I cannot but believe, will ultimately find a cherished abode in the youthful affections of this nation in whose history from the beginning the love of freedom, the love of philo-

[1] O. B. Frothingham in his book with that title (N.Y., 1876).
[2] See Frothingham. *Transcendentalism*, p. 286.   [3] Boston, 1838.

sophical inquiry, and the love of religion have been combined in one thrice holy bond." After describing the kind of philosophy that was needed at the time and by whom, he concludes: "The elements of a philosophy of this character, I venture to think, are contained in the doctrines of Cousin and his distinguished pupil Jouffroy as exhibited in the present volumes."

3. SIDE-TRACKING OF TRANSCENDENTALISM

The writer's hopes seem to have been fulfilled even more literally than he expected or perhaps desired. Speaking of the Transcendentalists six years afterwards, the first historian of the new movement could say: "So far as I can judge, they have merely taken up the philosophy of Victor Cousin, and, after comparing it according to their opportunity with that of the more recent German schools, have modified a little some of its dicta, and applied them freely to scientific and practical theology. . . . Of course, they differ considerably from one another: some following Cousin more closely, and others leaning more towards some German; some preferring one set of Cousin's terms, and others another, or coining new ones to suit their fancy. After all, Linberg's translation of Cousin's *Introduction to the History of Philosophy* may be considered the great storehouse from which most of them—*e.g.*, Brownson, Emerson, Parker, etc.— have derived their peculiar philosophical opinions, their modes of reasoning, and their forms of thought and expression."[1]

It was this fatal complaisance as to the foundations of their philosophy that more than anything else was the cause of the dissolution of the movement. Cousin did good service in the emphasis he laid on the history of philosophy and the comparatively detached spirit in which he expounded the work of Kant and his successors. For the rest, in his "Eclecticism" he showed no real comprehension of the philosophical situation in his time, and his "System" went down like a pack of cards before the criticism of Sir William Hamilton on the one hand and the new empiricism represented by Mill, Spencer, Taine, and Lewes on the other. Those who clung to it found themselves as much adrift as sailors at sea who had anchored their vessel to a floating mass of seaweed. While Cousinism was helpless before these attacks, there was nothing in the Hamiltonian dualism of reason and faith, or in the naturalism which seemed the

[1] James Murdock's *Modern Philosophy* (New York, 1844), pp. 177–179.

only alternative, to satisfy the deeper spirit of the age, determined to keep hold of the "eternal values", and yet convinced that, unless the Infinite were in some real sense knowable, there could be no rational justification of them.

But there was another important respect in which Transcendentalism showed itself inadequate to meet the demands of the time. Already in the middle of the century the causes which led to the Civil War were casting their shadow before. The next decade was to see the struggle between North and South which concealed the deeper issue of the unity or disintegration of national existence. What was wanted in the coming years was a philosophy which could do justice to the demand for local and individual freedom, while insisting on the value of the institutional side of life, of which the State was the fullest and most coherent expression. Perhaps it was easy after the events of the Civil War to see all this, but it was not so easy to see where such a philosophy was to be found; and those who, alone on the continent in the 'sixties, saw both are entitled to the credit of discoverers. "The national consciousness", wrote W. T. Harris in 1867, "has moved forward on to a new platform during the last few years. The idea underlying our form of government has hitherto developed only one of its essential phases—that of brittle individualism—in which national unity seems an external mechanism soon to be entirely dispensed with and the enterprise of the private man or of the corporation substituted for it. Now we have arrived at the consciousness of the other essential phase, and each individual recognizes his substantial side to be the State as such. The freedom of the citizen does not consist in the mere Arbitrary, but in the realization of the life which finds expression in established law. This new phase of national life demands to be digested and comprehended."[1]

It was just on this side that Transcendentalism proved itself most inadequate to meet the situation from the practical side. It was a philosophy of detachment from the old world rather than of attachment to the new. The spirit of aloofness from current politics and contempt for institutional life which characterized so many of its adherents is described not without a touch of irony by Emerson in his essay on "Transcendentalism". It is true that this was only one side of the picture. There were those who were profoundly

[1] *Journal of Speculative Philosophy*, vol. i, Address "To the Reader" (condensed).

interested in social reconstruction. "We are all a little wild here with numberless projects of social reform. Not a reading man but has a draft of a new community in his waistcoat pocket", wrote Emerson to Carlyle in 1840. "I am gently mad myself and am resolved to live cleanly. George Ripley is talking up a colony of agriculturists and scholars with whom he threatens to take the field and the book.[1] One man renounces the use of animal food; and another of coin; and another of hired service; and another of the State; and on the whole we have a commendable share of reason and hope."[2] But the forms which their zeal took in the attempt to found Utopian communities were in the spirit of a bygone age, and in the end brought the whole movement into derision. By the 'sixties there was little left of this side of it but the memory of what the Cambridge History calls a "transient experiment in civilization".[3] It was in this way that the time was not only ready but was crying out for a philosophy which should be prepared at once to speak with the new form of naturalism in the gate and to provide a sound intellectual basis for efforts of constructive statesmanship.

Traced to its source, the weakness of the Transcendentalist philosophy was the weakness of the Cousinian Eclecticism. In its "principle" or starting-point, no less than in its "process" of criticism, to use Cousin's own terms for the twin foundations of his system, this had failed to understand both what Kant had done and what he had left undone, while, in committing itself to the doctrine of an immediate and infallible "intuition", it ran the risk of reviving

[1] Preliminary to the experiment of Brook Farm.

[2] *The Correspondence of Carlyle and Emerson*, vol. i. p. 308.

[3] The failure of the most famous of these (Brook Farm, 1842–47) is attributed by Frothingham to its becoming connected with the economic socialism of New York. But the cause was deeper and consisted in the rooted moral individualism of the leaders of the movement. When A. Bronson Alcott (after Emerson perhaps the most outstanding representative of the school, and the author of an independent experiment at Fruitlands) visited England, a meeting was got together in the name of persons prepared to subscribe to the declaration: "We ignore human governments, creeds, and institutions; we deny the right of any man to dictate laws for our regulation or duties for our performance, and declare our allegiance only to Universal Love, the all-embracing Justice." Following naturally on this was "the restoration of all things to their primitive owner and hence the abrogation of all property", and "the substitution of the divine sanction for the civil and ecclesiastical authority". Where there is no organized thought, extremes meet. Alcott, who could apparently listen to all this unmoved, himself writes of the duty of the community to protect itself by the state-education of children against their parents' vices—a principle that would justify anything. See Frothingham's chapters, *op. cit.*, on "Practical Tendencies" and "The Mystic".

the worst features of the eighteenth-century doctrine of the all-suffi-ciency of private judgment.[1] Not only did it find itself in a blind alley, but it had its ears stopped to voices coming from the open road.

What was wanted to provide the basis of a sound idealism was a conception of the Infinite, which could be defended against Posi-tivism, not as a datum but as the underlying assumption of all knowledge, and against Hamiltonian Agnosticism as in a true sense an object of knowledge. It was just such a conception that the successors of Kant had sought to work out and that had taken stable form, for the moment at least, in the philosophy of Hegel.

[1] How this dogma struck an intelligent observer may be illustrated from James Murdock's account of its immense theoretical and practical effects: "It makes the Divine Being, his government and laws, and our relations to him and all our religious obligations and interests—every part of theology, theo-retical and practical—perfectly comprehensible to our Reason in its spon-taneous operation . . . we need no explanations and no confirmations from any books or teachers . . . we are, all of us, prophets of God, all inspired through our Reason, and we need no one to instruct and enlighten us." See the whole passage in this rare book, pp. 181–183.

CHAPTER II

HEGELIANISM IN AMERICA

1. Pioneers

In a former chapter we tried to trace the circumstances under which "Hegel came to England". So far as the same general conditions prevailed in the United States, and as American students of philosophy had access to the literature that was published in England on German philosophy during the first half of the nineteenth century, there was likely to be a general coincidence in the arrival of Hegelianism on both sides of the Atlantic, and it might be supposed that the same story would serve for both. As a matter of fact the movement in America took place under entirely different circumstances, and to a large extent was independent of what was taking place in England at the same time. Such coincidence as there was, was rather the result of the general spiritual requirements of the age, and the fact that in both countries there were found men sufficiently in touch with these requirements and sufficiently endowed with the enthusiasm and industry that were needed for any attempt to meet them. It is this that makes the American story another, and in its course and issue a not less romantic one, than the British.

Although divisions had broken out among his followers in Germany immediately after Hegel's death, and although Schelling had taken occasion to effect a diversion of men's minds in an altogether different direction, even earlier than in England there were those in America who understood the situation and were prepared to recognize Hegel's place as the lineal heir of Kant and the true representative of a philosophical idealism. Among these was Dr. Frederick A. Rauch, Professor in the University of Heidelberg, who got into trouble with the Government owing to the freedom with which he had expressed himself on its ways, had to flee the country, and settled in America in 1831. At first attached to the Theological Seminary of the German Reformed Synod at York in Pennsylvania, he became in 1836 President of Marshall College in Mercersburg. Rauch's familiarity with German philosophy and particularly with Hegel, as well as his thorough identification of himself with the country of his adoption, qualified him in a special degree to carry the life and spirit of German thought into America, and, as he himself expressed it, "to unite German and American mental philosophy".[1] Unfortunately he died in 1841, when he had just begun this work by the publication of his *Psychology or View of the Human Soul including Anthropology*, but not before he had imbued others with the conviction (as the author of the short biography prefixed to the second edition puts it) "that German Philosophy must in the end make itself deeply and extensively felt upon our system of thinking in one way or another"—as it ought to do, "for it embodies elements which are needed to give tone and vigour to our inward life". But the time had not yet come. American students heard of Hegel in the histories of philosophy.[2] Cousin, in the *Specimens* published by Ripley in 1838, had referred to him, with a note upon his works, as having "borrowed much from Schelling", but as starting with "abstractions of his own which in his view are the foundation and the type of all reality". But for twenty years to come he was little more than a name with a mark of interrogation affixed to it.

The earliest record of an attempt to read and understand him occurs in the chapter entitled "Pantheistic Philosophy. Hegel's Absolute Idealism: Logic the only Metaphysics", in Murdock's *Modern Philosophy*. After a short account of "Dr. Geo. Wm. Fred. Hegel, a professor at Berlin, who died in 1831 at the age of sixty-one", Murdock goes on to indicate the relation of his school to that of Schelling, which it "has of late altogether eclipsed". The difference between them corresponds to that between "a system of Absolute Idealism and a system of Realism". After referring to the two volumes of the *Science of Logic* of 1812–16, and the single volume of the *Encyclopædia* republished in 1830, which he has before him, Murdock goes on: "Hegel is the most unintelligible writer I ever read . . . although abundantly warned on this point, I had the temerity to take up his *Encyclopædia* and read it attentively from beginning to end, and some part of it a second, a third, and even a fourth time, comparing it often with his *Logic*, vainly hoping to get some of that logical analysis which he tells us is the basis of all philosophy. But after a fortnight's hard study I was nearly as ignorant of the whole process and of every part of it as when I first sat down." Murdock has the honesty (which some other reporters on Hegel would have done well to imitate) to admit defeat and to

[1] Preface to his *Psychology* (1840).
[2] In the allusions to him in Tennemann's, Morell's, and Lewes's histories, see Pt. II. Chap. II. above.

content himself with reporting the opinions of others, chiefly Krug
—himself a reporter of opinions mainly hostile to the Hegelian
philosophy.

But as in England, so in America it was not only the difficulty of
Hegel's language but the rooted prejudice in academic circles against
German influence that stood in the way of progress. The Eastern
centres of culture, Harvard, Yale, and Princeton, were all still under
the deadening influence of what Santayana calls "the genteel tradition" in its various forms. "Mental and Moral Philosophy", as it was
called, was not a free and independent study but a means of inculcat-
ing that tradition in the literal sense of stamping it in at the end of
the undergraduate course. What struck Emerson's contemporaries at
Harvard was not the inadequacy of Transcendentalism as a philosophy but its danger as a heresy. Yale turned away from Kant and
all his works as "subversive of morality". Princeton entrenched itself
behind the lines of the Scottish Philosophy—seeking, as its Trustees
announced in an address to the Inhabitants of the United States, "to
make this institution an asylum for pious youth in this day of general
and lamentable depravity".

2. Henry C. Brockmeyer

Under these circumstances it is not surprising that the effective
pioneers of the Hegelian movement were found in men who sat
loose to academic tradition and in a city at the time totally devoid of
it. St. Louis has been described by a writer who knew it well in the
'sixties as "different from any other city of the land, more foreign,
more cosmopolitan, more un-American in its conception of freedom".
It was "a Teutonic city of the radical type", in which "a party somewhat like the European Red Republicans had risen to the surface
and threatened for a while to re-enact the bloody deeds of the French
Revolution".[1] Though the freedom of its atmosphere was probably
a factor in the new movement, the Teutonic character of the popula-
tion had little to do with its origin, as the connection of the leader
and the main factor in it with the city was purely accidental.

If the man who first utters a name "with emphasis and even with
affection"[2] in a country may rightly be claimed as its discoverer

[1] Denton J. Snider in *A Writer of Books* (St. Louis, 1910)—himself ranked
by Riley along with Brockmeyer and Harris as one of the leaders of the
movement, of which he was the historian.
[2] Snider, *op. cit.*, p. 304.

there, the honour of discovering Hegel belongs unquestionably to Henry C. Brockmeyer, whom W. T. Harris met in St. Louis in 1858. Brockmeyer was a fugitive not, like Rauch, from governmental but from parental tyranny in his own country, who found his way to America while still little more than a boy, and without education to speak of. His chief qualification to become the leader of a new movement in philosophy was the restless energy that carried him in a short space of time through the stages of thought which had occupied several generations in the community in which he found himself. Though a rebel against the discipline, he brought with him the simple piety of his old home, and when, after making enough money to support himself at college, he felt the need of a wider education, it was to orthodox centres in Georgetown College, Kentucky, and Brown University in Rhode Island, that he betook himself. But he was not the man to be detained long with "the dead material of a dead past" that was then being offered by the teachers of these institutions, and when the "oceanic swell" of the Transcendentalist movement rose near by, he was more than ready to plunge into it. It was under the influence of its teaching that he took his gun and spent some years in the backwoods of Missouri, carrying out the doctrine, as his biographer says, to its bitter logical results: "the only one who did so"—even Thoreau's experiment being civilization itself as compared with his.

By the time we meet him in St. Louis in the 'fifties, he has entered on a third phase of spiritual development. If he was not and never could be an "unromantic", he had got beyond the crude romanticism of the transcendentalists, "transcended transcendentalism", and "emancipated himself from emancipation". It was the living insight, which he thus had attained for himself into the dialectic he was to find worked out in detail in Hegel, that led Harris to describe Brockmeyer as "a thinker of the same order as Hegel", who, before reading anything of Hegel's except the few pages in Hedge's *German Prose Writers*, "had divined Hegel's chief ideas and the position of his system".

Snider has described him as he appeared some ten years later: the centre, which came near to being also the circumference, of the group that was the nucleus of the St. Louis Philosophical Society, "with the quick almost wild eye of the hunter, his face unshaven, the chief feature an enormous nose, his body tall, arrowy, and lithe, raying forth agility and strength which was not only corporeal".

The description of the whole scene reminds the present writer of a similar group in Glasgow of the 'seventies, drunk like the St. Louis one with raw draughts of Hegel, incited and led by their own Brock-meyer in the person of Henry Jones.[1] In after days his restless genius carried Brockmeyer into politics, but not before he had executed a translation of Hegel's *Logic* that was at once the inspiration and the initiation of the younger men and the Bible to which he had himself continual recourse to the last.[2]

3. W. T. HARRIS

It was this man whom William Torry Harris met for the first time in 1858. Himself a man of an entirely different make both physically and intellectually,[3] this "active worker of the philosophical set and most devoted Hegelian propagandist that ever lived" was then a youth of twenty-three. Born at Killingly, Connecticut, he had studied at Andover and Yale, but left college without taking a degree to accept a position as teacher of shorthand in St. Louis.[4]

"He informed me that Hegel was the great man among modern philosophers, and that his large logic was the work to get", is Harris's own description of this fruitful meeting. "I sent immediately to

[1] See Hetherington's *Life of Sir Henry Jones* and Jones's own contribution to the *Life and Philosophy of Edward Caird*.

[2] See W. T. Harris's *Hegel's Logic* (Chicago, 1890), Preface, p. xi. The fortunes of this translation, which is still in manuscript, would alone be a romantic story. Snider, who was employed upon the revision of it, thought that "the catastrophe of the movement was its failure to make accessible to English readers at the pivotal time the creative book of its system", and that "what is true of St. Louis in this matter is true of the rest of the English-speaking world" (*op. cit.*, p. 327). A translation of the *Science of Logic* by British scholars has recently been published, but it would be an act of piety on the part of American idealists of whatever shade of opinion to secure the charge of so interesting a relic, now in the possession of Mr. D. H. Harris, brother of William Torry, in Los Angeles.

[3] "Pale, nervous, twitching, thin-chested and seemingly thin-blooded, sharp face and rather pointed nose, a needle that could prick keenly and deeply into things", is Snider's description of him as he first saw him in 1865 (*op. cit.*, p. 308).

[4] Subsequently he held the post of Superintendent of Schools in that city from 1867 to 1880, when he removed to Concord. In 1889 he was appointed Commissioner of Education for the United States—the fourth to hold that office. In 1889 he received the degree of doctor from the University of Jena in recognition of the work he had done as exponent of Hegel. On his retirement in 1906 the Carnegie Foundation for the Advancement of Teaching conferred upon him the largest permissible allowance for distinguished service. He died in 1909 at the age of seventy-four.

Germany for it, and it arrived late in the year." By the end of 1860 Brockmeyer had translated the whole of it, and Harris set about making a copy for himself, thus making sure that he had "read every word of it". But it made him equally sure that he "did not understand anything beyond the first part of the first volume, and could not follow any of the discussions in the second and third volumes or even remember the words from one page to another". It was "all over my head". Balked in the attempt to take Hegel by storm, Harris returned to the study of Kant's *Critique of Pure Reason*, on which he was already engaged.

If the course taken by the pioneers of thought possesses for another generation the same kind of interest as the trail of the first settlers in a country, the account that Harris gives of his pilgrimage deserves to be remembered. The two steps in it which led from Kant's *Critique* to Hegel's *Logic* were the discovery in 1863 of the meaning of *Für-sich-seyn*, or "independent being", as standing not for indeterminate but for self-determined reality,[1] and secondly, in 1866, of "Hegel's most important *aperçu* and highest thought"—the distinction "between negative unity or substantiality and *Begriff* or *Idee*". Arriving at them thus for himself and independently of the *Logic*, he was able to see that neither of these two doctrines was exclusively Hegel's, but that both went back to Plato and Aristotle, —Hegel's originality consisted merely in giving universal form to the expression of them.

The steps, on the other hand, by which Harris reached in 1879 "his final and present standpoint in regard to the true outcome of the Hegelian system" and the defects in it of which by that time he had become aware, belong rather to the story of the criticism of Hegel in America—the flight from him rather than the flight to him.

What here is of interest and importance for the history of philosophy on the American continent is that by the middle of the 'sixties,[2] by a singular coincidence there was a student of philosophy there, as in Scotland, who in entire independence of academic assistance had discovered what he regarded as the secret of Hegel, and was prepared,

[1] Howison, whose copy of Harris's *Hegel's Logic* was before me in writing the above, in a marginal note derides this "discovery" as "the common property, *e.g.*, of all theologians". This is to forget that to hold a truth as part of a dogmatic system is one thing, to arrive at it as the result of speculative insight is quite another. It is further to forget that there have been mystical theologians who have held quite another view.

[2] J. Hutchison Stirling's *Secret of Hegel, the Hegelian System in Origin, Principle, Form, and Matter*, was published in 1865. See above p. 166.

like his Scottish contemporary, to devote the rest of his life to the exposition of it as containing also the secret of the aspirations of his age. While the work of Hutchison Stirling, taken by itself, was undoubtedly the more massive, the American student possessed advantages denied to the other in his contact with a group of friends whom he was able to inspire with his own genial enthusiasm, and in the possession of funds that enabled him to establish an organ for the exposition and diffusion of the new thought. Certain it is that the foundation of the "Kant Club" in St. Louis and of the *Journal of Speculative Philosophy* (both the first of their kind in the Anglo-Saxon world) and his connection later with the Concord School of Philosophy and Literature,[1] of which, so far as philosophy was concerned, he was the leading spirit, provided Harris for the next twenty years with unique means of making his influence felt.

4. The "Journal of Speculative Philosophy"

In the address "To the Reader" in the first number of the *Journal*, Harris as Editor set forth what he and his friends regarded as the chief needs of his own generation. That which concerned America particularly—the demand for a philosophy which should provide the intellectual background of the political structures in which the national consciousness was struggling to embody itself—has already been referred to. But there was the wider need of a philosophy which should "close the vortex between traditional faith and intellectual conviction" by something that went deeper than an emotional mysticism devoid of real speculative insight. Deeper than both of these was the predicament created by the more philosophical writers on natural science, led by Herbert Spencer, who no longer appealed to sensory data for the foundations of the structure of the physical universe, but to the idea of the "correlation of forces", and thereby transferred the issue to the region of metaphysical speculation by raising the question of the adequacy of this conception as a basis of ultimate explanation. It was because Harris and

[1] The idea of the School dated from 1841 but did not materialize till the arrival in Concord of Harris as guest in 1879. In the following year the first large subscription to its funds was promised by Mrs. Elizabeth Thompson of New York, on condition that Harris should emigrate from St. Louis to Concord. (See F. B. Sanborn's *Recollections of Seventy Years*, vol. ii. pp. 486 and 489.) Without possessing the philosophical genius either of Hutchison Stirling or of Edward Caird, Harris was able to combine in a degree the work of both, and do by himself for America what they together did for England.

his companions thought they saw in the Hegelian philosophy a sword wherewith to smite the three-headed monster of anarchy in politics, traditionalism in religion, and naturalism in science, that they found the courage to undertake and the perseverance to carry through the task of naturalizing it in America.

With the address "To the Reader", the short preface on the "Speculative", explaining what the principle of the new departure must be, and the long leading article on "Herbert Spencer", giving a foretaste of what might be expected from the application of the principle to the chief intellectual problem of the time, Hegelianism may be said to have arrived and issued its first manifesto in America.

Harris himself seems to have felt that they marked the end of what he calls his "apprenticeship" and the beginning of what he foresaw would be a long "journeymanship". He was keenly conscious of the difficulties of the task. In addition to those mentioned above, there was the "popular demand for originality", the lack of which had been a recurrent reproach to American philosophy: "Why rifle the graves of centuries? Why desecrate the Present by offering it time-stained paper from the shelves of the Past?"[1] He had indeed his answer ready: "To examine the thoughts of man—to unravel them and make them clear—must constitute the earliest employment of the speculative thinker; his first business is to comprehend the thought of the world, to dissolve for himself the solutions which have dissolved the world before him." But it required courage and patience. Meantime he and his coadjutors could only express their belief that "our course in the practical endeavour to elevate the tone of American thinking is plain: we must furnish convenient access to the deepest thinkers of ancient and modern times. To prepare translations and commentary is our object. Originality will take care of itself. Once disciplined in Speculative thought, the new growths of our national life will furnish us with objects whose comprehension will constitute original philosophy without parallel".

How far this faith was justified time alone can declare but it explains why so much of the earlier numbers of the *Journal* was occupied with translations and expositions of Fichte, Schelling, and Hegel. Whether or not it was a mistake, as Snider thought it, to neglect the more solid work of the publication of the *Logic* may be a question. What is certain is that the *Journal* stimulated a wide interest in German philosophy and literature, and to a large extent

[1] *Journal*, etc., vol. i. p. 127.

provided the material for the series of more systematic treatises which in the 'eighties and 'nineties rivalled the similar series in England.[1] It was just such work ("spade" if you like) which was necessary to naturalize Hegel on the new soil. America was fortunate, and in its own way original, in being able to bring forth the men who had the power, and to provide for them the means of doing it.

[1] Grigg's German Philosophical Classics for English Readers and Students, edited by George S. Morris, may be said to be the American equivalent of Blackwood's Philosophical Classics. Besides Harris's book on *Hegel's Logic*, this series contained one by the Editor on *Hegel's Philosophy of the State and History* (1887; Second Edition 1892). G. S. Morris's adhesion to the movement is all the more significant as he had to fight his way to his final position inch by inch. (See R. M. Wenley's *Life and Work of George Sylvester Morris*, New York, 1917, which contains an interesting picture of the philosophical forces against which Hegelianism had to make its way in the years following the period referred to in this chapter.) In the 'nineties appeared *The Ethics of Hegel, translated Selections from his Rechtsphilosophie*, with an introduction by J. M. Sterrett (Boston, 1890); *Theory of Right, Duties, and Religion*, with a supplementary essay on Hegel's systems of Ethics and Religion, by B. C. Burt (Ann Arbor, 1892); S. W. Dyde's *Hegel's Philosophy of Right* and *Hegel's Educational Ideas*, by W. M. Bryant, both in 1896; in the new century *Hegel's Logic*, by J. G. Hibben, 1902; *Thought and Reality in Hegel's System*, by G. W. Cunningham, 1910; *Hegel Selections* in the Modern Students' Library, Ed. J. Loewenberg, 1929. If the work represented by these and other books falls short in mass of the work done in England in the same period, we have to set against this the more practical direction which it took. After Bradley's *Ethical Studies* (1876), little or nothing was published in England claiming to be an exposition of Hegelian ethics till the present century.

CHAPTER III

CHARLES PEIRCE

I ANTI-HEGELIAN REACTION

By the end of the 'seventies, in America as in England, the Secret of Hegel may be said to have been out. Hegelianism had had its school and its organ first at St. Louis, then at Concord. It had its Professors and their disciples, all over the country. Here, too, its victory had been almost too complete, and philosophy was in danger of passing into bondage not only to Hegelian ideas, but to the formulæ in which they were expressed. But in America as in England reaction had already set in from different sides.

There were those who from the side of religion took alarm at its apparent pantheism. Writing just of this time,[1] George Herbert Palmer may be said to have summed up the common view of at least one powerful group of New England thinkers when he tells us: "I have gained more from Hegel than from any other philosopher, but I never became a Hegelian. Hegel has too slender a sense of personality and practically none of sin or conscious wrongdoing, a fundamental fact. Freedom is his sacred word, but with him it means necessity, and has nothing to do with the alternative choice of common speech."

Even more ominous of coming reaction was the brilliant reconnoitre of William James in his 1882 article in *Mind*, "On Some Hegelisms".[2] "We are just now witnessing", he wrote, "a singular phenomenon in British and American philosophy. Hegelianism, so defunct on its native soil that I believe but a single youthful disciple of the school is to be counted among the *privat-dozenten* and younger professors of Germany, and whose older champions are all passing off the stage, has found among us so zealous and able a set of propagandists that to-day it may really be reckoned one of the most powerful influences of the time in the higher walks of thought. And there is no doubt that, as a movement of reaction against the traditional British empiricism, the Hegelian influence represents expansion and freedom and is doing service of a certain kind. Such

[1] *Contemporary American Philosophy*, edited by G. P. Adams and Wm. P. Montague (1930), vol. i. p. 39.
[2] Afterwards reprinted in *The Will to Believe*.

service, however, ought not to make us blindly indulgent. Hegel's philosophy mingles mountain-loads of corruption with its scanty merits, and must now that it has become quasi-official make ready to defend itself as well as to attack others. It is with no hope of converting independent thinkers, but rather with the sole aspiration of showing some chance youthful disciple that there *is* another point of view in philosophy, that I fire this skirmisher's shot, which may, I hope, soon be followed by somebody else's heavier musketry." James's shot, like that of "the embattled farmers" at Lexington, was to be "heard round the world".

But it was not only among those who had been trained in orthodox tradition or in other schools of philosophy that there was reaction. There were also among those who attached themselves in the main to the great idealistic tradition, of which Hegel was the last outstanding representative, men of sturdy individualism, determined indeed to go forward, but equally determined to do it from self-chosen ground *nullius addicti jurare in verba magistri.* Without abandoning the interpretation of Kant on which Hegelianism was founded, they felt that its main doctrine of the "identity of thought and reality" was either a monstrous paradox, or concealed under the term "thought some occult meaning entirely different from anything ordinarily meant by it". The "dialectic", moreover, was felt to have been greatly overworked. The old stupid mistake of supposing it to be founded on the denial of the law of non-contradiction was indeed no longer made. It was even accepted as a useful description of the zigzag character of human progress. But when put in the place of Providence as the controller of human destiny it was apt to appear to be the Juggernaut which von Hartmann saw in it, crushing out individual freedom as effectively as the materialism it was thought to have superseded. Finally, they were tired of a formalism that was content to repeat Hegel's jargon instead of following his great underlying thought and applying it freshly to new problems. What the writer on the movement in the *Cambridge History of American Literature*[1] says of Harris, "He thought he had gained insight when he had translated a fact into his own terminology", was felt to be more or less true of the whole generation. The general result was that Hegel seemed to many to have only "repeated the feat of Jonathan Edwards by constructing a system which none could refute and few could accept".[2] If the

[1] Vol. ii. p. 238.   [2] Garnett's *Emerson*, p. 59.

"objective idealism" for which Hegel stood was to have a future in America it must be recast in a new form.

Two of those who so thought were thinkers with special training in their own particular, though entirely different, departments and of peculiar philosophical genius. Though separated by some fifteen years in age, they were neighbours and friends for a considerable part of their lives in Cambridge, and exercised a profound influence upon each other's thought. It is because their names, and especially that of the younger of them, are more likely than those of any others of their contemporaries to be associated with the form of Neo-Hegelian doctrine, that most closely corresponds to the new developments which were taking place at the same time in England, that I have selected them for special consideration in these Studies.

2. PEIRCE AS GERMINAL THINKER

When the history of American philosophy in the nineteenth century comes to be written in greater detail than hitherto, the important place of Charles S. Peirce as a pathfinder in every one of the many fields that his work touched will have to receive fuller recognition than has as yet been accorded to it.

Born in 1839, his life covered the period which felt the influence first of the romantic idealism of the transcendentalists, then of the Hegelianism of W. T. Harris and the St. Louis group, later of the reconstructed idealism of which Royce was the chief representative, and finally of the more radical reactions against absolutism led by James and Dewey. With these movements Peirce was not only in intimate touch, but from one side or another in lively sympathy. It was for this reason that it was his fate, as it has been of few others, and those only the greatest, to be claimed as a founder by different schools of thought. By writers in logic he has been assigned a leading place in the development of the Logical Realism associated in England most conspicuously with the name of Bertrand Russell. He himself claimed the title of a "critical common-sensist",[1] reminding one both of the older, naïver realism of the Scottish school and of the critical realism of Santayana and his friends. Readers of Royce's later works are familiar with the frequent allusions to his debt for some of their more original features to suggestions derived from Peirce's writings. Finally, and with more popular éclat, his connection

[1] *Monist*, vol. xv. pp. 481 foll.

with pragmatism, first as the inventor of the name and of the often repeated formula of its method, and secondly as the advocate of its favourite doctrine of the essential indeterminateness of nature and "cosmic weather", has been exploited in the interest of that form of philosophy. It is in this sense that he figures in Woodbridge Riley's sketch of *American Thought* as the representative of what he calls "primitive pragmatism", that William James dedicates his *Will to Believe* to him, and that he has been claimed by Dewey in Professor Cohen's volume of selected papers[1] as "in the literal sense of the word pragmatist, more of a pragmatist than James". "If philosophic eminence", writes Cohen himself,[2] "were measured not by the number of finished treatises of dignified length but by the extent to which a man brought forth new and fruitful ideas of radical importance, Charles S. Peirce would easily be the greatest figure in American Philosophy."

While some may find in this many-sidedness an admirable feature marking Peirce out as the truly seminal writer that he was, and while Professor Cohen is within his right in contenting himself in his Introduction with drawing attention to it, others may find in it more of a challenge. Is it possible, they will be inclined to ask, that a writer, imbued with the spirit of logic as he was, believing as he did in the ultimacy of what he calls "concrete reasonableness" in thought and practice, claiming as he constantly does that "Synechism", or faith in the essential continuity of things, is the chief mark of his thought, should have left his own philosophy with so little internal coherence that like the empire of Alexander it fell at his death into a collection of warring satrapies? Is it not more likely that a closer study of his work in its origin and development as a whole will show it to have been governed by some central tendency that allied it more nearly with one or other of the great traditions of philosophic method and doctrine? This question is all the more pertinent, seeing that in the essay already quoted on "The Pragmatism of Peirce" Dewey ends his summary with the suggestive question "whether recourse to Peirce would not have a most beneficial influence on modern discussion". If Mr. Dewey's many admirers are going to take this call of "Back to Peirce" with the seriousness with which he obviously issues it, it is a matter of the utmost importance to have a clear

[1] C. S. Peirce, *Chance, Love, and Logic* (1923), edited by Morris R. Cohen.
[2] Article on "Later Philosophy" in the *Cambridge History of American Literature*.

idea as to which of these many Peirces is the real one from whom to take their start. The present chapter is a very imperfect attempt to set his thought in a truer perspective than seems to the writer hitherto to have been done, in the hope, which he shares with Dewey, of the beneficent effect that such an understanding may have on contemporary discussion. If it were to form the basis of a kind of Peace of Utrecht which might end the long and bitter war between pragmatism and its enemies, whether of the idealistic or the realistic camp, it were a consummation devoutly to be hoped.

What is here proposed is *first* to give a short sketch of the development of his ideas, as that may be gathered from the most accessible of his published articles, with special reference to their bearing on pragmatism, and *secondly*, setting aside in the light of this development the attempt to identify him with that form of doctrine as founded on misapprehension, to summarize the main influences that seem to have moulded his thought and as a matter of fact allied him with quite another tradition. If reference to his contributions to symbolic logic[1] is omitted altogether, and his theory of induction only lightly touched on, it is not because of any underestimate of their importance, but partly because of inability to do justice to them, partly because they seem to the writer, and probably would have seemed to Peirce, only of importance in so far as they threw light on his general philosophy. He himself reminded us of the priority of the more general problem when he wrote: "What sort of a conception we ought to have of the universe, how to think of the *ensemble* of things, is a fundamental problem in the theory of reasoning."[2]

3. Relation to Descartes, Berkeley, and Kant

Peirce's chief published articles fall into three clearly marked groups: (1) Those which he contributed to the *Journal of Speculative Philosophy* in 1868 (the second year of its existence); (2) those which were published in the *Popular Science Monthly* ten years later in 1877-78; (3) those which after the interval of another decade appeared in the *Monist* of 1891-93; to which as a kind of aftermath may be added (4) those which in the first decade of the present century he

[1] Ueberweg's *History of Philosophy* (Heinze's Edition, vol. iv. p. 554) speaks of his logical doctrine of relatives as "a link between Morgan's work and that of Schroeder in his *Algebra of Logic*".

[2] *Chance, Love, and Logic*, p. 108.

contributed to the *Monist*, Baldwin's *Dictionary of Philosophy*, the *Hibbert* and other journals.

The articles of the first of these groups possess a special interest for the student of American philosophy, not only because of the time and place of their appearance, but far more because of their contents. They were coincident with the new start that philosophy in America was then taking in the earnest first-hand study of German, and more particularly of Hegelian Idealism, of which the *Journal* was the chosen organ. On the other hand, they seem to have been quite independent of that movement for their inspiration, and are more truly regarded as representing an independent spring of fresh constructive thought. It was not only that, as was to be expected from one who, as he himself tells us, had been bred in the laboratory, Peirce approached philosophy from an entirely different angle from that of the St. Louis idealists, but that, in so far as he connected himself with the European tradition, he went to the great mediæval thinkers rather than either to Plato or Hegel. As if further to mark the independence of his starting-point, he took his bearings from a criticism of Descartes, the real "father", as he called him, "of modern philosophy", rather than from a criticism of Kant. It is to the correction of the errors of Descartes, as they affect both the nature of thought and the reality of the thinking self, that the first two articles, on the subjects respectively of "Questions Concerning Certain Faculties Claimed for Man" and "Some Consequences of Four Incapacities", are directed.

The "faculties" he chiefly attacks in the former are that of the direct intuition of truth, whether by external perception or by introspection; that of imageless or, as he would afterwards have expressed it, "signless" thinking; and that of conceiving of an incognizable absolute. With regard to the first of these he develops the doctrine which is the keynote of his whole theory of knowledge as consisting essentially in inference, conceived of as a continuous process in which it is a mere blunder of principle to ask for any first or last. Similarly in what he says of the second incapacity we have the germ of his later doctrine of signs. In a fuller account of Peirce's theory of knowledge, what he says about immediacy and inference with special reference to the question of the status of the sign would call for more detailed treatment.[1] For our present purpose it is to what he says

[1] The same holds of the matter of the articles of the same date as those under review, especially that "On a New List of Categories", which were published in the *Proceedings of the American Academy of Arts and Sciences.*

of the last of these incapacities, and the consequences which in the second article he deduces from it, that the main philosophical interest attaches.

He has already convinced himself that upon Cartesian principles, involving as these did the separation not only of matter or the *res extensa* from the *res cogitans*, but of the world of objects in general (including the mind itself) from the subject, "the very realities of things could never be known", and that any theory which contained the least vestige of these principles, including Kant's itself, was involved in the same condemnation. In this fundamental criticism he was at one with the Hegelians of St. Louis, but he had reached it by a path of his own and he connected it with a fresh interpretation (the result of a profound study) of the realism of St. Anselm and Duns Scotus rather than with Fichte and Hegel. He saw that his rejection of any immediate intuition of truth involved at once the rejection of the popular interpretation of the mediæval doctrine. ("Any given piece of popular information about scholasticism", he held, "may be safely assumed to be wrong.") What Duns Scotus taught and what any true realism must teach, was not the reality, before or side by side with particular things, of universals which might be the objects of intuition, but the existence of an as yet undetermined reality (a "vague", to use a later expression of Peirce's own) towards which the reason of man was on its way, however far short it may yet have fallen.

Here also we have the first sketch of a view of which his subsequent philosophy was only a fuller development. It rests on the distinction between the *ens* or reality which is relative to the limitations of our information and reasoning power, and the *ens* or reality to which full information and correct reasoning will bring us. Seeing that this fullness of knowledge is an ideal of the long future and one that is only conceivable in a society whose achievements are a corporate rather than an individual possession, it involves the belief in "a *Community* without definite limits and capable of an indefinite increase of knowledge". In this way "those two series of cognitions, the real and the unreal, consist of those which at a time sufficiently future the community will always continue to affirm and of those which under the same conditions will ever after be denied".

The doctrine, here sketched on the basis of a criticism of Descartes, is further developed in a careful article of about the same date in review of Fraser's edition of Berkeley, which appeared in the *North*

American Review of 1871. As a criticism of Berkeley the article is interesting as the first clear statement, so far as I know, in American philosophy of the real place of Berkeley in the history of thought as "the half-way station between Locke and Hume". "The innocent Bishop generated Hume, and as no one disputes that Hume gave rise to all modern philosophy of every kind, Berkeley ought to have a far more important place in the history of philosophy than has usually been assigned to him."

There has recently been a reaction against the treatment of Berkeley's philosophy as a mere transition phase of the empiricism of Locke, with a correspondent emphasis on the appeal to his doctrine of "divine causation".[1] What is particularly interesting in Peirce's account is the connection he established between these two phases of the Bishop's thought as an example of the strange but not infrequent historical alliance between nominalism and Platonism. It was just his denial of reality to sensible things which drove Berkeley to seek for it in an otherwise unknowable cause of phenomena. But to assert the existence of such a cause adds nothing to our knowledge. All that we can mean is that there are regularities in events in relation to what we call a thing, which have to be taken into account beforehand in the conception of that thing. What as a matter of fact we assert when we speak of the reality of a thing, is that there is a "general drift" of human thought which will lead to "one general agreement, one catholic consent", a consent which is not limited to men in this earthly life but extends "to the whole communion of minds to which we belong, including some probably whose senses are very different from ours".

By the object's independence of our thought is therefore meant not independence of all experience and thought. "It is a real which only exists by virtue of an act of thought knowing it, but that thought is not an arbitrary or accidental one, but one which will hold in the final opinion." This Peirce admits is phenomenalism of a sort, for it denies the reality of any unknown thing-in-itself, which is the cause of our sensations. But it is *not* the phenomenalism which makes the reality of a thing dependent on its being in *our* consciousness. Its standard of the truth of an idea or of the reality of an object is not its presence to perception, as with Berkeley, but its coherence with the general experience which "does not depend at all on its being actually present to the mind all the time".

[1] See G. A. Johnson's book referred to, p. 73 above.

On the other hand, it *was* the phenomenalism of Kant if we recognize *first* that Kant's "Copernican step was precisely the passage from the nominalistic to the realistic view of reality", and *second* that "It was the essence of his philosophy to regard the real object as determined by the mind: in short, as the normal product of mental action and not as the recognizable cause of it."

What is remarkable in all this is, in the first place, the sureness with which Peirce has arrived for himself at what is essential in the teaching of Kant as the doctrine that "the real object is determined by mind"; in the second place, the connection of this teaching with mediæval realism, interpreted not as the assertion of the independent existence of universals, but as the assertion of the existence of a conceptual interpretation of the particular thing, as experienced here and now, which would bring it into harmony with "the body of realities"; and thirdly, the decisiveness with which he identifies himself with this form of realism and thus links his own teaching explicitly with the great mediæval tradition of which Duns Scotus was the founder.

In the general conclusions to which he had thus been brought he was undoubtedly influenced by his reading of Kant, but going along with this there was the antipathy which the mathematician in him felt to a doctrine that excluded from reality everything of which an image could not be formed, and that closed the door on negative quantities and infinitesimals. By such an application of Ockham's razor he admitted that mathematics would be simplified, but it would be "simplified by never advancing to the more difficult matters". To the last with Peirce the decisive factor in the condemnation of all forms of nominalism, including pragmatism, was the denial which they seemed to him to involve of infinitesimals and therewith of the reality of the whole modern science of mathematics.

The second article closes with a criticism of the Cartesian view of consciousness and personality. Peirce accused himself twenty years later[1] of being still at this time too much under the influence of nominalistic views, but in the interpretation of consciousness as having its being, not in an unknown substance behind its manifestations, but in the continuity of the process by which the mind passes by aid of the sign (the only immediately given whether it be a word, an image, an action, or a mere feeling) from one meaning to another, he indicates sufficiently what he has in view. While it is

[1] See *Monist*, July 1892, p. 203.

true that "the phenomenal manifestation of a substance *is* the substance", yet the whole reality is never given in such manifestations. To know our minds as they really are, is, like all other true knowledge, something for which we have to wait upon the future. "Thought is what it is only by virtue of its addressing a future thought", which is only a more developed form of itself. He ends by quoting *Measure for Measure*:

> proud man,
> Most ignorant of what he's most assured,
> *His glassy essence,*

a phrase which was to be the title of a later important essay.

4. His "Pragmatism"

Any reader approaching the second group of articles mentioned above, with a knowledge of the first, ought to have been put on his guard against any interpretation of it that should seem to contradict the clear tenor of the latter. There was the less excuse for any such misunderstanding, seeing that the first article of this group is devoted to the clearest possible restatement of the results of the earlier group. Nominally concerned with "scientific method", these six articles, like all that Peirce ever wrote, have in view the results which emerge for our conception of the universe as a whole. What they do for us is merely to carry the Neo-Kantian conception as sketched above to a further stage of its development.

The first article is concerned with the test of truth, and is a particularly vigorous restatement of the hypothesis which underlies all scientific investigation, viz., that "There are real things whose characters are entirely independent of our opinions about them." Different as our sensations may be, corresponding to the difference of our relation to the object, our "perspective" of it, yet "by taking advantage of the laws of perception we can ascertain how things really are, and any man, if he have sufficient experience and reason enough about it, will be led to the one true conclusion".

If we inquire into the ultimate ground of this faith, it is to be found not in its pragmatic success in the settlement of accidental differences of opinion, but in the inner demand for consistency and the dissatisfaction to which contradictory propositions invariably give rise—a dissatisfaction having its source in turn *not* in the doubt that there is a reality (Peirce acutely remarks that if this were doubted contradiction could not be a source of dissatisfaction), but just in the conviction of its existence. The article ends (as though in view of future alogistic interpretations of its tenor) in an eloquent assertion of the supremacy of logic. "The genius of a man's logical method should be loved and reverenced as his bride whom he has chosen from all the world. She is the one that he has chosen, and he knows that he was right in making that choice."

It is in the second article that the passage occurs which was claimed by William James, in his Californian lecture of 1898, as that in which the standard of Pragmatism was first raised.[1] It would have been odd if it really had been so after all that had gone before and in view of all that was to come after. As a matter of fact the passage occurs in a paper not on the standard of the *truth*, but on the standard of the *lucidity* of concepts. It sets forth maxims for the *clarification*, not for the *verification* of ideas. It is certainly true that Peirce was at this time not himself wholly clear as to the importance of this distinction; and there are other unfortunate ambiguities in the article, chiefly as to the meaning and the scope he assigns to "active" and "practical", and again to "sensible effects". There is surely a certain irony in the fact that a passage which is concerned just with the question of clearness should have left crucial ideas in a state of obscurity when a word or two of definition in the despised formal sense of *genus* and *differentia* would have supplied precisely what was required. With regard to the most important of the above concepts, that of activity, whatever doubt might remain was finally set aside by the wholesale repudiation in later statements of the doctrine of pragmatism as commonly understood. "To say that we live for the sake of action", he writes in 1905, "would be to say that there is no such thing as rational purport." Still more decisively in the article on Pragmatism in Baldwin's *Dictionary of Philosophy*, he repudiates the doctrine that the end of man is action as "a stoical maxim which to the present writer at sixty does not commend itself so forcibly as it did at thirty." As

---

[1] It is too long to quote. The significant words are at the end. After insisting that "our idea of anything *is* our idea of its sensible effects", Peirce concludes: "It appears then that the rule for attaining the third grade of clearness of apprehension is as follows: Consider what effects, which might conceivably have practical bearings, we conceive the object of our conception to have. Then our conception of these effects is the whole of our conception of the object." *Cp.* W. James's *Pragmatism*, pp. 46 and 47.

though to take the last stick of support from misunderstanding, he ends by proposing to his readers, as the means for attaining the highest grade of clearness, that they should remember "that the only ultimate good is to further the development of concrete reasonableness".

But it is on the ground of the appeal to *sensible* effects in the passage before us that, as we have already seen, Dewey claims that "Peirce is more of a pragmatist than James". It is therefore all the more important to recall that here also he sought later to set himself right by a whole-hearted disclaimer of sensationalism. "Modern psychologists", he writes to Mrs. Ladd-Franklin,[1] "are so soaked with sensationalism that they cannot understand anything that does not mean that. How can I, to whom nothing seems so thoroughly real as generals and who regard Truth and Justice as *literally* the most powerful powers in the world, expect to be understood by the thorough-going Wundtian? The curious thing is to see absolute idealists tainted with this disease, or men who like John Dewey hover between Absolute Idealism and Sensationalism."

While there is no justification for attributing to Peirce even at this time anything at all resembling pragmatism as understood by James and Dewey, the articles before us are important as containing the first clear statement of what (as distinguished from this) he himself called Pragmaticism, a name which, as he fondly hoped, "would prove ugly enough to rescue it from the hands of kid-nappers". Alexander Bain had already called attention to the practical aspect of belief as a habit of action. "Belief", he had announced, "is that which we act upon." Kant had insisted that the categories of thought are rules of action in the sense of rules for the guidance of thought. Peirce's originality consisted in generalizing these suggestions. He frees Bain's doctrine from the nominalism of the sensational philosophy and from the narrowness with which Bain conceived of action; he frees Kant's from limitation to the categories and extends it to conception in general treated of as a form of habit or a preparedness of the mind to act in a particular way in the presence of the appropriate stimulus. The value, in his view, of this generalization was that it succeeded in co-ordinating thought with conduct as a form of control. "The theory of Pragmaticism was originally based", he writes in 1905, "as anyone will see who examines the papers of November 1877 and January 1878 upon

[1] See *Journal of Philosophy*, vol. xiii.

a study of that experience of self-control which is common to all grown men and women, and it seems evident that to some extent at least it must always be so based." "The machinery of logical self-control works on the same plan as does moral self-control in multiform detail. The greatest difference perhaps is that the latter serves to inhibit mad puttings forth of energy, while the former most characteristically insures us against the quandary of Buridan's ass. In moral life we are chiefly solicitous about our conduct and its inner springs and the approval of conscience, while in intellectual life there is a tendency to value existence as the vehicle of forms."[1]

Whatever is to be said of the assimilation of concepts to habits (and I suppose from the side of psychology there would be a great deal to be said), it is clear that Peirce has no intention of resolving logic into ethics. Logic has its own special interest, finely defined in this passage as "the value of existence as a vehicle of form", its own unlimited range "bounded solely by the limits of its own powers", its own decisive laws delivering us from the quandaries of Buridan's and other asses. What we here have is the first clear statement in American philosophy of the conational and purposive element in intellectual processes that was afterwards of such decisive importance. How far it influenced Royce in his philosophical development between the writing of the *Religious Aspect of Philosophy* and *The World and the Individual*, is a matter of surmise, but when the latter appeared Peirce was not slow to recognize in it the central feature of his own doctrine. In the same letter that contains his repudiation of psychologism he concludes: "Royce's opinions as developed in his *World and Individualism* [sic][2] are extremely near mine. His insistence on the element of purpose in intellectual concepts is essentially the pragmatic position."

The article ends with a return to the distinction between the clearness and the veracity of ideas which, in spite of ambiguities, he never wholly loses sight of. "Ideas may be ever so clear without

---

[1] *Monist*, vol. xv. pp. 483–484 and 482, condensed.
[2] In a review of the second volume which appeared in the *Nation*, vol. 75, Peirce writes of it: "As the first serious attempt to apply to philosophical subjects the exactitude of thought that reigns in the mathematical sciences, Royce's *World and Individual* will stand a prominent milestone upon the highway of philosophy." Where he still feels himself unable to entirely follow him is in the absolute idealism which consists in the denial of the distinction between being and being represented. "Royce", he writes, "is completely immersed in his absolute idealism. It is his element, and there is total reflection at the surface."

being true. How to make them so . . . how to give birth to those vital and procreative ideas which multiply into a thousand forms and diffuse themselves everywhere, advancing civilization and making the dignity of man, is an art not yet reduced to rule, but of the secret of which the history of science affords some hints." It was to developing these hints that his own logical articles here and elsewhere were devoted.

What further concerns us in the present group is not their contributions to logic, considerable as these are, but the speculation in that upon "The Order of Nature" on the source of the universality, and harmony with reality of our ideas of time, space, and force. He is aware of the suggestion that this is the result of natural selection "acting in favour of more and more correct ideas of these matters". But he only mentions it to put it aside on the ground that "it does not seem to account for the extraordinary accuracy with which these conceptions apply to the phenomena of nature". He adds: "It is probable that there is some secret here which remains to be discovered." He came himself to believe that it could only be explained on the ground of some such fundamental identity between the laws of thought and the laws of being as that which formed the main tenet of Royce's idealism.

5. TYCHISM

Up to this point in the development of his general philosophy Peirce had been mainly occupied with epistemological questions, and been chiefly influenced by antagonism to Cartesian ideas. But the time into which he had been born had other problems of a wider and more immediately pressing kind to occupy it. The advance of physical science and more recently of biology, which seemed to bring not only animal but human life itself under quasi-physical law, had raised in a new and acute form the age-old question of the relation of man to nature, and the possibility of vindicating his essential freedom and therewith the ideas on which (however imperfectly they as yet governed practice) the civilization of Christendom rested.

There were two ways in which this vindication might be attempted. It might take the form of insisting on "determination" of some sort as a fundamental concept—equivalent to the rationality of our world and therefore indispensable if we are to have any philosophy of it at all—while at the same time recognizing the necessity of distinguishing between different forms of determination according to the level of being that had been assumed—inorganic, organic, animal, or mental. It was this line that the German idealism, with which in the 'sixties and 'seventies both England and America were being inoculated, took. But Hegelian idealism was still imperfectly understood, and it was easy enough to mistake its doctrine of the dialectic of history for merely another attack on spiritual freedom in the interest of a "block universe". Even though its spirituality could be vindicated, there was still the question of the relation of the material to the spiritual in the process of cosmological evolution. There remained the other method of a frontal attack on the dogma of the exactness and rigidity of the *soi-disant* laws of nature and on the whole idea of determination as a universal mode of the world's being.

In the uncertainty, which in the 'eighties was beginning to prevail, as to the ultimate constitution of the physical world and the laws it followed, there was much to tempt to this method of attack, and it is not surprising that in these years both on the Continent and in England there were writers who were endeavouring to counter the mechanical view of the world by proving the existence of an element of spontaneity in the physical world itself, only masked by the uniformities which science for her own purposes and by a method of selection had succeeded in establishing. It was in this spirit that Boutroux wrote of the *Contingency in the Laws of Nature*, that Poincaré identified gravitation with a statistical law of averages, that Bergson wrote on *Creative Evolution*, and James Ward spoke of a Contingency that was discoverable in the heart of nature. The support that this view is supposed to get from the theory of quanta in physics makes it a particularly live issue at the present time.[1]

It was unlikely that a mind so alert to newer influences as Peirce's was should not share in this general movement, or, on the other hand, that one so original should fail to give expression to it in his own way. By the 'nineties he had begun to regard it as the main requirement for the "architecture" of a theory that it should come to terms with the scientific conception of law, which, he held, had "revolutionized the intellectual world". It is again all the more important to understand precisely the "Tychism" or theory of

[1] See, *e.g.*, Eddington's *Nature of the Physical World*, pp. 301 foll.

chance which he advocated in the *Monist* articles of 1891–3,[1] seeing
that this is the other element in his philosophy which was taken by
William James to lend support to pragmatism.

While it is usually assumed that what requires explanation is the
absence of uniformity in nature, Peirce held that, on the contrary,
what requires explanation is precisely the presence of uniformity.
While he saw no way of explaining diversity on the basis of a pre-
supposed determinate similarity, he thought he saw his way to
explaining determinate similarity on the basis of an initial indeterminateness. If the inorganic world of matter were taken by itself,
it might be difficult to find instances of the precipitation of uniformity
from diversity, but the mistake was to take it by itself. Bring in life
and mind, and we can see that it is one of their most universal
features that they tend to generalize themselves by the formation
of what we call habits. Starting with an initial spontaneity, they
tend to settle down into uniformities that economize effort and
regulate future action. Instead, therefore, of mind, with its apparent
spontaneity, being the offshoot of matter and its fixities, why should
not matter be conceived of as the precipitate of mind? Schelling
had already conceived of nature as unawakened mind. Peirce would
correct this by conceiving of it as partially "effete mind", and as
therefore containing the possibility of a renewal of the spontaneity
in which it had had its origin. He even suggests that (as Poincaré
and others had maintained) the so-called laws of matter are merely
statistical uniformities telling us nothing of the mode of action of the
ultimate elements.

A difficulty might be caused by the axioms of geometry and the
propositions founded upon them, which mathematics and, following
mathematics with its usual ape-like fidelity, metaphysics have taken
to be precise and universal. But recent advances in mathematics, he
held, had shown that there is no reason for supposing that what had
hitherto been claimed to be axiomatic truths, *e.g.*, that the three
angles of a triangle $= 180°$, are precisely true. Seeing then, as he
also held, that metaphysical axioms are imitations of the geometrical
axioms, "now that the latter have been thrown overboard, without
doubt the former will be sent after them".

[1] The first of these articles is on "The Architecture of Theories"; the second
on "The Doctrine of Necessity"; the third on "The Law of Mind"; the fourth
contains an ingenious speculation on cellular activity, under the title of
"Man's Glassy Essence"; the fifth, the application of the whole to a reinterpretation of biological evolution, bears the title "Evolutionary Love".

Peirce sums up the view of the universe which thus emerges in the words: "Like some of the most ancient and some of the most recent speculations, it would be a cosmogonic philosophy: it would suppose that in the beginning—infinitely remote—there was a chaos of impersonalized feeling which, being without connection or regularity, would properly be without existence. This feeling, sporting here and there in pure arbitrariness, would have started the germ of a generalizing tendency. Its other sportings would be evanescent, but this would have a growing virtue. Thus the tendency to habit would be started, and from this, with the other principles of evolution, all the regularities of the universe would be evolved. At any time, however, an element of pure chance survives and will remain until the world becomes an absolutely perfect, rational, and symmetrical system, in which mind is at last crystallized in the infinitely remote distant feature".[1]

We are not here concerned with the truth of this theory. Its importance has been largely discounted by the direction which recent anti-materialistic thought has taken, corresponding to the first of the two lines indicated above. Instead of trying to vindicate freedom by undermining the belief in the validity in its own sphere of mechanical law, stress is laid on the necessity of recognizing different levels of existence, each with its own kind of law as the subject-matter of the different sciences.[2] We are concerned merely with what he meant by the doctrine and with the type of philosophy with which, as developed by him, it allies him.

As stated in this form, there might seem to be a *prima facie* case for interpreting the doctrine in the sense of the pragmatic belief in

---

[1] *Chance, Love, and Logic*, p. 177.

[2] "Let us not", writes Gilbert Lewis as the summing-up of his brilliant book on *The Anatomy of Science*, "be confused by the double sense in which we use words like 'physics' and 'biology'. We may well suspect that the subject-matter of physics and the subject-matter of biology constitute a single continuum, but the *sciences* of physics and biology comprise postulates and laws which no more need to be compatible with one another than do the geometries of Euclid and Lobachevski. The science of physics rests upon the postulate of determinism; the science of biology, unless it is to ignore deliberately the phenomenon of behaviour, must abandon this postulate and substitute therefor a postulate of choice or freedom. As we continue the great adventure of scientific exploration our models must often be recast. New laws and postulates will be required, while those that we already have must be broadened and extended and generalized in ways we are now hardly able to surmise."

CHARLES PEIRCE 341

open possibilities in nature, *lacunæ* so to speak, in her laws.[1] But it is difficult to see how even so it could be of any "practical" significance. Nature to Peirce meant just the set habits into which the original feeling-stuff had fallen. Only as such a system of habits could nature be known. Only as such a system could it form a stable foundation for either thought or practice. If the end of all action, whether theoretical or practical, is, as he also held, that kind of harmony between our thoughts and the nature of things which he calls concrete reasonableness, "becoming governed by law, instinct with general ideas", nothing could be more impractical and self-defeating than to reckon on any remnant of caprice that an abstract metaphysic might find in things.

As a matter of fact, Peirce made no attempt to work out the theory consistently with itself. The *formation* of habit is itself described as the result of "a law of mind": law, in other words, is explained by the assumption of a previous law. Not less is habit dependent for its *efficacy* on the recurrence in nature of similar circumstances—in other words on pre-existing uniformities. Even the very existence of chance is conceived of by him as an imperfection in the universe, which will in the end be eliminated in a world which by the crystallization of mind in it has "become an absolutely perfect rational and symmetrical system". If, moreover, this faith in an ultimate tendency to rational system is to have any warrant in the nature of things, it must be founded on the presence in the feeling-substance itself of some deeper law of inherent *nisus* towards that consummation. To explain wherein such a law can consist is precisely the object of the last essay of this group, on "Evolutionary Love".

This essay is perhaps of all his published papers the one that is most characteristic of his many-sided and essentially human personality. The prophetic insight of some passages in it comes home to us with special force to-day. The question of the determining factor in evolution was not one on which biology had the last word. Darwinism had been pressed into the service of what he considered a particularly devastating social theory. The struggle for existence working on a basis of chance variations, when transferred to society, meant *laissez-faire* and a policy of Gradgrind. Peirce saw in this

[1] Peirce himself tells us that both the name and the doctrine of pragmatism were connected in their origin with Chauncey White's "Cosmic Weather". See *Chance, Love, and Logic*, p. xix *n*.

only ruin to the social order. "The Gradgrind banner", he declares in a prophetic passage, "has been this century long flaunting in the face of heaven with an insolence to provoke the very skies to growl and rumble. Soon a flash and quick peal will shake economists quite out of their complacency, too late. The twentieth century in its latter half shall surely see the deluge-tempest burst upon the social order—to clear upon a world as deep in ruin as that greed-philosophy has long plunged it into guilt, no post-Thermidorian high jinks then."

He gave the existing system too long a rope. A shorter, as we now know, was sufficient wherewith to hang itself. But he knew what he was speaking of, and there seemed to him no higher mission for philosophy than to cut away the props that it derived from a false interpretation of the law of progress. For this purpose he tries to show that, while Darwin appeals to chance variations, and Weismann to physical necessity, Lamarck was on truer lines than either in leaving room for a deeper law of inward striving after higher forms of being and growth by experience. The theory of "creative evolution" and the *élan vital* has since been made familiar to us by Bergson and others. The principle that underlies it, which Peirce calls "evolutionary love", has received too little attention. Perhaps not the least of the benefits that would accrue from Dewey's "recourse to him" would be the redirection of attention to this deeper *élan*.

Returning to Tychism, what is made clear in this concluding paper is that it is in reality intended to dispose of any purely necessitarian interpretation of evolution by the substitution for it of one that appeals not to chance and the absence of law, but to the subordination of both necessity and chance to the higher law of love.

6. TOWARDS RECONSTRUCTION

We have tried to follow the development of the general theory which Peirce, according to the phase of it which he is emphasizing, calls at one time Realism, at another Commonsensism, at another Schelling-fashioned Idealism, but most characteristically Pragmaticism—with the view of bringing out the difference between it and Pragmatism as that doctrine has taken form and is to-day widely held in America. The conclusion above arrived at finds confirmation from a summary review of the main influences which we know from his own references entered into the formation of his thought.

1. Passing over what he says of his early inoculation with the bacilli of Transcendentalism and his training in the laboratory, one of the earliest and perhaps the most fundamental of all these influences was that which, as we have seen, came to him from the study of mediæval logic and particularly of Duns Scotus. From him he learned the meaning and place of the universal in the being of things, not as another kind of intuitable particular, nor as a mere abstract notion that may form the content of a class name, but as the principle that is embodied in the particular and that gives it such individuality as it possesses: the principle that makes a tree a tree, a man a man "for a' that". Whether Peirce realized clearly the distinction between what his friend Josiah Royce, following Hegel, called the abstract universal (the common property in virtue of which names are given) and the concrete universal (the unity of principle that pervades the parts of any organic whole), may be questioned, but that the universals in which he believes as "literally the most real and powerful powers in the world" were of the latter type there can, I think, be no doubt. Just such universals he conceived it to be the object of the form of induction he calls "hypothesis" to reach. It was on the subordination of all human action to such universal principles in practice that all true progress, in his view, depended. It was such subordination, finally, both in theory and practice, that he meant by "concrete reasonableness", and that he declared to be the chief end of man.

2. Equally certain, both from what he has himself told us of his intellectual development and from the whole tenor of his writings, was the influence of the study of Kant's *Critique of Pure Reason*— the textbook, as it might be said, of the philosophically wise of his generation. From this he learned not, as pragmatism would have it, the subordination of all activity to practice and of logic to ethics, but first (what is a wholly different thing) the purposiveness of all activity, whether practical, theoretic, or æsthetic. It was the general view founded on the recognition of this purposiveness that, to distinguish it from pragmatism, he called pragmaticism, and that since his time has become, I suppose (though not under that (Peircean name), a commonplace of philosophy. In the second place, he learned from Kant the place of thought as the direction of intellectual and moral activity towards unity and organization in

the "matter of experience". Not all experience was perception
and thought. He complains (mistakenly, as Royce could have told
him) of Hegel's resolution of it into thought and immediacy. There
was feeling and there was will. Nevertheless, experience through
which there does not run a thread of thought, like a strain of music,
through notes (the metaphor is his) is a mere confusion and no
true experience of anything. The third thing he learned from his
study of Kant was the impossibility of combining the belief in an
unintelligible thing-in-itself with the real teaching of the *Critique*.
The place of the thing-in-itself had been taken once for all by the
thing at the determination of which we arrive when the process,
as just described, has been brought to completeness in an exhaustive
and harmonious experience. This for us must remain an ideal;
but its existence *as an ideal* witnesses to our belief in a community
of minds or in a common mind (Peirce believes that the one implies
the other) in which it will one day be realized. This was the farthest
he was willing to go in the attempt to prove the existence of a
universal mind, to which all truth was already present. He thought
Royce's attempt to take this farther step well worthy of consideration.[1] But he himself could see his way no farther than to an appeal
to the harmony which the belief in it brings into life both from the
side of theory and practice. Like Coleridge, he did not believe that
the being of God was demonstrable in any strict sense of the word,
but, like Coleridge, he was ready to say "assume it, and all becomes
clear".

3. The third of the influences, in the light of which his work must
be understood, was that which came from mathematics and the
study of the logic of mathematics, in which he was one of the
recognized leaders. If this had been the sole factor in his philosophical
development, or even if it had been a more decisive one than it
really was, there might have been a better case for allying him
with pragmatism. The Italian logician, Vailati,[2] in the same number
of the *Monist*, in which Peirce's "Prolegomena to an Apology for
Pragmaticism" appeared, wrote on the connection between "Pragmatism and Mathematical Logic", emphasizing this alliance. As a
matter of fact, in the autobiographical passage already quoted all
that Peirce claims for his mathematical conceptions is that they

[1] See his review of the *World and the Individual*, vol. ii; *Nation*, vol. 75,
No. 1935.
[2] See *Monist*, vol. xvi.

modified the "Schelling-fashioned idealism" with which he had previously been inoculated and which ended by coming to the surface. Whatever might be the points of alliance between pragmatism and mathematical logic, they were all outweighed for Peirce by the unforgivable sin of a nominalism that meant denying the reality of infinitesimals in mathematics and importing into logic what he calls "the trivial language of practical life".[1]

4. The last of the influences that deserve mention (like all those that go deepest in a man's mental make-up) is difficult to describe. Peirce would probably have rejected the description of it as Christianity. Perhaps he would have been less unwilling to have it called the Platonic tradition which underlies the Christian theology. However described, it was the conviction in his mind of two things: *first* the underlying unity of human society, the reality of what idealists have called the general will, and *secondly* the underlying unity between the community of finite souls and the soul of the world which they have called God. In respect to the first of these we may not be prepared to accept Peirce's mystical doctrine of the existence of a "spirit" in a people or an age which achieves results "beyond the powers of unaided individuals",[2] but the tenacity with which he held to it witnesses to the vividness with which he realized the dependence of individuals on the sustaining spirit of their corporate life. And with regard to the second, while, as we have seen, Peirce had little belief in the ordinary arguments for the existence of God, he yet held that "it would be folly to suppose that any metaphysical theory in regard to the mode of being of the perfect is to destroy the aspiration toward the perfect, which is the essence of religion. Am I to be prevented from joining in the common joy as the revelation of enlightened principles of religion which we celebrate at Easter and Christmas because I think that certain scientific, logical, and metaphysical ideas which have been mixed up with these principles are untenable? To do so would be to estimate these errors as of more consequence than the truth".[3]

It would not be true to say that Peirce ever succeeded in bringing the ideas that came to him from these different sources into a consistent whole. But that, like Coleridge again, with whom, both in his

---

[1] See his criticism of Dewey's *Studies in Logical Theory* in the *Nation*, vol. 79, No. 2046.
[2] *Chance, Love, and Logic*, p. 297.
[3] *Popular Science Monthly*, June 1878 (*Chance, Love, and Logic*, p. 130).

strength and in his weakness, we are often tempted to compare him, he felt the need of so doing, is abundantly plain.[1] Unlike Coleridge, he was fortunate in having as friend a companion thinker whom he had himself profoundly influenced and with whose development of his own ideas he was in profound sympathy.

The significance which the philosophical alliance of Peirce and Royce had for the future of American philosophy will call for more particular notice in the next Study. What I have tried to bring out in this one is the line in which the true affinities of the work of the elder of these thinkers are to be sought and the kind of benefit that might accrue to contemporary discussion from the "recourse to Peirce" to which Mr. Dewey summons us. The line lies, I believe, in a return to the great central philosophical tradition which for lack of a better name I have called Platonic; the benefit will be (what perhaps is most needed at the present time, in America perhaps as much as elsewhere) a sense that some firm ground has been won here as elsewhere by the best of the thinking that distinguished the end of the nineteenth and the beginning of the twentieth century, from which assured progress may be made.

[1] After the summary of "the materials out of which chiefly a philosophical theory ought to be built", in the paper on the "Architecture of Theories", he prays, "May some future student go over the ground again and have the leisure to give his results to the world."

CHAPTER IV

JOSIAH ROYCE (i). EARLY ESSAYS

1. APPRENTICESHIP

The man who with fullest knowledge and sympathy felt both what was owed to Hegel and what called for correction and restatement in him was Josiah Royce. Born in 1855, in education and general outlook he belonged to the older generation. As at the time he went to college in Berkeley, California,[1] there was no organized course of philosophy, his training there was chiefly literary. Sent to philosophy by the need he felt for a rational basis for beliefs which in their accepted form were no longer tenable, he viewed it from the first as having this for its chief motive. He would have accepted *fides intellectum quærens* as the best expression of the philosophical spirit. "The religious problems", he tells us in the Preface to his first book,[2] "have been chosen for the present study because they first drove the author to philosophy, and because they of all human interests deserve our best efforts and our utmost loyalty." He believed that relief from the pressure of these problems was to be won not by turning away from doubt but by carrying it to the farthest point. "Doubt", he wrote,[3] "for a truth-seeker is not only a privilege but a duty. Philosophic truth as such comes to us first under the form of doubt, and we can never be very near it in our search unless for a longer or a shorter time we have come to despair of it altogether." Out of the strong he believed cometh forth sweetness, out of the eater meat. The argument in the eleventh chapter of this his first book, to which he frequently afterwards refers as to the sheet-anchor of his idealism, was founded on the paradox that in the very question "what if all be error?" there lies the germ of a new faith.

He belonged to the older school of idealists also in the resoluteness with which he sought to put himself abreast of the best that had been thought and written on the central problems of philosophy both in ancient and modern times. Even as a youth he was equipped as few others of his generation were for the task he set before him-

---

[1] The University of that State has just done worthy honour to his memory in dedicating to it the great Hall in the new buildings at Los Angeles.
[2] *The Religious Aspect of Philosophy*, p. v.　　　[3] *Op. cit.*, p. 14.

self.[1] The writer who first exercised a decisive influence over his thought was John Stuart Mill, whose chapter on the Psychological Theory of the External World[2] he regarded as "one of the most important philosophical productions of English thought of the last century". Under Mill's influence he became what he calls a "decidedly sceptical critical empiricist". Though we all desire to discover the standards by which thought should be guided, these, he saw, cannot be found through intuitions which turn out to be mere "persuasions"; nor if we derive them from experience can they be anything "necessary". On the other hand, Herbert Spencer's effort to reinstate necessary truths on the basis of his evolutionary theory failed to satisfy him.

It was in such a mood he tells us that he turned to German philosophy, especially to Kant and Fichte, and, "by way of an episode", to Schopenhauer. Kant seemed to him for a while to have a very definite solution to his problem. But when he examined it, he found the difficulty of how you can know that the categories or laws of phenomena are the only or permanent forms of our world to be an insuperable one: what if my categories changed? The influence, on the other hand, of Fichte upon him was deepened by Lotze's teaching that a man's convictions were not his innate ideas but his postulates. But this only opened the way to another form of scepticism: "The postulates were his own assertion. He left it to God." His own solution seems to have come to him as a kind of revelation.

Granted that the postulates may be mere attitudes to the real, this means that error is possible. But what would be an error? "This led me to the doctrine of the nature of error as involving interpretation. I said this to myself: 'this view which I set forth about the nature and conditions of error is true or false. Whether it is true or false, we have here a teleological situation which brings the thought of the moment into contact with a type of consciousness which is not the merely human type'." It was this thought at which he had arrived by the year 1883, and which may be said to have marked the conclusion of his apprenticeship. He had not only left British empiricism behind him, but he had rejected the "radical empiricism" of some of his own contemporaries as failing to get

[1] For some of these references to the growth of his early opinions I am indebted to the very careful notes of the last course of lectures given to his senior students in 1916, taken by Mr. Ralph W. Brown, which, through his and Professor Hocking's kindness, I have been here permitted to use.

[2] *Examination of Hamilton.*

beyond momentary consciousness except by a postulate whose nature and ground it failed to explain. Finally, he had side-tracked the influence of Hegel by attaching himself rather to Fichte. But no mere restatement of another's philosophy could meet the situation of his time. "The need", as he expressed it in one of his earliest articles,[1] "seems to be that certain ideas, known, but in our age too much neglected, should be not simply revivified, but rather reformed to bring them into closer connection with modern progress." With this declaration of independence and in this conviction he was prepared to set out on a pilgrimage marked thenceforward by a continual, perhaps too feverish, striving forward to new points of view.

2. Life Harmony

It is fortunately possible to trace the successive stages of this pilgrimage, not only through the personal references in the Prefaces to his chief books, but in the articles with which, as a painter in his preliminary sketches, he prepared for each of them.

In what is apparently the first of these, written at the age of twenty in the *Overland Monthly* in 1875 on the subject of "The Life Harmony",[2] we find him already in revolt against the intellectualism that sought in knowledge rather than in feeling the stuff of life and the link that binds one age to another in harmonious growth. In opposition to Hegel's view of history as proceeding through conflict and continual self-immolation, he insists that "self-conflict is the very negation of harmony; self-immolation destroys the possibility of unity. Grand as Hegel's thought is, we cannot but think it one-sided. The conflicts of the soul are facts, but they are not alone. The mind of man is not a comet wandering from system to system in orbits of incalculable eccentricity. If it does not revolve in the fixed paths of the bound slaves of inanimate nature, it yet neither wishes nor has the power to do more than pass from member to member of the same system at every change, attaining a better and nobler position, but never forsaking its great objects". In this course it is not thought and reason that raise it to the higher level: "Reason can discover truth but it cannot unaided make life." It is the

---

[1] *Journal of Speculative Philosophy*, 1881.
[2] Among the many interesting parallels between him and Bradley is the early attraction of the problem of History. See above, p. 221.

emotional nature that "lies at the foundation of life", and that "is the true link binding mankind in a common brotherhood".

In this criticism it is not perhaps fanciful to find the germ of the form of idealism at which he himself ultimately arrived, with its rooted opposition to any attempt to place the essence of progress, whether in the race or in the individual, in the negative movement of self-transcendence, and with the emphasis falling more and more upon will and feeling, instead of upon thought. If, nevertheless, he ends this juvenile article with an account of the development of art, which makes it pass through the three stages of pure *objectivity* or concern with nature, *subjectivity* or concern with the personal self, and the *union of the two*, in which nature and personality, "sympathy and independence are completely and harmoniously united", we may see here also perhaps the strain of Hegelianism, that in spite of his frequent disclaimers permeates the best part of his own thought.

3. KANT'S RELATION TO MODERN PHILOSOPHIC PROGRESS

But it is in an article of six years later that we have to look for his first serious attempt to orient himself in relation to contemporary idealism. Already in 1881 he had become convinced, like so many of his contemporaries, that the foundation of any future metaphysic must be laid in a criticism of knowledge such as that to which Kant in the *Critique of Pure Reason* had led the way by his distinction between sense and understanding. He was not, however, convinced that Kant had given the right interpretation of that distinction, and, when asked to take part in the centennial of the *Critique* at Saratoga in that year, he took the opportunity to read a paper on "Kant's Relation to Modern Philosophic Progress",[1] in which he tried to substitute a better for it.

By taking the categories, notably that of causality, as a primary form of the *a priori* element supplied by the understanding Kant had involved himself in a dilemma. He had either to admit that uniformity was already contained in the sensory data or to deny it. In the former case the work of the understanding was unnecessary; in the latter case it was incomprehensible how it could be introduced into them, and what justification it could have from them. As a

---

[1] Published in the *Journal of Speculative Philosophy*, October 1881. The article on "Schiller's Ethical Studies" (*ibid.*, the previous year) has little philosophical interest

matter of fact, causality is a complex category which presupposes an earlier and more ultimate synthesis. This synthesis Royce finds in the reference of the present datum *first* to an ideally reinstated past, *secondly* to a similarly represented future, *finally* to a universe of truth, which is the common possession of the self and other conscious minds. Through these three classes or forms of activity, which he calls "acknowledgment of the past", "anticipation", and "acknowledgment of a universe of truth", he claims that "experience as a whole is created".

He believes that this threefold synthesis was what was really meant by Kant's "unity of apperception", but he differentiates his own "reform" from it in that, whereas Kant thinks of the unity of apperception as something which, "like a sea-fog, enters, pervades, floats through, and fills the world of experience conceived of as somehow given", he thought of it as "projected" into a conceived but not given space and time. On the basis of this analysis, which is in reality the corner-stone of all his subsequent thought, he proceeds to dismiss what he calls "the three imposters of the *Kritik*: the thing in itself, the transcendental object, and the noumenon", and to summarize the view of reality which should be substituted for the Kantian. The summary ends with the twofold conclusion: first, that "the great object of critical philosophy is not to toil in the vain hope of constructing an ontology, but to devote itself to the study of the forms of intellectual activity with a view to separating in these the insignificant from the significant"; and secondly, that "the goal can be reached only in an Ethical doctrine which will find the justification of intellectual activity in its moral worth".

There is much that is of biographical interest, but also much that is of doubtful omen, in this first sketch of what he was afterwards to expand into a whole system of philosophy. In his contribution to the volume of papers "In Honour of Josiah Royce", Professor John Dewey has criticized him for having in this early article stated a voluntaristic doctrine inconsistent with the teaching of the book which was to follow. While in the article volitional and ethical activity is put forward as the justification of cognitive and theoretic, in the *Religious Aspect of Philosophy* the order is reversed. "Acts of will are not self-justifying, the ethical is transcended in the cognitive."[1]

I think that this criticism is just, in so far as Royce has not yet

[1] *Josiah Royce*, p. 20.

reached any clear idea of the relation between practical and theoretic activity, and in this preparatory period shows a marked leaning to the voluntarism that was to dominate his thought in the middle phase of its development. But whereas Dewey regards the doctrine that takes its place in the immediately following period as a relapse from a truer insight, I believe, on the contrary, that it ought to be regarded as a return to the true line of the great tradition of which he never ceased to regard himself as an exponent. In justice to Royce, moreover, it is important to notice that by the "ethical" justification, of which he speaks, he means something demanded of us by our nature, whether as practical or cognitive, and that the "universe of truth", which is conjured up in response to an ethical requirement, is regarded as having independent rights of its own, and as only so being able to serve the purpose on which it is postulated. Neither here nor elsewhere does Royce give any countenance to a philosophy that seeks to subordinate truth to practice in the ordinary pragmatical sense.

Of greater immediate importance in this article for the understanding of the foundations of his idealism is the apparent acceptance of a view of Kant's work which had already been set aside by the best of his British and American critics as failing to do justice to the depth of Kant's thought and the results it had achieved. It is true that there are passages in the *Critique* which seem to treat the world of sense as a *given*, to which the understanding brings the logical forms, that introduce organization and unity into it, and that just at this time and in the *Journal*, in which Royce's article appeared, this was being somewhat stormily claimed by Hutchison Stirling as Kant's real view. On the other hand (also in the same *Journal*), Edward Caird in a devastating reply had shown that to accept such an interpretation of Kant's work as a whole was to reduce it to nonsense.[1] The real meaning of Kant was something quite different, and consisted in showing the impossibility of making any separation between sense and understanding except as different sides of the one concrete whole of experience. In order that there may be any experience at all, there must be a union of the particularity of the given and the universality of the ideal. There cannot from the nature of the case be first a given sensory experience and then, as a result of an intellectual activity, an ideal extension of it by the importation of elements from without.

[1] See p. 171 above.

Royce saw clearly the impossibility of such a doctrine in the case of causality; but, instead of drawing the comprehensive conclusion that the initial separation was at fault, and proceeding to reform the doctrine from that point of view, he accepts the separation and goes on to substitute a new interpretation of the nature of the intellectual activity. It is true that, before the article was published, he had become aware of the other view, and in the article itself makes his bow to it as probably "on the right lines"; but this did not prevent him from reproducing in his own theory of the nature of the ideal extension just the separation which these writers had criticized as untenable in itself and inconsistent with Kant's more mature and deeper teaching. To Royce there is still a present, given to individual consciousness, which by a "spontaneous" act of thought is expanded into a continuity of past, present, and future. But this was only to expose himself in a new form to precisely the criticism he had levelled against Kant. If the continuity of space and time is already an element in experience, the spontaneous extension is unnecessary; if it is not (and he assumes that it is not), the extension is something purely subjective without support in experience. The error in both cases was the same. We never start with a datum consisting of an experience here and now, exclusive of a then and a there. If we did, we should have on our hands the insoluble problem of explaining whence we obtain the materials for our construction. The associationists had their answer to this in the principle of similarity, but, by the time Royce wrote, this was pretty well exploded and he would have been the last to have availed himself of it. But with its disappearance the problem of the principle of the resuscitation returned, and on a subjectivist view, such as that from which Royce here starts, it must remain as insoluble as ever. Only if the form of a Whole beyond the here and the now is already in some sense present, and the "integration" is in some sense a "redintegration", could it be made at all comprehensible.

What was required in the "reform" of Kant, which Royce rightly saw was called for, was to realize that there is no immediate datum that is not pervaded by just such a "sea-mist" coming from afar as Kant had himself indicated, and to carry this out consistently by eliminating from Kant's presentation of it the survivals of the older doctrine. I believe that the failure at the outset to come to a clear understanding of Kant's teaching in this respect was the source of what students of Royce have always felt to be a central

z

ambiguity in his philosophy as a whole, and of the consequent doubt in the minds even of the most sympathetic whether in the end he had escaped the pitfalls of subjectivism.

4. MIND AND REALITY

The effects of this failure became at once obvious in the form which the problem of idealism took in his mind, and which in the article on "Mind and Reality" of the following year[1] he proceeded to state. Ontology (he had announced in the article on Kant and altogether in the spirit of that master), as a dogmatic theory without foundation in a theory of knowledge, is an anachronism. As he put it in the new article, "ontology is play, theory of knowledge alone is work. Ontology is the child blowing soap bubbles, philosophical analysis is the miner digging for gold". But an ontology, or at any rate a metaphysic of some sort, is a necessity, if for no other purpose than to clear away theories that, like those of mind stuff and of unconscious or monadistic mind, were cumbering the ground, and he proceeds to give a hypothetical sketch of a purified Berkeleianism which might take their place.

Starting from Berkeley's assumption that "all direct data are internal facts", and that "in the strictest sense all data are direct", he concludes that to reach the idea of an external world we require "an addition to the data of consciousness". This addition consists not merely in the introduction of order into present data, as Kant supposed, but in the "active production of non-data. We do not receive in our senses, but we posit through our judgment whatever external world there may for us be". In the end the existence of the external world rests on nothing else than our will to have one. "The ultimate motive is the will to have an external world. . . . The certainty of an external world is the fixed determination to make one." Once started, however, the activity continues under the general law "that the external reality is conceived *after the pattern of the present data*", the aim of the whole process being "to reach as complete and united a conception of reality as is possible, a conception wherein the greatest fullness of data shall be combined with the greatest simplicity of conception", in other words, with "the greatest

---

[1] *Mind*, 1882. It was preceded by one in the previous year on the "Mind Stuff" theory, which only concerns us as showing the care with which Royce sought to clear the way for his own reconstruction.

definiteness of organization". After repeating his own reform of Kant's doctrine as the substitution for it of the postulate of likeness of my present state of consciousness to a past or future state of my own, and again the likeness of my present state to the conscious state of another, he goes on to add to it "the familiar postulate of natural science": the likeness of its conclusions, beyond the actual experience of any one, to a "possible experience". By these two postulates, the likeness to the actual, and the likeness to the possible, he claims that "the whole notion of external reality is exhausted", and that this position is the one that is "more or less purely maintained by the whole body of modern idealists".

Agreeing though these[1] do in accepting this general account, they have nevertheless failed to inquire what an experience which is not actual but only possible means. Yet (if it be true that the real is only for consciousness) this is the question that is now forced upon us. Beyond actual experience it would seem as though *either* there were no reality at all, *or* what is called "possible experience" must be actual in some universal or absolute consciousness. Royce is here content to put forward the latter alternative merely as an hypothesis, as an hypothesis, moreover, that brings with it no emotional satisfaction, and gives us only "the cold deadness of a universal knowing one". But he claims that it has the advantage over all others of being simple and adequate, and further in being "plastic", leaving room for something more, if an ethical theory could be established. Such a theory would only have "to speak the word and our Universal Consciousness will be transformed into what it now is not—an active Spirit". We are thus left with the twofold question of whether anything of the nature of a proof can be given of the hypothesis: whether, that is, it can be shown that these postulates are more than arbitrary assumptions; and of whether, were the Being, hypothetically assumed, proved to be real, it could be endowed with emotional quality. It is these questions that he sets himself to answer in the book that was published three years later under the title of *The Religious Aspect of Philosophy*.

Meantime, what we have to note is that while in this article, equally with the earlier one, we have the view that in experience we start from the small island of present experience which has to be

---

[1] He gives a list of them (repeated in *The Religious Aspect of Experience*, p. 362), which includes philosophers so diverse as Hegel and J. S. Mill.

expanded by a fiat of the will (equally it would seem islanded in the present and in the individual mind) into a world, intermixed with this there is the new idea of a "similarity" forming a bridge between past and present, the individual mind and the mind of others, finally between actual and possible experience. The writer seems wholly unconscious of the difference, ultimately the incompatibility, between these two ideas. According to the former we have disconnected elements, an actual and an ideal, a mere unrelated, formless datum on the one hand, and relations or form on the other, united by an arbitrary act of will. According to the latter the datum has somehow acquired a "pattern" of unity and completeness which gives a standard to which the mind in the further development of its world has to approximate—*that* being true and real which most completely conforms to the ideal pattern. In the one case we are tied up with a present moment, a merely individual mind and a merely possible beyond, and there is no escape but by an arbitrary fiat of the will. In the other we have as our starting-point a world, somehow present to us, into which we have not yet fully entered, but into which more and more fully we are to enter by following the clue which it itself supplies. In this case there is no need to cut the knot but merely to unravel it, according to the principles of extension and organization which he has himself indicated. The question raised by this article is—Which of these two is Royce's real meaning? On which side, if or when he becomes conscious of the contradiction, will be choose to take his stand? I believe that he never became clearly conscious of the contradiction, and that the tragic element in his philosophy and the cause of its unconvincingness, when taken as a whole, is the ambiguity which continued to attach to it in this respect to the end. Meantime we are concerned with the form his thought took in the first of his chief works and its relation to the divergent tendencies which these preliminary studies indicate.

CHAPTER V

ROYCE (ii). THE RELIGIOUS ASPECT OF PHILOSOPHY[1]

1. THE ETHICAL APPROACH

The influences already mentioned as coming to him from his earlier studies, combined with that of William James, his colleague in Harvard, make it all the more significant that in the first developed statement of his philosophy he shows comparatively little sign of them, and follows rather the line of his own deeper philosophical insight. It is for this reason that the book has appeared to some to give a more favourable impression of the type of idealism by which he would himself have desired to be remembered than any of his other books. It lacks the elaborateness of detail that characterizes *The World and the Individual*; it is less concerned with the form of the religious consciousness which interests us chiefly in the West than *The Problem of Christianity*; but besides the comparative freedom from the pressure of his immediate environment already mentioned, it had the additional advantage of being free from the lecture form which offered peculiar temptations to a writer of Royce's expansiveness, which he was not always able to resist.

Whatever doubt the writer may have had as to the place of will as a metaphysical principle, he was convinced that it was an essential element in religion. However much it may be concerned with beliefs about existence, "so much at all events seems sure about religion: It has to do with action. It is impossible without some appearance of moral purpose". It is by this relation to a moral purpose that the philosophy of religion is distinguished from general philosophical theory. Theoretic truths have to be acknowledged, but there remains the question of their value in view of the end or ideal of human life. It is through the study of this ideal, therefore, that our problem has to be approached. "The ideal ought to be studied first, since it is the ideal that is to give character to our whole quest among the realities."[2]

This consideration determines not only the order of questions but the kind of answer to the first of them that we shall be prepared to accept. The realist's appeal to the fact that a thing *is* can never be

[1] Boston, 1885 (Seventh Edition, 1887). Referred to below as *R. A.*
[2] P. 17.

an answer to the question of what it ought to be. Reviewing the main types of answer that had been given to the ethical problem of the foundation of the "ought", Royce finds their chief defect in their failure to recognize this fundamental inadequacy. Plato, Aristotle, the Epicureans, and Stoics all appeal in the end to some brute fact, whether of human nature or the cosmic order. Even the Christian ideal of love to God "seems to have for its sole theoretical foundation the physical [sic] fact that man often feels gratitude". Similarly with the modern appeal to conscience, or to sympathy, or to the facts of evolution. We are shown what may be, not why it ought to be, felt or done. To the rejection of the appeal to fact in favour of that to the ideal, the realist has his reply in the caprice and chaos, the scepticism and pessimism to which romantic idealism has once and again brought us—a scepticism to which Arthur J. Balfour's recently published *Defence of Philosophic Doubt* had given "a final and perfectly cold-blooded" expression. But between the alternatives which that writer offers us of the acceptance of the non-moral world of science or a blind faith there is a third alternative: the possibility of establishing a criterion of ends which shall be independent of caprice without being realistic.

To this, the main question of ethical and religious philosophy, Royce's answer consists in a fresh and original application of the old principle, that a scepticism which is in earnest with itself cannot rest in mere indifference. It is bound at least to affirm *itself*—at once the doubter and the doubt. It is because the self is one and seeks unity that doubt is possible. Applied to the will, this means that we feel the conflict of wills within ourselves because we are ourselves one will and are committed to the search for harmony among our multifarious ends. What therefore is pointed to is, not the renunciation of the will to live, which is the logical issue of a complete scepticism, but the *insight* that will show us the way to harmonious life. Division with conflict is indeed a phase or moment in this insight, and this phase finds expression in the distraction which we feel "when we contemplate two opposing aims in such a way as momentarily to share them both". But deepen insight by reflection, and you see that underneath the division of aims there is an aim of aims, an "ideal of ideals", to which you are committed by your nature as a voluntary being. Finally, what holds of the conflict of wills within ourselves holds also of the conflict between our own will and the will of others. Here too, and by virtue of that same nature, we are committed to the ideal of a world of individuals acting as one Being, having a single Universal Will,[1] and to be realized through the same deepening insight into one another's lives. Altruism, devotion to others merely as others, is not enough apart from insight into the ends which give both self and others significance as joint partners in a larger life and a common task. The only thing that can give satisfaction to a self of the kind we know ourselves in our deepest consciousness to be is the life of devotion to ends that bring harmony into the different wills which we find within ourselves, while at the same time uniting us with the wills of others in common endeavour. These ends are too diverse and absorbing to be pursued all together or any one of them to its ultimate goal. The main thing is the *insight* which reveals their essential worth and their general relation to one another in the whole of human life. When in working for any one of them, truth or beauty, material production or social improvement, we have this insight, we have revealed to us that in which and in which alone we can feel ourselves most truly affirmed.

In all this something might be said in criticism of Royce's interpretation of the great ethical philosophies of the past as appealing to mere brute fact, and of his failure to see that in the end he has himself to make the same appeal in what he says of our "nature as voluntary beings".[2] But his main contention of the implication in human life of the ideal of a unity or totality of purposes, as the central and significant fact with regard to it, is in the true line of idealistic thought; and it is doubtful whether the meaning of "moral nsight" as the condition of realizing that unity has ever been better stated than in the chapter with that title.[3]

2. THE SEARCH FOR RELIGIOUS TRUTH: PHYSICAL AND METAPHYSICAL REALISM

The first half of the book is only preliminary to the statement of the religious problem. Granted that the Good is to be found in things which, like beauty, truth, and justice, bring our wills into harmony

---

[1] Pp. 143–145.
[2] See the contemporary review of the book by S. Alexander in *Mind*, vol. x. pp. 599 foll. This early division of the elements of experience into ideals and facts as into sheep and goats is ominous of what was to come later in the apotheosis of the "ought".
[3] See especially pp. 148–156 and 161–162.

with themselves and unite them with the wills of others, the question becomes immediately pressing: have we any ground for believing that the world is such as to be able to guarantee the objective reality of this Good? Is the universe itself pledged, as it seems to pledge us, to a moral order of which our finite lives are only the partial embodiments under the form of time? or are we here in a region in which our sole light is faith in our own ideals projecting themselves as *possibilities* into an unknown and unknowable future? It is here that Royce takes up the argument from the point where, as we have seen, he had left it in the earlier articles.

Antecedent to the question of the discovery of some aspect of reality that shall have religious significance, there is the question of how we know reality at all. Meeting us here at the outset is the realist's conception of an external nature to which our thoughts have in some way to conform. Royce was to return to this again and again. His philosophy may be said to be one long wrestle with realism in its Protean forms. In this first bout with it, he is concerned to show not so much its falsity as its worthlessness for religion. As he had shown in the former part of the book that the facts of nature can of themselves give no standard of moral value, so here he tries to show that, granting the truth of the realist's conception, all that we have is a "world of powers", that are either totally indifferent to our ideals, or at best can be shown here and there accidentally to further them. Even although physics had any right to speak of progress at all, it could only show that nature permits progress; it does not necessitate it. History may tell us of "a power that makes for righteousness", but the power moves upon the changing evanescent background of earthly existence. History tells us nothing of that which changes not "wherein is no variation or shadow of turning". As little can metaphysics, whether monistic or pluralistic, whether offering us mind-stuff, unconscious Will, or the "intensive atom", give us what we want. Even Reason fails: "The first starving family, or singed moth or broken troth, or wasted effort, or wounded bird, is an indictment of the universal reason." Equally unsatisfying is the conception of a Creator who has made the world and us as free creative beings in it. On such a view there is clearly something higher than the Creator in the uncreated laws under which He works. There may be mysteries that we have reverently to accept, and creation may be one of them. "But if creation is indeed such a mystery, at all events a self-contradiction about creation is not

such a mystery."[1] Finally, with the advent of the theory of evolution, the argument from design has lost its force. Behind evolution
there may be a designer who works through it. But experience tells
us nothing of this. "To study English literature in the rubbish heaps
of a bookbinder's workshop would seem to a wise man a more
hopeful undertaking than to seek any one notion of the real plan on
which this world is made from a merely empirical study of our little
fragment of nature." In a word, "the world of powers is the world of
the children of the dragon's teeth."[2]

3. RELATIVE IDEALISM

But recent thought has opened up a different method of approach
in emphasizing the place of postulation or "ideal construction"[3] in
the work of science, and Royce devotes a chapter to prove that both
in practice and theory "the wise shall live by postulates". In this
sense the uniformity of nature is something that we postulate rather
than find, and we postulate it because it answers our highest intellectual need, the need for simplicity and absolute unity of conception. The view is here put forward, as in the *Mind* article, not
as something established, but as something possible, carrying along
with it the suggestion that, if postulates are permissible in science,
why not in morals and religion? If science postulates the truth of
the description of the world that at once includes the given phenomena and attains the greatest simplicity, why may not religion
assume the description of the world that, without falsifying the
facts, arouses the highest moral interest and satisfies the highest
moral needs?

So far Royce might seem to be merely preparing the way for a
pragmatism of the type that was to "precipitate itself out of the
air" in 1898,[4] with its claim to have unlimbered the external reality
and rendered it plastic to our needs. But he was too well aware of

[1] P. 279. This criticism had a special interest at the time as aimed at the
doctrine advocated in Professor Bowne's recently published *Metaphysics*,
still quoted as providing the basis of the personalistic form of idealism. See
below, p. 368.
[2] P. 287. S. Alexander's remark (*loc. cit.*) that "the most striking quality of
Royce's style is its imaginativeness" is nowhere better illustrated than in
these sections.
[3] Royce quotes G. H. Lewes as the originator of the phrase (p. 361).
[4] The date of the Californian Address; see above, p. 334. The phrase is
James's own in the Preface to his *Pragmatism* (1907).

what was required by a true philosophy of religion to be content to
leave it there. He saw that "postulating into the void" was "a
dangerous business", and that so far what the world of reality "had
gained in plasticity it had lost in authority". Can this authority be
re-established on the new basis? It is this question to which Idealism
was the answer—the only possible answer; and in the following
chapter with that title he develops the account, more or less already
familiar to us from the *Mind* articles, of his own intellectual pilgrimage to it, apologizing, by the way, for what he modestly fears
his fellow pilgrims may think the ease and directness of his path.
However easy and direct, it was not taken without due caution.

First the Berkeleian conception, purified of causal and teleological
elements, is sketched as a possible, and, compared with others, a
simple and plausible hypothesis. Next the steps are traced by which
it is "suddenly transformed from an hypothesis into a theory, and
from a doctrine of an eternal, normal thought into a doctrine of an
all-embracing spirit".[1] The first step is the rejection of causality as
a primary postulate. To make this principle the ground of our
belief in an external world is to end in the "disfigured realism",
which reduces it to an unknown and unknowable x. Causality is
only one of the ways in which the mind seeks to realize its ideal of
"a conception wherein the greatest fullness of data shall be combined with the greatest simplicity of conception . . . the greatest
richness of content with the greatest definiteness of organization".[2]
The fundamental postulate therefore is not that there shall be a
cause for our ideas, but that reality shall be like our idea of it. How
define this likeness?

Here the Kantian analysis comes to our aid with the idea of that
which is a "possible experience", not in the sense of one which we
may arbitrarily imagine, but of one which under certain conditions
according to the laws of nature would necessarily be ours. As he has
told us, it was Mill's statement of this in his account of matter as
the "permanent possibility of sensation" that had enabled him to
take this second step. Since then he had found it in a multitude of
thinkers,[3] taking the more general form of the doctrine that "thought
when it inquires into its own meaning can never rest satisfied with
any idea of external reality that makes such reality other than a
datum of consciousness and so material for thought. . . . I see an
apple fall, and no more than that. But I postulate that, if I could have

[1] P. 354.   [2] P. 357.   [3] See above, p. 355 *n.*

had experience of all the facts, I should have observed a series of material changes in the twig on which the apple hung that would have sufficed to restore the broken uniformity and continuity of my experiences. There is something beyond our experience, namely, another experience; that is the first postulate. Experiences form a uniform and regular whole of laws of sequence; that is the other postulate subordinate to the first".[1] Science stops here. It is concerned merely with the extension of experience according to this second postulate. Philosophy has other work. It has to ask what all this points to as to the nature of "the something beyond", the "other experience"? It would seem therefore as though, arrived at this point, we have a third postulate. "We want a hero. Not a Don Juan, but a hypothetical subject of the possible experiences." Can we establish one as an Absolute knower? Granted that we can, have we a right to transform this Knower into something of religious value for single conscious lives that are to get truth by agreement with him? It is to the first of these questions that the argument of the central chapter of the book on "The Possibility of Error" is devoted. It contains the final step in the evolution of his own idealistic creed. He frequently refers to it as containing a statement from which he had never knowingly departed. It will be sufficient to recall it in the form in which Royce himself gives it in his preliminary statement, therein (as so often with him) attaining a clarity that his more elaborate expositions sometimes lack.

4. ABSOLUTE IDEALISM

If we start from the assumption that each of us is shut up in the circle of his own ideas, there seems no way by which we can pass from *our* ideas about things to a judgment of their truth and falsity. We can say that these ideas are sincere or insincere, not that they contain truth or error; and the reason is that their objects are not really "objects" at all, but only other, still merely subjective, ideas. On such a supposition "controversy, progress towards truth, failure to get truth, error, refutation, even doubt itself, will all cease to have any meaning whatsoever". But if (reversing the original assumption that I can be concerned only with my own ideas) my thought is related to a higher thought, even as the parts of one of my thoughts are related to the whole thought, then truth and error as objective

[1] Pp. 363–366.

are possible since my thought and its object, both as I think it and as it is, are together in the universal thought, of which they form elements, and in which they live and move and have their being. As my thoughts are postulated as having a unity more or less complete in themselves, so all thoughts and objects must be postulated as in unity in that thought for which the universe exists as a whole. On this view the statement that straight lines are the shortest between their extremities "is true objectively, and its contradictory false only in case both the world of possible straight lines and my thoughts about the world of possible straight lines are known to a higher thought—are in fact members of a higher thought, which, comparing what I cannot compare, making a synthesis of what is to me separate, unifying what is for me diverse, finds my thought really true or false."

So stated, the theory is put forward, not as giving an *a priori* account of facts of experience or as one for which science has any use in its own particular work of discovery, but as a theory of that which makes experience as a whole possible, and put forward on the sole ground that "no other offers any chance of a philosophy nor any hope of even a rational scientific notion of things".

5. ETHICAL AND RELIGIOUS APPLICATIONS

Having arrived at the reality of an infinite thought of perfect *insight*, we may advance to the conception of it as absolutely *good*, seeing that "the infinite thought must know what is desirable, and knowing it must have present in itself the true objects of desire". As the sense of error is the guarantee of the reality of a truth we do not yet fully possess, so the sense of evil is "just an evidence to us finite beings that there exists something desirable which we have not and which we just now cannot get".[1] Moral evil can only be unmixed badness, as error only unmixed untruth, if it be taken, as it never can be, in its separateness. Rebel as the bad will may, its badness is condemned and overcome in the Whole, which in its very rebellion it asserts. On the other hand, in overruling the bad will in itself, the good will realizes in part what is no mere ideal of its own, but the veritable life of the whole. It is in this way, the author concludes, that it may be said that "consciousness has given us in concrete form solutions of our two deepest philosophic problems. That the

[1] P. 444.

possibility of error necessitates an inclusive thought is illustrated for us by our own conscious thought, which can include true and false elements in the unity of one clear and true thought at any moment. And the possibility of moral evil, demanding a real distinction between good and evil, is illustrated for us in a way that solves the whole trouble, namely, in the unity of the conscious moral act. There at the one moment are good and evil warring, implacable, yet united in the present momentary triumph of the good will. A world in which this victory is the supreme fact is the perfect world that religion needs".[1]

Little though the Universal Thought whose existence is here demonstrated had in common with traditional theology, it was the God of Plato, St. Augustine, and the whole idealistic tradition. Resting as the proof does simply on an analysis of the nature of truth and error, it is independent at once of arguments from design and of what science may discover or fail to discover in the laboratory. A genuine, as contrasted with a "mendicant" idealism, looks to these not for confirmation but merely for "illustrations of rationality". Once for all it knows that the Whole is divine.[2]

The present writer can remember the impression which this book on its publication made on himself and others in England. It wanted the massiveness of thought of Bradley's *Ethical Studies* and Green's *Prolegomena to Ethics*; it wanted the air of a manifesto which gave a certain authority to the *Essays in Philosophical Criticism*. But the author had found a way to Idealism for himself, and was determined to get forward from Kantian and Hegelian formalism to something that Anglo-Saxon philosophy might call its own. There were traits in his statement of his results: the exaltation of ideals above experienced fact, and the emphasis on "postulation", that reminded one too much of Fichte and Royce's own early flirtation with activism. But, in the emphasis laid on "insight" throughout, it seemed as though these were on their way to be replaced by something in which volition and the process it implied were, as he himself puts it, "mere minor facts happening at a moment of time, insignificant elements in the infinite life in which as a whole there is and can be no progress, but only an infinite variety of the forms of the good will and of the higher knowledge"[3]; and in which the postulates are no longer either the "spontaneous" departures from an otherwise secure basis of

[1] Pp. 467-468.   [2] P. 482.   [3] P. 467.

experimential data that they were in the earlier articles, or merely something forced upon us by our higher needs, as in the earlier tentative chapter of the present work. We are to be led beyond "the world of postulates" and to find a "more excellent way". These become "expressions of the spirit of devotion to the highest"--itself no mere postulate, but a veritably experienced reality. It is true that the highest finds no perfect verification in experience, "dwelling" as it does "in part in the unseen and being itself the condition of all verification". But this does not take it *out of* experience, where it certainly dwells in part.

6. New Influences

This strain we might have expected to find deepened by the course of British thought, especially by Bradley's later work, whereby idealism was being remodelled on a wider basis of psychology and metaphysics. In the interval between the *Religious Aspect of Philosophy* and his next constructive effort in 1895 Royce as a matter of fact was deeply influenced by the latter, and was prepared to adopt not only Bradley's rejection of thought in favour of "experience" in the definition of reality, but his identification of the supreme reality with a completely inclusive and unified experience.[1] But there were influences coming to him at this time, partly from his own studies, partly from his immediate surroundings, that were powerfully diverting him in another direction. The preparation of his *Spirit of Modern Philosophy*[2] had led him to a deeper study of Fichte, of whom he there writes with a sympathy and gusto not elsewhere to be matched in that brilliant book. Contrasted with this, we have a treatment of Hegel which takes its departure from the *Phenomenology* rather than the *Logic*, and finds his main contribution, not in the march of the dialectic through the intellectual forms of the categories, but in "the logic of the passions", and in his description of "the paradoxes, the problems, and the glories of the spiritual life".[3] But an even more powerful influence was that which was coming to him from contemporary psychology, particularly that of his colleague William James.

As early as 1877, while still a student at Johns Hopkins University, Royce had been impressed with the doctrine of the nature of ideas

[1] See *Conception of God*, pp. 32 and 46.   [2] Boston, 1892.
[3] This does not prevent him from going with considerable fullness into Hegel's "formulation of the inclusive nature of the universal", or from characterizing it as "one of his own peculiar contributions to philosophical theory".

as explained in a course of lectures which he there heard from William James on Knowledge and its character, and especially with the opening sentences which he was accustomed to quote in his own college seminar.[1] "I call your attention to the fact that our minds are never engaged in merely copying objects; we are always reaching, responding, making over our world; it is our response to the world that constitutes our consciousness, and, if you define the mind in terms of the response in question, you will understand it better." By the time of which we are speaking the conative or "intentional" interpretation of ideas may be said to have become a commonplace of psychological theory. James himself had developed it in his own incomparable way in the chapter on "The Stream of Thought" in his *Principles of Psychology*, especially in the section on "Feelings of Tendency" in what he calls the "cognitive function". Not less revolutionary was the psychological analysis of volition which led to its identification in the last resort with attention. In this also James had been a pioneer in his chapter on Will, in which he had developed the view that "effort of attention is the essential phenomenon of will", and that "consent to the idea's undivided presence is that effort's sole achievement".[2] It was in the indeterminateness of this act, if anywhere, that freedom was to be found.

It was in these two psychological doctrines as to the nature of ideas and of will that Royce was to find the starting-point for a fresh statement of his idealistic philosophy. But it was only gradually that he came to realize their metaphysical importance, more gradually still that he came to make them the explicit foundation of his thought. His first book, as we have seen, shows comparatively little trace of their influence. That which we have now to notice represents the transition from what might be called the "logical" to the "ethical" view. Even in it the ideas on which it is founded are rather assumed than explicitly stated. It is not till we come to the First Series of the Gifford Lectures on *The World and the Individual* that it is made the explicit foundation of the whole argument; not till we come to the Second Series of these that the full result of this Fichtean strain makes itself manifest.

[1] MS. notes above referred to.
[2] *Op. cit.*, II. p. 564; really a revival of an old view. See above, pp. 67 and 69.

CHAPTER VI

ROYCE (iii). NEW STARTING-POINT IN "THE CONCEPTION
OF GOD"[1]

1. The Address

The first challenge to what was known as "Absolute Idealism" came
in America, as it did in England, in the name of "personality", to
which, it was held, it had failed to do justice.[2] Under the influence
of G. H. Howison a form of personalistic idealism in the interest of
theism had established itself on the Pacific coast. In 1895 Royce
was invited to give an address before the Philosophical Union of the
University of California, in which his book upon *The Religious Aspect
of Philosophy* had been the special subject of study for the year.
In the address he aimed at something more than a restatement of
his former argument: "A tradition", he finely says, "may be true, but
only a present and living insight can be philosophical." His own
insight had been quickened in the interval by Bradley's *Appearance
and Reality*, which had been published in 1893. From this he had
learned the inadequacy of the terms "thought" and "knowledge" to
denote the kind of experience for which identity with reality could
be claimed, and he set himself to bring his argument in this respect
into line with Bradley's phraseology, while at the same time retaining
the emphasis on selfhood in the Absolute. It came to him as all the
more of a surprise when, in the discussion which followed the close
of his address, he was vigorously attacked by his supposed friends.
"I had come into that field", he told them, "not to war with fellow-
idealists, but to criticize the Realism of ordinary tradition."[3] But
here, within what he had thought their own camp, he found a form of
the old realism reasserted in the apparent interest of the moral order.
"In terms of this form of Idealism", Howison had declared, "no manifold of selves is provided for or can be provided for." The very
meaning of goodness as a moral attribute "is lost unless there is a
society of selves to every one of whom Goodness, to be Divine, must

---

[1] *A Philosophical Discussion concerning the Nature of the Divine Idea as a
Demonstrable Reality*, edited by G. H. Howison, New York, 1897; referred
to below as *C. of G.*
[2] See above quotation from Palmer, p. 324, and what is said, p. 361 *n.*,
of the influence of Bowne.
[3] *C. of G.*, p. 142.

allot an unconditioned reality and maintain it with all the resources of infinite wisdom".[1]

We are familiar in these Studies with the answer that lay to the hand of anyone prepared to follow the main line of idealistic thought. Personality is the central fact of the modern world, and any philosophy which fails to recognize its importance is self-condemned. But persons, like all other first things, have their place in a larger world which permeates them at every pore, and in reaction with which they live and move and have their being. The word itself, like the word "thing", may be used to denote the least as well as the most that can be claimed for its correlate in respect to significance. We have the least when the term is used to indicate a mere particular and exclusive centre of feeling; we have the most when it means one who has opened his life to the influences that come to it from nature and society and brought them to unity in devotion to some comprehensive purpose. It is here, at the end, rather than at the beginning, of moral development that true individuality and freedom are to be sought. Even so there is nothing unconditioned and absolute about them. Everywhere they are conditioned by human limitations. The greatest can appropriate only a small part of the wealth of the whole: at the end, as at the beginning, the wholeness or integrity in which individuality consists is an ideal.

Royce was aware of all this and was prepared to denounce "the illusion that the category of Individuality is definable in terms of the segmentation of contents. . . . Chasms do not individuate".[2] He knew too that "the finite individuals are as real as the moral order requires or permits them to be", while at the same time "no finite individual possesses the wholeness, the grade of reality, which the Absolute possesses".[3] But he was by this time too deeply impressed with what he conceived of as the metaphysical bearings of the new psychology to be content with this as an answer to his opponents, and in the main portion of the Supplementary Essay on "The Absolute and the Individual" he develops his argument on a line which was really inconsistent with it.

2. THE SUPPLEMENTARY ESSAY AS ANTICIPATION OF LATER PHILOSOPHY. THE ARGUMENT

The Essay has permanent interest as the first sketch of the form that idealism was to assume in Royce's hands in his chief book.

[1] *Op. cit.*, p. 105.   [2] *C. of G.*, p. 331.   [3] P. 337.

Like others of his first sketches, it possesses a clarity that the fuller development lacks, and is worth dwelling upon on that account.

Nothing apparently could be assumed to be done with in philosophy, and the first part is devoted to rehearsing the dialectical steps by which, he held, ordinary realism, if it is in earnest with itself, must be driven first to a half and then to a wholehearted idealism.

The problem is not that of the implied presence in all knowledge of something other than our process of knowing. This is common ground. The real question is how this otherness has to be interpreted. Realism in all its forms says that it means "independence". This too may be granted; but what *sort* of independence? and how do we know it? It is no use appealing to mere *feeling*. This may give us *some* kind of independence, but it cannot tell us *what* kind.

Giving up the appeal to immediate feeling and coming to mediate knowledge reached somehow from what *is* felt, we have three alternatives: to seek for a *cause* of what consciousness does not of itself produce; for a *logical ground* of what is generally admitted to be an appearance; or, lastly, for that *which will give meaning and value* to what would otherwise be a senseless dream. Of these the appeal to causality breaks down, seeing that what is meant by causality is a relation between terms that may be known in experience. But how can this apply to an object or term, which *ex hypothesi* is never presented in experience? It was under the pressure of this dialectic that philosophy passed from causal nexus to logical ground. By "independent reality" we are now to mean that which under certain statable conditions we logically infer would be experienced—in fact Mill's doctrine of matter as the possibility of sensation generalized and applied to reality as a whole. But here logical ground merges into what you *mean*, and to tell what you mean is to transform your "Beyond" into something within the world of experience. Realism becomes half-idealism. But it remains half, so long as it holds that there is something that is merely possible, that can never become an actuality, and that opens the door to the admission of something transcending all experience. Out of this see-saw there is only one way—"the half-idealist must become a thoroughgoing idealist", by asking whether what we mean to express by *independence* is not in the first place that all our actual experience is fragmentary and partial, and in the second place that we know it to be so because we are conscious, along with it, of the reality of a completer form of experience than our own—even of a complete and perfect one. The realist may attempt to escape from this conclusion by shifting his ground to the extent of appealing, not directly to the sense of the independence of the object, but to its sameness at all times and for all subjects. Enlightening though this appeal is and convincing against all forms of scepticism founded in the denial of anything the same for all, none, Royce thinks, is "more adapted for an immediate transformation into the Absolute Idealism maintained in his original paper". For, if we ask what this confessedly unique reference to something which is the same for different thinkers or for ourselves at different moments really *means*, the only answer is that it is a reference to a kind of experience that brings our fragmentary experiences into relation with one another, rationalizes them and justifies their claim to be objective in the sense of valid for all.

So far we are on lines that ought by this time to have been fairly familiar. But just here what he had learned from the new psychology seemed to Royce to give the clue to a fresh statement of the result. We are concerned with the *meaning* of an idea. Interpreting then the conception, as the new psychology requires us to do, in terms of *intention*, and following it out into its consequences, we see the old conception of the relation between our knowing and an independently existing object transformed before our eyes into that of the relation between two aspects of the intention: the one subjective, the empirical consciousness of our individual ends, the other objective, the consciousness of that which in its wholeness is such that it is able to *fulfil* the subjective intent of the moment. But "To suppose such a relation (the relation between idea and meaning) objectively realized (as we do in every act of knowing) without a transcendent objective unity in which it is realized, is to suppose a question answered without an answer being given, a wish fulfilled without any concrete fact of fulfilment."[1]

The step is here hastily made—almost as a parenthesis. It was to be more fully explained in hisnext great book. Meantime his concern is with the application of the main argument to the ethical realism, or more properly pluralism, of his critics by pressing the logic of the situation. "Logic is not ethics, but the ethical categories must be logical", and the category on which the ethical realist must depend is the *sameness* of the moral individual, as to his independence and his rights, with the society which Howison had called the "city

[1] *Op. cit.*, p. 179.

of God", to which his allegiance is due. Howison's mistake was in failing to ask what this sameness means and how it is experienced, and in conceiving of it as the property of a transcendent object beyond our experience like Kant's thing-in-itself or Spencer's unknowable, instead of as the element of permanent purpose in our social experience which we share with one another in fragmentary and imperfect form.

Royce does not pause to develop the point, and introduces a polemical note into his statement of it from which as a rule his writings are singularly free. This is all the more to be regretted, as the idea of a moral order and of the kind of society, that should embody it, is particularly well suited to illustrate his own doctrine of the union in social morality of the immediate purpose or intention of an action and the underlying sense of a system of rights and duties with which that intention has to harmonize, and which may be said to be that in which it finds its full realization. Passing this over, what is here noteworthy is the original use he makes of the volitionist psychology to reaffirm what he calls "the universal presupposition of rationality"[1] as the corner-stone of a complete idealism. But, if we accept the first part of the essay in this sense, it is all the more surprising that in the second part, dealing with the "Conception of the Will and its relation to the Absolute", by which he prepares the way for his doctrine of individuality, he also seems to be preparing the way for a capitulation to the pluralism, ethical and other (which he here condemns), by finding the essence of free will in the element of indeterminate choice in the act of attention, instead of in determination by rational ideas as the objective element in meaning.

His aim in this part is, as he tells us, to supplement the conception of the Absolute as the All Knower, which had been prominent in the *Religious Aspect*, by vindicating its title to free volition. Taking his cue again from the psychology which found "the one element which is constantly present and which has central significance in our voluntary experience", not in "the largely illusory sense of power and of free control", but in selective attention, Royce looks to this to provide the basis of freedom. To select and limit attention to one set of possibilities rather than another is a free act. "In der Beschränkung", he quotes, "zeigt sich erst der Meister." But possibilities are in themselves mere ideas, general types. To become more they have to be realized in the concrete. Hence attention may be said to be the

[1] P. 178.

sacrifice of ideal possibilities for the sake of realizing ideas. The life in which this process ends is one of sharply "differentiated fact, discrete realities". Transferring this to the Absolute Experience, we shall attribute to it "just such an individuation of its contents, just such an attentive precision whereby" its ideas, as universal types, "get discrete expression".[1] In Royce's new terminology, the Absolute has to be conceived of as fulfilling ideas in a way that on the one hand is counter to no idea (in other words that is absolutely rational), and on the other hand that "cannot be conceived as determined by any of the ideas, or as necessitated by thought. . . . In this sense the individuality, the concrete reality of the contents of the Absolute Experience, must be conceived as on the one hand fulfilling ideas, but as on the other hand freely, unconstrainedly— if you will capriciously—embodying their universality in the very fact of the presence of this life, this experience, this world".[2]

It is from this point of view that we can speak of the "Divine Will", which is "simply that aspect of the Absolute which is expressed in the concrete and undifferentiated individuality of the world"; while the world appears "not as a barely abstract world of pure ideas, but as a world of manifested individuals". Finally, seeing that there is an unexplained element in the selection of this world as the one fulfilment of absolute ideas and ideals, there is a place for what has been called the "Divine Love", the generalized expression for "an affection or colouring of consciousness which involves a selection of some content as valuable for reasons that can no longer be abstractedly defined in terms of this content". All that is clear to the loving consciousness is that "no other object fills the place or could fill just the place occupied by the beloved object". It is in this way that Royce seeks not only to supplement the conception of God as "thought" with the attributes of will and feeling, but to subordinate it to them. Thought is a mere abstraction from the whole of an experience which transcends it, and the proof is that in thought we are subject to logical necessity expressed in a "must". But "there *must be* what is beyond every must. The *must* is our comment. The *is* expresses the ultimate fact. . . . It is this aspect of the ultimate situation which defines the world as a whole, and which, without introducing an external cause, or a mere force, does, as it were, colour the whole unity of the Absolute consciousness with a new character, namely, the character of Will".[3]

[1] P. 201. [2] P. 202. [3] P. 212.

Coming to the problem of Individuality, on which the Californian discussion had concentrated attention, after complaining of the neglect of it in modern philosophy, Royce proceeds to give an interesting account of the opposing views of Aquinas and Duns Scotus. This we might have expected to lead up to an analysis of his own, reflecting something of their thoroughness. But instead of this he goes on to assume, rather than prove, that the essential element in the idea is "uniqueness", and, leaving this also unanalysed,[1] proceeds to ask how it is *known* and to what it is *due*. His answer to these questions is that individuality as thus defined is not knowable either through sense or inference. Sense gives us what is here and now, but there are many "heres" and "nows", and, to fix this one as individual, it has to be related to something already so recognized, and this is just that of which we are in search. So with inference. This is from a universal, and can only give us what is an instance among many, and is not therefore unique. The conclusion is that "the concept of the individual in its primary and original sense is distinctly an ethical concept, whether you speak in terms of knowledge or of being". From the side of knowledge we know a thing as individual only through our instinctive emotional attitude of interest in it—an interest which is essentially exclusive and demands an exclusive object. "One stands in the presence of an object concerning which one simply feels that there shall be no other of this particular value."[2] He admits indeed that *all* interest is not individualizing, and this leads him to distinguish between "organizing interest" and other types, but he does not develop a line of thought which might have led to a deeper view of the nature of the individuality of which he was in search, and he goes on to apply the same idea to the question of the source of individuality in the world.

Taking the world itself as a unique whole, and without asking how we know it as such, he explains it as the result of the selective act of a being to whom interest or love and its fulfilment are one and the same thing. "Such a being would say: There shall be but this one world; and for him this one world would be fact." And so with individual objects within the world. "Objects are individuals in so far as they are unique expressions of essentially exclusive ideals, ends, Divine decrees." But again the idea of a mere *fiat*, as the source of individuality, is qualified by that of organization. Exclusive choice is

[1] I know of no thoroughgoing attempt at such an analysis of the idea of uniqueness either in England or America before Bradley's in the Second Edition of the *Logic*, vol. ii. pp. 647 foll.

[2] P. 262.

not enough either in the case of the world as a unique whole or of the things in it. Will in the Absolute cannot be conceived, in the case of the former, in abstraction from what he calls the various interests which "together constitute the organism of the Divine Will".[1] Similarly in the case of finite things, *e.g.*, in biology, there must be enough organization "to represent apparently unique variations of a type", something therefore, one should have supposed, of which uniqueness is a function or consequence instead of a primary attribute.

Accordingly it is only what we might expect when in the discussion of self-conscious individuality the emphasis shifts back from spontaneous acts of choice to the degree in which organized unity of content is achieved. In the excellent section dealing with the question of the "Reality of the Ego" he makes it clear that, apart from the unity of a life-plan, "the empirical ego can be as truly called a thousand selves as one self". Selective attention is the condition of the unity and continuity of this plan, but what gives it substance is the coherence of its parts and the actual embodiment of it in a consistent and energetic form of life—unique in so far as it is his own, but his own, not merely because he has chosen it, but because he has realized himself in it.

Coming to the question raised by Bradley of self-consciousness in the Absolute, Royce recognizes the difficulty that, while in finite individuals it involves the contrast between ideal and fulfilment, self and others, it is just the absence of these contrasts that characterizes the absolute experience. To it there can be no unfulfilled idea nor any other to itself. How then can self-consciousness be attributed to it? His answer consists in showing that, while these and other like contrasts cannot exist in the Absolute as they do in us, seeing that we must conceive of them as there transcended, yet *in order that they may be transcended they must be there, and there to consciousness as different aspects of one self.* In this sense we have within the Absolute the two aspects of thinking and experiencing, two selves, "as we might metaphorically call them", of Thinker and Seer, contrasted with and mutually related to each other, and only transcended as so conceived. It is for this reason Royce concludes that "with all my indebtedness to Mr. Bradley's discussion of the Absolute I am unable to view the categories of self-consciousness as 'mere appearance', or to regard them as 'lost' or 'absorbed' or

[1] P. 270.

'transformed' into something unspeakably other than they are as soon as one passes to the absolute point of view". The argument was to be restated at greater length and with new illustrations in the later treatise. Meantime he has to apply it to the relation of the Absolute to the finite individual, which it was the object of the whole Essay to define.

3. APPLICATION TO HUMAN FREEDOM

However valid as a statement of idealist doctrine, he was aware that his argument was open to the charge of merely confirming the indictment of the critics of the Address. It had only succeeded in proving that: "There is one Individual, and that is the Whole. The parts are predestined in the Whole. Each part is determined. 'Only one is free, and that is Zeus'."

The answer to this criticism, one might have supposed, was not far to seek for anyone who had himself risen above the conception of the Whole as either a Destiny or a Divine Will, determining man from without, to that of it as an ideal, prompting (in the language of religion "pleading with") him from within, and bestowing freedom and individuality upon him in the degree in which wholeness was realized in his own life. But having committed himself in the earlier part of the essay to the view of the Absolute as Will, and to indeterminate choice as of the essence of will, both in the Absolute and the finite individual, Royce has to take another line. In order that there may be a moral world, "no one simple free act suffices, but many such acts are needed in order to account logically for the individuation actually present in any such world". But "A world of so-called 'infinite' free agents is at best a polytheistic world. At worst it threatens something more diabolical." The solution must therefore consist in limiting this freedom, and he ends with the hoary compromise, "The free agents of a moral world are free only in so far as their essential moral relations leave them free. They have their place and must stay in it. They have their individuality and must subordinate it."[1]

No wonder that Howison was able to agree and to claim that his own doctrine of individuality as consisting in *self*-activity, and therefore as the highest category, "is not only the clear implication, but the real significance of Professor Royce's whole argumentation

[1] P. 321.

for the presence of what he calls 'will' at the heart of reality";
guarding himself at the same time from the imputation of meaning by *self*-activity "boundless self-will" by adding the saving word
"rational".[1] He does not see any more than Royce (who would have
agreed to the qualification) that by laying the emphasis on "rationality" rather than spontaneous choice he has altered the whole
situation. Whether in the sense of choice of alternative courses of
conduct or of alternative objects of attention, will in that case could
no longer be claimed as the source either of the being or of our
knowledge of individuality. It is only the elementary condition of
that form of self-determination which consists in the progressive
organization of life in accordance with the ideal of wholeness that
alone entitles it to be called rational. To stop short of this must
result either in the identification of the spontaneity of the individual
with that of the Absolute and the acceptance of a non-moral monism,
or in surrender to the ethical pluralism which Royce had set out to
undermine.

The more, in fact, the idea of the priority of will in the sense
defined by him is worked out in detail, the more is he likely to
involve himself in this dilemma. What was necessary was, in *the first
place*, that he should make a more careful analysis of the idea of
individuality than he had as yet anywhere done, in order to define
more clearly the relation of the two elements of uniqueness and
internal unity, which are alternately emphasized in his actual
treatment of it; and *secondly*, that he should make up his mind
whether the principle was to be looked for in unexplained beginnings
or in an ideal end: in the multifarious acts of selective attention, or
in the degree of organization that it is possible to realize through
the controlling "insight" which he had so well characterized in *The
Religious Aspect of Philosophy*; whether, in a word, individuality
was or was not on all fours with reality itself as a teleological idea.
The interest of the student, who is trying to follow the movement
of Royce's thought during this the central period of its development,
centres round the question how far he is prepared to make his
position clear in these respects, and, in case of his failure to do so,
where the logic of the ambiguity we have noted tends to carry him
when he is faced with ultimate metaphysical questions.

[1] Pp. 321 and 333, Editor's notes.

CHAPTER VII

ROYCE (iv). THE WORLD AND THE INDIVIDUAL[1]

1. MYSTICISM AND LOGIC

In the Californian Address and Essay Royce had tried, under the inspiration of criticism, to restate the argument for Idealism with special reference to the problem of Individuality, and had begun the transformation of it into terms of Will. But he had been taken unawares. The new terms were there, but they had not the prominence they deserved. His space, moreover, was limited. With the invitation to deliver the Gifford Lectures in the University of Aberdeen came the opportunity of putting the volitional basis in the foreground, as well as of developing the argument in fuller detail.

He was the first American thinker to give these lectures,[2] and there was no one in either country better fitted, alike by sympathy with the Founder's conception of "God the only Substance" and by philosophical training, for the task. The resulting book has been with justice described by the writer on Philosophy in the *Cambridge History of American Literature* as "The nearest approach to a philosophical classic that the American continent has produced". For an analysis of its contents the reader may be referred to the reviews that appeared at the time of its publication, more particularly to the two by J. Ellis McTaggart which appeared in *Mind*.[3] What we are here concerned with is the expansion which his voluntaristic theory of the nature of reality receives in its pages, and the new illustrations of it derived from the studies which in the interval had been occupying his attention, and of which two deserve special mention.

By the time Royce went to Harvard in 1882 the Transcendentalism of the Concord group had become little more than a tradition. The place of his own birth and training had been in regions remote from it. But his temperament allied him with the mystical element in that movement, and he realized keenly the close connection between it and his own form of idealism. "Mysticism as a mere

---

[1] *Gifford Lectures.* First Series, New York, 1900; Second Series, New York, 1901. Referred to below as *W. and I.*

[2] William James's *Varieties of Religious Experience* were not given till the following year.

[3] N.S., vol. ix. pp. 258 foll.; and vol. xi. pp. 557 foll.

doctrine for edification", he held, "was indeed no philosophy. Yet a philosophy has been based upon it." "The mystic is a very abstract sort of person, but he is usually a keen thinker."[1] Already, in *The Spirit of Modern Philosophy*, he had devoted considerable space to the contrast between the idealistic and the mystical point of view. "On the other hand," he writes in the Preface to *Studies of Good and Evil*,[2] "it is unquestionable that the mystic and the idealist have much in common, and there can be no doubt of the enormous historical importance of mysticism in keeping alive the sense of intimacy of our human relation to the divine Reality." He had himself made a careful study of some of the mediæval mystics, particularly of Meister Eckhart,[3] and in his college lectures he was accustomed to illustrate the mystic attitude both from what was most ancient and from what was most modern in literature. In *The World and the Individual* the treatment of it has rightly been regarded as a triumph of sympathetic interpretation.

The other influence that had by this time[4] begun to make itself felt in his thought was the study of the new logic of mathematics, of which his friend Charles Peirce was the chief exponent in America. What especially interested him in it was the conception of the infinite as containing determinate results within an indeterminate series, and offering an illustration of the way in which the One and Many might be united in an intelligible manner both in the Absolute and in finite consciousness, and therewith an argument by which Bradley's sceptical view founded in the "infinite process" might be successfully met. Too technical for the lectures, he relegates the exposition and application of it to a long "Supplementary Essay" at the end of the First Series.[5] In spite of the involved form of the essay, nothing he ever wrote is more important in bringing out the difference between the type of doctrine with which his name is associated and the more orthodox idealistic tradition to which, with all his radical scepticism, Bradley on the whole sought to remain faithful.

---

[1] *W. and I.*, vol. i. pp. 77 and 81.   [2] New York, 1902.
[3] See the paper on him in the book just quoted.
[4] See already *C. of G.*, p. 208, where the mathematical conception of the "group" is used with effect to illustrate the idealist's conception of the Total System of possible thoughts.
[5] Whether he was able to satisfy experts that he was really master of the subject may perhaps be doubted in view of the remark he humorously quotes from the letter in which Peirce acknowledges the gift of this book: "When I read you, I do wish that you would study logic. You need it so much" (*Problem of Christianity*, vol. i. p. 117).

2. Theory of Being

We have already referred[1] to the effect of Bradley's writings on Royce's mind in respect to the use he had made in his first book of "thought" as that form of experience in which truth and emotional satisfaction are attained. By this time he is fully convinced of its inadequacy to express the unity of God and the world which still remains his "central assurance". "While this term", he writes in the Preface, "was there so defined as to make Thought inclusive of Will and of Experience, these latter terms were not emphasized prominently enough, and the aspects of the Absolute Life which they denote have since become more central in my own interests. The present is a deliberate effort to bring into synthesis, more fully than I have done before, the relations of Knowledge and of Will in our conception of God." What made this effort important was the further conviction at which he had arrived, that it was only in terms of Will that the existence of Individuality, whether in God or man, could be explained.

It was in virtue of the clearness he had reached on this subject that he also saw that the foundation must be laid in a fresh analysis of the meaning of ideas. "I am one of those", he writes, "who hold that when you ask the question: What is an Idea? and How can Ideas stand in any true relation to Reality? you attack the world-knot in the way that promises most for the untying of its meshes."[2] "First our account of the nature of Being and of the relation between Idea and Being is to be founded explicitly upon a theory of the way in which ideas possess their own meaning. Secondly, our theory of the nature of meaning is to be founded on a definition in terms of Will and Purpose. We do not indeed say, Our will causes our ideas. But we do say, Our ideas now imperfectly embody our will. And the real world is just our whole will embodied."[3]

We are already familiar with what he means by this distinction between the imperfect and the complete embodiment of will, and need not follow the fuller exposition that is here given of it. All that it adds is the designation of the partial and passing purpose as the "internal", the reference to something with which the idea has to correspond as the "external" aspect of ideas. The doctrine previously sketched in the *Conception of God* thus becomes expressible in the form: "Let my process of determining my own internal meaning

[1] Pp. 366 and 368. [2] *W. and I.*, vol. i. p. 16. [3] P. 39.

simply proceed to its own limit, and then I shall face Being. I shall
not only imitate my object as another, and correspond to it from
without; I shall become one with it, and so internally possess it"[1]
—words on which the constructive part of the argument rings the
changes. But first he has to apply the view thus reached to other
classical theories reduced to the three main types of realism, mysticism, and critical rationalism.

3. REALISM AND MYSTICISM

By one of those sudden expansions of his thought, which he so
engagingly records, Royce had come to see that the first reaction
both in logic and history against ordinary realistic conceptions was
not in the direction of idealism in its modern form, but of mysticism.
The dialectic which he had tried to trace in the *Conception of God*
thus takes a wider sweep, beginning in this reaction as we have it in
the Upanishads and the Vedanta, passing thence to the West first
into Greek then into Christian thought, Catholic and Protestant
alike, and ending in a philosophical theory having significance, not
from the things to which it applies the predicate "real", but from
the view it takes of the fundamental meaning of "the very ontological
predicate itself". As realism takes hold of the reference in our immediate experience to something "other", on which it depends, but which
is independent of it, mysticism takes hold of immediacy as itself the
sign-manual of reality. It consists in asserting that "to *be* means
simply and wholly to be *immediate*". While to others, therefore, *ideas*
may be the path that leads to reality, to the mystic they can only
lead to illusion. The mystics in fact, "are the only thoroughgoing
empiricists in the history of philosophy".[2] Combining this with his
own account of the meaning of ideas, Royce is able to find in realism
and mysticism "the polar opposites of each other". In realism the
whole stress falls on the "external" meaning of ideas: it "defines
real being as a total independence of any idea, whose external object
any given being is". In mysticism the whole stress falls on the internal
meaning. It "defines real being as wholly within immediate feeling".[3]
What therefore he has to show is that "These two conceptions, both
of them false abstractions, are still both of them fragmentary views
of the truth—hints towards a final definition of the other, of that
fulfilment which our finite thinking restlessly seeks."[4]

[1] *Ibid.*, p. 38.   [2] P. 81.   [3] P. 86.   *Ibid.*

Royce is never better than in sketching the movements of philosophical thought in large historical outlines, and it was with justice that the chapter in which all this is set out appeared at the time to its ablest and best informed critics "admirable both as metaphysics and as literature".[1] Not less admirable are the sections that follow in which the abstractness of these points of view is demonstrated first by insisting, in Socratic fashion,[2] that the ideas of independence and immediacy must be taken in their purity, and secondly by showing that when so taken they "both end in a *reductio ad absurdum* of every definite idea of the Real".

If to be real means to be totally independent of ideas, what, we ask, becomes of ideas themselves? They surely are beings, and as such, according to realistic interpretation, without inherent relation to the other being which is called "reality". And (seeing that realism as a doctrine is itself a system of just such ideas) what is this but the disappearance of the doctrine itself? As having no essential relation to its object, it becomes at once an account of anything or nothing. Similarly from the other side with regard to mysticism. Being is to be that which we reach when we have been delivered from all definite and particular experience. But to define the reality which we are to experience as only the negation of all the experience we actually have is to define a mere nothing. In order that the Infinite may have any meaning we must retain the contrast-effect, and this can only be done by regarding the particular experience as embodying something of positive value which nevertheless by its defects points to something beyond itself. "If Mysticism is to escape from its own finitude and really is to mean by its absolute Being anything but a Mere Nothing, its account of Being must be so amended as to involve the assertion that our finite life is not mere illusion, that our ideas are not merely false, and that we are already, even as finite, in touch with Reality."[3] So to amend it Royce conceives to be the special mission of Idealism as a world philosophy. What attracts him in mysticism and marks it as an advance upon all forms of realism, is the assistance it gives to thought in this enterprise. Instead of

---

[1] McTaggart, *loc. cit.* So Dewey: "Personally I have found the discussion of mysticism one of the most interesting and enlightening portions of the book" (*Philosophical Review*, vol. ix. p. 315 *n.*).

[2] "Heavens, my dear Glaucus, how energetically you polish them up for a decision, first one and then the other, as if they were two statues" (Plato, *Republic*, p. 361).

[3] P. 182.

dogmatically refusing, as realism commonly does, to consider the paradoxes in which it involves itself, mysticism "expounds its own paradoxes and glories in them". It is, moreover, essentially "a practical doctrine. It observes at once that you merely express your own need as knower when you regard an object as existent", and that, when you define that need, you find that it is nothing else than yourself: "You want yourself—the self in its completeness, in its fulfilment and final expression. In brief, when you talk of reality you talk of self-possession, of perfection, and of peace."[1]

4. CRITICAL RATIONALISM

While he has thus come to find in mysticism the first solvent of crude realism, Royce holds that the historic precursor of modern idealism was the modified form which realism took when it was perceived that reality could only be defined in terms of possible experience. This was Kant's great discovery. It was the statement of it in his own way that made Mill's work so important.[2] The general outcome of the criticism of realism, for which these names stand, is the impossibility of defining Being without including a reference to knowledge ("The real is that which fulfils our idea of knowledge"), and what we have in the lecture on "Validity and Experience" is merely an expanded version of the exposition in the *Religious Aspect of Philosophy*. It is only when, after the long and crucial chapter on the "Internal and External Meaning of Ideas", the writer turns to the criticism of this Third Conception of Being, that the argument assumes a new form corresponding to the new orientation of his thought.

The defect of "Critical Rationalism", as explained in the earlier book, was in effect that it did not perceive that possibility logically involves actuality. There is no such thing in logic as mere possibility. State the conditions of your hypothetical judgment, and you inevitably have a categorical judgment of real existence. But Royce had meantime become dissatisfied with any merely logical statement of the case for idealism. He was pledged to state it in terms of will and purpose. He was pledged also (for was not this the whole object of his treatise?) to state it in a form that would be consonant with the demand that the real should be concrete and individual. "There is an ancient doctrine that whatever is is ultimately something

[1] P. 186.　　　　　　　　　　[2] See above, p. 348.

individual" are the words with which he opens his lecture on the "Fourth Conception of Reality", and he makes it clear from the outset that he takes his stand with ordinary realism on this axiom. But, having rejected the doctrine of individual objects given to us as an "other" which is independent of our ideas, he has to find the ground of both the otherness and the individuality within the four corners of the ideas themselves. We now know how this is to be done. The real appears as an "object" because our ideas have a meaning, aim, or intention. It appears as "another" because it is thought of as an object to which our ideas, as ours, only partially conform, but to which they "mean" wholly to conform. And the reason of this partialness is that, as ideas, they are general and fail to include the particular and the individual, and so to complete themselves. "This completion is for us another, solely because our ideas, in their present momentary forms, come to us as general ideas —ideas of what is now merely a kind of relative fulfilment and not an entire fulfilment." For their entire fulfilment we should need to have all the instances in which the general becomes embodied—the *omnitudo realitatis*, as something determinate. "This want of ours not only sets us looking for Being, but gives us our only ground and means for defining Being."[1]

If, from this way of stating the problem, we return to critical rationalism, we see that its error consists in defining the "other" by what are merely general characters. The real is to be such that we should have this *kind* of experience (sensation or thought) of it. It is that which, under certain conditions, we should have. But in the end it gives us nothing really other than our ideas. All that is thus defined about the object is its mere *what*, not its Being. "If", Royce concludes, "you have once observed this defect of any assertion of a bare possibility of experience, you will have seen why the mere definition of universal types can never reach the expression of the whole nature of real Beings, and why, for that very reason, the realm of Validity is nothing unless it is more than merely valid, nothing, too, unless it takes individual form as a unique fulfilment of purpose in a complete life."[2]

Such a view finally, he claims, is a synoptic one, giving a place to what is true in its rivals, while correcting what is false. With realism it asserts that what completes is other than and authoritative over any of our finite ideas; but it differs in insisting that the otherness

[1] P. 347. [2] P. 357.

and authority are conferred upon it by the will itself. With mysticism it asserts that the reality is one with the true meaning or purpose of the idea: the otherness is in the end appearance. But it holds against it that the true purpose of the idea is never its own extinction, but its extension, so that it may correspond to and embrace what at first appears as its other, but is in reality its own completion. With rationalism, finally, it holds that the real is defined, and can only be defined, in terms of valid ideas, but what validates ideas has always to be conceived in terms of a real individual experience, in which "the what turns into the that".[1]

It is impossible not to admire the ingenuity which the writer shows in making his distinction between the internal and external meaning of ideas do service as a criticism of Kantian idealism. But it is impossible also to escape the suspicion that it is only by a *tour de force* that he succeeds in doing so. The whole point of the distinction is that, in the search for meanings in which our whole life consists, we start from something immediate and, so far, subjective, which has to be interpreted so that it shall correspond to or express something not immediately given and yet be the confirmation of it as objective. He says too little of the precise logical process whereby this confirmation is effected. But where he does touch upon it he rightly sees that it is a process of elimination of possibilities by universal judgments which take the form of disjunctions. "The purpose of our universal judgments is that, by the aid of disjunctive judgments, they enable us to determine the world of Being"[2]; a determination which must consist in finding one or other of the alternatives confirmed in particular experiences. If there is any doctrine clearly attributable to Kant, it is that there can be no truth that does not consist in the union in this way of universal and particular. It is therefore with some surprise that we find the view of truth and reality which originated with Kant described as one that leaves us with mere universals. Kant's mistake was not this, but consisted in holding that truths whose validity was thus established held only of our "experience", and failed to give us "reality". No wonder that critics like Dewey at the time[3] found the whole argument fallacious, on the ground that it confuses the three notions clearly distinguishable in Kant of reality, the valid idea and possible experience, and then uses this confusion to condemn the theory in question.

[1] P. 358. [2] P. 278.
[3] See his review of this work in *Philosophical Review*, vol. ix. pp. 311 foll.

Not less in the establishment of his own theory is there something clearly missing. So long as this is made to depend merely on a distinction within our wills, it is open to regard the "external meaning" as no more than the requirement to go beyond the momentary and immediate to something more in accord with the internal or subjective meaning. To attribute this something to an Absolute experience does not help us, seeing that it is still an experience of our own that we are in search of. Dewey's gibe at a theory which seemed to imply that all possibilities are real in the Absolute[1] may be unfair, but he was within his right in showing that Royce blows alternately hot and cold on finite experience, and that by the argument, as we here have it, we "either do not get to the Absolute—what we get to is the necessity of reinterpreting our own experiences—or if we get it (our meanings being presented in the Absolute), what boots it us?" This criticism could only be met by showing that the necessity for reinterpretation comes, not from any element supplied by our will in setting an object before itself beyond immediate experience— this may still be, as the pragmatist holds, something particular, and, as such, still "internal" in Royce's sense of the word—but from the presence in all experience, whether thinking or willing, of the idea of a reality which exercises constraint on our thought and will, requiring their expansion into more adequate, and in the end more individual forms. Royce's whole position, as opposed to that both of Kant and Dewey, depends on the assertion of this principle of objectivity, and it is nothing less than a surrender of it to resolve the "object" into anything that our wills can be said to supply.

We shall have to return to this. Meantime we have to follow the author as he turns from the conception of Being, at which he has thus arrived, to its application to the question of the Individual.

5. THE PROBLEM OF INDIVIDUALITY

What, he asks, does that conception imply as to the reality of individuals? In one respect it seems to deny it, seeing that the essence of this conception is that all meanings are only partial expressions of one all-inclusive meaning: "The One is in all, and all are in One. All meanings, if completely developed, unite in one meaning, and

[1] Speaking of economic possibilities: "we prefer the solid gains for ourselves and to leave the experiences of bankruptcy and bad investments to God", *loc. cit.*, p. 317 *n*.

this it is which the real world expresses."[1] In another aspect it seems to imply the reality, not only of a multiplicity of private meanings corresponding to the multiplicity of ideas, but also of a multiplicity of free individual thinkers or selves: "The world then is a realm of individuals, self-possessed, morally free, and sufficiently independent of one another to make their freedom of action possible and finally significant."[2] Can these views be reconciled?

The chapter on "Universality and Unity" is devoted to the development of the thesis (on the lines and often in the terminology of the argument of the *Religious Aspect*) "that the whole world of truth and being must exist only as present in all its variety, its wealth, its relationships, its entire constitution, to the unity of a single consciousness, which includes both our own and all finite conscious meaning in one final eternal present insight". If it is true that "all which has Being exists only as known object", then, whatever the relation of the many knowers to one another may be, it must be known to a consciousness which includes them all. Even if they be sundered from one another, "their very sundering implies their common presence as facts to a knower who consciously observes their sundering as the fulfilment of his own single meaning".

But Royce is not content with the abstract statement of this side of the case, and goes on, in one of the best sections of the book, to show that the world of ordinary experience and of science, in spite of its apparent refractoriness, "has already a provisional unity" which contains "a genuine, if fragmentary, hint of a final unity". The most obvious illustration of this unity is the implication in all present experience, of whatever kind, of a reference to a past and a future, which, though different from it, as the ideal from the actual, are yet indivisible from it. Whatever the object you please to observe in a world of time and change, "the question, What is it? is logically and inseparably bound up with the two questions, What was it? and Whither is it tending?" Consistently with this, he is prepared to conceive of the whole of Nature, in one of his most interesting speculations,[3] to be more fully worked out in the Second Series, as a vast society with an indefinitely enlarged time span, "in whose transactions finite processes of evolution, when viewed, not with reference to the eternal meaning of the whole, but with reference

[3] Already anticipated in the essay on "Self-consciousness, Social Consciousness, and Nature", in *Studies of Good and Evil* (1895).

to the temporal series of facts, are presumably mere passing incidents". It is this conception[1] also which he finally applies in his definition of the eternal consciousness as "one for which all the facts for the whole time-stream have the same type of unity that your present momentary consciousness even now within its little span surveys".

In this emphasis on the time-relation, and particularly in the treatment of simultaneity (the *totum simul*) as the characteristic feature of the absolute experience, we may perhaps see a survival of that "incomplete idealism" which we have already noted in Royce's earliest writings. But the uncompromising statement of the unity of reality as consisting in the interrelations of content transcending time, and not in any supposed unity of times in the act of will as such, is in line with the better idealistic tradition. It leads us to expect a treatment of the problem of individuality, to which he now returns, more in harmony with that tradition than the one which we met with in the *Conception of God*, and in one respect we are not disappointed.

He still commits himself dogmatically to the primariness of the element of uniqueness. "By an individual being, whatever one's metaphysical doctrine, one means a unique being, that is a being which is alone of its own type, or is such that no other of its class exists." But he illustrates the thesis from the effort of science to discover the one meaning which the facts will bear, *e.g.*, in the diagnosis of disease, where clearly the judgment is an inference from the complete survey of the conditions and trained insight into their systematic relations with one another, and where it is quite indifferent whether this is a unique case in any other sense. He adds, moreover, that for individuality in the full sense of the word there must be complete inclusiveness. Long before we have any idea of unique experiences "our restless finite will itself has demanded that the real world wherein our will seeks, and logically speaking ultimately finds its fulfilment, shall be altogether determinate, both in so far as nothing further is needed to complete it, and in so far as nothing else could meet the needs which constitute finite ideas".[2] From such a position the way would seem to be clear to a view of finite individuality which should make it consist in the *degree* in which our minds and wills approximate to this ideal of determinateness.

But just at this point Royce drops the clue that the definition

[1] P. 425.   [2] P. 457.

puts into his hand and reverts to the guidance of the psychology of selective attention, as he had done in the *Conception of God*. "Owing to our finitude, will in our own case far anticipates its own fulfilment. The individual, therefore, as a conceived object of inquiry, of desire, and of knowledge, appears to our finite human thought as something that we early define much more in terms of selective exclusion than of empirically observed completeness." It is accordingly in "our selective attention embodied in our exclusive affections" that we must look for the assurance that we are in the presence of individual beings.[1] Lest, finally, there should thus appear to be a gap between his account of individuality in the Absolute and in the finite, he goes back upon his former definition and asserts that "The world as a whole is an individual fact not merely by virtue of the completeness of the contents of the Absolute, but by reason of the selection of that object which shall be permitted to fulfil the final meaning." In a word, "It is will in God and man" (not any completeness and unity of content) "that logically determines the consciousness of individuality."[2]

With this the question of the relation of these two wills is at once again raised and answered again, as in the *Conception of God*, by what is little more than a restatement of the problem. Our wills are doubtless in God, but they are not lost in God. "You are at once an expression of the divine will, and by virtue of that very fact the expression here and now, in your life, of your *own* will, precisely in so far as you find yourself acting with a definite intent and gaining through your act a definite empirical expression."

It is difficult to conceive of anyone who is in earnest with the idea of individuality, whether in an absolute or relative sense, finding himself satisfied with the argument as here presented, any more than with its earlier form in the *Conception of God*. If the uniqueness claimed for the finite individual in the act of will belongs to him as independent of any other will, we are still in the grip of an absolute pluralism. If, on the other hand, the uniqueness is something that at every moment is sustained by the divine act of choice, it is difficult to see how we escape from an all-devouring monism. It is useless to appeal to "internal meanings" as "typical instances of facts and of precisely the facts of whose unity the world consists".[3] These "meanings" are just what Royce himself means by acts of will in us, and their unity what he means by the Divine Will. Unless, there-

[1] P. 458.   [2] P. 460.   [3] P. 464.

fore, they have a being as facts independent of that unity, as ordinary realism holds, they remain, in spite of their apparent pluralism, acts of God and not of us. So long as he continues to lay the stress on uniqueness as the fundamental element in individuality, and finds the basis of the uniqueness of wills in their spontaneous activity, he more and more involves himself in this dilemma.

If we inquire more closely into the source of this difficulty, we shall find it, I believe, to be the same as that noted in the previous section—the obscurity in which he has left the relation between universal and particular. Without a clear understanding on this fundamental point, it is impossible to give any satisfactory account of what is meant by individuality. It was towards a truer understanding of it that the whole movement of post-Kantian idealism had been moving. What had been emerging in the course of it was that we are on the wrong track when we look for individuality, whether in things or persons, in any mere particular immediately given fact, whether of outer or inner sense, apart from its relation to a wider whole which it shares with others. Being-for-self and being-for-other, as Plato had long ago seen, and modern idealism had been gradually rediscovering, are not opposed to each other, but play in and out of every thing as inseparable elements in its constitution. To know a thing as truly individual, we have to see it in its place in the whole or system to which it belongs—as a reflection of the world of which it is a part. To ask for any other individuality is to ask for we know not what.

To this it is no answer to accuse, as Royce does, the concepts by which we seek to define things of generality and applicability to other things as well as this, and thus as failing to define any one thing. For, in the first place, universals, as an element in the actual process of thought, are never merely general with the indeterminate sense they have in a dictionary, but take definiteness from the context in which they occur, the subject of which they are predicated. The green of the sea is not the green of the trees; the sweetness of the nightingale's song is not the sweetness of Melba's. In the second place, such predicates are not the only kind of universals. With equal right we speak of the whole or system to which a thing belongs, the organism which gives its place and meaning to its members, as their universal. It is these and not the abstract universals or class names of ordinary logic that are the real objects of science. Hegel called them "concrete universals". The phrase has gone out of fashion, but the thing is as alive as ever in the science and philosophy of our time.[1]

Even more obvious has it become with regard to persons that no mere particularity can give us what we want. If this is all that is necessary, we can have it, and its equivalent uniqueness, in being this particular centre of feeling—in other words, in being nothing distinctively human at all. To be a determinate person one has to leave the privacy of feeling and share through perception and idea a world that is common to oneself with others.

It is to this kind of inclusiveness that his nature both as a natural and a rational being commits every man. He has to die in order to live. Mere inclusion is, of course, not enough: this might mean mere distraction and dissipation. What is taken in, the "interests" with which a man identifies himself, must be brought into unity in some sort of harmonious whole. He must "either be a whole or join a whole", and his nature is such that he cannot do either without doing both. This is why in ordinary human life the path to individual personality is through the discovery of a place or station in society. When a man has found this he finds something that he can make his own in the sense that no other can really take his place, that he is, if you like, unique. But the uniqueness is secondary. The essential thing is the place and the "proper service" which the poet tells us

> every place on earth
> Was framed to furnish man with.[2]

To be a person one has, as the mediæval use of the word "persona" or "parson" signified, to be representative of what is more than a private self. No one, it may confidently be said, who has learned this lesson cares in the least whether he is unique or not so long as he is in this sense himself. Both in thought and action the important thing is not to think or act differently from other people, but to think and act for oneself. "The reasonable", Hegel said, "is a highway on which all go and no one distinguishes himself."

Returning to Royce, what we find ambiguous in his account of individuality is the persistent emphasis on the element of uniqueness instead of on the inclusiveness and organization which all real self-affirmation involves, and of which uniqueness is merely a function. He is well aware that for ethics there can be no true self-realization

[1] It is what Professor Whitehead, for instance, means by the "system" to which a thing belongs and apart from which it cannot be understood.
[2] See Bradley, E.S., p. 183.

except in so far as the individual identifies himself with the society of which he is a part, shares its thoughts, lives its life, makes its cause his own. This was the whole burden of the argument of the first part of the *Religious Aspect of Philosophy*. He was to return to it, as, in the last period of his life, he became again dominated by socio-ethical conceptions. But in this middle period he is so occupied with finding a place for the exclusive aspect of individuality that the other takes more and more a subordinate place, and in the end is in danger of disappearing altogether.

6. THE SUPPLEMENTARY ESSAY: THE QUESTION AT ISSUE AND ROYCE'S ANSWER

The book of the decade of which we are speaking was Bradley's *Appearance and Reality*. Its thesis was that, assuming individuality to mean complete inclusiveness and indivisibility, in other words comprehensiveness and coherence of content, this is something that in the end can only be predicated of the Absolute. The proof was that any attempt to stop short of the whole of reality and seek individuality in a part is bound to leave us with insoluble contradictions on our hands. We are always left with elements which we are forced to believe coherent, yet which we cannot *see* to be so. The crucial instance Bradley found just in that conception of relationship on which some Neo-Kantians had sought to found their faith. Be relations as "internal" to the terms as they may—and Bradley was bound to insist on the contradiction involved in separating between a term and its relations—yet to our thought the terms are different from their relations, and the question of their relation to the relations again rises, and so on *ad infinitum*. Applied to the idea of individuality, this meant that it could never be completely verified in any finite thing, and that this held even of the conscious self. The individuality we attribute to it turns out to be "appearance".

It is not evident why Royce should have been so much concerned to meet this argument. He had himself come to the conclusion that it was impossible by way of thought to arrive at the individuality which we must attribute to everything we characterize as real, and he had been engaged of recent years in finding a new ground for this attribution in will and feeling—in the *postulate* that my object shall be unique. This might seem to have removed him beyond the reach of Bradley's dialectic, which only proved in its own way what he, in

his, had already arrived at. It is a witness to the influence that
Bradley's book was exercising at this time upon his thought, perhaps
also to Royce's failure to realize fully the implications of his own
theory, that he still feels it incumbent on him to meet Bradley on
his own ground. In trying to follow him in what is perhaps the most
difficult of his writings, it is important to make clear the precise
point of attack, by distinguishing between that part of the argument
which is really relevant to Bradley's doctrine and that part of it
which is founded on a mistaken interpretation of his meaning.

It is not surprising that Royce, like others, should have been mainly
impressed with the negative side of Bradley's dialectic, and shown
himself ready to interpret him as meaning that conscious experience
was "mere" appearance in the sense that it simply disappeared in
the life of the Absolute.[1] In opposition to any such doctrine he was
justified in insisting that we have a right to use "any rag torn by our
imperfect knowledge from the living garment of God to give us, if
so may be, a hint of the weaving of the whole. The hint may prove
poor. But only the trial can tell. . . . Mysteries still surround us; but
we see what we see".[2] As a matter of fact this is just what Bradley
intended to say. What he is arguing for was not the unreality of the
finite, but its failure to correspond with our ideal of complete reality.
It was a doctrine of degrees of reality and unreality, and of the only
way of ascent from one degree to another as through the light which
these themselves supply. When you come to the highest in self-
consciousness, it is still in the light of it that you must try to go
farther. Irrelevant also to the main issue is Bradley's particular
argument as to the unreality of relations. This may or may not be
sound. It is legitimate to hold that, in his own proof of the impossibility of severing terms and their relations and in his recognition of
forms of experience, in which the relational element is subordinate,
he largely himself succeeded in turning the edge of his own criticism.[3]

The questions raised by Royce are: *first*, whether we can arrive, by
the way of thought with its demand for consistency, at a completely
coherent view of the world: whether, that is, we can anywhere see
plurality emerge from unity and return to it; *secondly*, whether the
fact that an affirmative answer to this question may, without loss
to its validity, involve an infinite process; and *thirdly*, what bearing
our answer to these questions has upon the individuality of the self.

[1] See p. 477 and his use of the metaphor of the sponge, *passim*.
[2] Pp. 491 and 498.   [3] See above, pp. 265 and 283.

His answer consists in trying to show, in reply to the first, that we have instances in our finite experience of thought moving, *proprio motu*, to further determinations of its object in a way completely comprehensible; in reply to the second, that, although this involves an infinite process, the result is not merely negative in the sense that it fails to give us the individuality of which we are in search, —on the contrary, it gives us results which are novel and unique; in reply to the third, that we do not escape from such a process in the Absolute itself: in it we must have knowledge of its own knowledge to infinity; and that, in this way, self-consciousness *ipso facto* survives in it.

The instances he relies upon in proof of these contentions are drawn partly from ordinary experience, partly from mathematical processes. To the former belongs the attempt to make a complete map which, in order to be quite complete, must include the map itself, and so on *ad infinitum*; to the latter belong such operations as the selection within a series, *e.g.*, the cardinal numbers, of another series, *e.g.*, 2, 4, 6, etc., each, member of which stands in a one to one relation with the members of the first series. In all these instances of what may be called "self-representative systems" we have *first* our thought, *by its own movement*, developing multiplicity out of unity in "an order which shall be transparent to the intellect or which shall appear to it as its own deed"[1]; *secondly*, and in spite of the infinite process, we have, in each case of repetition, *something positive* in the sense of being novel and unique; *third*, we have a precise parallel to what we must suppose to be present as an element in the absolute experience: while granting that the absolute transcends self-consciousness, we must still conceive of it as experiencing its own transcendence, and therein experiencing something novel and unique at each repetition: "It can escape from selfhood only by experiencing as its own this escape; by no device can we avoid conceiving of the realm of Being as infinite in precisely the positive sense now so fully illustrated. The Universe, as Subject-Object, contains a complete and perfect image or view of itself. Hence it is, in structure, at once One as a single system and also an endless Kette."[2]

There is much that is suggestive in the Essay; something, too, in the last part of it that anyone who sought to deny the reality of self-consciousness as an element in the Absolute would have to take account of. For the rest it is full of difficulty, if taken seriously as a

[1] P. 558.　　　　　　　　　　　　　　　　　　　　[2] Pp. 550 foll.

contribution to the further determination of what is to be understood by the Absolute of idealist philosophy in general, and of
Royce's form of that philosophy in particular.

Putting aside the apparent inconsistency, above referred to, of the
attempt to find the conditions of individuality in the ideals of logical
thought already rejected by Royce as insufficient for the purpose,
what strikes the reader in the argument, taken as a whole, is the
begging of the question involved in looking for light on the kind of
individuality which we must conceive of as typical of the Absolute,
in the "self-representative", which are also self-repetitive, series here
pressed into the service. Granted that, in the instances on which
Royce relies, it is transparent how the One breaks out into the Many,
the reason of the alleged transparency is to be found in the abstractness of the content (in the one case the idea of an absolutely complete map, in the other the idea of a merely numerical series) which
is just that which is absent in dealing with the constellations of
objects and their distribution in the world of concrete experience.
Not less from the side of the return of the multiplicity into unity do
the examples fail to bring conviction. The map-making and the
mathematical operations alike commit us to an infinite and so far
to a non-unified process, to which an end is put only by the concrete
purpose of having a map of the territory, to which the map itself as
a physical object is irrelevant, or of reaching in mathematics a result,
to which again the indefinite repetition of the operation is irrelevant.

It is useless here to appeal, as Royce does, to the uniqueness and
novelty of the determinations. It is not this kind of determinateness
that is sought, but such as comes from the interrelation of elements,
the organization of the parts into a real whole or system. This
ambiguity is obscured by the use of the word "system" to indicate
what is at best only an indeterminate series. Royce is aware, and has
done well to emphasize the fact, that merely to assign a boundary
does not give individuality. "When and upon what ground", he asks,
"could one say: *I have seen an individual whole?* Never, I must insist,
upon the ground that one has seen a group of facts with a sharply
marked boundary. A finished series of data does not constitute an
individual whole merely by becoming finished."[1] But this is not the
question. The question is whether the absence of a boundary is the
negation of individuality. Royce's argument is directed to show that
it is not. This we may grant to be true, but on one condition, namely,

[1] Pp. 584–585.

that we can explain this boundlessness as the result of an abstraction —the abstraction involved in "letting oneself go" along the line of repetitive additions—and are thus able to include the indefinite in the definite, and so cancel its power either to give or take away. If, on the contrary, we leave the repetition standing, still more if we take it as the proof that we have what we are in search of, we simply entangle ourselves anew in the contradictions which beset us when we seek for completeness in that which is by definition incomplete. It is this vacillation between the true and the false conception of the kind of individuality and wholeness to which our intelligence commits us that the reader of the Supplementary Essay finds so puzzling; all the more so that Royce had in his own idea of selective purpose just what was required to side-track the endless process as something essentially purposeless.

If, returning to the text of the Lectures and reviewing the doctrine it expounds, we look for the source of the instability of which the vacillation in the Supplementary Essay is only another illustration, we shall, I believe, find that it has nothing to do with the selection of Will as the point of departure. If we know what we are talking about, it is indifferent whether we take that as sensation, will, or feeling. All roads lead to Rome, and it was an interesting, if not an original, experiment on Royce's part to try the road of the will. But he had to make sure that he was on it. It was his failure to do this at the outset by a deeper analysis of what is meant by will than he anywhere gives us, that is the ultimate source of his difficulties. Far more fundamental than the psychological question which he had raised and discussed at length, as to whether we are to look for the source of volition in the choice of overt acts or in the direction of attention, is the question of the content of the will and its mode of operation.

Granted that attention to an idea precedes the identification of the self with it in which voluntary action consists, the act of attention is never the arbitrary "spontaneous" thing that Royce, here following James, represents it to be. It is itself the expression of an interest—the "concernment" of the self with this idea rather than with another. To treat it as spontaneous in any other sense than that it is that which we choose as in the line of that interest, temporary or permanent, is to cut it off from all connection with the self and commit us to chance, in other words to determination from without. Behind the will defined in terms of spontaneity, going deeper than it and giving meaning to it, is the consciousness of some wholeness of life that is to be realized in the act. Royce of course knows this. No one has insisted on it more strongly when occasion offers. It is indeed what he means by the "external" meaning, however inadequate that phrase is to express what is in reality the more deeply internal side of the life of will. It is all the stranger that he seems to forget it when he seeks to lay the foundations of his theory of individuality on the appeal to "internal meanings, selections, and expressions" as "typical instances of facts, and of precisely the facts of whose unity the world consists". We have seen where that leads.

What was wanted was to reverse the situation and insist upon the external meaning, interpreted in the above sense, as containing the direction in which individuality and freedom are to be sought. Individuality then appears in its true light, not as something coming at the beginning, but as the end towards which the will strives in the effort to give some sort of wholeness to the life of the self; in other words, not as an immediate experience, whether as *datum* or *actum*, but as an ideal. True it is an ideal which can never under the form of temporal life be fully realized, but there may be progress towards its fuller realization according to the comprehensiveness of the interests which form the principles of conduct. There may thus be degrees of individuality corresponding to moral growth from the child, who is a bundle of impulses, to the man with a dominant life-purpose; from the man, dominated by some narrow interest forcing him to constant inconsistency, to the man who strives not only to contemplate but to live in the light of "all time and all existence". It is because Royce stopped short in his analysis of the will at the point at which it is resolved into an act of attention, that he is unable to bring the two sides of his theory together and to reconcile the idea of *God* or the Absolute as "the universal presupposition of rationality" with the idea of Him as spontaneous creative will, the idea of *man* as pledged by his own nature and the nature of the world he inhabits to rationalize his life with the idea of him as summoning that world spontaneously into existence as something which his will requires for its fulfilment.

What made it possible for some of the critics of the *First Series* to overlook this fundamental ambiguity, and say, as McTaggart did in his review of it already quoted, that "it may be considered as based upon Hegel", is the survival in it of phrases which could be read in the sense that reality is conceived of as given to experience, in some sense, in its wholeness, instead of being, as a thoroughgoing voluntarism of the Fichtean type must hold, created by the will. Added to this was the habitual use in the text of the lectures and in the Supplementary Essay of illustrations, such as that of the reproduction of a melody or a mathematical operation, that failed to raise in an acute form the question of the essential "otherness" of the object and its recalcitrance to our will. It is only when he comes, as he does at the beginning of the *Second Series*, to the treatment of Nature, that it becomes impossible to ignore this element of opposition, and that the question of the adequacy of the theory to which Royce had committed himself, is raised in its most crucial form.

7. THE TEST OF THE EXTERNAL WORLD

In his book on *The Spirit of Modern Philosophy* Royce had drawn the distinction between the "World of Description" and the "World of Appreciation",[1] the world of facts which are the same for all, and are the object of the theoretic consciousness and the world of acknowledgements and valuations which depend on individual response and are the basis of our volitional life. Royce had there found the psychological basis of it in the social nature of man, and had sought to show that the conception of a world which was the same for all had its roots in the social consciousness, and the necessity, if cooperation is to be possible, that there should be truths which are valid for all—in a word, in what James Ward called "intersubjective intercourse".[2] Since that time he had come to realize the inadequacy of this account, and in the essay in *Studies of Good and Evil*, above referred to, had tried to carry the analysis farther. In the Preface to the present volume, after referring to his own former treatment of the problem, he goes on to point out that "The power to make this abstraction (of a world of mere fact), however much social intercourse is needed to give it definition, must have its logical roots in the common consciousness of the individual." Accordingly, after a further development of the distinction between these two worlds, he goes on in the text to give what he calls "a logical deduction of this primal contrast".

[1] Too uncritically, as we may think, if he intended, in adopting the former phrase from Mach, (see *W. and I.*, vol. ii. p. 27 *n.*) to indicate acceptance of Mach's definition of the purpose of natural science as merely exact description to the exclusion of explanation.

[2] In the Preface to the Second Series of the Gifford Lectures Royce refers to the influence which Ward had exercised upon his thought.

We have to recognize at the outset that in the world of fact are included both the world of nature and the world of society, and that between these two there arises a secondary contrast which itself has to be explained. Taking first the social world, Royce holds that the belief in the objective reality of our fellow-men is not to be deduced, as it was the fashion to say, from the analogy of what we know in ourselves. Our consciousness of their reality he holds to be based on our discovery in them of an "endless treasure of more ideas", and of the source from which we may draw "the constantly needed supplement to our fragmentary meaning". For this reason the social world readily falls into line with the Fourth Conception of Being as expounded in the first series of lectures. It is in fact explicable as a part of the external meaning of our ideas and as providing the standard of their fullness and truth.[1]

Nature, however, presents itself in no such complacent aspect. Far from being obviously a part of my will, it appears as that which is "foreign" and "stubborn" to it.[2] How is this appearance possible if the world of fact is merely one aspect of the will's own purpose? Royce seems to feel that he has here reached the crucial test of his theory, and bends all his energy to reply to this question in the terms which it demanded.

The "otherness" to my will is an obstinate fact, which is not to be gainsaid. "But it is equally important from our idealistic point of view to remember that, in so far as I purpose, intend, pursue, or find myself accomplishing, it is of the very essence of my will to demand its own Other, to set its fulfilment beyond its present, and so to define its own very life as now in some sense not its own, or as in some wise now foreign. Our rational purpose in living as we human beings now do is essentially and always the wanderer's purpose. We seek our home, our city out of sight, our lost truth. But in the very search itself lies the partial embodiment of what we ourselves will. It is not then *merely* our fate that makes our home far off, or the truth a lost truth. It is we ourselves who demand our object as the Beyond; and we are pilgrims and strangers in a world of seemingly foreign facts, not only because the facts, as such, are stubbornly foreign, but also because we insist that ours shall be the wanderer's portion." After referring in illustration to the lover and the mistress

---

[1] *Cp.* Bosanquet's account of civil society as the "standing criticism" of our ideas.
[2] P. 28.

who rejects him and "controls his will by his own connivance", he concludes: "All this we saw in general in our former consideration of the concept of Being. It follows however that no account of the categories of experience, which founds our consciousness of facts solely upon our experience of their compulsory or foreign character, can be just to the nature of knowledge. What we experience is, in one aspect, always *our own will to be compelled by facts*."[1] The "other" that limits my will is thus something that *must* be, if my will is to be something whose summons is felt as an "ought" rather than an "is",—an "ought" which (as elsewhere and always) is "my own will more rationally expressed than at the instant of a capricious activity I as yet consciously recognize". What determines us to acknowledge as real one particular fact or system of facts rather than another is that this system, while conceived of as constraining our acts, is also conceived of as "thereby enabling us even now to accomplish our will better than if we did not acknowledge it". In a word, everywhere the "ought" goes deeper than the "is". It is the "ought" rather than the "is" which is "the first determining principle", the first of the categories to which all others, including objectivity, subjectivity, and teleology, are subordinate.[2]

Returning to the contrast between the world of fact and the world of appreciation, the result is to have shown that the limitation, that seems to be imposed by the world of fact, in reality arises within the world of appreciation, in other words within the circle of the will itself, and that the constraint it exercises, which to the observer appears as an overwhelming fate, is only "the overwhelming fate of his own intelligence".[3]

The rest of the book is devoted to the application of the exposition of the central thesis, thus completed, to the interpretation of Nature, Man, and the Moral Order. What concerns us here is the uncompromisingness with which Royce is here led by the logic of his position to commit himself to a doctrine which seems to make the whole choir of heaven and the furniture of earth emerge from the fiat of the will disguised under the name of a postulate.

It was little wonder that, with this result before them, the ablest of his colleagues should have been filled with distrust of his whole method. It was only perhaps what was to be expected that to William James with his radical empiricism Royce's Absolute should

[1] Pp. 28-30.   [2] P. 41.   [3] Pp. 325-326.

appear more than ever a gratuitous apotheosis of what he preferred to call Experience; and that to Santayana, imbued with the Latin craving for the lucidity of clear-cut distinctions, it should seem the Nemesis of a florid Romanticism. But even Peirce, who might have been expected to be attracted by the use to which his ideas had been put in the Supplementary Essay, and who otherwise felt himself in sympathy with the mystic element in his friend's idealism, could never, as he tells us, rid himself of the suspicion that it had failed to vindicate the objectivity of the world with which science and mathematics have to do.[1] A fortiori was a theory that found in the "ought" a more fundamental category than the "is"—the demand of the will upon reality more basic than the demand of reality upon the will, likely to rouse suspicion in idealistic contemporaries familiar with the logic by which philosophy had been forced, even in Fichte himself, beyond the conception of Act.[2]

To us who have been engaged in the attempt to trace the course of Royce's thought from the beginning, this last development may seem to connect itself with his early interpretation of the teaching of Kant. We had occasion, in referring to his 1881 article,[3] to note the pitfalls that surround any view which takes its start from a mere particular here and now as the datum of experience and conceives of the extension of this into a world of systematic relations as the work of spontaneous intelligence. In the development of the voluntarism of the *World and the Individual* into a view that summons the world of objective reality from a *Weissnichtwo* in obedience to the unsupported imperative of a mere idea, we seem to see the Nemesis of this youthful indiscretion. If the history of Idealism has taught us anything, it has taught us that unless the ideal is somehow given as an actual, unless it is in some sense actually present in what the mind meets and does not create, the "ought" must not only remain, as it does in Kant, without a content, but also without foundation of any kind. In order that there may be an "ought" there must be a sense, however elementary, of something defective or contradictory in what already is and some resultant discontent with it. Apart from a sense of conflict between a larger world, in some way here and now apprehended as real however little as yet fully ours, and the narrower world which we here and now possess, there can be no

---

[1] See *Nation*, vol. lxx. 1900, p. 267, and vol. lxxv. 1902, pp. 94–96.
[2] See Henry Jones in *Hibbert Journal*, 1902–3, pp. 132–144.
[3] Above.

ground on which to erect our ideal. It is not sufficient to reply that this larger world is present as part of the will and purpose in us. A purpose is never something in the air, as a mere wish may be. What is purposed is always an extension of a reality already partly ours, the fuller realization of a self already partly realized. Royce knew this, and is constantly restating it in unexceptionable terms.[1] But this does not prevent him from going on, sometimes in close juxtaposition, to speak of the will as though it were the creator of the "ought". We might be inclined to urge against a view of this kind the infinite regress in which it appears to involve us, seeing that Royce seems to argue that the "ought" *has* to be created in order that we may have purpose at all and begin really to live, while, on the view which he takes, it *can* only be created in response to a previous "ought", and so on indefinitely. But Royce, as we have seen, is prepared to meet this argument in a way of his own, and it is better to content ourselves with noting the inconsistency between the position he here takes up and the sounder one which we found in the *Religious Aspect of Philosophy*. His criticism of the Kantian conception as resting on the view of the facts of science as merely "valid" (that is as merely what we *ought to believe*), is there founded upon the argument that actuality goes deeper than validity, what is there to be believed deeper than the duty of believing it. It was to go back on the whole burden of that teaching to suggest, as he finally does in this book, that we should invert that order, and make the "is" wait upon the "ought". It may well be true (and Royce is here on firm ground) that our *knowledge* of what is real is founded on what we *ought* in logic to believe, but we are speaking now not of the *causa cognoscendi*, but the *causa essendi*; and here it must needs be true that the order is reversed, if for no other reason than that the "ought" itself is a form of "being".

[1] See, *e.g.*, *W. and I.*, vol. ii. pp. 23 and 25, in the chapter immediately preceding the Fichtean utterances quoted above.

CHAPTER VIII

ROYCE (v). LAST PHASE: THE PROBLEM OF CHRISTIANITY

1. The Philosophy of Loyalty

In more than one sense Royce's thought may be said in the last period of his philosophical activity to have come full circle. His first book was dominated by his interest in ethics and religion. In the intermediate period, though this was never far from his mind, he had been chiefly occupied with logical and metaphysical problems. In his last period, to which *The Philosophy of Loyalty*[1] and *The Problem of Christianity*[2] belong, he became more and more preoccupied with this interest, though never without an eye to the metaphysical basis or without reactions upon his metaphysical conceptions. As it is these reactions with which we are mainly concerned, and as the former of these works contains little that is significant from this point of view, we can afford here to touch only lightly upon it.

Already, in the first part of *The Religious Aspect*, we have the germs of the later theory. He had there shown that what calls for our devotion, what constitutes in Fichte's phrase our "vocation", is not the increase of happiness in any direct sense, but the promotion of human solidarity by the service of art, science, truth, and the state. The supreme virtue, because that which most fully expresses the will to further the chief end, is faithfulness to the causes these represent. He has not yet given to this virtue the name he afterwards chose for it, but the sense is there, and, when he returns to the subject in this book, we have merely an expansion of the same idea.[3]

Seeing that what we mean by a "cause" is just one of these ideal objects conceived of as "a live spiritual unity", and seeing that the word for the willing and entire devotion of a self to a cause that unites many selves in one, and which is therefore the interest of a community, is "loyalty", the simplest statement of the principle of the good life is "Be loyal to your cause". It is true that these causes are different and may come into conflict with one another, but this

[1] New York, 1908.
[2] New York, 1913; referred to below as *P. of C.*
[3] Afterwards again contracted in the essay on "Loyalty and Insight" in *William James and Other Essays* (1912), and that on "The Religion of Loyalty" in *The Sources of Religious Insight* of the same date.

only means that our loyalty must be accompanied by insight; and Royce held that the ideal of an all-embracing human society was the all-sufficient criterion. Finally, as this social unity is a spiritual matter, and can only be attained by loyal wills, our loyalty must be loyalty to the loyal. "Hidden from you by all the natural estrangements of the present life as this common life may be, the one cause of all the loyal is that for which you live. In spirit you are really sundered from none of those who themselves live in the spirit."[1]

All this implies that while the object is personal to us, it is also superpersonal. It may indeed be held that what is called superpersonal is merely that in ourselves which makes union with other selves possible. But this did not satisfy Royce. The natural history of societies seemed to him to show that, united from the first, they are always being organized into unities of a higher order; psychology proved that societies have minds of their own, acting on different principles from the minds of the individuals who compose them. Wundt (and nearer home Charles Peirce) held that scientific and social progress could only be explained on the basis of the real existence of such a superpersonal mind. In fact, "few ideas had been more fruitful in their indirect consequences for ethical doctrine as well as for religion".[2] His object in the later and more important book was to bring out the significance of this idea for religion and metaphysics.

2. THE BELOVED COMMUNITY

He had little difficulty in tracing the belief in the existence of such a spiritual unity in the literature of Christianity, as in the Gospel teaching about the Kingdom of Heaven, and in the Pauline and Johannine conception of the Church, or in expanding it, in harmony with modern ideas, into "the company of all mankind in so far as mankind actually win the genuine and redeeming life in brotherhood, in loyalty and the beloved community".[3] The idea appealed to the preacher in Royce, which was never very far from the surface, and he makes the most of it. What scandalized his more orthodox readers was the subordinate place which his way of working it out seemed to assign to the central figure of the Christian religion. Instead of the "real body", of which the Church was only the symbol, Christ becomes the symbol of a unity in no wise dependent on Him.

---

[1] *William James*, etc., p. 78. [2] *P. of C.*, p. 63.
[3] *Op. cit.*, vol. ii. p. 367.

Our own interest in this development of his philosophy lies, not in its relation to orthodox dogma, but in the metaphysical application which, in the latter portion of the book, he makes of the idea and in its relation to previous statements of his doctrine of reality.

With his usual eagerness to utilize any hint coming from his contemporaries to give freshness to his own expositions, he seized on Peirce's analysis of the cognitive process into the three factors of perception, conception, and interpretation,[1] which fell into line only too well with his own earlier reading of Kant. Without noticing the analogy that in Peirce's suggestive exposition the idea of "interpretation" bears to Hegel's concrete universal, Royce goes on to apply it *first* to reflection in general wherein the present self may be said to interpret its past self (*e.g.*, in a promise or resolution) to his future self; *secondly* to secular history, where he thinks that "the most general distinctions of past, present, and future appear in a new light when considered with reference to the process of interpretation"; *finally* to history as a spiritual process, in which "an endless time-sequence is controlled by motives, which, endless in their whole course, interpret the past to the future. These motives express themselves in an evolution wherein to every problem corresponds in the course of endless ages its solution . . . to every tragedy the atoning triumph which interprets its evil. . . . The salvation of the whole world, the consciousness that in its wholeness the world is and expresses and fulfils the divine plan and is wholly interpreted and reconciled—this is something that is never completed at any point of time. Yet the unity of the spirit, this consciousness of reconciliation, occurs in our world of interpretation through our insight into the meaning of all that occurs in time. We do not declare in our metaphysical doctrine that the divine consciousness is timeless. We declare that the whole order of time is interpreted, and so interpreted that, when viewed in the light of this goal, the whole world is reconciled to its own purpose".[2]

The book in which this doctrine is developed suffers even more than Royce's other later works from being written in the form of lectures. An otherwise sympathetic critic notes that the argument in it for the reality of the Community "differs *toto cælo*, from the closely articulated, logically ordered reasoning of his strictly metaphysical works".[3] Nevertheless, Royce himself believed that there was

[1] See above, p. 332.   [2] *P. of C.*, vol. ii. pp. 376–378, condensed
[3] Mary W. Calkins in the volume published under the title of *Papers in Honour of Josiah Royce* (1926).

no other work in which he had "told his tale more fully or with more approach to the far-off goal of saying something, sometime that might prove helpful to students of idealism".[1] It is this and not its logical form that gives the book importance in the attempt to trace his thought in this last phase of its development, and find the relation in which it stands to the earlier.

3. Relation of the Community to the Individual and to the Absolute

In the marked omission (not entirely explicable by its popular object) of references to the Absolute it might seem to represent a step farther in the movement away from his earlier point of view, had it not been for the equally marked absence of the voluntaristic language of the middle period. It is true that we only come to know the community by a process of ideal construction, analogous to, and indeed continuous with that by which we construct the world of time by the synthesis of past, present, and future; but we hear no more of the objective world—now "the community of interpretation"—as the creation of the will or a product of the "ought". The moral ought and the will that is loyal to it spring from the social being of man, rather than the social being from them. So far from having the ego-centric world of Fichte to start with, we have a world of which the soul of society is the centre, and of which the individual finds the interpretation only as it enters into a communal relation with it. "Whatever my purposes or my ideas, whatever will to live incites me to create and believe, one truth stands out clear: Practically I cannot be saved alone; theoretically speaking I cannot find or even define the truth in terms of my individual experience without taking account of my relation to the community of those who know. The community then is a reality."[2] What we have is a new interpretation of the Absolute as an objective reality in terms of the community, which raises at once the question of the precise relation of these two ideas to each other and of both to the human individual. Does Royce mean to attribute concrete selfhood in the full sense of the word to the Community? and, if so, how is this related to the selfhood on the one hand of the Absolute, on the other hand of the finite individual?

[1] In a letter to the author of the article mentioned above. See *op. cit.*, p. 68.
[2] *P. of C.*, vol. ii. p. 312.

In the critical paper and correspondence mentioned above, these were just the questions that were raised. With reference to the first of them the writer of the paper suggested that Royce's statement was compatible with the view that the community is not a self or person in the full sense of the word, but that it merely behaves and is treated "as if it were a person". This being so, it was further suggested that the proper reading of his doctrine was that the community is merely an "expression" of the divine, having a different degree of selfhood from that which we find in the individual soul. " 'To be expressed by' does not mean to be 'constituted by', and the divine life would be distinguished from that of the community and from the world, though not external to them." After quoting passages from the text in support of this view, the writer concludes: "The plain implication of these passages is that the 'interpreter spirit' not only includes but transcends world and Church."[1] To this criticism Royce replied in a letter to the writer of it, in which we have, so far as I know, his last written utterance upon the subject, and which we have every reason, both in respect to what he says and what he omits to say, to regard as conclusive on the question of his meaning.

After an interesting reference to the consistency of his philosophical statements, he goes on expressly to repudiate his critic's interpretation of his claim for the community and to insist that "a genuinely and loyally united society is in a perfectly literal sense a person", and that, as applied to the Church, his statement is "a scrap of theology which serves as a hint of what I have been trying to formulate in this recent phase, not merely of my thinking but of my experience". He adds: "I do not know any reason why this phase of my thinking should attract any other interest than what may be due to its actual relations to a process which has been going on in human thought ever since Heraclitus remarked that the Logos is fluent, and ever since Israel began to idealize the life of a little hill-town in Judea. I stand for the importance of this process which has led Christianity to regard a community not merely as an aggregate but as a Person, and at the same time to enrich its ideal memory of a person until he became transformed into a community."

It is impossible to mistake the drift of these statements. They commit the author to the doctrine of the mystic personality of human society, carrying with it the identification of the life of God

[1] *Papers in Honour*, etc., p. 59.

as Logos with its life and the relativity and imperfection of individual persons, except in so far as they expand their life into and identify themselves with this larger selfhood. But this answer only raised, in a more definite form, the difficulties from which his sympathetic critic was seeking a way of escape. What is implied as to the relation of the individual to the community, may be taken as a correction of the individualism in which his doctrine of the will in *The World and the Individual* was in danger of involving him. But it clearly went farther. Does he or does he not identify the Absolute with the Community? If he does, the "problem of Christianity" remains unsolved. It may be true, as he says, that "Christianity needs a philosophy", but it is not likely to be content with one that leaves God's transcendence in any doubt. Comte's "religion of Humanity" was wittily defined as "Catholicism without Christianity". Royce's religion of "the Beloved Community", if thus interpreted, is bound to appear to be Christianity without either God or Christ. If, on the contrary, Society is only, as his critic suggests, one of the modes in which the Absolute expresses itself, the Beloved Community as thus interpreted cannot be the highest form of unity which we know, or the social consciousness in the individual, however perfected, the highest he can attain. Idealism *may* have to come to be merely an up-to-date form of Positivism, but it will be at the price of giving up what from the beginning has been its fundamental and inspiring principle —the presence in man of the consciousness of a totality of Being, of which Nature and Society are only finite and partial embodiments.

Not less ambiguous than the theory of the community itself is the theory of the community of *interpretation*. The distinction on which it is founded carries with it the same suggestion of an arbitrary separation of perception and conception, which, we have seen, infected Royce's early reading of Kant, and brought confusion into his later statements. It is doubtful whether either he or Peirce, from whom he had borrowed the logical formula, had ever really taken to heart the deeper meaning of Kant's doctrine, according to which the concrete thing which is the object of knowledge contains in itself elements of particularity, universality, and the synthesis, or, if you like, the "interpretation" of them. These may be separated in analysis, but it is a mistake even to suggest that the one only enters when the work of the other has been completed. What it is important to realize is that there can be no perception which is not implicitly conception, and no conception which is not implicit interpretation; and this is obscured when language is used which seems to imply that one supervenes upon the other as a separate act. Royce doubtless would have repudiated any intention of separating them except as distinguishable aspects of an indivisible process. But this merely raises the question of the appropriateness of the whole metaphor and his application of it in this and other fields. Is it really true, as he seems to hold, that life always consists in "interpreting the past by the present and merging both in an address to the future"? Doubtless all present life, in so far as it consists in action, has both a backward and a forward aspect. As Bergson puts it, "it reclines upon the past and inclines to the future". But a philosophy which is not committed to a pragmatism of the baser sort, must surely insist that life has other aspects than practical activity bent on altering things, and that, where this is the case, it is a matter of accident or particular interest whether we interpret the past by the present, the present by the past, the future by either, or either by the future. Wordsworth's protest against the doctrine that

> Nothing of itself will come
> But we must still be seeking

had long been before the world, and Royce, when he was in the mood, knew as well as anyone else what it meant. For religion and philosophy, at any rate, the important thing is not the psychological analysis of our processes of interpretation, but the logical principle according to which the meaning of our world is to be interpreted. Here Royce himself has taught us that the principle is one that carries us beyond the distinctions of past, present, and future. To use language that suggests the reinstatement of time as an ultimate reality, is to falsify the whole deeper meaning of his philosophy.

In spite of these ambiguities and the obsession by phrases which he had pressed into the service of the restatement of his philosophy in this last book, it is possible to see in the comparative absence of the language of voluntarism, already noticed, along with the emphasis on the *content* of social experience, the beginning of a return to the truer, because more objective, point of view of his first book. In his case, as in Bradley's, we are reminded of Browning's lines in "Apparent Failure":—

> That after last returns the first
>   Though a wide compass round be fetched
> That what began best, can't end worst.

4. SUMMARY

Looking back on Royce's work as a whole in the light (if it is a light) of this Study, we see it inspired, as Idealism from the first has been, by the necessity of justifying to the reason the special characters and the validity of the different forms or worlds of experience, which we know as knowledge, morality, and religion, against sceptical or mechanical theories that would reduce them to illusions. He had early convinced himself of the general validity of Berkeley's principle of the priority of mind to matter, but this had to be interpreted in view of the critical philosophy of Kant. Dissatisfied with what he conceived of as the dualistic element in Kant—the thing-in-itself as something independent of the work of the mind, and, in the work of the mind, with the place assigned by Kant himself to causality— he sought to remedy these defects by conceiving of the world we experience as built up out of present data into a continuity of time, space, and other consciousnesses. But this doctrine was clearly am- biguous. Was the pattern of the building somehow also "given", and was the subsequent work inspired and guided by the suggestions it contained, or was it something supplied by a creative *fiat* of the mind itself? Royce, I believe, failed to realize this ambiguity, and wavered between these two interpretations. In his earliest sketches he leaned to the latter alternative. But in the *Religious Aspect of Philosophy* he has come so far under the influence of Hegel as to lay stress upon the implication in all our knowing and thinking, even the most elementary, of the reality of a complete insight related to our incomplete ideas as whole to part.

Becoming conscious, in the succeeding years, of the difficulties that surrounded any interpretation of this "whole of Insight" in terms of thought alone, we might have expected him, following the line of British thought as represented by Bradley and Bosanquet, while hold- ing to the background of totality on which all experience rests, to have proceeded to correct the abstraction by which reality was identified with thought, by insisting on the inadequacy of this, as well as of all other forms of experience, including will and feeling, when taken by themselves, to express the full content of the Whole. He was pro- foundly influenced by Bradley, but was repelled by what he conceived of as the negative results of his criticism, particularly of his destruc- tive criticism of the idea of the self. From these results he hoped to escape by laying the emphasis upon will and feeling as that which, in contrast to sense and thought, alone can give selfhood to things and persons, and preserve it as an attribute of the Absolute. This was the text of his chief book. It is a magnificent *tour de force*. It may be said to have left rival types of philosophy, in the forms in which they were then advocated, in ruins. But it cannot be said to have convinced his contemporaries that he had substituted one that, either from the realist or idealist side, could "stand by its own weight." Its foundations were felt to be too narrow to support the massive structure he tried to raise upon them. From the side of realism, it still seemed to be infected with the subjectivism from which it had taken its departure. From the side of idealism, it seemed in substituting "Will" for "thought"—Fichte's Akt for Hegel's Begriff—merely to have substituted one abstraction for another, to the neglect of the givenness of reality in its wholeness, which must be the basis and starting-point of all attempts, whether in knowledge, conduct, or production, to find individuality and, through that, significance in experience.

If complete success was denied him in the central and most vigorous period of his life, it was perhaps hardly to be expected when his health and strength had begun too early to fail. His work during this period still showed much of his old fire, and darted new light into the fields of ethics and religion with which it chiefly dealt. There was moreover in it, especially in all that he had to say of the Community, a partial return to his early sense of the Totality, as that in which alone what appears to us in the form of the separate independent individual has substantial and significant being. But here again, so far as he seemed to be merely substituting society for the individual as the name of the ultimate reality, he was only exchanging a narrower for a wider abstraction. If there is an "ultimate" or "absolute" reality, this must be the name of a Being in and through which society is indeed a reality—more of a reality, if you like, than the individuals who compose it—but which itself is of richer content than any that is revealed to us in the form of human society. Royce had indeed had the notion, in *The World and the Individual*, of a larger society which should include all nature as well as humanity, and which would be only another name for the Totality of Being, but he cannot be said to have there worked it out into clearness, and in the later book he seems to drop it altogether out of view. Whether, had he lived, he would have been able to orient himself to this wider point of view, and bring the different sides of his philosophy into harmony with one another, we cannot say. What seems to the present writer true is that no future worker on idealist lines in America can afford to neglect the service he did in clearing the ground and laying at least part of the foundation of the structure the vision of which was his life-long inspiration.

CONCLUSION

WHAT IS DEAD AND WHAT IS ALIVE IN IDEALISM

1. THE QUESTION AS RAISED BY THESE STUDIES

THE text of these Studies has been that, side by side with the Empiricism which is commonly considered to have been, since the time of Bacon, the chief note of British philosophy, there has been, from the first, another embodying an entirely different tradition. Side by side, and in open conflict with the Sensationalism of Hobbes, there was the Intellectualism of the Cambridge Platonists. Emphasized, if not called forth by Locke's "new way of ideas", we have in the next generation that other way which the Oxford writers, John Norris and Arthur Collier, had learned from Malebranche. For nearly a century thereafter, this idealistic note may be said to have died down, except in so far as it reappeared as a faint echo in Berkeley's later speculations. At the beginning of the nineteenth century, it was powerfully revived by Coleridge, the significance of whose work was not so much that it introduced German methods of thought as that it revived the Platonic tradition in English philosophy. It was from the Neo-Platonists that Coleridge got his first sight of a wider world than that of Locke and Hartley, and he probably owed not less to Cudworth, John Smith, and Henry More than to Kant, Fichte, and Schelling. It was to keep alive this tradition in the form in which the poet-philosopher had left it: in his own words, "to review the grounds of the National religious belief", that his disciple J. H. Green laboured in the years that followed Coleridge's death.[1] In the generation that followed, it was the threat to what men most valued in morals and politics, art and religion, which came from the empiricism of Mill and the naturalism of Herbert Spencer, that gave its edge to the Neo-Kantian movement. But, so far as Oxford, its main centre, was concerned, the new thought owed as much to the revival of Platonic study, inaugurated by Jowett, as to the more intensive study of Kant and Hegel. There was a momentary danger that the German element, with its high-sounding claims and elaborate formalism, might swamp the more distinctively British traits of caution and modesty.[2] But these were excesses which the critical and conserva-

---

[1] See *Coleridge as Philosopher*, Appendix II.
[2] Perhaps the caution came from Scotland, the modesty from England.

tive atmosphere of the University might be trusted to correct, and it was precisely to clear the ground for a more distinctively British growth that Bradley came forward in the 'seventies and 'eighties with a searching logic, combined with a lucidity of style unknown since Hume, to try the reins both of Germanizing and of degenerate British schools in the interest of a more comprehensive form of the tradition they represented. The paradox of the situation created by Bradley's work was that the very strength of its reaction against prevailing foreign influences brought with it the danger of a new incaution, and that, in protesting against the enslavement of British philosophy to Continental models, he might himself seem to be embracing an element in these which threatened what was best in it.

What was central to nineteenth-century idealism in England and America, was its determination to have done with the dualism of a here and a beyond, whether this took the form of the two worlds in religion, the "ought" and the "is" in ethics, the individual and the community in politics, or the relative and the absolute in metaphysics. Carlyle did not do much for constructive philosophy, but in Teufelsdröckh's "here or nowhere" he struck the keynote of all sound idealism. Yet it was just this "here or nowhere" that much in Bradley's work had the appearance of undermining.

It is for this reason that watchful enemies of the whole philosophy were prepared to welcome the new development which he initiated as just what was wanted to bring its inherent logic full circle and expose its remoteness from the concrete interests of life. All that was now needed was a metaphysical Karl Marx to show that Absolutism, like the Capitalism with which it had taken its rise, had overreached itself, or, in language nearer to our time, a philosophical Einstein to do for the Hegelian idea of reality as a whole what the new physics had done for the Newtonian idea of space and time. It is for this reason also that those, on the other hand, who claim a reversionary interest in the idealistic tradition, recognize that a crisis has been reached in its development which can only be met by a review of the whole situation. Is it true, as its critics assert, that the foundations have been removed and that the building is in ruins, leaving nothing but salvage work for its former inhabitants to do? or, in spite of threatening structures that have been erected upon them, do the foundations remain as a part of the living rock, perhaps even some of the structure as material for the future builder? It is this question which I have ventured to put in the form which is the title of this concluding Study.

2. The Platonic Tradition

A good *a priori* case in favour of the latter of the above alternatives might be made out on the ground of the length and depth of the tradition which idealism, as we know it to-day, seeks to carry on, the variety of the directions in which it has broken new ground and the brilliance of its achievements in all of them. With the exception, perhaps, of the Philosophy of Nature,[1] there is no department in which its contributions to philosophy will not bear comparison with the best that have been made from any other point of view. In an interesting reference to its American critics, Bradley complains of their failure "to realize the wealth, the variety, and the radical differences which are to be found in that outburst of German philosophy which came after Kant".[2] A similar and far stronger plea might be made on behalf of that continual outburst of fresh thought, which throughout the whole history of philosophy has followed a return to the principles for which idealism from the time of Plato has stood. After all that has been said in the course of these Studies, it is unnecessary to dwell on this *prima facie* case. But there is one circumstance, in the midst of the present reaction against idealistic methods, which is itself sufficient to suggest that they may be more than a withered stalk and may still contain the seeds of a new life.

The centre of the reaction, as it is the characteristic mark of the modern spirit in general, is the determination at all hazards to be true to fact. But fact is a large word, and it is also a characteristic discovery of the modern mind, and even of the "modernism" of which Nietzsche is the acknowledged high-priest, that besides the facts of *existence*, there is the fact of a worth, goodness, or value in things, and that the chief problem of philosophy is the reinterpretation of all other facts—the "transvaluation" of all values—in view of it. It seems, to say the least of it, unlikely that a philosophy, which had made this problem its main concern from the time that Socrates sat on the prison bench and propounded it in almost modern form to his friends, should have nothing which is itself of value to contribute to its solution. Bearing in mind what has been said above as to the double root of present-day idealism, we might even be tempted to find a short and ready answer to our question by setting

[1] Even here, in view of the work of such writers as Dr. J. S. Haldane, the exception would have to be qualified.
[2] *Essays in Truth and Reality*, p. 153.

aside the Germanic elements in it on the ground that they have merely side-tracked the true course of Anglo-Saxon philosophy, and taking as our motto, not "back to Kant," but "back to Plato". But this would be to jettison not only the fruitful developments from the second root, with which much of these Studies has been concerned, but an element, which it is necessary to add to the Platonic tradition itself, in order that the principles for which it stands may be applicable with any profit to the world as we know it to-day and the problems which it forces upon us. It may therefore help to put our subject in its true perspective if, before going on to this addition, I begin by trying to state more fully the ideas which seem to me to have been, whether in explicit or implicit form, the living core of that tradition and the source of its undying power. If I seem to some readers to be here going back to very rudimentary things—the food for babes in philosophy—it may at least be interesting to see how, after wandering in the wilderness for over half a century, an elderly inheritor of these ideas returns to them as the sincere milk of the word. While no one of them, taken by itself, can be said to be the exclusive property of Platonizing philosophy, yet, taken together, they may, I think, be claimed as characteristic of it in contrast to others.

1. Starting from the simpler and more fundamental, we have the distinction between things that seem, or things as they seem, and things that are or as they are. In his recent Gifford Lectures[1] Professor Eddington has some excellent chaff about "reality with a halo", and as it is received "with cheers" in philosophical perorations. But the distinction between the aspect of things as presented to sense, or represented in sensuous imagery, and the aspect of them as apprehended by thought or reason, between the phenomenal and the noumenal, lies at the root of science itself, as no one has shown more clearly than Eddington.[2] The difference between the noumenon of science and the noumenon of philosophy is simply the difference between what he calls a "domestic" variety and what we might call the "cosmic" genus of reality. Whatever else philosophy is, it is the contemplation "of all time and all existence", in view of which this time and this existence must receive their interpretation.

2. Coming nearer to doctrines more definitely characteristic of Platonism, we have that which finds in the separateness and apparent

[1] *The Nature of the Physical World*, by A. S. Eddington, 1929.
[2] For an excellent statement of this ontological reference in all science see Professor F. Orestano's *New Principles*, especially chapters xv and xvi.

independence of things a feature which falls to the side of the apparent or phenomenal. To see things as they are apprehended by reason and in their reality, we must see them *sub specie unitatis*. Neither science nor philosophy can ever be happy with a world merely "full of a number of things". They are both essentially synoptic— philosophy again with the wider synopsis. They both find, as White-head, perhaps the most Platonic of present-day scientific writers, puts it, that "a thing is only itself in drawing into its own limitations the larger whole in which it finds itself".

3. Leaving this for fuller statement and defence at a later point, we have the complementary principle that, though *independence* is phenomenal, *difference* is not. Plato had "laid hands on his father Parmenides" to good purpose, and the tradition he established may be said to have been ever since in its best representatives immune from the monism which seeks either to absorb difference in identity, the *existence* of things in their *essence*, or, granting difference, to find that it is *indifferent* in the sense that things all stand on the same level as regards an essence which is "as full and perfect in a hair as heart".[1] There are real differences in things, corresponding to the degree in which they are permitted, or permit themselves, to be dominated by the form or "idea" of the whole. There is not only *Being*, but there are *beings*, and these constitute a hierarchy of "degrees of reality". It was for this reason that, when this doctrine was revived in our time by Bradley, there were those who, like Bosanquet, were prepared to recognize and welcome it as in the true Platonic line.

4. This order has an outer and inner side. It shows itself under the outer forms of space and time. But these are only the appearances of an inner form. What gives things their being is not the position they occupy in space, but the function they perform, the purpose they serve in a whole which has no place in space but in which all spaces are.[2] Call the space body and the function "soul", and it is in the soul or, as the greatest of the Platonists called it, the "entelechy" that you find the reality of the body. Both words have suffered from

---

[1] It is important to insist on this opposition between the Parmenidean and the Platonic tradition in view of attempts like that of Emile Meyerson and other French philosophers to represent the *nisus* of science and philosophy as towards an abstract identity.
[2] In the well-known passage in the *Timæus*, p. 36 fin., the physical is placed within the soul, not the soul within it. *Cp.* the suggestive passage on the nature of space, pp. 50 foll.

the use of them by a Vitalism which unites the soul from without to something which is supposed to have substantial existence apart from it. But, purified of such dualistic and materialistic associations, they express perhaps better than any others the noumenal as opposed to the phenomenal reality of the body. Take the soul or entelechy from the body, and it is no longer the body which it was. It may be that the same may be said of the soul. But if, as we must hold, the soul was more than its body from the first, and has other affinities than those which it has with its body, it will remain this more, and have these affinities, body or no body.

What is true of space is true of time. Time is only "the moving image"[1] of the eternity in which it is, but which itself is not in time. To be prior in time is therefore no sign of priority in being. Paradox as it has always seemed to the image-loving mind, there is nothing more vital to the Platonic tradition, or that distinguishes it more sharply from its Democritean rival, bent on explaining the whole in terms of the parts into which "victorious analysis" resolves it, than that, in the Order of reality, the whole precedes the parts. From this it further follows that to know the reality or essence of things we have to look at them not in their feeble beginnings, but in the light of what they are when most fully developed, when the parts or phases which they exhibited are most completely permeated with the form or idea of their function in the whole—a form or idea which they are rightly regarded as perseveringly seeking to express.

5. Applying this to Man, it is in the light of what we know of his soul and of what is most characteristically human in his soul, that we must try to read the meaning both of the material and the psychical world of which he is a part. What we there find is that the principle of the Order appears in him as conscious purpose. His soul is "the place of ideas" in a new sense. What in the rest of the world appears as a blind drive, *élan*, or *nisus*, towards wholeness of being, appears to him in the form of Good. What in the rest of the world has to be regarded from the outside as an order of higher and lower according to the visible complexity and unity of structure, shows itself in him from within as an order of domination by narrower or more comprehensive ideas and ends. What works in him is the idea of another, more total and integral, self to be realized in another, more approximately total and integral object; and he is so formed that nothing

[1] Plato, *loc. cit.*, p. 37.

which is not absolutely and entirely "good" will satisfy him.[1] He knows this in different forms, corresponding to different sides of his nature, intellectual, practical, or æsthetic, in the ideas of truth, moral goodness, and beauty, but he knows too that these are only partial forms of a reality that includes them all.

While these old Platonic doctrines formed the foundations of all later Idealism, they were insufficient so long as the relation between the ideal and the actual was left not only obscure but insoluble, as in reality it was on the presuppositions of Greek philosophy. The "chorismus", separation or apotheosis, of the Platonic ideas was only one aspect of a deeper dualism between appearance and reality, which ancient philosophy was never able completely to overcome. The development of such hints as there are in Plato and Aristotle of the immanence of the real in the actual, and the union of them with Christian theology in the doctrine of the Logos and the Real Presence, may be said to have been the work of the Middle Ages, their retranslation into philosophical terms the work of modern, especially Hegelian, metaphysics. As far as English and American idealism is concerned, this development is by far the most important element which it assimilated from German philosophy. That it had to go there for it, was not so much because it was not to be found in older indigenous writers as because it had largely forgotten the rock of Neo-Platonic speculation from which it had itself been hewn.[2]

But the important point with regard to this and the other elements here mentioned is not their origin, whether Greek or Christian, British or German. What is important is that it was in the power of them, and particularly of the last of them, that the main fields of philosophy were revolutionized in the latter part of the nineteenth century, and that, if taken all together and by themselves, their vitality (in and far beyond technical philosophy) could only be doubted by anyone who was prepared to repudiate the whole spiritual background of modern civilization. But they have been developed by philosophical writers in a complex intellectual environment, and have been partly enriched, partly obscured, by the assimilation of

---

[1] "Yes," she said, "and you hear people say that lovers are seeking for the half of themselves; but I say that they are seeking neither for the half nor for the whole unless the half or the whole be also good. There is nothing that men love but the good"(Plato, *Symposium*, p. 205 fin., Jowett's translation).
[2] To have reminded us of this seems to the present writer the chief service that what we now know of Coleridge's work does for us. See *Coleridge as Philosopher*, chap. iii.

elements not wholly homogeneous with them, some even contradictory of them; and it is these outgrowths and overgrowths that have drawn the main fire of the critics of idealistic philosophy as a system in our own time and led them to question the permanence of the structure to which they seem to be organic. The object of this Study is not to defend any structure that can be said to exist to-day, but to clear the ground for future construction by trying to distinguish what in these developments has enriched, what has obscured the vision of the design as it has haunted the mind of the centuries from Plato to the present day.

3. MODERN DEVELOPMENTS. (i) NEO-KANTIAN. (a) THE IDEA OF THE SELF

In submitting those modern adhesions to criticism, with a view to discovering which can be accepted as organic to the central tradition as above defined, it will be convenient to adopt the division with which the preceding studies have familiarized us between the earlier or more distinctively Kantian form of doctrine and the later, which is itself founded largely on a criticism of it. After what has been already said of the movement from one to the other, and by way of criticism on our own account of the point that has been reached, a more cursory review of particular doctrines than would otherwise have sufficed, may be here excusable.

The emphasis on the idea of the Self, as something primary in experience and providing the basis of an ontology, may be said to be the keynote of modern as contrasted with ancient and mediæval philosophy. It was this that Descartes had the merit of being the first to bring into prominence, and thereby, as Whitehead puts it, of making "the greatest philosophical discovery since the age of Plato and Aristotle".[1] For the moment lost in Spinoza, this note was recovered and raised to *fortissimo* by Leibniz. In another form, and with even more reverberating effect, it was struck in England in the subjectivism of Berkeley and Hume. Kant, indeed, sought to readjust the balance between subject and object by insisting on the quasi-objectivity that the sensory data receive from the form-giving power of the understanding. But he ended with a surrender to the subjectivist principle in teaching that the only world which we can *know* is a construction of the self or ego.

Earlier post-Kantian idealism took up the problem where Kant

[1] *Process and Reality*, p. 222.

had left it, and tried to carry out what it took to be his real intention by substituting for the unknown thing-in-itself as the criterion of reality the universe of inclusive and coherent thought to which Kant's ideas of the reason pointed. It is this substitution which realistic critics, who identify the form which the doctrine thus took with the older subjectivism, whether that of Berkeley or of Kant, and the "egocentric predicament", have commonly failed to understand. The idealism which is the subject of these Studies has from the first been as insistent as realism (*is* a form of realism in insisting) on the presence to consciousness of a non-ego. Where it differs from ordinary realism is in insisting also on the *relativity* of the distinction and in refusing to join with realism in the attempt to evacuate the object as non-ego of every element of subjectivity. How science, which starts from the legitimate abstraction of subjective elements, must in the end interpret the physical objects is its own concern. Recent well-known developments, which bring home the impossibility of interpreting it in terms of either the secondary or the primary qualities of realistic tradition, can hardly be said to support that evacuation. Yet the above-noted criticism, mistaken though it may be as applied to an intelligent Neo-Kantism, will retain a value so long as scientific writers, unfamiliar with the history of philosophy, continue to try to rehabilitate Berkeleianism as the alternative. Huxley's surrender to Berkeley's subjectivism in his book upon Hume may be paralleled to-day by Eddington's rejection of materialism on the ground that "no one can deny that mind is the first and most direct thing in our experience".[1]

It is not from this side that the Neo-Kantian doctrine of the primacy of the idea of the self is open to criticism, but from the side of subsequent advances in psychology which have sought to do more justice, first, to levels of experience at which the distinction between self and not-self has not yet developed or has been transcended, and, secondly, to the presence at all levels of the feeling of value with its accompanying conation. If we call the failure to recognize either or both of these "intellectualism", it is to this charge rather than to that of subjectivism that the older idealism threw itself open. The

[1] *The Nature of the Physical World*, p. 281. This, two pages later, is identified with the entirely different proposition: "The only subject presented to me for study is the content of my consciousness." This may be accepted, yet it may be denied that *mind* is the only content of that consciousness. See also J. H. Jeans' *Mysterious Universe*, p. 148, "The universe begins to look more like a great thought than a great machine."

error, in fact, consisted not in the failure to do justice to the objective element in experience, but on the contrary in the failure to do justice to an element which may be said in a sense to be peculiarly subjective. On this idealistic writers of such diverse types as Bradley and William James, James Ward and Josiah Royce, may be said to be agreed,[1] and so far we may be content to follow them.

Yet, while the Kantian attempt to start from the idea of selfhood and make it the foundation of the whole structure must be given up, there remains an element of truth in it which it is vital to understand and retain.[2]

Granting that the idea of the self has been proved to be a construction, and, psychologically regarded, a late one, seeing that it emerges from a more developed level of experience than that of anything which appears to sense-perception, we must still hold that it has been constructed *out of* a reality and *by* a reality, which is not *less* than it, and that, as the highest of its constructions, self-conscious life contains the best clue which we have to the inner nature of its parent, the best "representative" (to use a phrase of the older English Platonism) of it. The most powerful argument against the idea of the self as a stable, self-consistent being is probably that of Bradley's celebrated chapter in *Appearance and Reality* on this subject. But the argument there proceeds on the assumption that this idea is derived negatively from the contrast between the subjective and the objective aspects of experience from which psychology starts. It ignores that larger knowledge of the self which comes to us through reflection on its positive achievements in the work of civilization—the self-realization of mind as thinking, willing, and feeling, in knowledge and morality, social structure and law, art and religion. It is in these, and not in the abstraction which psychology investigates, that the essential features of human selfhood reflect themselves. Even in the psychological analysis of the life of the self, whether in knowledge, conduct, or production, we may not forget that the most valuable thing which we discover is the presence in it of the criterion it brings to the judgment of its achievements in these fields—a criterion that is none other than the degree in which through them personality attains fullness and harmony of expression. It is in virtue of what we thus come to know of it that Bradley

---

[1] Though of course with important differences, see, *e.g.*, Bradley and Ward above, p. 282 foll.

[2] What follows should be taken along with what is said, pp. 276 foll., in criticism of Bradley.

himself, in spite of the fierceness of his polemic, could still say that "his whole view may be taken as based upon the self", and that "he cannot doubt that a self or a system of selves is the highest thing that we have".[1]

If this is so, and if the highest includes and epitomizes all that has gone before,[2] it must be from what we find in self-consciousness, individual and social, that we obtain the completest idea of the elements for which room must be made in the attempt to discover what reality in its fullness means. The question may indeed be raised how self-consciousness can supply a criterion by which its own claim to ultimate reality is judged. But the question is unanswerable only if we begin by treating reality as falling outside of the self, as Bradley's polemic had the appearance of doing.[3] If, on the other hand, as Bradley himself really held, reality is present and operative in self-conscious mind as something that is always carrying it beyond any of the finite forms it may assume, and if therefore the soul's reach may be said to be always farther than its grasp, what we have is not self-consciousness judging itself, but the greater than the self in the self, of which we are conscious, judging that which is less than itself in its wholeness. It is only in the engineer's world that water can never rise above its own level. In the biologist's world and with the water of life this is what is always taking place. And it is so because in the actual living thing there is always working a reality that is carrying it beyond itself, a reality which we only hesitate to call "ideal" because it does not necessarily take the form of an idea, but may be felt as a blind *nisus* or instinct. It is the characteristic mark of self-conscious life, on the other hand, that this reality does appear in the form of an idea, and it is to this that an idealism that knows its business and would remain true to its central tradition must hold—not as an assumption or an intuition, but as patent fact forced on us by the most elementary analysis of what is before us.

We shall have to return to this question when we come to the idea of the Absolute. Meantime our conclusion is that, reject as we may the idea of the self as, on account of its origin and implied limitations, inadequate to express what we must take as the ultimate reality, it seems impossible to part with the clue which it gives to the nature of that reality.

---

[1] *A. and R.*, p. 558. [2] Above, p.393.
[3] It was this appearance that moved Caird to write that Bradley's knife was "all blade and no handle" (*Life and Philosophy*, p. 206).

4 (b). The *a priori* Element in Knowledge

Connected with the idea of the self as the source of the unity of our world is that of the *a priori* origin of the forms in which that unity finds expression. It was indeed an error to suppose that Kant himself ever meant that Nature was created by man's intellect. He had guarded himself against misunderstanding in declaring "macht zwar Verstand die Natur, aber er schafft sie nicht": Nature, as we might say, is a construction but not a creation of our minds. But there remained the doctrine that the formal or "eidetic"[1] element in what *we* know as nature is supplied from the mind's own resources, and it is not surprising that it found a lodgement in Neo-Kantianism.

Against this whole line of thought the reaction in our time has been widespread and profound, both from the side of realism and the later idealism. Modern realism is Platonic in its assertion of the reality of universals and in its refusal to treat them as in any sense mental as contrasted with a non-mental object. As little can idealism afford to admit the Kantian doctrine in this form. To emphasize the activity of our thought in the development of knowledge is one thing, to regard this as something for which *we alone* are responsible is quite another. As Kant's doctrine of the ego left it a miracle how the self could produce in the world a unity that was not to be found in it, so his doctrine of the categories left it wholly inexplicable why our *a priori* forms should receive any countenance from the sensuous material which comes to us from without: why the cheques we draw upon the bank of experience should be honoured in any form at all. Whatever the value of his psychological empiricism, Berkeley had the advantage over Kant here in being able to appeal to the mind of God as the source at once of nature and of our ideas of it. Unless the Kantian thesis of the activity of thought is supplemented by a doctrine of the unity of our thought with one that is immanent in things, it leaves the problem of how his categorically "constructed" nature can be guaranteed any connection with "created" nature: how in his own language the categories can be taken to be valid for all possible experience.[2] In view of the change of outlook to which both realism and idealism have contributed, it

---

[1] Husserl's term in his *Ideen*.

[2] See for an excellent statement of the contrast between Kant and Berkeley in this respect H. W. B. Joseph's lecture to the British Academy, *A Comparison of Kant's Idealism with that of Berkeley* (1929).

is impossible to found anything that can hold its own upon Kant's supposed Copernican revolution in the sense of assigning a merely *a priori* origin to the formal element in experience. To return to this, whether in the name of critical realism or critical idealism, is to involve ourselves in the old paradox of a thing-in-itself which, in Bosanquet's phrase, becomes "more unknowable the more it is understood". It is for this reason that Kantian epistemology in this sense must be regarded as a withered branch.

But there remains a side of Kant's work which connects itself not with the subjectivism, which in reality it was Kant's special work to undermine, but with the Platonic tradition from which we started by referring us to the "ideas of the reason", in other words to the ideal of a completely integrated whole of experience, for our standard of depth and reality. Kant himself sought to limit the scope of this ideal to the "regulation" of thinking experience in contrast to the constitutive function he assigned to the forms of the understanding. But, in thus removing it one step farther from the reality that is experienced, he really brought it back to it. For what other definition of reality can there be but that which controls and regulates our thought about it? or by what authority can the ideas of the reason regulate except by the sign-manual of reality itself?

It is this more thorough Copernican revolution, and not the shifting of emphasis from object to subject, from theory of things to theory of knowledge, for which the deeper thought of the idealism of our time stands. The reality both of subject and object is indeed given to intuition from the first. Any philosophy which overlooks this immediate contact with Being is self-condemned. But the undifferentiated experience in which the world is thus given to sense and feeling is only the point of departure of the mind which, as continuous with the felt reality, is pledged to follow its movement as it expands into a form more adequate to express the fullness of the differences and the fundamental unity of its contents. To assert, with some forms of realism, that all reality is "out there", or with some forms of idealism that it is all "in here", dependent on selection and emphasis as guided by passing interest, is to falsify the most elementary convictions of common sense, the constructive work of science and the achievements of the human mind in the worlds of art, morality, and social life. These worlds are all real, and, if we are to hold that they embody a higher truth and so possess a higher reality than the world of sensory appearance or instinctive reaction, and again that within them there are differences of level, whereby

> In dignity of being we ascend,

our standard must be quite other than correspondence with anything that is given either from without or from within us.

Idealism, without always being conscious of it, has been a long training in this point of view in the field of knowledge. Its most conspicuous recent successes have been won in a Logic, based upon the conception of inclusion and organization as the twofold test of validity in the "morphology of thought". Hardly less in the fields of Law and Morality has this conception been instrumental in effecting a revolution in men's minds as to the ends at which these aim, and the criterion by which they have to be judged. If in these fields the criterion is no longer taken to be correspondence with anything merely given either from without by force or authority, or from within by an infallible inner light, but the extent to which action and institution make for the widest and most harmonious form of human life, it is to the work of statesmen and writers who have followed the lead of this idea that it is mainly due. It is here that the idea of selfhood, discussed in the last section, gets its most convincing illustration. The phrase self-realization has recently fallen into disrepute because of the ambiguity attaching to it. But if it be freed from ambiguity, and the "self" be taken in the full scope of its meaning as personality, it would be difficult to find a better one to express at once the content of the world of practice and the unity of the actual and the ideal elements in it.[1]

It is on these grounds that I should be prepared to accept the claim put forward on behalf of historic idealism by one of its ablest living exponents. "It is the peculiar merit of idealism to have led the way in the philosophical study and appreciation of these worlds which the mind not only contemplates but creates and sustains as organs of its own self-realization. The 'Philosophy of the Human Mind', which in the hands of David Hume and the English Empiricists had remained within the limits of introspective psychology, went out (so to speak) into the world under the leadership of Kant and Hegel and their followers in Germany and England, and drew within its

---

[1] Like many of his readers, I have found Husserl's idea of the pure ego, which is the starting-point of his Phenomenology, somewhat evasive; but I do not think that we should be wrong in taking it as in the line of the above interpretation of the permanent element of truth in Kant's doctrine.

compass the whole achievement of mind in Society and Civilization. Abandoning the 'subjective' point of view of psychology, it acknowledged not only the reality of Nature, but also the reality of the Spiritual Worlds which mind has erected on the basis of and through mastery over Nature."[1]

5 (c). THOUGHT AND REALITY

We can understand how, in the analysis of knowledge, the emphasis upon the constitutive function of judgment and the substitution of systematic unity in thinking for correspondence with an external given object, as the criterion of truth and reality, in which Neo-Kantians found the real meaning of Kant's work, should have exercised a fascination for men eager to follow up what they took for an all-revolutionizing discovery and drive it home even at the expense of paradox. How better impress it on an unbelieving generation than by the formula of the "identity of thought and reality"? For the moment this became the shibboleth of philosophical enlightenment. It was in vain that Green protested[2] that this was either to use "thought" in an altogether new meaning, or to put forward a wholly unwarrantable claim for what our thinking could accomplish. In his own emphasis on relations as constitutive of reality, yet as nowhere found except in thinking consciousness, he seemed to commit himself to something dangerously like it.

We have seen in our study of Bradley that it was one of the main objects of the systematic attack upon current ways of idealistic thinking in *Appearance and Reality* to dissociate himself from this dictum by insisting on the immediate apprehension of reality in sensory experience at a level below anything that could by any stretch of language be called thought, and by pointing to the worlds of feeling and will as possessing a reality which it was impossible to equate with the world of rational theory. Whatever else might be doubtful in his teaching, these contentions were too much in line with the general advance in psychology and metaphysics to permit of any return to the old formula, and by the end of the century the doctrine of the identity of thought and reality may be said to have been dead. Yet before it is committed to the grave, and in view of the opposite abstractions of an unthought or thought-less reality to which we have merely to submit as something here and now given,

[1] R. F. A. Hoernlé, *Idealism as a Philosophy*, p. 74.   [2] See above, p. 209.

it is important to remember what it was in the doctrine which once gave it life, and in which, though dead, it yet speaks.

Freed from exaggeration, it stood, in the *first* place, for the indissoluble union, in anything for which in knowledge we claim reality, of two factors best describable as the actual and the potential or ideal. As there can be no conception of potency entirely divorced from that of actuality at some point, so there can be no conception of the actual that can stand by itself without a penumbra of content, which, if it cannot at certain levels be said to be "thought", yet, where it is a question of *knowing* it, is ideal in the sense that it appeals to and is supported by the mind's power of completing in idea what is otherwise mere passing appearance. While I cannot "deduce Krug's pen" from any idea of it in my head, neither, when I see it, can I keep out of it that which exists only in idea, even though it be merely its own past and future. Reality is never given as contained in the moment which alone is actual. It is along this line that realism itself has been driven from its uncritical to its critical form, and been forced to recognize a side of the real world which is supported in an atmosphere wider than any that can be described as immediate, sensory, or perceptive experience—a world of potential, enveloping the world of actual being, if not constituted by thought, yet revealed and, as far as we can see, revealable only to thought. In the *second* place, the doctrine stood for the fact that the more of this penumbra of content that passes into idea in the sense of conception, and is organized in this form into a coherent whole of meaning, the deeper the mind's grasp of the underlying reality. The system of ideas, grasped as theoretic truth, is only one aspect of that reality. Reality has other aspects as something that is felt and appeals to active tendencies. But in its own field, and so far as it goes, the thought we call "true" is so, as continuous with reality and as carrying its own portion of the real world with it.

In spite, therefore, of criticisms, which, like Bradley's, dwell upon the "divorce" between thought and existence, or, like James's, upon the abstractness and greyness of the world of theory, as contrasted with the fullness and greenness of the worlds of will and feeling, we must maintain the solidity of the experience that comes to us through thought, and further (as a corollary) the added solidity which thought gives to these other worlds. They fall beyond the world of truth in the narrower intellectual sense, but they depend upon it for what they contain of truth in the larger sense in which we may be said to will and feel, or more generally to live "truly". Will is different from, if you like, more than thought, but all that is properly called will consists in the realization of *ideas*, and the more embracive and coherent the ideas we have about the objects that are willed (the more that is of reality they take up into themselves), the more our wills pass into the texture of the real world and become continuous with it, as what religion calls the Will of God. And what is true of will is true of the feeling of the value of things, whether in nature or in art. Art has been defined by Pater as "fundamental conception". Artists, like their public, differ in the amount of *conscious* thought that goes to their creations and appreciations.[1] But, in the higher forms of art, what gives permanence to their creations is the depth and significance of the thoughts of the artist which they embody; while, from the side of their public, the depth of the emotional reaction to them is in proportion to the amount of experience and reflection that has gone to make up the receptivity of its mind. Spinoza's "intellectual love of God", Spenser's and Shelley's "intellectual beauty", are no mere poetic phrases, but point to the place that the logic of the intellect, which is the "spirit of totality", holds in fields otherwise far removed from its theoretical expression.

How far down in the scale of creation this logic extends, how far animals and plants, cells and atoms can be said to "think", is matter of speculation. But, granting there is an element of subjectivity or internality in them all, there is no reason for, but every reason against, interpreting this in terms of feeling and conation in any sense that excludes the apprehension of meaning which is the germ of thought.[2]

6 (ii). Neo-Hegelianism.[3] (a) Reality as Experience

While these Kantian and Neo-Kantian elements have had to submit to the criticism of a later generation, in the most recent developments other features have come into prominence which have seemed to the critics of idealism to connect it with an even more ambiguous

[1] Leonardo da Vinci and Raphael, according to a well-known story, are instances in point.

[2] The ambiguity of "feeling" as the word for both sense of value and un-differentiated presentation has too long haunted this whole discussion. Once cleared up, the above contention would seem to follow for anyone who would hold to the facts and hold them together.

[3] Professor Hiralal Haldar has used the term in the title of his book for the whole British post-Kantian movement. It is used here to indicate the later phase of it, more particularly associated with F. H. Bradley, who, as that author rightly sees, has a closer affinity to Hegel than to Kant.

past. Subjectivism, whether of the Berkeleian or the Kantian type, is gone; but reality is asserted with new emphasis to consist for each of us of Experience, and, since he has no other, apparently of *his* experience. The transcendent ego is gone, but the Absolute remains as something transcending anything interpretable in terms of the experience which we know. Subjectivity has come to its own as against Spinoza's substantivity, yet the only subject we know still appears as an "adjective" of the Absolute.

We have seen how, when first announced by Bradley, the former of these doctrines roused the suspicion of idealists themselves. Bradley, as we have also seen, had his answer in that the experience he appeals to is not that of the Berkeleian self and its states. It is an experience that reaches both at the lower and the higher end beyond the distinction of subject and object, and therefore one within which the self and its states are arrived at only by an act of analysis and abstraction. But the answer was incomplete. For if this is so, why should we call it "experience" any more than "the experienced"? The double reference in the word probably had an attraction for Bradley, and may be the reason of his choice of it. But how slippery the ground was, is seen in the sentence already quoted, "Nothing in the end is real but what is felt, and for me nothing in the end is real but what I feel", where he seems to start, not with a neutral simply "felt,"[1] but with "I feel", which, on his own showing, is a very different thing.

This ambiguity has been sufficient to cause misgiving even in Bradley's most sympathetic readers, and to suggest that the really significant part of his doctrine is to be looked for elsewhere than in the direct identification of reality with experience in any sense of the word to which, from the point of view of "finite centres", we can attach a definite meaning. Following this suggestion, we may ourselves find the living element in it to consist in the emphasis it lays upon the fact, *first*, that our minds from the beginning are not only everywhere in contact with reality (though the metaphor of "contact" is inadequate to describe the situation), but are continuous with it; and *secondly*, that if you take away from reality all that it means to consciousness, whether from the side of sensation, idea, will, or emotion, you have left on your hands not even a thing-in-itself but a nothing-in-itself, what Kant called an *Un-ding*.

To dwell for a moment on these two points, it is reality which, as present to us and in us from the first, feels, thinks, and wills in our

[1] See for this and what immediately follows p. 289 above.

feeling, thinking, and willing. Mystics have used this primitive *rapport* with the larger life of the world—this "wisdom", as Plato called it, "even of our meaner parts"—to illustrate the soul's deeper religious insight, as Bradley himself used it to illustrate the kind of experience he meant by the Absolute. We are not here concerned with this, but with the humbler application of it in the fact that from the first there is more *in* the mind than there is *before* it, whether as object or subject, and that by far the most important thing that is *in* it, is not any subconscious or subliminal self but the vast hinterland of being—neither subjective nor objective, neither subconscious nor superconscious, but simply *there* extending indefinitely and colouring all that is before it. In contradiction, then, to the pluralism that takes its start from disjointed appearances, we must say in a new sense that the whole precedes the parts, and that all analysis and abstraction proceed from a basis, not, as Kant would say, of *unconscious synthesis*, but of *apprehended totality*.

And so of the second point. In spite of dualistic criticism, we must hold to the fact that we can have no idea of a reality which is not suffused with the characters it bears to experiencing minds. This contention is not to be met by appealing to the conviction, shared by common sense and science, of the distinction between knower and known and of their *prima facie* independence of each other. This, from the level of common sense and science, is not denied, but it is not the point. The point is the impossibility of conceiving of anything from which all the elements it owes to sensory, intellectual, emotional, and volitional experience have been eliminated, as more than a mere *x* of which anything or nothing may be said. A theory which asserts this impossibility may be very far from having proved that the universe is the expression of a mind. Perhaps idealists have been overhasty in drawing theistic conclusions from their premises. But hostility to theological deductions ought not to blind us to the difficulties involved in the attempt to treat experiencing mind as an epiphenomenon or as something that is merely "compresent" with a non-mental object, as a table may be compresent with a chair. In spite of the high authority of this phrase,[1] it does not seem a particularly happy one at a time when science in every field is in revolt against the admission of coexistence as a category in which it can rest. There is no respect in which Hegel's thought has passed more decisively into the logic of the sciences than in what he says about

[1] As in S. Alexander's *Space, Time, and Deity*.

the conjunctions "and" and "also"[1] as a mere cloak for our ignorance of real relations. Philosophy merely carries this a step farther in insisting on the connection between experiencing mind, and the world that is experienced, as more than a verbal correlation. Against the realist's repudiation of knowledge theory as "a magic key to open the door of the mysteries of the universe",[2] and his appeal from it to the "plodding investigations of science", we may therefore set the scientist's own confession that his method ends in a mere "shelving of the inquiry into the nature of the world of experience", that another method is necessary, and that what this leads to is the view of physical entities as of "a nature continuous with our own".[3]

That there are difficulties in the theory goes without saying. Chief among them we have to meet the contention that "there is not the slightest reason why there should not be objects which are not known to any mind".[4] Idealism has doubtless its reply in the counter-contention that there is not the slightest reason why there should be; or again, in speculations as to a larger cosmic life, in which our physical order is only the body of a mind with a wider time-span than ours. But we shall still be asked to stick to facts which assure us of a time when as yet mind was not; and in the end our safest ground will be the Platonic principle with which we started, itself the fact of facts: that what to us appears as an order in time is only the "moving image" of another order which is not in time. In modern language, the time order is only the scheme through which to our eyes the real order which is one of values unfolds itself. To us it appears as though mind and its knowledge were an after-thought in the evolution of things; to that which is beyond time there is no before and after: what is last may be first and the first last.[5]

7 (b). THE IDEA OF THE ABSOLUTE

If we had only the older Kantian or Neo-Kantian form of Idealism in view, as that took shape in England and America in the third

[1] *E.g. Science of Logic*, Eng. tr., vol. ii. p. 123.
[2] See B. Russell in *Sceptical Essays* (1923), p. 71.
[3] A. S. Eddington's *The Nature of the Physical World*, p. 321. *Cp.* pp. 280 foll.
[4] B. Russell, *ibid.*
[5] For this view also affinity with that of Husserl may perhaps be claimed. If, as he says, "to have a meaning or to have something in mind is the cardinal feature of all consciousness" (*idem*, § 90), and if the real world is inconceivable except under the form of meaning, in other words except as significant, we are carried a long way towards the view that consciousness is a cardinal feature in the make-up of that world.

quarter of the nineteenth century, we might have been content to leave the Absolute, like Mahomet's coffin, suspended between earth and heaven.The word had first been naturalized in modern philosophy by Schelling,[1], and, since Coleridge's revolt against the pantheism of the Philosophy of Identity, had come to be regarded with a certain suspicion by English writers, even when most influenced by Hegel. But, in the more recent developments on both sides of the Atlantic, the Absolute has taken a central place both in word and idea, and challenges criticism as nothing else does.

That there are ambiguous features in the doctrine is clear, not only from the violent reaction against it outside the lines of idealism, but from the reception it had, when it first appeared full-fledged in the work of Bradley, from idealists themselves, by whom it was suspected of being a revival of Spinoza.[2] Hegel had claimed that modern philosophy in passing "from substance to subject" had transcended this form of monism. But the new emphasis seemed to be nothing less than a return to the lower category. The writers most deeply committed to it were doubtless prepared to disown the comparison, and to appeal to its affinity rather with the Platonic doctrine of degrees of reality. With Hegel they were even ready to claim that the Absolute is not something far away in a world beyond, but "is directly before us, so present that so long as we think, we must, though without express consciousness of it, always carry it with us and always use it".[3] But so long as they continued to speak of all forms of finite individuality as "adjectival" to the Absolute, the one supreme and only real individual, there was bound to be protest. It is not therefore surprising that we should have had on both sides of the Atlantic a powerful reaction in the direction of what has been called Personalism or Spiritual Pluralism, and that we seem faced with the alternative of either accepting a philosophy

[1] It seems to bate back to Nicolas of Cusa, who uses it of God as the *esse absolutum* or *ipsum esse in existentibus*. Kant used "the Unconditioned" for the metaphysical conception of God, and he was followed in this by Fichte, except as he was in his later work influenced by Schelling. See William Wallace's useful note in *The Logic of Hegel*, translation Second Edition, p. 410.
[2] "The end of the book" (*A. and R.*), wrote Caird in 1895, "is a kind of reversion to Spinoza, and I think a manifest self-contradiction. For the very idea that is set up as the test of truth seems to be finally dissolved in the absolute, which, as with Spinoza, is presented as complete reality, and yet as the negation of all the 'reals' we know" (*Life and Philosophy*, p. 206). *Cp.* p. 123: "We might perhaps say that his theory is a new Spinozism."
[3] *Logic of Hegel* (Wallace's tr.), p. 50; *cp.* Bosanquet, *The Principle of Individuality and Value*, p. 27.

which attributes to finite existences, as such, a veritable ultimate and absolute being, or of finding some more satisfying way of interpreting the relation between the one Absolute and the finite individual.

The reasons against the acceptance of the former alternative (characterized by Hegel as "undeserving the name of philosophy"[1]), as parting not only with everything for which idealism has stood in the past, but with everything to which the deeper spirit of our own time, as that is manifesting itself in every field of thought, appears to point, seem to be overwhelming. On the other hand, it is possible to state the truth contained in the Absolutist doctrine in a way that is compatible with all justifiable claims on behalf of human personality.

Taking the idea in general, it merely stands for the highest and most inclusive form of the principle of totality. Emphasize as you may the manifoldness of the world in space and time, the separateness and apparent contingency of the constellations which experience reveals, whether in matter, life, or spirit, once there and accepted, the many begin to display their essential relationship with one another. No individual thing remains apart or continues to seek what is merely its own, without in the end ceasing to have anything which it can call its own to seek. If there is anything to which modern thought is everywhere coming, it is this conception of a wholeness, integrity, or individuality, to be attained by things, *not* by maintaining themselves in an impermeable shell of private particularity, but by opening themselves to the influences that seem to come to them from without, and *re*forming themselves with the material which they thence appropriate. Philosophers have to exercise caution in claiming support for their theories from the new trends in science. But when physicists tell us that "Nothing is isolated; everything makes reference to everything else. Every event by reason of its very nature requires the whole universe in order to be itself",[2] and when biologists are everywhere disowning the dualism between organic and inorganic[3] in the interest of a deeper unity and continuity between them, we may be justified in feeling that an old dream of

[1] *Science of Logic*, Eng. tr., vol. i. p. 168.
[2] J. W. N. Sullivan in *The Basis of Modern Science* (1928), p. 240; *cp.* Whitehead quoted above.
[3] For a striking statement and application of the view that "surrounding nature is not an influence outside our lives but within them", see J. S. Haldane's Gifford Lectures on *The Sciences and Philosophy*.

philosophy is coming to have a new meaning through the patient observations of the laboratory.

When we come to human life, the essentially social nature of man and the reality of the social mind and will are, in spite of pluralistic reactions, the most living notes in the ethics and politics of our time. By society and the social, moreover, we are coming to understand something far wider than any mere chance collection of human beings.[1] *Totus mundus agit histrionem* was taken, by a fine inspiration, as the motto of the New Globe Theatre. But all the world's a stage, and if we read the motto in the form *totus mundus agit hominem*, we should again be expressing an old dream of the philosophers.

Coming back, therefore, to the roots of idealism in human consciousness, we have the fact that this call of the Whole comes to us in the form of an ideal. It "agitates" us as something to be realized at every point at which we take hold of our world, whether in science, in art, or in social life. Science seeks for something which will hold all the facts and will hold them together. Art has to make a little space into a reflection of the unspaced harmony of things. In society a man has "to be a whole or join a whole", and to discover in the end that he can do neither effectively without doing both. It is this call of the Whole, experienced as an ideal, and as nevertheless having a reality beyond anything which appears in time or for which actuality can anywhere be claimed, that is the vital element in the idea of the Absolute. Instead, therefore, of seeing it as something that falls *beyond* our experience, we ought to see it as the deepest element in it, and as that which we experience most intimately when we are living to any purpose. If we cannot claim that with this idea we can unlock all doors, we can, I believe, say that without it we cannot unlock any.

8 (c). SUBSTANTIVE AND ADJECTIVE

More serious than the criticism of the idea of the Absolute in general, that has come mainly from the side of pragmatic empiricism, is the criticism of the idea of the Absolute as Substance, which comes from the side of recent developments of realistic philosophy. After infecting metaphysics from the time of Aristotle and surviving in Spinoza the blow dealt it by Descartes, this idea might be supposed to have been finally exorcised from idealistic philosophy by Hegel's claim to

[1] See Whitehead's suggestive use of "society" in *Process and Reality*, pp. 123 foll.

have passed "from substance to subject". Nevertheless, in Bradley's conception of everything finite as "adjectival" to the Absolute as the one eternal substance, it seems to have found its way back into it—a resurgence all the more remarkable in view of the rejection by that philosopher of the corresponding logical idea of subject and predicate as failing to lead us beyond the abstractions of thought. The inadequacy of the metaphysical conception has already been noticed.[1] What was there said is reinforced by the criticism that has recently been directed against the whole idea from the side of the conception of nature as a system of space-time events and Whitehead's Philosophy of Organism. In view of all this, it seems impossible to be satisfied with Bradley's use of the conception. But the question returns whether, apart from the distinction for which "substance and adjective or accident" is a linguistic and metaphorical expression, there can be any philosophy "organic" or other at all.

If what has already been said of the distinction between real and apparent, and with it of that between degrees of satisfyingness or adequacy to represent reality in the apparent, is to stand, can this, we may ask, be better expressed than as a distinction of "substantiality" in things? To be substantial is to be something in which the soul can feel itself *bene fundata* and be at rest. It is difficult to see how a philosophy can claim, as the Philosophy of Organism does, to be carrying on the tradition that "the things which are temporal arise from participation in the things which are eternal", and that "the two sets are mediated by a thing which combines the actuality of what is temporal with the timelessness of what is potential"[2] without this idea. We do not get rid of it by substituting "potential" for substantial. In reality we thus drop out an element which is essential to our meaning by using a word which, in common language, suggests something that falls short of full concrete reality. If we are to hold, as again we are assured that we must, to the Aristotelian principle that, "apart from things that are actual there is nothing—nothing either in fact or efficiency", and on the other hand that the things that are actual to our apprehension reflect only a fragment of the whole actuality, we cannot afford to part with the one word that expresses the degree in which they succeed in reflecting it.

One cannot help suspecting that the failure to recognize this deeper use of the category of substantiality is bound up with the failure, under pressure of the newly found immensities of space and time and

[1] P. 236 above.   [2] Whitehead's *Process and Reality*, p. 54.

energy, to keep hold of that which alone for us gives meaning to them as the staging of the form of life we know as spirit and the standards of goodness and truth which this brings with it. Unless "process" is the vehicle of progress, and unless progress means bringing more of the substance of the eternal into the accidents of the temporal, we have parted not only with the spirit of Plato and Hegel, but with the spirit of faith in anything that philosophy can do for us. On the other hand, with the reciprocal correction here suggested, there is no reason why we should not accept the younger writer's claim that "the final outcome" of his own philosophy "is not so different" from that of Bradley's, and the prospect thus opened up of a concord in our own time between realism and idealism in their higher developments.

9. IDEALISM AND THE PHILOSOPHY OF VALUE

Reference at the outset was made to the problems raised by the prominence given in recent philosophy to the idea of value and the hope that comes to us from this side that we are within sight of the end of the reaction against the great central tradition, which we have been studying in its historical varieties. But, if this hope is to be realized, the conception of the Absolute, as above interpreted, must win its way by the light it is able to throw on the two most fundamental of these problems: that of the criterion of value, and that of the relation of value to existence. In the discussion of them, it looks indeed as though all the old battles would have to be fought over again.

Already a singularly active and ably supported form of realism has taken the field with answers to both of these questions founded on the attempt to explain value in terms of interest.[1] Value, we are told, depends on interest; interest, in the end, depends on instinct and appetite, and these are their own justification. It is the old hedonism in a new form. But as hedonism was dead when the fact of the qualitative difference of pleasures and the necessity of having another criterion than pleasure to judge of pleasures were recognized, "interestism" (as we might call it), in view of the patent fact of the difference between the value of interests themselves and the

[1] See R. B. Perry's able book on *Value*. The criticism that follows would apply only to the starting point of the subtle theory he propounds. In appealing (p. 687) to "An *order* of satisfactions whose form is prescribed by reason", he is not far from the Kingdom of Plato.

need of some objective standard by which their relative values can be appraised, may be said to be still-born. Granted that it is human values with which we are concerned, and that we have no right to treat the human "frame of reference" as absolute for the rest of the universe, yet within human life, if there is to be any order of values, there must be something in the make-up of that life that sets its mark on one object of interest as preferable to another. More and more it seems bound to appear that to interpret values in terms of subjective interest—the ideal element in life in terms of actual feelings—is to put the cart before the horse. Things interest because they have value for us; they do not have value because they interest us. Interest, like the feeling which is an essential element in it, is the sign, but can never be the criterion of value. Unless there are *real* interests, things, as the word signifies, that "concern" us, and concern us more deeply as they touch what is deeper in ourselves, value ceases to have any meaning except as a synonym for what happens to stimulate feeling and reaction in an individual organism. It is idle to appeal to the universal interest in *life*. One seems to remember similar appeals and what came of them in the ethical controversy.[1] As there, so here, this is only to push the question a stage farther back. Life, apart from the contents of life, is as much an abstraction as pleasure or interest. It is the life of a man, not of an oyster, that it concerns us to live, and the question returns as to the intrinsic nature of such a life and what it is that makes one man's life of greater value than another's.

It is just here that idealistic conceptions, as they were able to bring to a conclusion the long controversy with hedonism as to the nature of moral good, may be expected to have something conclusive to say on the standard of good in general. Can this in the end be other than the degree of wholeness which an object of interest gives to the subject of it? Can there be any other rule than this: in order to find the value of anything to anything—in other words what is that thing's good—find the particular kind of wholeness of which it is capable? For man the good or that which is of real value is the affirmation in him of that wholeness to which his ideals, economic, moral, political, æsthetic, religious, commit him. Language is oddly poverty-stricken in expressions for these ideals, but the familiar trilogy of truth, goodness, and beauty are sufficient illustration of what is meant. Man's finiteness may in the end doom him to

[1] See above, Bradley on *Sidgwick's Hedonism*.

dissatisfaction in the sense that there is always for him a beyond. But his dissatisfaction itself comes from his already possessing in a positive sense a foretaste of what he seeks, and he shows his more-than-finiteness in his power of identifying himself in anticipation with this fullness and living at least momentarily in the sense of attainment. Define this wholeness as we may, as perfection, the real self, individuality, the Absolute, postpone it as we may as an ideal unrealizable in anything we can conceive of as existing in the form of time, it is difficult to see how it can be dispensed with by any philosophy which would remain true to patent facts and the reality of the values we call spiritual.

Difficulties doubtless remain—the chief of them that above referred to as the relation of value to existence. But in what has been already said we have at any rate a point of view from which it is possible to see generally where "the weld" between the ideal and the actual may come. We can see that, while it is impossible to explain value in terms of existence, it may be possible to explain existence as the temporal side of the ideal, and as necessary to give it complete reality. It is a dream at once of Platonic and Christian theology that the divine perfection is only fulfilled in being communicated to finite beings; in modern language the ideal requires embodiment in the actual in order to be fully itself. Idealist and realist may perhaps here be content to meet on the basis of Professor Whitehead's statement which I have elsewhere quoted.[1] "There is no such thing as mere value. Value is the outcome of limitation. The definite, finite entity is the selected mode which is the shaping of attainment; apart from such shaping into individual matter of fact there is no attainment."

The fact that there is a supreme value, whatever name we give it, may be something ultimate, and in that sense inexplicable; but if it has the reality that idealism claims for it, it must, as Hegel says of it, at least have the power to *be*. In the form of it, which we call truth, it must from one side be taken as inhabiting eternity, but it is only as that shapes itself in knowledge and becomes a quality of an existent mind that it can come into any world that we can conceive of. And so with goodness and beauty. To be real in the full sense goodness must take form in character and action, and so qualify existence; to have real beauty we must have it here and now

---

[1] "The Real and the Ideal" in *University of California Publications in Philosophy*, vol. viii, 1926.

in sense-given things. The beautiful thing is indeed, as it has been called, a thing "twice-born"; but it must have been born once before it can be born again; it must have the lower before it can have the higher power. It is true that in our ordinary lives there is a division which secular experience fails to heal. But we are not confined to secular experience, and in religion we have another, in which the division is at least momentarily broken down, and in which the ideal is experienced as fact and as the essence of fact—in a word, as Nicolas of Cusa's *ipsum esse in existentibus*.

Coming back from this discussion to the question with which we started at the beginning of a previous section, and interpreting the Absolute in this sense, we can see that so far from absorbing human personality it is the very principle of its reality. Anyone who asks for more substantiality than that which comes from self-identification with it asks for he knows not what. On the other hand, from the side of personality, as we know it in ourselves, we can see this as that by which the Absolute is brought into the world of existing fact, and thus becomes real in every way. To seek for anything higher for oneself than to become the bearer in a world of persons of values that come from beyond himself is surely to pursue a shadow.

In a passage at the end of the last of the Terminal Essays in the Second Edition of his *Principles of Logic*, Bradley, shortly before his death, wrote: "Everything that is worth our having is (you may say) our own doing, and exists only in so far as produced by ourselves. But you must add that in the whole region of human value there is nothing that has not come down to us from another world—nothing which fails still to owe its proper being and reality to that which lives and works beyond the level of mere time and existence." The twofold aspect of personality could not be better expressed. We are made to feel that it is this wholly Platonic doctrine, and not any revival of Spinoza's Substance, that is the vital element in the later development of idealistic philosophy, and, in spite of criticism from a lower level of thought, remains to us as a living inheritance from it.

I have been trying to indicate certain principles underlying the mode of philosophizing commonly known as idealistic, for which I am prepared to claim a survival value in the sense that, taken all together, they represent a definite achievement of the thought of the past and offer a secure base for future advance. But I recognize that this and all similar metaphors are misleading if taken to mean that even for a "base" all that is necessary is merely to accept them, put them together, and proceed to deductions from them. I am even prepared to say that, taken as merely inherited doctrines, they are one and all as dead as the bones in the Valley of Jehoshaphat. It is only as they are breathed upon and vivified by the spirit of a thinker, himself inspired at once by a knowledge of the best that has been thought in the past and by sympathy with the deeper intellectual needs of his own time, that they can really live again. But I should be false to my own convictions if I did not add that they *can* be so made to live, and that, if they do not give us any final solution of the riddle of the universe, they can at least give us the assurance that we are working in the line of the great tradition of the Western world, and thus save us from despair.

INDEX OF PROPER NAMES

GEORGE ALLEN & UNWIN LTD
LONDON: 40 MUSEUM STREET, W.C.1
CAPE TOWN: 73 ST. GEORGE'S STREET
SYDNEY, N.S.W.: WYNYARD SQUARE
AUCKLAND, N.Z.: 41 ALBERT STREET
TORONTO: 77 WELLINGTON STREET, WEST

The Structure of Thought

by LUDWIG FISCHER

Demy 8vo.   TRANSLATED BY W. H. JOHNSTON   16s.

This book is a philosophy of philosophies. The world is treated as a whole which is intelligible only by virtue of the order which is immanent in it, and the author makes it his first task to trace the outlines of this order. Having reached this "natural order" of the universe, he proceeds to the main part of the book—an attempt to treat the different philosophies as different systems of axioms within one great system of the natural order. His survey ranges over human thought from the Pythagoreans to Dreisch and Vaihinger, a survey significant because it is not a chronicle but a dissection of the logical interrelation between systems.

The Revolt Against Dualism

An Inquiry Concerning the Existence of Ideas

by ARTHUR O. LOVEJOY

Professor of Philosophy in the Johns Hopkins University

Sm. Royal 8vo.   15s.

The purpose of this work is not to present a private and original speculation but to give a critical survey of the philosophy of the greater part of a generation, in both America and Great Britain, upon two important issues, and to show that certain definite conclusions have been reached on these issues.

The Quest for Certainty

A Study of the Relation of Knowledge and Action

by JOHN DEWEY

Demy 8vo.   *Gifford Lectures*, 1929   10s. 6d.

"Deserves great praise for its penetrating analysis of the present state of philosophical thought, and clear presentation of the problems with which . . . the traditional philosophies are beset"—*Spectator*
"A stimulating book which should have an audience far wider than that of those whose main interest is in technical philosophy."—*Manchester Guardian*

Science and the Unseen World

by Sir ARTHUR EDDINGTON, Ph.D.

Author of "The Nature of the Physical World," etc.

Swarthmore Lecture, 1929

Cr. 8vo.   *Fifth Impression*   Cloth 2s. 6d., Paper 1s. 6d.

"One of the most remarkable contributions made during the present century to the controversy over the relative value of the scientific and religious outlooks as guides into apprehension of truth."—*Morning Post*
"It should find its way into the reading of every household, for in its short space it deals with the realities which face every thoughtful mind."—*British Weekly*

All prices are net.

LONDON: GEORGE ALLEN & UNWIN LTD

LaVergne, TN USA
02 August 2010
191691LV00001B/150/A